British Government in an Era of Reform

British Government in an Era of Reform

Edited by W. J. Stankiewicz

Professor of Political Science
University of British Columbia

COLLIER MACMILLAN
LONDON

A Collier Macmillan book published by
CASSELL & COLLIER MACMILLAN PUBLISHERS LTD
35 Red Lion Square, London WC1R 4SG
Sydney, Auckland, Toronto, Johannesburg
An affiliate of Macmillan Publishing Co. Inc.
New York

First published 1976

Printed in Great Britain by
Northumberland Press Ltd., Gateshead

I.S.B.N. CASED   0   02   977240   0
        PAPER   0   02   977250   8

Contributors

STANLEY ALDERSON (born 1927): Freelance writer; author of *Britain in the Sixties: Housing* (1962) and *'Yea or Nay? Referenda in the United Kingdom'* (1975).

N. T. BOADEN (born 1934): Lecturer in Social Administration at the University of Liverpool; author of *Urban Policy Making* (1971); preparing books on 'Politics in Merseyside' and 'Community Development in Liverpool'.

SIR RICHARD CLARKE, KCB, OBE (born 1910): Permanent Secretary of the Ministry of Aviation and Technology, 1966–70; author of *The Economic Effort of War* (1939); *The Management of the Public Sector of the National Economy* (Stamp Memorial Lecture, 1964); *New Trends in Government* (1971).

PATRICK COSGRAVE (born 1941): Political Editor of *The Spectator*; author of *The Public Poetry of Robert Lowell* (1969); *Churchill at War. 1: Alone* (1974); preparing a book on 'The Breaking of the Prime Minister'.

BERNARD CRICK (born 1929): Professor of Politics at Birkbeck College, University of London; author of *The American Science of Politics: Its Origins and Conditions* (1959); *In Defence of Politics* (1962, 1964); *The Reform of Parliament* (1964, 1970); *Political Theory and Practice* (1972); editor of *Essays in Reform* (1967).

MARGARET P. DOXEY: Associate Professor of Politics at Trent University, Peterborough, Ontario; author of *Economic Sanctions and International Enforcement* (1971); preparing a book on the contemporary Commonwealth.

The Rt Hon. LORD HAILSHAM OF SAINT MARYLEBONE (Quintin Hogg), (born 1907); Fellow of All Souls College, Oxford, 1931–38; MP for Oxford City, 1938–50; St Marylebone, 1963–70; Minister for Science and Technology, 1959–64; Lord High Chancellor of Great Britain from 1970–74; author of *The Law of Arbitration* (1935); *The Times We*

Live In (1944); *The Purpose of Parliament* (1946); *The Case for Conservatism* (1947); *The Conservative Case* (1959); *Science and Politics* (1963); and other books.

JOHN W. HOLMES (born 1910): Director General of the Canadian Institute of International Affairs since 1960; Visiting Professor of Political Science at the University of Toronto and at Glendon College, York University; Assistant Under-Secretary of State for External Affairs, Ottawa, 1953–60; author of *The Better Part of Valour: Essays on Canadian Diplomacy* (1970); preparing a book on 'Canadian Foreign Policy: The Establishment of an International Presence 1945–1968'.

DENNIS JOHNSON (born 1929): journalist on the staff of *The Guardian* since 1961 (special interest: politics outside Westminster).

G. W. JONES (born 1938): Senior Lecturer in Political Science at the London School of Economics and Political Science; author of *Borough Politics* (1969); co-author of *Herbert Morrison: Portrait of a Politician* (1973).

ENID LAKEMAN: Director of the Electoral Reform Society, London; author of *Voting in Democracies* (with James D. Lambert) (1955, 1959); *How Democracies Vote* (1970, 1974).

ANTHONY LESTER (born 1936): currently special adviser to the Home Secretary, and practising barrister, writer and broadcaster; co-author of *Race and Law* (1972), and writer of various other articles and pamphlets on politics, race relations and international law.

LORD MACDERMOTT (born 1896): Lord Chief Justice of Northern Ireland, 1951–71.

JOHN PITCAIRN MACKINTOSH (born 1929): Professor of Politics at Birkbeck College, University of London; MP for Berwick and East Lothian; author of *The British Cabinet* (1962); *Nigerian Politics and Government* (1966); *The Devolution of Power* (1968); *British Government and Politics* (1970).

J. D. B. MITCHELL, CBE (born 1917): Salvesen Professor of European Institutions at the University of Edinburgh; author of *Contracts of Public Authorities* (1954); *Constitutional Law* (1964, 1968).

EDWARD MORTIMER (born 1943): Foreign Specialist and Leader Writer with *The Times*; author of *France and the Africans 1944–1960* (1969); preparing a book on 'The Rise of the French Communist Party'.

O. HOOD PHILLIPS, QC (born 1907): Vice-Principal, Pro-Vice-Chancellor and Barber-Professor of Jurisprudence at the University of Birmingham; author of *Principles of English Law and the Constitution* (1939); *Constitutional and Administrative Law* (5th edn 1973); *Leading Cases in Constitutional and Administrative Law* (4th edn 1973); *A First Book of English Law* (6th edn 1970); *Reform of the Constitution* (1970); *Shakespeare and the Lawyers* (1972).

W. A. ROBSON (born 1895): Professor Emeritus of Public Administration at the University of London; author of *Justice and Administrative Law* (1928); *The Development of Local Government* (1930); *The Government and Misgovernment of London* (1939); *The British System of Government* (1940); *Problems of Nationalised Industry* (1952); *Nationalised Industry and Public Ownership* (1960); *Local Government in Crisis* (1966); *Politics and Government at Home and Abroad* (1967); and other books.

C. H. SISSON (born 1914): Director of Occupational Safety and Health, Department of Employment, since 1972; author of *The Spirit of British Administration* (1959); *Art and Action* (1965); *Essays* (1967); *The Case of Walter Bagehot* (1972).

BRIAN C. SMITH (born 1938): Senior Lecturer in Public Administration at the University of Bath; author of *Regionalism in England I: Regional Institutions* (1964); *Regionalism in England II: Its Nature and Purpose* (1965); *Regionalism in England III: The New Regional Machinery* (1965); *Field Administration* (1967); *Advising Ministers* (1969); *Public Administration* (with Jeffrey Stanyer), in press.

The Rt Hon. MICHAEL STEWART, CH (born 1906): MP for Fulham; Secretary of State for Foreign and Commonwealth Affairs, 1968–70; author of *The Forty Hour Week* (1936); *Bias and Education for Democracy* (1937); *The British Approach to Politics* (1938); *Modern Forms of Government* (1959).

M. J. C. VILE (born 1927): Professor of Political Science and Dean of the Faculty of Social Sciences at the University of Kent at Canterbury; author of *The Structure of American Federalism* (1961); *Constitutionalism and the Separation of Powers* (1967); *Politics in the U.S.A.* (1970, 1973); *Federalism in the United States, Canada and Australia* (Research Paper No. 2, Royal Commission on the Constitution) (1973).

IVAN YATES (1926–1975): The late Chief Leader Writer and Leader-page Editor of *The Observer*.

Contents

To David Corbett

I finally had to realize that all the states of our time without exception are badly administered. For, in regard to the laws, the condition in which they are is almost beyond recovery, so that only some quite extraordinary effort, accompanied by exceptionally lucky circumstances, could possibly change it; and I was forced to say ... that it is philosophy that enables us to recognize the claims of justice both in public and in private life.

PLATO *to Dion's Relatives and friends*

Introduction

The fragmentation of constitutional thought in Britain, and the rejection, for good reasons, of older political theories, without their being replaced by any comprehensive view of the structure of our system of government and the values it is intended to safeguard, leaves us to drift before whatever wind of expediency may blow.

M. J. C. VILE

It is typically British to imagine that it is possible to reform local government – or any other institution – without first being clear about its purpose, without first settling the value judgements and working out the objectives of the reformed institutions. It is assumed that by looking at the particular machinery, by taking evidence about how the present arrangements work, inconsistencies will emerge, obvious changes will suggest themselves and the problem will be solved.

J. P. MACKINTOSH

The present anthology is a sequel to my earlier *Crisis in British Government* (1967): the two books are linked by a common theme – reform. A similar chapter structure has been followed but the contents of the two collections differ. While encouraging the reader to refer to the earlier volume, *British Government in an Era of Reform* is meant to continue the debate of a number of issues which were discussed in the first anthology; yet it is conceived as an entity in itself.

Taking stock of constitutional and political developments in the UK in the last seven or eight years calls for a re-appraisal and a restatement of the editor's initial position. The word 'crisis' has raised questions and may need a word of explanation. The issue is primarily one of the identity of the Constitution and its adaptability to social change. It is not directly concerned with the politics of the government in power (although the situation may be aggravated by the policies of that particular government).

The problem of 'crisis' is also institutional in the sense that many inadequacies and failures of the present system can be expressed in terms of institutional practices. Among these are: confusion regarding ministerial responsibility, the lack of effective control over the executive, the unimaginative use of committees by the House of Commons, uncertainty regarding parliamentary control of the nationalized industries, the lack of an adequate system of long-term planning, inequities of the electoral law, etc. What is at issue, however, is not just the façade of political institutions, but their inner framework.

'Reform' likewise relates to fundamental structural changes. It is seen as an all-embracing design which accommodates those particular constitutional and administrative innovations that are consonant with public purpose. It also serves as a testing ground for constitutional principles.

The tasks faced by those engaged in constitutional reform are extensive: to reconsider and enumerate the many inadequacies and failures of the present system; to identify the main principles of the Constitution and the extent to which they have been 'eroded'; to emphasize the desirability of discussing particular reforms in terms of first principles; to analyse the actual proposals relating to the machinery of reform as well as the reform measures themselves. These tasks define the scope of the present symposium.

Must one still justify the need for reform as a comprehensive undertaking? (That a great number of particular reforms are needed few seem to contest. But the proposal for an all-embracing constitutional reform is regarded differently.) What is it that militates against the general acceptance of this type of approach – the lack of a sense of public purpose among politicians, the empirical malaise of the scholars (and their acceptance of what 'is' as what 'ought to be'); dissatisfaction with parliamentary government and the inertia and cynicism of the public?

The failure even to consider the problem of major reform is a consequence of the approach – frequently adopted by modern academics – which focuses on an explanation of *what is* and on a description of the existing state of affairs. This school of thought – represented (insofar as the British constitutional system is concerned) by Samuel Beer, Richard Rose, Gabriel Almond and Sidney Verba among others – is fundamentally opposed to the views of thinkers such as M. J. C. Vile, Alfred Cobban, E. C. S. Wade and J. P. Mackintosh, who insist on considering the principles or theories underlying practice, and whose writings are prescriptive.

Professor Beer, in particular, considers that the British system has changed 'markedly from period to period'[1] – radically over the last two and a half centuries – that it has responded to new conceptions of what constitutes legitimate representation. Today, according to him, the system reflects a predominant acceptance of the legitimacy of group representation (the spirit of corporatism?). But this does not worry Beer: he fails to relate corporatism to instability within the political system and does not see the need for a new constitutional framework to accommodate new institutional arrangements; indeed, he is oblivious of the very existence of a constitutional crisis. He focuses his main attention on the political process and is unwilling to consider the latter in relation to constitutional problems.

Samuel Beer's case is not an isolated one. In his discussion of contemporary British politics, Professor Rose acknowledges what he calls 'the secret of stable representative government'[2] and then glosses over the need to discuss the constitutional situation. Absorbed in a study of the British political process, he seems to assume that one can disregard the problems of constitutionality or unconstitutionality of government as long as interests are being effectively 'aggregated' and the legitimacy of government is widely accepted. Nor does the problem worry Professor Almond and his associates. The role played by theoretical (and institutional) considerations in the joint work of Almond and Verba is minimal.[3] Their surveys stress the essential stability of British political culture.[4] In another work, Almond and Coleman implicitly use the British system as the model of a developed area and a 'more or less stable democracy'.[5]

The present editor, on the other hand, is inclined to stress, as Professor D. C. Corbett has pointed out,[6] the 'precarious, contingent character of present-day stability' in Britain. He believes that events have outpaced the self-regulating mechanism of the Constitution and that a major erosion of principles has occurred. He urges a general reformulation of constitutional thinking. He advocates an overall reform with reference to fundamentals and a careful restatement of the latter. He believes that piecemeal change, without reference to constitutional principles, will have short-lived and ineffective results.

The need for a new blueprint stems from inaccurate and partial perceptions – and consequently mistaken interpretations – of the system. The focus of the existing 'descriptive' texts – usually concerned with the functioning of various components of the political system or with the reactions of individuals to the latter – acts as an obscuring factor which has delayed recognition of the current British constitutional predicament. Stressing the tradition of 'gradual change', their authors have minimized the need for reform and placed it in a wrong perspective. How can such a reform – any reform – succeed, unless there is agreement on the general objective? How can there be such an agreement unless the general objective is clearly formulated; unless fundamental principles are regarded as templates and seriously debated? 'A continual restatement of political principles', says Alfred Cobban, 'is both necessary and inevitable.'[7] Professor Vile goes even further when he speaks of a 'unified reconciling theory of constitutional government'[8] – a prerequisite to proper reform. Instead of this, there exists in practice an essentially anti-'holistic' tradition which has jeopardized the idea of considering the system in its entirety and re-defining its principles with a view to reform. Obviously aware of the problem, A. H. Hanson and Malcolm Walles speak as follows of the inhibiting effect of the force of tradition:

> Only once has the attempt been made to look at British government as a whole, with the object of elucidating certain general principles to guide the hands of those anxious to bring it fully 'up-to-date'. This attempt, recorded in the Report of the 'Haldane' Committee of 1918, failed to produce a fully practicable scheme of politico-administrative reform ... *Improvisation, with a bias towards the minimum* rather than the maximum amount of institutional change, has been the favoured method of adaptation.[9] [Editor's italics]

It is a pity that Hanson and Walles did not go beyond their shrewd diagnosis.

Constitutional principles have been either taken for granted or discussed in a highly compartmentalized context of constitutional law separated from the sphere of politics. A different approach is suggested by Professor E. C. S. Wade: 'Like Dicey we must never lose sight of what are the rules of the constitution in any endeavour to bring up to date the application of the sovereignty of Parliament and the rule of law to modern conditions.'[10]

J. P. Mackintosh deplores the atomization of institutional reform which has prevented the inclusion of 'broader issues':

> At the moment of writing [1968], some ministers, MPs and members of the public are considering methods of Parliamentary reform. Meanwhile, totally disconnected, the Fulton committee examined the personnel, professional structure and recruitment of the civil service. Both parliamentary and civil service reform closely affect local government but it is being reviewed in a totally separate compartment subdivided into three boxes labelled London (which has been 'done' by the Herbert Commission), England (the Maud Commission) and Scotland (the Wheatley Commission) ... By subdividing the consideration of reform and failing to state the overall objectives clearly, many of .. possibilities and interconnections were omitted.[11]

This indictment was formulated some six years ago but the situation has remained almost unchanged. The Commission on the Constitution (the Crowther Commission) set up at the beginning of 1969 had rather limited terms of reference and its work overlapped with that of the Maud Commission.

It has been suggested elsewhere[12] that it is ultimately the theorists who, through their interpretations, are chiefly responsible for institutional change. Walter Bagehot is an obvious example of how a constitutional interpreter can both shape constitutional trends and influence the thinking of future generations about the Constitution. (His errors of judgement do not seem to have reduced this influence.) It might be argued that the 'efficient secret' of the system lies in the freedom it gives to those who are determined to give a new turn to customary interpretations. This system – shaped by Bagehot, Dicey, Laski and Amery – will in future be affected by the writings of J. P. Mackintosh, Geoffrey Marshall, J. D. B. Mitchell, Graeme Moodie, W. A. Robson, M. J. C. Vile and others.

It is from these and other theorists that the decisive impetus will come. If, on the one hand, their role in some instances has been decisive in the sense that they have inflicted a 'bias' of interpretation[13] there have been, on the other hand, examples of the seminal involvements of the theorists in a reform movement and consequently their other – more direct – impact on social and political change. W. Friedmann speaks of the interactions of legal and social change in the nineteenth century: 'It was Bentham's philosophy, and that of his disciples, which turned the British Parliament ... into active legislative instruments, affecting social reforms, partly in response to, and partly in stimulation of, felt social needs.'[14] Bentham's proposals extended to law, government and the administration. His influence on nineteenth-century legislation – through his works on evidence, on civil and criminal procedure, and through his proposals to reform prisons and put the existing system of conflicting jurisdictions in order – was particularly strong.[15] His Constitutional Code was a systematic application of his principle of utility to the modern State. He also applied himself to a full-scale study of the structure of local government as well as to some concrete administrative problems, especially that of Poor Law reform.

The age of Bentham, Bagehot, Dicey and others like them is gone and yet the crucial role of the theorist in shaping the character of the British Constitution has not changed. A system which has no written constitution places a special obligation on the shoulders of constitutional interpreters. In an age which lacks theorizing, the very content of the Constitution is impoverished. Instead of evolving naturally, reform becomes a piece of social engineering: a series of *ad hoc* measures, a palliative – not a cure.

The need for a re-interpretation of the system parallels the need for reform. These needs are interlinked, and not merely in the realm of academic speculation. One of the practical recommendations offered in the previous anthology[16] was the setting up of a Royal Commission or Council for Reform, a body with very broad and comprehensive terms of reference encompassing the entire field of government – constitutional practices as well as administrative arrangements. Such a body could give constitutional theorists an opportunity to formulate a major statement on the present meaning of constitutional principles and to relate the latter to desirable recommendations for reform. The type of questions to which the Commission could initially address itself is indicated by the issues discussed in Part I of the present anthology (and in *Crisis in British Government*): What are the guiding principles of the Constitution? What is the meaning of parliamentary sovereignty? How can the decline of the rule of law be arrested? What is the nature of the functions of government? Should there be a Bill of Rights? How can the theory of law and the theory of government be reconciled? Should a system of public law be established? How serious is the abuse of arbitrary power? Is a statutory code of administrative procedure needed? How can we reconcile judicial and parliamentary controls of administrative action? How can maladministration be prevented?

No reform measures should be undertaken unless these questions are first answered. 'The question is not', said Quintin Hogg, 'whether we reform, but how.' This, of course, implies 'according to what principles'. The particular questions relating to concrete reform proposals are posed or implied throughout the anthology. Some examples are: Why has parliamentary reform been mainly unsuccessful? (Which reform measures have worked?) How can we revive parliamentary debate? Should one give renewed consideration to reforming the House of Lords? How much devolution of power is feasible? What are the effects of the civil service reform in the post-Fulton era? and many others.

W. J. Stankiewicz

University of British Columbia
December 1974

1. Samuel H. Beer, *British Politics in the Collectivist Age* (New York 1965), p. X.
2. Richard Rose, *Politics in England* (Boston 1964), p. 1.
3. Gabriel Almond and Sidney Verba, *The Civic Culture* (Princeton 1963).
4. 'One gets a feeling that what the surveys have revealed about British political culture may last forever.' Professor D. C. Corbett in a letter to W. J. S. dated 5 July 1967.
5. Not only do they show a lack of interest in constitutional matters but a tendency to make questionable assumptions based on their theoretical model. Cf. Gabriel Almond and James Coleman, *The Politics of Developing Areas* (Princeton 1960), especially pp. 44–45 where they say 'the aggregate function in the British political system is distinctively performed by the party system' etc.
6. Source quoted. Cf. Note No. 4 above.
7. Alfred Cobban, *In Search of Humanity* (London 1963), p. 20.
8. M. J. C. Vile, *Constitutionalism and the Separation of Powers* (Oxford 1967), p. 315.
9. A. H. Hanson & Malcolm Walles, *Governing Britain* (London 1970), p. 25.
10. A. V. Dicey, *Introduction to the Study of the Law of the Constitution*, 10th edition (London 1961), p. XX.
11. J. P. Mackintosh, *The Devolution of Power* (Harmondsworth 1968), pp. 39 40.
12. See my Introduction to *Crisis in British Government: the Need for Reform* (London 1967), p. XVIII, from which this paragraph has been taken.
13. Here the example of Dicey is striking: the mold into which he had cast the Constitution prevented later generations of students of public law from considering adequately the state of the law and practice of the Constitution in their own time. Cf. E. C. S. Wade's Introduction to Dicey, *Introduction to the Study of the Law of the Constitution*, p. XIX.
14. W. Friedmann, *Law in a Changing Society* (Harmondsworth 1964), p. 19.
15. Cf. J. Redlich & F. W. Hirst, *The History of Local Government in England*, ed. by Bryan Keith-Lucas (London 1958), p. 91.
16. *Crisis in British Government*, p. XXI. I was delighted to have my views on the need for such a Commission, or a similar body, confirmed in the Editorial 'The Machinery of Government' (*The Political Quarterly*, July-Sept. 1968) and by the Rt Hon. Quintin Hogg, MP in his article 'The Constitution: the Right Road to Reform' (*The Spectator*, 10 January 1969). 'A modernized form of inquiry instead of the traditional Royal Commission' was recommended by a group of politicians, civil servants, academics and publicists who met under the auspices of PEP (Political and Economic Planning) in 1969. Cf *Renewal of British Government* (PEP Broadsheet 513, July 1969). They were urged to discuss proposals for reform by Max Nicholson, author of *The System: The Misgovernment of Modern Britain* (London 1967). Cf. also J. H. Robertson, *Reform of British Central Government* (London 1971), Ch. XI.

Part One
Constitutional Principles and the Road to Reform

M. J. C. Vile

The Rise and Fall of Parliamentary Government

... Walter Bagehot's *English Constitution*, first published in 1865 as essays in *The Fortnightly*, and as a book two years later,[1] has undoubtedly had great influence over the course of constitutional thought during the past century. That this book is still, a century after its publication, perhaps the most oft-quoted work on the cabinet system is quite remarkable, in view of the extent to which the practice of British politics has changed during that period. No doubt the explanation of this continued popularity is that his style is so much superior to that of more academic works. As Mr Richard Crossman pointed out in 1963, it is the journalistic quality of these essays which has made them so consistently popular.[2] But if one of the defects of even the very best journalism is to exaggerate the points the writer wishes to make, then this is in fact just the major defect of Bagehot's famous book. The author wished to drive home a point, and in order to do this he misrepresented the theory he was attacking, and he exaggerated his conclusions, so as to make as clear and as great a gulf as possible between the two positions. But it is not merely Bagehot's journalism that we have to guard against. He was writing with a very strong political purpose in mind, and although this gives to his work a vehemence and a conviction which others lack, it also gives it a misleading character. Bagehot wished to warn, indeed to frighten, his middle-class readers, by pointing out to them what would be the effects of extending the franchise. He was, as he himself said in 1872, 'exceedingly afraid of the ignorant multitude'.[3] The American Civil War, seen in England so much in terms of a battle between the democratic North and the aristocratic South, had, in Earl Grey's words, increased 'the wholesome dread' of an extreme alteration in the English Constitution.[4] If the franchise were to be extended so that the lower classes gained control of the Commons, what check would there be to their power? Bright and Forster were accused of wishing to introduce the

American pattern of government into England. The result would be either an uncontrollable legislature or 'Caesarism'. For, as a writer in *The Quarterly Review* of January 1866 pointed out, 'The feeble and pliable executive of England is wholly unsuited to such an electoral body. A government that yields and must yield to the slightest wish of the House of Commons is only possible as long as that House of Commons is the organ of an educated minority.'[5] This was the point of view to which Bagehot was determined to give his utmost support. He wished to make it as clear as possible to his readers that the reform of 1832 had not, as some had argued it would, restored the balance of the Constitution. It had confirmed, in fact, that there were no longer any checks or balances in the system. Whoever controlled the Commons had absolute power. The balanced constitution was dead, and the middle class should have no illusions about it.

This determination to stress the absence of restraints to the exercise of power led Bagehot into considerable difficulty. He did not distinguish clearly between the Constitution as it actually worked in the hands of an educated minority, and how it *might* work in the hands of the representatives of the ignorant multitude. Nor did he, in spite of all his claims to factual realism, distinguish clearly between the legal and practical aspects of English government. As a result he presented a picture of the English system which was mangled and exaggerated. Ignoring almost everything that had been written on British government during the previous sixty years, Bagehot affirmed that the 'literary theory' of the Constitution, 'as it exists in all the books', was erroneously based upon the two principles of mixed government and the *entire* separation of the legislative and executive powers. In fact, wrote Bagehot, the efficient secret of the English system of government is 'the close union, the nearly complete fusion' of the legislative and executive powers. Thus he represented the extreme doctrine of the separation of powers as the accepted theory of the Constitution, and then replaced it with an equally extreme principle, the fusion of powers. In order to make this point Bagehot used the comparison with the United States, and quickly proved that Britain did not have the same system of completely separate personnel for the two branches of government as the presidential system. The difference lay in the role of the cabinet, this 'new word', said Bagehot, with sublime disregard of the writings on English politics from Paine to Grey. The demonstration that the complete separation of powers in all its aspects did not exist in Britain was, of course, readily established, but this did not necessarily mean that the powers of government were 'fused'. These alternatives were presented by Bagehot as if they presented the only possibilities. But, as we have seen, virtually the whole history of English constitutionalism has been characterized by the recognition of the need for a *partial* separation of the personnel of government, and a *partial* separation of the functions of government. Such subtleties did not exist for Bagehot, however.

Naturally enough this extreme view of the 'principle' of British government did not square very well with the facts of its operation in the 1860s, and this led Bagehot into very difficult waters. On the same page as he writes of the fusion of powers, he uses expressions quite incompatible with that idea. Thus his famous metaphor of the cabinet as 'a hyphen which joins, a buckle that fastens' the two parts of the State, is itself somewhat different from the idea of fusion, and elsewhere he writes of the necessity of 'the constant co-operation' of the two parts of the government – a very different matter indeed![6] His most remarkable misuse of words comes in the following passage: 'The chief committee of the legislature has the power of dissolving the predominant part of that legislature – that which at a crisis is the supreme legislature. The English system, therefore, is not an absorption of the executive power by the legislative power; it is a fusion of the two.'[7] This might be seen as an attempt to combine the ideas of Park and Aiken, so close is the language to that used by the earlier writers, but as a piece of logic it is very difficult to follow. How does the conclusion follow from the premiss? The fact that the cabinet has the power to dissolve the Commons surely does not prove that they are fused, but that they are not. Indeed it seems that Bagehot was trapped by his own use of language. His description of the cabinet as a committee with power to destroy its parent body did not lead him, as one might expect, to discard the idea of a committee, which is entirely inappropriate here, but to insist even more strongly upon the idea of a fusion of powers. A similar confusion is found in this statement: 'The regulator, as I venture to call it, of our single sovereignty, is the power of dissolving the otherwise sovereign chamber confided to the chief executive.'[8] Here we are close to the root of the confusion in Bagehot's work. The legal idea of sovereignty can be attached to the King-in-Parliament, of which one part, the government, can use its power to dissolve the other, the Commons, and appeal, as Bagehot says, to the next Parliament. But the Commons alone is certainly not sovereign in the legal sense. In the political sense, if the term 'sovereignty' can usefully be applied in this connection, again it is not the Commons that is sovereign, but the electorate, which judges between cabinet and Commons in case of a difference of opinion that ends in a dissolution. It is true of course that the Commons must be satisfied with a cabinet if it is to continue in office, but to attribute 'sovereignty' to the Commons is to misunderstand the powers the ministers exercise on the one hand, and the role of the electorate on the other. Bagehot, in fact, adopted a view of legislative sovereignty or supremacy more like that of the proponents of *gouvernement d'assemblée* than any earlier view of legislative supremacy in England; a fact which helps to explain why his ideas were so well received in extreme republican circles in France in the early years of the Third Republic.

When Bagehot turned to the description of the working of parliamentary government he dropped his preconceived framework of a 'fusion' of powers, and wrote in terms of the balance between government and parliament which earlier writers had stressed. The fate of the government is determined by the debate in parliament, he wrote, but, on the other hand, 'either the cabinet legislates and acts, or else it can dissolve. It is a creature, but it has the power of destroying its creators.'[9] A perfect description, but not one of a fusion of powers; rather of a subtle division and inter-dependence of two arms of government, each with its proper function to perform. Indeed Bagehot summed up the position perfectly when he wrote: 'The whole life of English politics is the action and reaction between the Ministry and the Parliament.'[10]

Bagehot's influence upon the study of English politics has been great. His emphasis upon the need to concern ourselves with the real working of government, and not with irrelevant 'principles', has contributed to the tendency of modern students of British government to concentrate upon the day-to-day working of institutions without relating them to the over-all structure of the Constitution. Constitutional considerations became almost exclusively the domain of the lawyers, something that had never formerly been true in England. Furthermore, his characterization of the fusion of power in England seemed to become more and more relevant as the details of the system he claimed to describe changed out of all recognition. The growth of mass political parties and of party discipline in parliament created a situation in which the fusion of power seemed much more of a reality than it ever was in the period between the two Reform Acts. The concept of concentrated power that he supplied suited admirably the needs of that society, the emergence of which he had most wished to prevent. Of course, the idea of a balanced government did not die overnight. Sidgwick described the British system of government in terms of the essential balance between government and legislature, with an appeal to the electorate,[11] and Bryce wrote of 'the exquisite equipoise' of parliamentary government.[12] In more recent years L. S. Amery relied upon this concept for his analysis of British Government,[13] and Herbert Morrison maintained that it was the existence of a balance between cabinet and parliament which distinguished the British system of government from that of the Third and Fourth Republics.[14] But the trend of thought was against them. It was Bagehot who was read, and still is read, and who seemed to suit the mood of the age, in spite of the fact that the predominance of the Commons over the cabinet as he described it, has, in the view of present-day observers, been replaced by the predominance of the cabinet over the Commons, or indeed of the Prime Minister over both.

English constitutional thought over the past century has, therefore, been extraordinarily fragmented. The functional concepts of the theory of parliamentary government have not been jettisoned, for we still think of the function of the Commons as that of exercising control over the government, and discussion turns upon the way in which this can best be achieved, if at all. Yet the idea of a *balance* between government and parliament has almost entirely disappeared. The mechanisms of this balance as Grey saw them, dissolution and ministerial responsibility, have almost wholly ceased to play the role envisaged for them in the classical theory of parliamentary government. The tacit acceptance of Bagehot's view of a fusion of powers has not, however, entirely replaced the functional categories upon which the doctrine of the separation of powers was based. Both that theory, and the theory of the balanced constitution, had been created upon a functional analysis of the acts of government, which classified them into legislation and execution, the making of laws and the putting of these laws into effect. The idea of a rule of law was, as we have seen, closely bound up with this functional view of government acts. The theory of parliamentary government had a different functional basis, whilst Bagehot suggested that there was really no significant functional distinction to be made. These two functional analyses of the eighteenth century and the nineteenth century did not, of course, coincide. The idea of 'government' and of 'execution' are radically different. Yet the categories of 'government' and 'control' could not wholly supersede the old categories of 'legislation' and 'execution'. For the former related only to a *theory of government*, whereas the latter had, in the seventeenth and eighteenth centuries, been part of both a theory of government *and a theory of law*. The insistence that the executive should obey the legislature was the institutional expression of the demand that the law was supreme, over King, Protector, Governor, and President alike. This view of the supremacy of the law did not come to an end with the rise of the theory of parliamentary government, and indeed it was strongly reasserted by Dicey at the end of the nineteenth century. The proponents of parliamentary government did not for a moment assert that the government was no longer subject to the restraints of the law; it was subject to the law, although it played a decisive role in the process of legislation, and in the general business of government, which bore no relation to the idea of a 'mere executive'. The new categories overlaid and ran parallel to the old.

It is true that the idea of a 'mere executive' power had never been fully accepted in England. The King's prerogative, the discretionary powers of the Crown, had never been lost sight of in the theory of the balanced constitution, in the way in which the French and the Americans had, for a time at least, assumed that discretionary powers were unnecessary in a constitutional government. Nevertheless the insistence upon the supremacy of the law, and relegation of the royal power over legislation to a quiescent 'negative voice', had made the application of the term 'executive power' to the King and his ministers seem not too inappropriate. In the nineteenth century, however, the explicit recognition of the role of the government in formulating, initiating, and indeed securing the passage of legislation, made the term 'executive' quite inadequate as a description of the role of ministers of the Crown. That we still use the term today is indicative of the extent to which we attach a dual role to the same body of persons.

The continued vitality of the principle of the rule of law implied also a continued adherence to the ideas which had lain behind the separation of powers. Twenty years after Bagehot's articles had been published in *The Fortnightly* A. V. Dicey restated the basis of the English theory of constitutionalism with unprecedented vigour, expounding the rule of law without any concessions, in a way which would have been acceptable to the most fervent anti-royalist of the seventeenth century. For Dicey the absolute supremacy of the regular law excluded arbitrary rule, prerogative, or even wide discretionary authority on the part of government.[15] Dicey was no advocate of the separation of powers; indeed he fired a few shots at the doctrine himself. Yet once again it was the extreme doctrine that was under attack, the doctrine 'as applied by Frenchmen', the doctrine which gave birth to the dreaded *droit administratif*. Nevertheless, the whole burden of *The Law of the Constitution* was that the making of law, and the carrying out of the law, were distinct and separate functions, and that those who carry out the law must be subordinated to those who make it. On the one hand the executive might act only with the authority of the law; on the other, Parliament might not exercise direct executive power, or even appoint the officials of the executive government.[16] Dicey did not fully explore what this meant in terms of the separation of functions among different *persons*, but if the subordination of the executive to the law was the keynote of his work, it would be to reduce this principle to nonsense to assume that legislators and executives were identical, that the powers of government were 'fused'. Not unnaturally, therefore, an attachment to the ideas of the separation of powers in the twentieth century has been associated with lawyers rather than with students of politics, whilst the latter have preferred a point of view derived rather from an amalgam of the ideas of Grey and Bagehot. At certain points these views have come radically into conflict, and the areas in which these points of view did not overlap have become critical. The extreme, almost hysterical, criticisms made by Lord Hewart in *The New Despotism*, and expressed also in a more balanced way by C. K. Allen, were met, before the Second World War, with strong assertions of the need for co-ordinated, decisive government action. Since the War, however, there has been a change of tone. Lawyers are no longer so apt to think in terms of bureaucrats lusting for power, nor are students of politics so unheeding of the dangers which arise from the characteristics of modern government. There is some recognition today that there is virtue in both the theory of law and the theory of government. How to reconcile them is the great problem.

At the end of the nineteenth century the ideas of Grey, Bagehot, and Dicey seemed to run along parallel lines. The theory of parliamentary government, with its balance between government and parliament, the fusion of the legislative and executive powers, and the subordination of the executive to the law were all quite cheerfully accepted as principles of British government. They were in fact all capable of being reconciled to a considerable extent. The reconciliation between the theory of law and the theory of government was achieved through the principle of ministerial responsibility. This idea enabled the two theories to be knitted together, and the differing functional concepts they embodied to be brought into a working relationship. The 'executive' must act according to the law, the 'government' must exercise leadership in the development of policy; but if the government was subject to the control of parliament, and the executive to the control of the courts, then a harmony could be established between the two roles of the ministers of the Crown. Ministerial responsibility, legal and political, was thus the crux of the English system of government. Whilst it remained a reality the whole edifice of constitutionalism could be maintained; should it cease to be a workable concept the process of disintegration between the legal basis and the operation of government would begin.

At the end of the nineteenth century the view that ministers could be held responsible to Parliament for the actions of 'government' and 'executive' alike seemed reasonable enough. The Civil Service was seen as a passive instrument of the will of Parliament under the supervision of ministers. The tasks of government were still relatively simple and could be assumed to fit, without too much difficulty, into the categories either of policy or of administration. The development of new tasks of government, however, which consisted of active intervention in the economic and social life of the country, presented a very different picture. The difference between 'government' and 'executive' became even more marked. It was no longer possible to restrict the discretion of government by insisting upon the adherence to detailed rules laid down by Parliament. 'Delegated legislation' and 'administrative justice' were the inevitable accompaniments of the expanded role of government in society. Furthermore, the 'executive' could no longer be seen to be composed of responsible ministers who decided 'policy' and civil servants who carried it out. The new demands upon government had called into existence an extensive, complex bureaucracy, within which important decisions were taken by anonymous civil servants. The extreme critics of these new developments suggested that a nominally responsible government could, by its control over the legislative process, obtain for the so-called executive power the right to draw up its own rules and even to free itself from the control of the courts by excluding their jurisdiction. The potential power of the government, they suggested, was being used to destroy the rule of law. More important, perhaps, than these factors was the character of the twentieth-century party system. The close links which had been forged between the government and the majority in Parliament seemed to destroy all idea of balance between cabinet and legislature, and even to throw doubt upon the possibility of a general control of government business. The assumption underlying the system of parliamentary government had been destroyed, and the reality of ministerial responsibility was therefore thrown in doubt. Once this essential principle was questioned the whole edifice began to show cracks.

In 1929 the Committee on Ministers' Powers was appointed, with the task of rebuilding the bridge between the two concepts of the Constitution, which had come to be represented on the one hand by politicians and administrators, and on the other by lawyers. The Committee's terms of reference instructed it to consider the powers exercised by or under the direction of ministers of the Crown by way of delegated legislation and judicial or quasi-judicial decision, and to report what safeguards were desirable or necessary to secure the constitutional principles of the sovereignty of Parliament and the supremacy of the law. There was, therefore, explicit in these terms of reference the remarkable admission that it was conceivable that the decisions of responsible ministers, or of their servants, *could* operate in a way which offended the rule of law. There was a recognition, therefore, that the rule of law must mean something more than the mere formal sanction of some legal authority for every act of government, for no one suggested that ministers or civil servants had been acting illegally. The attempt of the less sophisticated of Dicey's critics to equate the rule of law with mere legality misses the point that the supremacy of the law in English thought since the seventeenth century has included, and must include, certain ideas about the articulation and separation of the functions of government, as well as 'due process'. The evidence and report of the Committee on Ministers' Powers illustrate the difficulty they had in reconciling this view of the Constitution with the needs of modern government, which seemed so much better served by the categories of the theory of parliamentary government than those inherited from the theory of the separation of powers.

The argument that the separation of powers was being destroyed by the way in which the ministers and civil servants were usurping the functions of the legislature and the courts was met by the Committee with the counter-argument that the doctrine of the separation of powers, whilst very important, had never been completely accepted in England, and that some deviation from its precepts was perfectly safe, acceptable, and indeed essential. The Committee in its Report stated: 'The separation of powers is merely a rule of political wisdom, and must give way where sound reasons of public policy so require.'[17] The delegation of legislative and judicial power to the executive was a necessary feature of modern government and so had to be tolerated, but it must be kept within bounds and surrounded by the necessary safeguards. With true British pragmatism the Committee concluded that the granting of judicial powers to a minister or ministerial tribunal 'should be regarded as exceptional and requiring justification in each case',[18] although of course they could not suggest what would be regarded as sufficient justification. Nevertheless, the Committee was quite definite in its adherence to the rule of law, and stated its belief that it was 'obvious' that the separation of powers is *prima facie* the guiding principle by which Parliament when legislating should allocate the executive and judicial tasks involved in its legislative plan.[19] The problem was, therefore, to determine the criteria for distinguishing between administrative and judicial decisions.

Thus the Committee became embroiled in a discussion of the

nature of the functions of government. Everyone agreed that it was impossible to draw precise boundaries, and numerous examples were cited to illustrate this difficulty. Nevertheless, the upholding of the rule of law seemed to necessitate definitions, and the Committee strove to find them. The problems they faced are well illustrated by the following excerpt from the minutes of evidence. The representatives of the Association of Municipal Corporations, W. J. Board and Sir William Hart, were discussing with members of the Committee whether or not ministers should be required to give the grounds for their decision following a public enquiry:

Sir William Holdsworth: Still I suppose a department where it has been given judicial powers and has been exercising those judicial powers does decide things on principle, and would it not be a help to the public to know what the principle was?

W. J. Board: These are not judicial decisions, they are administrative. There may be certain times when they may have the appearance of a judicial decision, but we think they are of the nature, and should be of the nature of administrative decrees and should be treated as such; they are not therefore comparable with what takes place in the Law Courts.

Sir Wm. Holdsworth: When you say 'administrative decisions' you mean they must apply their minds to them and decide them justly?

W. J. Board: Certainly.

Sir Wm. Holdsworth: I do not see why the fact that they are administrative should be a reason why no reasons should be given. They are decisions whether administrative or judicial.

Professor Laski: May I put it another way? The result may be administrative, but surely the process is judicial?

Sir Leslie Scott: Or to put it another way still, if the issue is a justiciable issue, either because the facts are disputed or because the law applicable is disputed, that is essentially a matter for judicial decision.

Sir Wm. Hart: I agree.[20]

From this confusion the Committee retreated to a simple, if indefensible, criterion. Administrative decisions, they concluded, were concerned with the application of policy and therefore involved the exercise of a wide discretion, whereas judicial decisions simply applied fixed rules of law. Quasi-judicial decisions were, therefore, in the Committee's view, essentially administrative decisions which had some element of a judicial character in that they involved disputes. Such disputes, however, were not regulated by rules of law, and so remained administrative in character, and were to be determined by the minister's free choice.[21] This device enabled the Committee to solve its problem. Justiciable issues, except in exceptional circumstances, should be left to the courts, administrative and quasi-judicial decisions to the executive. Ministers should be subject to the appellate jurisdiction of the High Court in regard to judicial decisions, and subject to the control of Parliament and public opinion in the exercise of their quasi-judicial and administrative functions. Ministerial responsibility, legal and political, remained the keystone of the Constitution. As the Treasury-Solicitor, Sir Maurice Gwyer, had warned the Committee, any departure from the principle of ministerial responsibility would imply the adoption of a new theory of government.[22]

The most ardent antagonist of the Committee's view was W. A. Robson, who published his *Justice and Administrative Law* shortly before the Committee was appointed, gave evidence before them, and in later editions of the book took issue with their Report. Robson flatly rejected attacks upon administrative law and justice originating from the doctrine of the separation of powers. The doctrine, he said, was an 'antique and rickety chariot ... so long the favourite vehicle of writers on political science and constitutional law for the conveyance of fallacious ideas'.[23] Like A. F. Pollard some years before, Robson demonstrated that the separation of powers had never been completely accepted in England, and that administrative and judicial functions have been mingled in the same offices since the beginning of English history. His objections to the doctrine went much deeper than those of the Committee, who had accepted it as a general guide to the distribution of governmental functions. Furthermore, he objected to the distinction the Committee drew between law and policy, which, as we have seen, really stems from the dual character of English constitutional thought.

The root of Robson's attack upon the separation of powers was his antagonism to the ideas associated with Dicey's formulation of the rule of law. The implicit commitment to some form of separation of powers in Dicey's work was the basis of his rejection of *droit administratif*, and the basis also of the claim of the ordinary courts to a monopoly of judicial power. Robson, however, was interested in the creation of a system of administrative courts, similar to those in France, and his attack was, therefore, directed at a doctrine which was used to argue that judicial powers ought not to be entrusted to administrators. The most important aspect of judicial institutions, Robson believed, was the development of the 'judicial mind'. If a similar state of mind were to be cultivated in the minds of administrators who have to deal with judicial problems, then 'we need spill no tears of regret because they do not bear the institutional characteristics of the former courts of law'.[24]

Robson's attack upon the views of Dicey, and upon the conclusions of the Donoughmore Committee, might be taken as the final attack upon the separation of powers in Britain, and a rejection of it in its last stronghold, the power of the judiciary to settle judicial matters. Yet there is something of a paradox in this position, which illustrates how the *values* implicit in the doctrine have survived into the twentieth century, and how the precepts of the doctrine have doggedly refused to die. As with Duguit in France and Goodnow in America, Robson's rejection of the extreme view of the separation of powers was only one side of his argument. He was forced to fight on two fronts at the same time. Whilst attacking the vested interests of the ordinary courts in the exclusive exercise of judicial power, his attachment to the idea that there is a proper sphere of action for administrative courts forced him to adhere to the basic functional concepts which Montesquieu had enunciated. He rejected the view that the definition of government functions was logically impossible; it was only the institutional articulation of these functions that he wished to challenge. And even then, like the American opponents of the extreme separation of powers, he did not relish the idea of a single man being policeman, prosecutor, and judge on the same issue. 'The exercise of judicial functions by administrative bodies can be rationalised and disciplined only by the introduction of specific institutional reforms and procedural safeguards.' When it is necessary to confer legislative, administrative, and judicial powers on a single department, he wrote, it is *always* possible and desirable to separate these functions within the department.[25]

It is a remarkable fact that after the great weight of criticism that had been poured upon the Montesquieu categories of the functions of government they still remained, in the 1930s and 1940s, the basis of the discussion about the structure of government. The simple fact, of course, is that if one abandons the Montesquieu functions altogether, closely related as they are to the concept of the supremacy of law, one is left without any criteria for the orderly conduct of government business. Day-to-day expediency becomes the only guide for action, and few people would be prepared to admit that expediency alone should determine the organization and powers of government. The uncomfortable fact remains, however, that these categories have failed to provide the detailed guidance that would enable us to allocate the functions of government properly, i.e. in a way that is immediately seen to be efficient, and at the same time to safeguard the values inherent in the separation of powers. The attempt of the

English courts to apply these categories has led, in the opinion of one authority, to a position 'riddled with ambiguities'.[26] The conclusions of the Committee on Ministers' Powers were of little help in determining the later allocation of government powers. It is significant that when the Franks Committee on Administrative Tribunals came nearly thirty years later to retread some of the ground covered by the Donoughmore Committee they refused to be drawn into the discussion of the nature of the functions of government. Whilst noting that the distinctions drawn by the earlier classification of government functions were constitutionally of great importance, the Franks Committee in their Report regretted that they had been unable to fix upon a valid principle of the practical allocation of powers between ministers and administrative tribunals. The only approach that seemed to them to be useful was an empirical one, which ignored the problem of the general principles involved.[27] The difference between the approach of the two Committees is perhaps symptomatic of the more sceptical approach to political principles which had evolved during the intervening thirty years, and also reflects, possibly, the chairmanship of an Oxford-trained philosopher over the deliberations of the later one.

The 'separation of powers' remains, therefore, a central problem in the English political system, for the problem of the controlled exercise of power is still, and probably always will be, the critical aspect of a system of government which hopes to combine efficiency and the greatest possible exercise of personal freedom. The basic problem remains, in spite of all the changes since the seventeenth century. If our system is to remain essentially a system of government by 'law' then some form of control must be exercised over the agents of government. If we abandon this philosophy of law how do we prevent mere expediency from degenerating into arbitrary government? Not the arbitrary rule of a Charles I, a Cromwell, or a Hitler, but the arbitrariness of a great machine staffed by well-intentioned men, possessing, of necessity, a limited range of vision, and a limited ability to judge where a succession of expedient decisions will lead. The fragmentation of constitutional thought in Britain, and the rejection, for good reasons, of older political theories, without their being replaced by any comprehensive view of the structure of our system of government and the values it is intended to safeguard, leaves us to drift before whatever wind of expediency may blow.

NOTES

1. *The English Constitution*, London, edn of 1963 used here.
2. In his Introduction to Walter Bagehot, *The English Constitution*.

3. *English Constitution*, p. 281.
4. *Parliamentary Government*, new edn, 1864, Preface, p. vii.
5. *Quarterly Review*, Vol. 119, No. 237, Jan. 1866, pp. 278–279.
6. *English Constitution* (London 1963), pp. 68 and 72.
7. *English Constitution*, p. 69.
8. *English Constitution*, p. 221.
9. *English Constitution*, pp. 69 and 73.
10. *English Constitution*, p. 151.
11. *Elements of Politics*, 2nd edn (London 1897), p. 436.
12. *The American Commonwealth*, 2nd edn (London 1890), Vol. I, p. 281.
13. *Thoughts on the Constitution* (London 1947), pp. 15–16.
14. *Government and Parliament*, 3rd edn (London 1964), p. 107.
15. *The Law of the Constitution*, 8th edn (London 1931), p. 198.
16. *Law of the Constitution*, p. 404.
17. *Report of the Committee on Ministers' Powers*, Cmd. 4060, 1932, p. 95.
18. *Report*, pp. 115–16.
19. *Report*, p. 92.
20. Committee on Ministers' Powers, *Minutes of Evidence*, 1932, Vol. II, p. 265. I am indebted to Miss S. Conwill for having drawn my attention to this discussion.
21. *Report*, pp. 74 and 81.
22. *Minutes of Evidence*, Vol. II, p. 6.
23. *Justice and Administrative Law*, 2nd edn (London 1947), p. 14.
24. *Justice*, p. 34.
25. *Justice*, p. 333 and 473.
26. S. A. de Smith, *Judicial Review of Administrative Action* (London 1959), p. 29.
27. *Report of the Committee on Administrative Tribunals and Enquiries*, Cmd. 218, 1957, pp. 28–30.

J. D. B. Mitchell

1965 - from
Public Law.

The Causes and Effects of
the Absence of a System of Public Law
in the United Kingdom

The task of a constitutional critic is not simple. Detachment is perhaps more difficult for him to attain than it is for the scientist. His material is more difficult to measure, and often provokes emotions within himself, since he has a personal relationship with it in a way which it is almost impossible for the scientist to have with his materials. So the lawyer may too easily fall into an uncritical acceptance of the virtues of another system, or too readily dismiss that system with the spoken or unspoken thought – 'That would not work with us.' With equal ease he may see nothing but the virtues or nothing but the faults of his own system. He is too close to it....
If what follows is critical of the state of public law in the United Kingdom, let it be said at the outset that much could be said of present and enduring virtues in other aspects of our constitutional structure. Of those virtues or believed virtues much has been said, perhaps indeed too much, for many of our present difficulties may be attributable to past virtues of a system, praise of which has led us to be too reluctant to change or adapt it. Nevertheless at the outset it should be emphasised that virtue exists.

Within small compass it is intended to assess the present state of public law with us and to examine the causes which have produced that state. General constitutional devices intended to control governments in a political sense (wherein many of the virtues are to be found) are therefore beyond the scope of this article, except in so far as they may incidentally affect detailed rules. Attention must also be drawn to the title of the article. It is concerned with a system of public law. Inevitably public law exists in some form wherever the machinery of government operates. The necessities of government have a way of making themselves felt, whether one likes it or not. The proud declaration of section 2 of the Crown Proceedings Act, 1947, that 'the Crown shall be subject to all those liabilities in tort to which, if it were a private person of full age and capacity, it would be subject'

Reprinted from *Public Law* (Summer 1965), pp. 95–118. By permission of the author and the publisher.

is inevitably made 'subject to the provisions of this Act'; and those other provisions are those wherein the necessities of government appear, and perhaps appear too strongly. The argument is then about the fact that public law is too often regarded as a series of unfortunate exceptions to the desirable generality or universality of the rules of private law, and is not seen as a rational system with its own justification, and perhaps its own philosophy.

There was certainly at one stage an embryo system of administrative law, which perhaps developed too early or too quickly for its health. Both in England and in Scotland the Privy Council exercised a jurisdiction over the administration, in ways which could have produced, by the process of evolution, a genuine administrative jurisdiction. In exercise of its supervisory powers, the Privy Council of Scotland is to be found requiring the Town Council of Edinburgh to hear each month complaints against its officers and to redress injuries[1] or hearing a complaint that the magistrates of Linlithgow were 'slack, negligent and remiss', and imposing a supervisory officer.[2] Abuse of power was checked, notably in relation to matters which could affect liberty such as the right of quartering soldiers or deportation,[3] and public officers who were failing to perform duties, such as that of maintaining roads or bridges, were corrected and threatened with severe penalties should the default continue.[4] The Exchequer was also exercising (though feebly) an administrative tutelage over local authorities.[5] In England the Privy Council exercised both aspects of an administrative jurisdiction, protecting officials from suits in the ordinary courts, and protecting individuals from abuse of power.[6] Even in so far as such bodies were concerned simply with the efficient administration of justice, it is easy to visualise the possibility of the development of that supervision into a more general supervision and control of administrative activity as the latter activity developed. Such an evolution was, however. frustrated. In both countries the jurisdiction of the Council and of conciliar courts, whatever virtues they had had at one time in protecting citizens from corruption and oppression, tended themselves to become the instruments of oppression. Indeed the neglect of the magistrates of Edinburgh referred to above was a neglect in the enforcement of oppressive laws. The Court of Star Chamber was abolished in 1641 and with the revolution of 1688 other conciliar courts were abolished in England. In Scotland the Privy Council lingered on, but after the Union of 1707 its abolition came in 1708 (an abolition which had been foreshadowed in the Acts of Union) and its amalgamation with the Privy Council of England (now without this supervisory jurisdiction) resulted from the same Act. The end of the Privy Council in Scotland caused little grief to those who remembered its character in its latter years before the revolution of 1688, by which time it often acted not as a bulwark against the oppressive use of power but as an accomplice in illegality.

The characteristics of these special courts were not, of course, peculiar to them; they were shared by like institutions elsewhere and, as Dicey perceived, there was in them the germ of something which could have evolved into an institution akin to the Conseil d'État.[7] Nor were the abuses of such bodies peculiar to our history. The peculiarity, and, perhaps, the tragedy is to be found in the time and setting in which the crisis in relation to such courts occurred. It is one of our pieces of good fortune as well as one of our misfortunes that we had our overt revolutions early. The whole revolutionary process which can be generally designated by the phrase 'the revolution of 1688,' happened early enough for it to be achieved with little bloodshed, and on the whole with little obvious upheaval in society. These things are all to the good. On the other hand that process happened at a time which, in retrospect, was unfortunate both as to the then current climate of thought of lawyers and as to the scope of governmental activity and the nature of constitutional machinery.

The abolition of the conciliar courts in the revolution of 1688 meant the unchallenged dominance of the ordinary courts, the courts of common law, in both jurisdictions, and in those courts there was the dominance of the concept of private property. It has been said that 'unlike the conciliar courts, the common law courts were only concerned with the fulfilment of legal obligations, and not with the execution of policy. In controlling governmental acts they were necessarily limited to considering the letter of the law.'[8] This concern with property rights certainly had its merits. It aided greatly in cases such as *Ashby* v. *White*[9] where the right to vote was treated as a property right, or in the great case of *Entick* v. *Carrington*,[10] wherein the defence of private property against invasion by agents of the government lay at the heart of the dispute. On the other hand its disadvantages became apparent once, for example, local government was no longer based essentially on a grant or charter to a borough (which clearly had a proprietary aspect) but was based on a system of authorities created by a legislative scheme. Not merely was thought confined within the ideas of property (of which more must be said) but available remedies were, on the whole, limited to those appropriate to property rights, or to those which were appropriate to the hierarchical control by a superior court of an inferior court. Thus limited, remedies became inappropriate to the control of administrative activity. So even where, as in Scotland, it was accepted that the supreme civil court should assume the jurisdiction formerly exercised by the Privy Council,[11] the exercise of jurisdiction was bound to be confined by reason of the available techniques even if it had not also been limited by other circumstances. The full consequences or even the existence of these limitations were not immediately apparent; rather did the immediate advantages (demonstrated in cases such as those which have been mentioned) catch and hold attention so that the attitude of lawyers tended to harden. The disadvantages only became apparent when the nature of governmental activity had changed and once the rudimentary constitutional machinery of 1688 had evolved.

There was inherent in the ideas of the revolutionary settlement a double control of governmental activity: control of legality in the courts and political control in Parliament. The broad limits of each form of control (but particularly of the first) were established in relation to the central government at a time when governmental activity in an internal sense was limited. Issues were either those of foreign affairs or, in relation to home affairs, were issues of policy of the most general order; issues of administration were rare. By the time that such issues had in the late seventeenth century become frequent and important to individuals, there had evolved what appeared to be an effective system of parliamentary control. That system was held in respect, a respect which grew as Parliament itself became more democratic, as a result of the process starting with the great Reform Act of 1832. This dependence upon parliamentary controls can be seen operating in the steady suppression of public boards in favour of administration through machinery of government cast in the mould of a department headed by a Minister who was himself subjected to parliamentary control through the doctrine of ministerial responsibility. It can also be seen in the steady rise in the popularity of Parliamentary Questions, a rise which reflects both this reliance on parliamentary controls, and the need for a mechanism for dealing with individual grievances.[12] While it may be true that individual grievances are now not normally raised as Questions in the first instance, but are first raised in correspondence with the Minister, the Question is the unspoken threat which adds weight to the latter. Belief in the efficacy of Questions grew among the public and among members, and indeed their value does not, in many ways, need argument. As a means of securing redress in an ordinary case of maladministration in its simpler forms, the Question could be admirable. The disadvantages are of two sorts. There is first the remedy which may result. The answer, even when it is followed by a rectification of an administrative error, lacks the quality of a judgement in two respects. It lacks the enduring and formative quality of a judgement which enters into a system of jurisprudence, and it lacks the ability of a judgement to decree compensation. Very often the mere rectification of an error without compensation is today an inadequate remedy. In the second place, the disadvantages spring paradoxically enough from the forum wherein questions are asked. When one speaks of a Parliamentary Question, one thinks above all of the House of Commons. That House is, above all, a political House, and it is right that it should be so. Yet the forum for political debate may often not be the appropriate place to argue a question of maladministration. The question is not a political one in the true modern sense of the word 'political'. Moreover, the reliance upon parliamentary controls has its effect (which is possibly disadvantageous) on the structure of government. It necessarily imposes, since Parliament is in one place, a high degree of centralization upon the machinery of the national government, even in relation to administration. The forms of parliamentary control, even if they do not require it, make it highly desirable that the answer can be found speedily in the Minister's department in London.

Clearly, however, at the time when the modern administrative state was emerging, not merely were these disadvantages not apparent, but even their existence might reasonably not be suspected. For the moment it appeared that parliamentary controls could be adequate. This situation had, and continues to have, its effect on the law, as well as on the practice of the administration in ways which are relevant to the present theme. The respect for, and belief in, the efficacy of parliamentary controls moved courts to assume an attitude of restraint in the exercise of their admitted powers of control, which otherwise they might not have assumed. The point may be made by three sentences from the opinions in *Liversedge* v. *Anderson*.[13] The majority of the House of Lords clearly accepted the finality of the certificate of the Secretary of State and in the majority opinions the parliamentary background stands out. Lord Maugham, in coming to that conclusion, emphasized that the Secretary of State was 'a member of the Government answerable to Parliament,' and that 'he would be answerable to Parliament in carrying out his duties'. Lord Macmillan equally emphasized that the Secretary was a high officer of State 'answerable to Parliament for his conduct in office'. Lord Wright emphasized the same point, adding, 'the safeguard of British liberty is in the good sense of the people and in the system of representative and responsible government'. It was Lord Atkin, who, in his dissent, emphasized the continuing role of courts and who clearly was not so satisfied of the perfection of parliamentary control. So too, in *Duncan* v. *Cammell Laird Co.*[14] the acceptance of the finality of ministerial certificates was undoubtedly helped by the emphasis upon the fact that the Minister was the 'political head of the department' and as such subject to the doctrine of ministerial responsibility. The insistence on the continuing role of courts came only with *Glasgow Corporation* v. *Central Land Board*[15] as a result of an insistence on the need for justice. Subsequent events (which will be discussed later) have demonstrated the need for that insistence, and also the fact that the House of Lords was over-optimistic in its reliance on parliamentary control.[16] It should not be thought that Scotland was unaffected by the other line of thought. Lord President Normand in *Pollok School* v. *Glasgow Town Clerk*[17] says, 'I am of opinion that the question whether the supply of houses is a purpose within Regulation 51 (1) is a political question and thus the exercise by the competent authority of a discretion in deciding it may be controlled in Parliament but cannot be reviewed in a court of law.' This attitude affected not only the decision of such large matters but even questions such as that of a right to a pension. Lord Sorn, speaking in the context of a claim to a naval pension, said,[18] 'In execution of its delegated power the Crown is answerable to Parliament, but I doubt if it becomes answerable to the subject.' That is to say that the subject might enforce the duty (which admittedly existed in some form) by parliamentary or political pressures, but not in a court of law.

These are modern cases illustrating the hardening of principle, but the same deference can be seen in the formative years. In *Institute of Patent Agents* v. *Lockwood*,[19] the source of the modern cases on delegated legislation, Lord Herschell opened the critical passage of his judgement with the assertion 'it must be remembered that it' [*scil.*: a wide discretionary power of legislating] 'is committed to a public department, and a public department largely under the control of Parliament itself'. This point was one of the main foundations for his argument limiting judicial control. It was coupled with the point that the rules made by the department were to be laid before Parliament and hence it was said Parliament had 'full control'. This second point illustrates another aspect of deference to Parliament, which in origin may have been justified but, as things have developed, is certainly no longer so. There is here the refusal of courts to examine the realities of parliamentary life, and hence their inevitable tendency to build the law upon the fictions rather than the realities of that life. Clearly, the pressures arising from the increase of legislation which is inescapable in a modern society have meant a diminution in parliamentary scrutiny of primary legislation and a still greater diminution in the scrutiny of delegated legislation. Yet the law, and the operation of courts, is based on the theory of 'full control', implying, as that phrase does, full scrutiny. In the same way at the time when a Minister became more and more a judge of disputes, whether between inferior public authorities or between citizens and public authorities, and the legal rules governing this situation were being settled, the same influences were felt. In *Local Government Board* v. *Arlidge*[20] the key to the decision may reasonably be said to be found in two sentences: 'My Lords,' said Lord Shaw of Dunfermline, 'how can the judiciary be blind to the well known facts applicable not only to the Constitution but to the working of such branches of the executive? The department is represented in Parliament by its responsible head.' From that fact, coupled with the dependent fact of the anonymity of the civil service, flowed the judicial answers that the individual was not entitled to know or see the individual official who decided (this being, it was considered, immaterial, since the Minister was responsible) and that decisions need not be reasoned. The last was an acceptance of administrative practice which was itself dependent upon the doctrine of ministerial responsibility. The decision, it was thought, should, if need be, be justified in Parliament but not elsewhere. Once the pattern of judicial activity had been set in this mould the shape of the more recent decisions became predictable.

It is necessary at this point to link the two elements already emphasized in relation to the revolution of 1688. The concern with private law ideas and techniques might by itself alone have stimulated this reliance upon parliamentary controls. Private law operates between parties who exist in the same plane, and are thus equal. Rights are in issue. In public law properly conceived there is an inequality; private right is in conflict with public interest in a quite different way.[21] The mechanisms appropriate to striking a balance in the one condition will of necessity be inappropriate or inefficient in the other. Therefore, relief in the second state of affairs would tend to be sought by other means. Yet, to an extent, the two causes, the legal and the parliamentary background coinciding as they did, increased the effect which either alone might have had. Each cause increased the effect of the other. That point is made by contrasting the vast evolution of private law in the nineteenth century which was necessary to absorb the industrial revolution (an evolutionary process which, to some extent, at least, continues in the field of private law) with the failure of lawyers to produce a similar evolution in the field of public law even when the needs for such an evolution had become apparent.[22] Instead, such evolution as there was came in the area of parliamentary techniques, an evolution which, it seems, was perhaps accelerated by the failure of the courts. The latter failure was also attributable to the remedies at the disposal of the courts. When it is said that administrative issues did not arise at the critical formative period, that is true of the central government. It was not true in relation to local government, in relation to which the disappearance of the conciliar courts had also meant the disappearance or weakening of central controls. In relation to the counties, wherein (in England) local government was largely conducted through the justices in quarter sessions, a degree of supervision by the courts could exist, but through mechanisms, in particular the prerogative writs or orders, which were appropriate to the control *en cassation* of an inferior court. The subsequent reforms of these remedies were reforms which contemplated exclusively their operation in the field of judicial proceedings properly so called, and had the effect as time went on of severely limiting judicial control in the field of administration just when the need for that control was growing. The supervision of the superior court could only be effectively invoked when the lower 'court' had stated reasons and those reasons were in error. Normally, because of procedural reforms, reasons were not stated.[23] This necessity for a 'speaking record' was particularly important since here again the lawyers and Parliament combined to the same end—silence. If the Minister were to answer in Parliament the decision was often not a 'reasoned' one. To give reasons could be to give hostages to fortune. Thus the process of administration tended to be a closed rather than an open one.

These procedural matters had a special significance in England, but had not, in strict theory, the same importance in Scotland. There there was a more general basis for judicial control. Perhaps this arose because of the circumstances commented on by Lord Kames, perhaps also because in Scotland Parliament was until recently felt to be more remote than was the case in England. The Court of Session, it was said, must be open to anyone who complains of a wrong done by an inferior body,[24] and, more clearly than the English courts, it could insist that decisions should be taken in such a form as would facilitate review by the courts.[25] Nevertheless, the scope of such review in Scotland tended not to be greatly different from that in England. The fact that the House of Lords was the ultimate court of appeal in both jurisdictions had an obvious effect,[26] and the same attitude towards Parliament was operative, as the cases cited above demonstrate. Indeed, the Scottish cases show clearly the effects of the evolution discussed. In 1843 in *Pryde* v. *Heritors of Ceres*,[27] in which the court was asked to review the rates of payment for poor relief, the court accepted jurisdiction, although it was conscious of the difficulty and the delicacy of the task. The greatest difficulty envisaged was that of ascertaining the facts necessary for a decision, but it *was* assumed that relief from the decision of a statutory board must be found in the courts. Three things should, however, be noted. The heritors were a local body; secondly, in 1843 no simple means of parliamentary redress was apparent; thirdly, the matter was finally regarded as fit for decision in a court as a pecuniary claim; it was not regarded as a political matter. In contrast, the *Pollok School* case indicates a very marked change of attitude. The full effect of the use of the parliamentary arena for seeking redress has had its consequences in broadening the scope of what can be comprised within the term 'political'. Essentially the issues in *Pryde*'s case were social, yet at that time a court would deal with them. A century later the interpretation of words, normally a lawyer's province, was treated in a similar context as quite outside the competence of a court. The forum for redress had had the effect of changing the classification of problems. Moreover, the decline, if one should not say the decay, of local government had accentuated that change. Increasingly all matters of principle involve the central government, and it is the central government which is represented in Parliament and amenable to challenge there. Hence, granted the constitutional background, in this way also the range of matters with which courts will feel a reluctance, and often an overwhelming reluctance, to concern themselves, has increased greatly. One could almost say that the philosophical questions about what is a 'political question' and what is a 'justiciable issue' have become the burning questions which lawyers must debate before it is too late.[28] Put in lawyers' terms it could be said very briefly that we have no system of public law because reliance upon parliamentary redress (a reliance fostered both by the growth of Parliament and the reticence of the courts), has made development of such a system impossible.

Before turning to some of the more detailed consequences in law which flow from the causes which have produced that general result, one may perhaps, though the dangers are obvious, emphasize the significance of this general constitutional background by contrasting it with that in France. There a revolution similar in basic principle to our own was delayed for a century. As a result it was more violent and the disturbance of political life was deeper and longer lasting. Yet, occurring when and how it did, there could be born or reborn in that revolution an institution, the Conseil d'État, which could develop those beneficent functions of a Privy Council which our history condemned to frustration. The troubled history of parliamentary evolution in France enabled, and perhaps encouraged, the development of those functions in the nineteenth century whereas the different parliamentary history with us had the opposite effect. No doubt the law of 3 March 1849 (which decisively affirmed the character of the Conseil d'État as a court), is important in that history, but, to a stranger, much more significant is the reaffirmation of the same

33

principle in the law of 24 May 1872, Article 9, which indicated more fully the scope of the jurisdiction, followed as it was by the decision in *Blanco*,[29] which opened the door to wide extensions of the work of the Conseil. The reaffirmation of the existence of an administrative jurisdiction and the reformulation of its basic principles came at the time when the modern state was already starting to have effect (the facts of *Blanco*, in that it could be said in modern times to involve a nationalized industry, alone show that). The jurisdiction could develop to keep pace with the development of that state, having not merely this philosophic basis, but also having behind it already a long history. Even if much of that history was in the quiet field of contract, that quietness had its advantages for the future. If with us the conciliar courts could have been quieter and duller their history might have been longer.

To return to the other side of the Channel, one must first note the ways in which the modern state drew itself to the attention of lawyers. Even that most far-seeing man Maitland, lecturing in 1888, while he emphasized the possible importance of contract in suits against the Crown, could also write: 'The Queen and her officers are no longer in the habit of seizing land upon all manner of pretences; there are few pretences available.'[30] He did not clearly foresee compulsory purchase for schools, hospitals, electricity installations and all the other 'pretences' available to a modern state which must exist but which may be abused. Beyond the field of contract he was content that the plea 'act of state' was excluded and for the rest to leave matters on the basis of private law. At the critical stage attention was fixed upon two matters, delegated legislation and administrative tribunals. The prominence of *Lockwood's* case and *Arlidge's* case in the history of English administrative law is significant, as is the contrast between them and *Blanco*. One consequence of this was the tendency to regard 'administrative law' as confined to these two issues. Dicey's article 'The Development of Administrative Law in England'[31] does not go beyond these bounds; the first book entitled *Administrative Law* in this country—that of Dr Port—was similarly confined, and the tendency to think in these restrictive terms was fortified by the two great inquiries: the Committee on Ministers' Powers and the Committee on Tribunals and Inquiries,[32] which concerned themselves exclusively with these matters, and were themselves the centres of debate, focusing interest upon their own subject-matter.

The emergence of these two issues, delegated legislation and administrative tribunals, as the central ones, is clear, yet needs further explanation. It is only a partial explanation to say that it was in this context, and most clearly in relation to inquiries, that the problem of reconciling judicial and parliamentary controls of administrative action became apparent and demanded solution. A fuller explanation is to be found in the technicalities of remedies which have already been mentioned. Especially in England the prerogative writs or orders were available, inefficient though they might be. Through them, in these contexts some relief could be sought. Elsewhere it was difficult to find a starting point. What was sought in *Arlidge's* case was a writ of *certiorari*. Yet this circumstance had further consequences. The availability and effectiveness of these remedies depended largely upon procedural matters. Hence the tendency has been for courts to be concerned not with substantive merits but with procedural defects involved in the matter in question which may or may not have had any real significance. What is attacked is not the substance or the merits of a decision, but the procedure by which it has been reached. It is certain that procedural rectitude can have advantages. In the Middle Ages insistence upon procedure was one means of securing regularity of administration. Too close a concern with procedure is probably only appropriate to an early stage of development, and in this context this concern with procedural questions has had a series of disadvantageous consequences.[33] First, and perhaps most importantly, it has the effect of producing technicality rather than generality in the law, a technicality which may sometimes do injustice to the individual, sometimes to the administration. The incidence of injustice is random. In order to come within the scope of *certiorari* a function had to be classified as judicial or quasi-judicial, terms which have never been satisfactorily defined.[34] As a result, since they are not classified as quasi-judicial, decisions may surprisingly escape judicial control. The cases wherein the courts refuse to intervene in 'disciplinary' proceedings are perhaps the outstanding examples.[35] Technicality is increased by the fact that while stages in the process of taking one decision may be classed as quasi-judicial, so that certain minimum standards of conduct are required during those stages, the later stages which are classed as administrative escape this requirement.[36] This can mean, then, that the whole decision is not subjected to review even on procedural grounds, and while the subtleties of distinguishing between stages may appeal to the lawyer, the result of these subtleties is likely to be a feeling of dissatisfaction in the mind of the citizen, to whose eyes the decision is a decision—an indivisible whole. Technically and concern for procedure may have other results. It may mean that an order is upset when in substance it is recognized as correct, and when in fact it is recognized that no injustice has been done. Thus in one case a misdescription in the area of land subjected to an order under schemes for regulating agriculture was sufficient to upset the order, even though it was clear that every-one knew what farm and what land was under discussion, and even though the misdescription was slight, referring to narrow strips at the edge of the farm in question, which could not affect the decision in question.[37] So also, although it appears that in substance a decision was right, and had been properly arrived at, an error in drafting the formulation of the decision may result in its overthrow.[38] In these cases it is the reasonable needs of the administration which are unreasonably impeded. In other cases, such as those of the type of *Errington's* case, it may be that the individual is left with a strong conviction that although certain procedural rules have been rigidly followed, substantial justice has not been done. Both of these types of consequences can be serious, and it is probable that too little thought has been given to the first type – the neglect of the needs of government, in the efficiency of which we too have an interest.

This neglect of a fundamental consideration of the nature and purposes of judicial review which flows from the concern with procedure is itself responsible for a second disadvantageous consequence, which has a double aspect. There grew, almost accidentally, a belief that if procedural safeguards could be strengthened, if more administrative decisions could be taken in a form which could be called quasi-judicial, then all would be well. That belief was fostered by the circumstance that it came to be thought that if the method of reaching a decision could not be described by the magic words 'quasi-judicial' (which had the effect of the incantation of 'abracadabra', opening the cave of judicial review), then rules of fair-dealing, such as the *audi alteram partem* rule, were excluded or inapplicable. Clearly these two things are related, the first (the belief in procedural safeguards) being prompted by the second. The second may be illustrated (apart from *Ex p. Fry*, already mentioned) by *Nakkuda Ali* v. *Jayaratne*.[39] That the Controller of Textiles, exercising his power to grant or revoke licences to trade in textiles, could be said by the Judicial Committee of the Privy Council to be 'taking executive action to withdraw a privilege' had the effect that he was under no obligation to regulate his action by any analogy to judicial rules. Hence, in the absence of any provision in the particular regulations there was no obligation upon him to serve notice on the trader or hear him before revoking the licence. Because the act was executive or administrative it was unencumbered by procedural rules, and in a system of judicial review so concerned with procedure, the serious consequences to an individual of such an attitude are sufficiently obvious. It is equally obvious that pressure would therefore arise to change the mode in which decisions were taken to avoid these consequences, even though procedural complications in the process of taking decisions may well render the process of government slow and cumbersome, when a modern age demands speed with safety. It is not always remembered that governments are expected to do something, or that at the end of the day complex procedures may not be the best protection for individuals. Nevertheless, evidence of these pressures is to be seen in the report of the Committee on Tribunals and Inquiries, and in the consequential Tribunals and Inquiries Act, 1958; both of which are essentially concerned with trimming the mode of taking decisions to fit an inadequate system of law rather than being concerned with that law itself. Indeed, the scope and terms of reference of the Committee are in themselves sufficient evidence of a belief that the vital issue was conceived to be a procedural one rather than being one of the whole nature of administrative law. The Report and the Act were limited by the circumstances of their origin and it has already become apparent that an awareness of the limitations of the reforms brought about by the Act is growing. The fact that that awareness often takes the form of pressure for other administrative palliatives, such as the appointment of an Ombudsman, is in part a result of the limited concepts of the role of public law induced by these procedural considerations. Thus blinkered, we cannot see the real scope of administrative law.

That this reliance on remedies which, as they have developed, focus attention on procedure has inhibited the courts in fulfilling their traditional role in a modern society can be demonstrated even by resort to internal sources.

In England the sudden growth in the popularity of an action for a declaration instead of, and in substitution for, applications for *certiorari* is one mark of this, for the former action is free of some of the limitations of the latter.[40] Indeed, it has been claimed to be a perfectly general remedy available where one party 'has a real interest to raise, and the other to oppose'.[41] It may, however, be doubted whether it can break free from the shackles of thought created by the older forms of action, and in any event it is a remedy without result. The action produces at the end of the day simply a declaration of rights. It cannot of itself be productive of redress, let alone compensation. Even our concepts of what is a real interest are fragmentary, rudimentary and underdeveloped. In Scotland, as has been said above, remedies were more general. The standard form of action is one for reduction, which is available wherever there exists a document or decision which can be quashed, where in effect there is something on which the order can act. The problem of classification of an act does not arise in an acute form, for the same remedy can be used whether it be administrative or judicial. In *M'Donald* v. *Lanarkshire Fire Brigade Joint Committee*[42] another fireman had been disciplined, and he too appealed to the courts, but this time with success. 'The irregularity of the proceedings and the unlawfulness of the penalty are sufficient grounds of action,' said Lord Guthrie. He had had *Ex p. Fry* pressed upon him in argument (which is one sign of how decisions in one jurisdiction may affect those in the other), but he avoided following that decision. Although he did, in fact, class the proceedings of the Fire Brigade Authority as judicial or quasi-judicial, this classification was not, it seems, fundamental to the decision; the bare grounds quoted above sufficed, as indeed they should. The case illustrates not merely that varying decisions can be reached on what are essentially similar facts, but it also perhaps demonstrates how different might have been the state of our administrative law had it been possible to maintain a generality of approach, particularly in the dominant jurisdiction of England.

One further result may here be noted. Since the most familiar field of operation of the courts was in relation to quasi-judicial decisions, the law in relation to the control of administrative acts has a hesitant or tentative air. Certainly there are to be found broad declarations of principle. There is the much-quoted dictum of Lord Greene. 'The court is entitled to investigate the action of the local authority with a view to seeing whether they have taken into account matters which they ought not to take into account, or conversely have ... neglected to take into account matters which they should have taken into account.'[43] The practical application of such declarations is however much more limited than these terms suggest. In that case Lord Greene was speaking of a local authority, and in respect of such authorities there is certainly a much greater readiness to examine their actions, though even in relation to such authorities it is likely that the courts in this century are much less ready to examine decisions in depth than was formerly the case. In relation to activities of the central government, it is even more true that a like reluctance has increased very greatly. The reasons for it are clear; once a court is concerned with questions other than those of *ultra vires* in a narrow sense, but is being asked to concern itself with the motive or propriety of an act, all those secondary influences of the development of the system of parliamentary control which have been noticed become operative. So, where the court was asked to declare unreasonable part of a town planning scheme confirmed by a Minister, Lord Greene himself said,[44] 'The common law does not control Parliament, and if Parliament confers on a Minister a power to make regulations, how can the court enquire into these regulations beyond ascertaining whether they are within the power?' adding, when cases dealing with local authorities were pressed upon him, 'We are dealing with a totally different class of subject-matter and one in which the ultimate arbiter is the Minister himself.' Thus, it is parliamentary influences which have ensured the perpetuation of the concept of the Minister-judge.

The full significance of such phrases is realized when inquiry as to the scope of any power is considered in the light of statements such as those in the *Pollok School* case referred to above. The definitions critical to the determination of that scope may be determined by a Minister, not the court. These difficulties become abundantly apparent when questions of motive become important. In *Earl Fitzwilliam's Wentworth Estates* v. *Minister of Town and Country Planning*[45] the majority in the Court of Appeal, and all judges in the House of Lords, were of the opinion that once a proper motive could be established, then the existence of other motives which might not be proper was irrelevant. Denning L.J. vigorously dissented: he regarded the other purpose as dominant and therefore the order was bad. In a short space it is necessary to express the decision in sharply contrasting colours, though there are, of course, subtleties of shading which can be found by a careful reading of the judgements. Even so, the case indicates the difficulties which face courts, as at present organized, when they attempt to probe in depth. Partly the difficulties spring from the fact that the traditional forms of judicial review, which have already been discussed, have encouraged an attitude of mind which is not inclined to such probing. Partly they spring from the fact that the techniques available to the courts, being those appropriate to ordinary civil litigation between private parties of roughly equal status and interests, are not appropriate to this form of litigation when one party may be in a dominant position in relation to essential information. The second of these propositions is more easily understood when the basic concepts upon which the equivalent rules have been built in France are considered.

In France the preponderant character of the administration has been recognized and compensated for. So, in the most critical area of *détournement de pouvoir* the private citizen is required only to raise such a case as will raise sufficient suspicion to merit investigation, and to counterbalance the dominant position of the administration the Conseil d'État has inverted the normal burden of proof, putting upon the administration the burden of proving innocence,[46] and has supplemented this general attitude by derivative rules such as that in *Barel*[47] whereby the silence of the administration is construed against it. Again, because of the recognition of the peculiarity of the public service, it has been possible to evolve rules of considerable subtlety and effectiveness on the control of motives,[48] which have the effect of striking a proper balance between the interests of the administration and those of the individual. All these rules are, however, dependent on a deliberate effort to achieve rules appropriate to a public-law situation. The contrast is sufficiently indicated by the rule in *Duncan* v. *Cammell Laird Ltd.*[49] and its subsequent developments. The leave granted to a Minister to reformulate a claim to privilege[50] indicates at the same time a concern for formalism and an attitude radically different from that of the Conseil. Even when protests are made against undue formalism,[51] in the sense that a particular set of words should not be regarded as automatically and necessarily sufficient justification for a claim by a Minister to withhold documents, it does not appear, on an examination of the judgements, that any real power of the courts to press their own inquiries is contemplated, or perhaps is possible under the existing system. The impression remains that '*vox et praeterea nihil*' may yet prove to be an appropriate summary simply because the courts will be unable without a major reorientation to achieve the necessary subtlety of procedure and of rules. Without such a power the element of ritual or formalism which will make such a claim unchallengeable will remain even though the formula used may be an expanded one, as compared with the formula currently in use.

This same line of cases may be used to illustrate one further difficulty which springs from the peculiar history of the role of courts in relation to the administration with us. Already it has been noted that judicial review, the control by a court, is dominated by the concept of a judicial or quasi-judicial decision. The concern in the Tribunals and Inquiries Act, 1958, s. 12, was to ensure that reasons, if required, should be given in decisions falling within that category, or where a decision was taken by a Minister in cases where a preliminary inquiry could be required by law. Clearly it is as important, or perhaps more important that reasons should also be given for administrative decision, especially when the preliminary stages in reaching the decision have not been in public. It is curious, and perhaps significant that section 12 does not impose any obligation to give reasons where any inquiry which precedes the decision is not one which could be compelled by law. The difficulty arising both from the absence of an obligation to state reasons in a fully significant way and from the reticence of the court once it is outside the familiar territory of the quasi-judicial, is apparent from the cases just discussed. In effect the tragedy is that the peculiar evolution of judicial review by artificially segregating one group of decisions from another has prevented the courts from creating and applying any general concept of administrative morality. The artificiality can be said to exist because in essence the decisions in either group have normally the same nature, and the process by which the decision is now reached is the result of historical accidents. The tragedy (perhaps the word is not too strong) is there because this question of administrative morality is a fundamental and general one; the mechanisms of the law have prevented the question being approached in the way that is necessary even though the question is, at times, seen to exist.[52] The approach must be as general as the problem and not as particular a one as the available remedies dictated.

The possibility of achieving a generality of principle has hitherto been denied by one other major consideration. Increasingly the services of government are becoming unified, because problems have become national. Neither education nor the relief of the poor can any longer be regarded as local issues. The nation as a whole has an interest in the quality of education in each part of the country. Increasingly there is talk of regional planning, in the interest not merely of the particular region but of the country as a whole. Thus economic and other forces compel a unification of services (which need not mean centralization) but the theory of our law conflicts with these facts. The 'administration' does not exist. Instead the law contemplates two things: 'the Crown' – which is very broadly the central government, and other public authorities – largely local authorities, with public corporations existing in an uncanny half-world. To the ordinary citizen it does not matter whether or not the public authority with whom he deals is or is not regarded in law as 'the Crown'. To him it is simply 'the government' or the administration. In law this classification matters a great deal. It affects profoundly the remedies which are available, since section 21 of the Crown Proceedings Act makes inapplicable certain remedies otherwise available; it affects also, as has been noted above, the way in which courts regard the activities of public authorities, since courts are much less ready to scrutinize closely the actions of the Crown. These things may matter a great deal in particular cases,[53] but they probably matter even more since they also are responsible for impeding the formation of general ideas.

Certain rights, because they are associated with the Crown, are called prerogatives, and because of this appellation and association they tend to be regarded as peculiar to the Crown. This has a double psychological effect. The rules are not clearly seen as being rules peculiar to government in general and in a practical sense: instead, they have, through the word 'Crown' with its overtones of feudalism, a mystic air of being related to monarchy (an air perhaps all the more dangerous when monarchy has become innocuous, but the rules are in truth applicable to a government with much greater power than a monarch ever had). This unrealism has the effect that the rules are allowed to operate when in some sense the Crown is involved even though that operation is to the detriment of the government and community. In the notable instance, the immunity which properly the Crown, in the sense of government, has from taxation, was allowed to operate even where the effect of its operation was exclusively to benefit a private individual at the expense of the government, because there was involved an official, the Custodian of Enemy Property, who could be regarded as a servant of the Crown.[54] Thus on the one hand the terminology tends to prevent, or at least to impede, the application of realism and common sense to rules affecting the central government. Equally the rules tend to have a universal effect in relation to that government, because it is 'the Crown', and so it is impossible to achieve those subtleties of application dependent on the character of the governmental act in question which are clearly necessary if a proper balance between the needs of government and the rights of individuals is to be struck. Because the rules are too absolute they are inappropriate to the varied activities of a modern government which acts in many characters.[55] On the other hand, because of terminology such as 'prerogative' or 'Crown' rules which are in truth general are not seen to be so. Local authorities as much as the central government perform governmental functions, yet this characteristic is only with difficulty recognized because terminology has obscured thought. The rule in the *Amphitrite*,[56] that the Crown cannot fetter its future executive action, is normally seen as distinct. The cases in which local authorities are faced by the same problem are regarded as somehow being different.[57] Similarly in relation to local authorities the consequences may be that the governmental or public character of their acts is not seen to exist and thus the frustration of their proper functions results.[58]

If appropriate rules are to be evolved to deal with modern government, then modern government must be seen in the round and not fragmented, yet again history has proved to be an obstacle. Again, too, it must be emphasized that that history has its own sound justification. At a period when the full impact of modern government could not be clearly seen the issue of the treatment of government became acute in relation to tax exemption. Many bodies were claiming exemption which was sensibly enjoyed by the Crown. A convenient way of limiting these claims to exemption was to deny the character of a Crown servant. So, for example, the University of

Edinburgh was (rightly) denied this character.[59] By these means the distinction was built into the law and has had enduring consequences. Once again, though the origins may be justified, the consequences can be deplored. The split which has been engendered affects all branches of the law. The servant of the local authority has some remedies when he is unjustifiably dismissed. The servant of the central government has none at law. An employee who changes between the two services does much more than change his master. The whole character of his relationship with his master is changed, even though the essential character of his duties is not. It is this aspect of public service which as much as anything shows the limiting effect on thought of this artificial division. Clearly it is impossible that all the developments in state activity should have left no mark in law. The advent of the National Health Service, which meant that hospitals became part of a service under the ultimate control of a Minister, was found to alter pre-existing rules relating to medical fault, particularly fault of consultants.[60] Yet the recognition of changed conditions has been slow and irregular. The fact of the existence of a National Health Service meant, among other things, that the potential employer of doctors in the hospital service was a near monopolist. Moreover, the conditions of employment of doctors bear strong marks of a service: they are for the most part governed by regulations. Yet in England the relationship of doctors to the hospital board has been regarded still as being the same as the relationship between a private master and his servant, with the result that the remedies available to the wrongfully dismissed servant were unreasonably limited. The character of service was entirely neglected.[61] In Scotland, however, more recently[62] full weight was given to this service character with the result that remedies *were* appropriate to the condition of employment.

This aspect of employment in the public service is but one illustration of a further major consequence of the lack of generality of ideas. Here they are to be seen the combined consequences of the dominance of private law (or its converse, the rejection of a specific public law) which has earlier been noted as one part of the revolution of 1688, and of the limitations upon thought imposed by the forms of action of judicial review. Ideas of general utility and significance such as that of *res extra commercium* or even ideas about the organization of a public service[63] have been lost, and appear too strange to be given effect.[64] As a result ideas of public contracts are ill-informed, so that although the compulsions of the needs of government may make themselves felt, the legal machinery to compensate the individual who has contracted with the government may be lacking.[65] The same

43

may well be said to be true of delictual liability,[66] though it is probable that much less hardship arises on this score. More important is the fact that ideas about what will suffice to give a good title to raise an action, particularly when general duties of public authorities are involved, are seriously underdeveloped. In part this is attributable to the fragmentary character of public law, to the absence of a system, since there has been little incentive to work out any general theory. In part this is again attributable to the ideas of property, and hence the insistence upon something akin to a proprietary right before the court's aid can be invoked.[67] That concern with property is readily understandable in the perspective of history, yet clearly the modern operations of government require, if law is to play its proper place in the regulation of society, a clarification and expansion of this particular concept.

In effect it is this question of the place of law in society that is at the heart of the matter. Some of the consequences of the absence of a system of public law which have been mentioned seem small and technical, but when all are cumulated the real problem becomes apparent. Other consequences which are more nearly constitutional could be mentioned. The relationship between central government departments and either local authorities or nationalized industries demonstrates limitations upon the use of law which have like causes to those limitations which have been discussed or mentioned in the context of the 'external' operations of government – its operations in relation to individuals. Enough, however, has probably been said to indicate the crisis which exists. Recently. there have been signs of the fact that recognition of the existence of a crisis is growing. 'We do not have a developed system of administrative law – perhaps because until recently we did not need it,' said Lord Reid,[68] recognizing in the same breath both the absence and the need. Earlier Lord Devlin had written,[69] 'I believe it to be generally recognized that in many of his dealings with the executive the citizen cannot get justice by process of law. The common law has now, I think, no longer the strength to provide any satisfactory solution to the problem of keeping the executive, with all the powers which under modern conditions are needed for the efficient conduct of the realm, under proper control.' Elsewhere the recognition is apparent in the continuing malaise which is felt by the public at large about the present situation ... in the absence of a system of public law the law has proved itself incapable of meeting the demands of a modern state and, because the inadequacies of the existing law are seen or felt, albeit instinctively, no longer do people turn to the law for relief but instead to administrative palliatives. But the problem to be solved, like the seventeenth-century problem of prerogative, can only be solved by courts and Parliament, by law and politics. Neither alone is effective, for as has been shown the popular remedy of an Ombudsman, operating of necessity in a parliamentary arena, could not deal with the central problems. Relief, in the end of the day, can be found only through law.

Thus, though much history enters into this theme, the theme is essentially modern. The crisis exists. It remains to be seen whether we must remain the prisoners of the unhappy consequences of some aspects of an otherwise happy history. Undoubtedly, the creation of an effective system of public law would be a major undertaking, involving as it would the rejection of many deep-seated ideas. It would probably require the creation of a new system of courts to break the fetters upon those which now exist. It is those fetters which have led to the acceptance by too many of a feeling of judicial impotence. Perhaps it is because the author is a lawyer that he does not accept the current despair about law. Recognition of the defects of the existing state of affairs need not lead to that despair.

One further word might be added. Just as at the outset it was said that many of the good aspects of our constitutional arrangements would not be mentioned, though they exist, so in conclusion it should be said that the criticism in what has been said is aimed at law and lawyers. Overall the administrative morality, especially in the civil service, is remarkably high and it is not that which is criticized. It must, however, be recognized that the best of men need from time to time a stimulus to their conscience. That stimulus can best be provided by the law.

NOTES

The basic text of this article was prepared for publication in *Études et Documents* (The Conseil d'État). The Editor of that journal has kindly allowed the publication of an English version. In the text that follows, the generality and relative lack of annotation dictated by the original form has been preserved, and, save where alteration was required by the different place of publication, the text remains close to the original and references have largely remained at the stage at which the original text was settled.

1. Fountainhall, *Decisions*, Vol. I, p. 301. In the same volume at p. 234 we find John Forbes sued before the Privy Council for oppression in collecting the excise and fined 900 merks.
2. Fountainhall, *Decisions*, Vol. I, p. 208.
3. See *Register of the Privy Council of Scotland* (3rd Series), Vol. II, pp. 4–6, or at pp. 512–513 for examples, or see Vol. VIII, pp. 3 and 6, for an order to release one improperly detained by the magistrates of the Canongate.
4. *Register of the Privy Council of Scotland* (3rd Series), Vol. III, p. 466.

5. *Conn* v. *Magistrates of Renfrew* (1906) 8 F. 905 at p. 911.
6. Holdsworth, *History of English Law*, Vol. IV, pp. 87–88.
7. For a discussion and defence of Dicey's views, see Prof. Lawson, 'Dicey Revisited' (1959), Vol. VII: *Political Studies*, pp. 112–120.
8. Keir, *Constitutional History*, p. 234. The emphasis of Locke, in his justification of the revolution, upon the fact that government has no other end but the protection of property (*Second Treatise on Civil Government*, Chap. VIII, § 94) should be noted.
9. (1703) 2 Ld.Raym. 398.
10. (1765) 19 St.Tr. 1029.
11. See Lord Kames, *Historical Law Tracts*, p. 228: 'The Court of Session has, with reluctance, been obliged to listen to complaints of various kinds that belonged properly to the Privy Council while it had a being.'
12. See Chester and Bowring, *Questions in Parliament*, with Howarth, *Questions in the House*. In modern times the device of a question is supplemented by the letter to the Minister from a Member on behalf of one of his constituents. From 1870 to 1900 the number of questions in a Session rose from 1,200 to over 5,000.
13. [1942] A.C. 206.
14. [1942] A.C. 624. See too Lord Greene M.R. in *Point of Ayr Collieries Ltd.* v. *Lloyd George* [1943] 2 All E.R. 546 at p. 547.
15. 1956 S.C. (H.L.) 1.
16. See the *Grosvenor Hotel Case* [1964] Ch. 464, discussed below.
17. 1946 S.C. 373.
18. 1950 S.C. 448 at p. 451.
19. [1894] A.C. 347.
20. [1915] A.C. 120.
21. Compare the development of ideas in Sandevoir, *Études sur le Recours de Pleine Jurisdiction*.
22. British jurisprudence remains essentially a philosophy of private law.
23. *R.* v. *Northumberland Compensation Tribunal, ex parte Shaw* [1952] 1 Q.B. 338.
24. *Jeffray* v. *Angus*, 1909 S.C. 400.
25. *Robb.* v. *School Board of Logiealmond* (1875) 2 R. 698.
26. Though *Magistrates of Ayr* v. *Lord Avocate*, 1950 S.C. 102 shows a departure from the English pattern set in such cases as *Franklin* v. *Minister of Town and Country Planning* [1948] A.C. 87, see Mitchell, 'The Scope of Judicial Review in Scotland' [1959] *Juridical Review*, 197.
27. (1843) 5 D. 552.
28. Clearly we are not alone in the Anglo-Saxon world in this. The issue is sharply posed in *Baker* v. *Carr*, 369 U.S. 186 (1961), and in the later cases in the same line the debate continues.
29. 1873 D. III 20. The evolution of ideas is admirably described in Sandevoir, *Études sur le Recours de Pleine Juridiction*.
30. Maitland, *Constitutional History*, p. 483.
31. (1915) 31 L.Q.R. 148. It may be noted that in that article (at p. 152) Dicey criticized the reliance on the doctrine of ministerial responsibility in *Arlidge's* case.
32. The Reports were respectively published in 1932 as Cmd. 4060 and 1957 as Cmnd. 218.
33. Many of which can be exemplified by *Johnson & Co.* v. *Minister of Health*

[1947] W.N. 251; [1947] 2 All E.R. 395, and could be prophesied from *Errington* v. *Minister of Health* [1935] 1 K.B. 249.

34. See de Smith, *Judicial Review of Administrative Action*, Chap. 2. Rightly the author remarks that in this area of law 'an aptitude for verbal gymnastics is obviously an advantage'. It may be doubted if a body of law which demands that aptitude so strongly is the best that can be devised in this field.

35. *Ex p. Fry* [1954] 1 W.L.R. 730; see, too, *R.* v. *Metropolitan Police Commissioner* [1953] 1 W.L.R. 1150.

36. The process of division is apparent in *Errington's* case above, wherein the Minister was in some sense deciding between a local authority and an individual. The difficulties of course came to a head in *Franklin* v. *Town and Country Planning* [1948] A.C. 67. Rare exceptions to the generality of what is said above, such as *Hoggard* v. *Worsbrough U.D.C.* [1962] 2 Q.B. 93, exist but they do not substantially affect the validity of the statement.

37. *R.* v. *Agricultural Land Tribunal, ex p. Benney* [1955] 2 Q.B. 140. The whole history of the litigation starting at [1955] 1 All E.R. 123 indicates the degree of technicality which may exist.

38. *R.* v. *Minister of Housing, ex p. Chichester R.D.C.* [1960] 1 W.L.R. 587.

39. [1951] A.C. 66. Although criticized in *Ridge* v. *Baldwin* [1964] A.C. 40, it is by no means certain that this unhappy case is dead; *cf. Vidyodoya University of Ceylon* v. *Silva* [1965] 1 W.L.R. 77.

40. See *Vine* v. *National Dock Labour Board* [1957] A.C. 488 and Zamir, *The Declaratory Judgment*.

41. Lord Denning, *Pyx Granite Co.* v. *Minister of Housing, etc.* [1958] 1 Q.B. 554 at p. 571.

42. 1959 S.C. 141.

43. *Associated Provincial Picture Theatres Ltd.* v. *Wednesbury Corporation* [1948] 1 K.B. 223 at pp. 223–224.

44. *Taylor* v. *Brighton Borough Council* [1947] K.B. 736; see, too, *Sparks* v. *Edward Ash Ltd.* [1943] K.B. 223. The steady fusion, in fact, of central and local government obviously increases the importance of this tendency.

45. [1952] A.C. 362; [1951] 2 K.B. 284.

46. See Auby and Drago, *Traité de Contentieux Administratif*, Vol. III, p. 322 *et seq.*

47. C.E. 28 May 1954; 1954 R.D.P. 509. Note Waline, and see in particular the *conclusions* of M. Letourneur at p. 522 for the admirably deft approach to the administration which combines understanding, firmness and a deep concern for administrative morality. The extension of this line of cases in the *conclusions* of M. Braibant in Poncin, C.E. 17 June, 1964; 1964 R.D.P. 811 should be noted.

48. Auby and Drago, *Traité de Contentieux Administratif*, Vol. III, p. 49 *et seq.*, where a similar approach is demonstrated.

49. [1942] A.C. 624.

50. [1963] 3 All E.R. 426; [1964] 1 All E.R. 92 (C.A.). The sense of inadequacy of these decisions was enhanced by reading them in the library of the Palais Royal.

51. *Merricks* v. *Nott Bower* [1964] 1 All E.R. 717 and *Re Grosvenor Hotel (No. 2)* [1964] 3 All E.R. 354.

52. The Franks Report says at § 405, 'We wish to emphasize that nothing can make up for a wrong approach to administrative activity by the admini-

47

strative servants.' Because of the circumstances discussed consideration of the enforcement of this necessary morality was not open to the committee.

53. In *Nottingham (No. 1) Area Hospital Management Committee* v. *Owen* [1958] 1 Q.B. 50 the quick effective and necessary remedy was excluded for like reasons.

54. *Bank voor Handel en Scheepvaart N.V.* v. *Administrator of Hungarian Property* [1954] A.C. 584.

55. The rules (mentioned above) dealing with the disclosure of documents in litigation between the government and an individual are typical of this; see Mitchell, *Constitutional Law*, p. 261.

56. *Rederiaktiebolaget Amphitrite* v. *The King* [1921] 3 K.B. 500.

57. *Cory (William) and Sons Ltd.* v. *Corporation of London* [1951] 2 K.B. 476.

58. *Western Heritable Investment Co.* v. *Glasgow Corporation*, 1956 S.C.(H.L.) 54.

59. *Greig* v. *University of Edinburgh* (1868) 6 M.(H.L.) 97.

60. *Hayward* v. *Edinburgh Board of Management*, 1954 S.C. 453.

61. *Barber* v. *Manchester R.H.B.* [1958] 1 W.L.R. 181.

62. *Palmer* v. *Inverness Hospitals Board of Management*, 1963 S.L.T. 124.

63. *Farrier* v. *Elder and Scott*, 21 June, 1799 F.C.

64. This emerges clearly in the opinions in the Inner House in the *Western Heritable Investment Co. Case*, 1956 S.L.T. 2.

65. The *Amphitrite* case above is the outstanding example. A more recent one may be found in *Commissioners for Crown Lands* v. *Page* [1960] 2 Q.B. 274. See generally Mitchell, *The Contracts of Public Authorities*.

66. *Hester* v. *MacDonald*, 1961 S.C. 370.

67. *D. and J. Nicol* v. *Dundee Harbour Board*, 1915 S.C.(H.L.) 1.

68. *Ridge* v. *Baldwin* [1964] A.C. 40 at p. 72.

69. 'The Common Law, Public Policy and the Executive' (1956) 9 *Current Legal Problems* 1 at p. 14.

Anthony Lester

Redress for the Citizen against the Abuse of Power

Unlike our Continental neighbours, we have neither a written constitution nor a sophisticated system of administrative law. Unlike the United States, Canada, and most new Commonwealth countries, we have no Bill of Rights protecting fundamental rights and freedoms, and enforceable in the courts.

The gap in our legal system is not accidental. The Victorian reformers who built the machinery of our modern government rightly believed that representative democracy was a safer guarantee against the abuse of state power than judicial remedies. Unfortunately, they also regarded democracy as the sole guarantee. Their deep distrust of any judicial scrutiny of governmental actions, together with their idealized theory of the democratic process, have left individual and minority rights and liberties dangerously exposed in our increasingly technological and bureaucratic mass society.

Today, the main restraint against wrongdoing by government departments is political rather than judicial : the doctrine of ministerial responsibility by which the minister in charge of the department is answerable to Parliament for the collective workings of his department. Civil servants are accountable to the Minister, and rarely owe a legal duty to members of the public. Characteristically, the main weapon against maladministration in the Civil Service is parliamentary and extra-judicial. Complaints of maladministration – of bias, carelessness, corruption, delay, unfair discrimination, excessive secrecy, and so on – are investigated by the Parliamentary Commissioner only after they have been referred to him by an MP. As his title indicates, the Parliamentary Commissioner exists to help Parliament to review of work of the executive. His investigations may result in a ministerial apology, or ex gratia compensation, but the victim of many forms of maladministration has no protection from the courts.

While at the centre of government, blatant injustice is likely to be attacked by conscientious MPs and the national press, at the local level the situation is far more bleak. Local government is less

Reprinted from *The Times* (3 October 1970), p. 22 By permission of the author and the publisher.

49

genuinely democratic, less politically accountable, and less exposed to healthy publicity than central government. The noble ideal of representative democracy bears little resemblance to real life in the average town hall. Our Utopian vision of a system of local government, genuinely responsive to the popular will as well as to the public interest, leaves local authorities free to allocate public housing to tenants or to place children in state schools virtually on whatever basis they care to adopt, without fear of challenge in the courts. The by-laws which they frame may interfere with basic personal liberties, without being set aside for want of reasonableness.

We are justifiably proud of the integrity and efficiency of public officials in this country. But abuses and injustices occur in the best systems of government; when they do, there should be effective redress for the victim. The administrative process cannot be a succession of justiciable controversies, but the scope of judicial review could be extended well beyond its present narrow limits without impairing the strength or efficiency of public administration. Although there has been a radical shift of attitude in the appellate courts in the last decade, and there are certain to be further examples of judicial creativity in this field, ultimately only Parliament can carry out the considerable programme of reform which the situation demands.

The principles of good administration, already inherent in the Parliamentary Commissioner's case-law, need to be embodied in a statutory code of administrative procedure, applicable both to central and local government. It could require, for example, that decisions should be taken within a reasonable time, after carefully considering relevant facts and the representations of those concerned: that a written statement of the reasons for a decision should be supplied upon request: and that the decision itself should be properly publicized. The proposed code could also be used to translate into English law the rights and freedoms guaranteed by the European Human Rights Convention: including the right to liberty and security of the person, to due process of law, to respect for private and family life, to freedom of thought and conscience, expression and association, to marry and found a family, and to be treated without unfair discrimination.

Britain, like every other contracting state, is obliged to secure the benefits of the Convention to everyone within its territory, and to provide an effective national remedy for violations of the Convention. It is regrettable that successive British governments have failed to implement this modest international Bill of Rights in this country (while writing its provisions into the constitutions of many new Commonwealth countries).

An extensive network of tribunals has been constructed to decide whether various social welfare benefits should be allocated to claimants. The system has several advantages: speed, informality, expertise and the avoidance of undue technicality. However, in spite of the efforts of many tribunals to help the layman who cannot afford a lawyer, the absence of legal aid for tribunal cases is the source of major injustice. Crucial facts or legal arguments can easily be overlooked in the course of the proceedings, and, to add insult to injury, the claimant who is aggrieved by a tribunal's decision may sometimes be debarred from arguing a point of law on appeal if it was not argued before the tribunal itself.

There is something wrong with our social priorities when four-fifths of legal aid for civil cases is spent on divorcing married couples, while not a penny is available for tribunal proceedings dealing with industrial injury and national insurance benefits, criminal injury compensation, rent levels, unemployment benefits, and redundancy payments. The extension of legal aid to cover these matters would be an important advance towards greater enjoyment of their legal rights by the poorest and least educated section of society. This simple if costly change would do almost as much to redress the balance between the citizen and the state as the grander reforms outlined earlier.

There remains the formidable problem of protecting the individual against the despotism of private institutions, which are barely touched by the democratic process, although they may exercise comparable power in their own domain to that of government itself. To the extent that government defers to these 'private governments' – the great industrial or commercial concern, the professional association, the trade union – to that extent do they enjoy autonomy over their own affairs and those subject to them. The danger of abuse of power is certainly no less in the private than in the public sector. But, here again, legal protection is uneven and ineffective. Significantly, perhaps, the courts have recently been willing to encroach upon the autonomous power of one particular type of private government – trade unions – insisting that they should act fairly in controlling the right to work in a closed shop.

If an administrative code or a Bill of Rights cannot be applied to private bodies exactly as though they are branches of government, there is no reason why the principles of good administration and fair dealing cannot be applied to them by means of familiar legislative techniques. It is becoming widely accepted that the rights and liberties of the subject need to be better protected, but it is difficult to win recognition that the necessary reforms should have high political priority. Some of the proposed reforms are controversial; others inevitably involve increased public spending on the administration of justice. They have a common aim: to translate the ideals of a just and democratic society into measures which can be enforced and relied upon by the individual. That aim cannot be realized by lawyers or the courts without the active intervention of Parliament.

Lord MacDermott

The Decline of the Rule of Law*

... The expression 'Rule of Law' is in common use by the good citizens of today as they protest against an increasing lawlessness; but few even of the best of them have much interest in constitutional matters and the expression is generally employed vaguely and without any close regard for its implications. My plan, therefore, will be to say something about its meaning and then to consider its virtues and its value. After that I shall seek to establish that the Rule is in decline, and finally I shall invite you to consider some ways and means of restoring it to health, with particular reference to Northern Ireland.

THE MEANING OF THE RULE OF LAW

In this Kingdom and in some other countries – mostly common law countries – the term 'Rule of Law' is used in two different though not exclusive senses. It may signify little more than the law of the land that maintains an ordered society – that is to say, the law which for us supports the Queen's Peace and regulates the rights and duties of her subjects. This – the primary meaning – is now that more commonly in use. It connotes respect for the law and an obligation to obey it. It holds the door against anarchy. Its strongest support lies in the consent of the people: but sanctions remain necessary and its greatest problem at present is that of enforcement

The second meaning makes for a free as well as an ordered society. It focuses not so much on the letter and requirements of the law of the land as on the characteristics of what, in the United Kingdom, we consider desirable in our constitutional law and practice. It is mainly concerned with the supremacy of law in the relationship

* This is the text of a public lecture delivered by Lord MacDermott at the Queen's University of Belfast on 5 December 1972.

Reprinted from *Northern Ireland Legal Quarterly*, vol. 23, no. 4 (Winter 1972), pp. 475–495. By permission of the author and the publisher.

between the state and its subjects. Its essence is not just a distillation of the law's commands but arises rather from a philosophy of law which this nation has long accepted. This deeper meaning – the constitutional meaning – was brought to public attention by Professor Dicey in 1885 in the first edition of his famous *Law of the Constitution*. Dicey, of course, did not invent the Rule of Law in this sense. In proclaiming it he was building on the decisions of centuries and pronouncing, with much insight and analytical power, on a body of law and custom which, without being cast in a completely rigid and unalterable mould, had become part and parcel of the spirit of our unwritten law of the constitution. So, though not bound to treat Dicey's every view as infallible, we cannot regard the constitutional meaning as merely a matter of academic theory. We must accept its substance as an established part of our legal tradition which goes back a long way and reflects to a considerable degree the kind of society the British people have come to want as theirs.

Although the constitutional meaning has been widely discussed since 1885, a precise and satisfactory definition has never been achieved. But we need not wait for this to happen. It is too much a matter of the will and the spirit to be contained in a box of words. Yet the ideas and ideals which the constitutional meaning embodies have a value all their own and we can get a fair picture of them, despite their elusive qualities, from what Dicey wrote and from the later commentaries of himself and others. For present purposes I must limit myself to two of the main 'conceptions' which he included in his analysis of the Rule as a feature of the British constitution.

The first of these is that 'no man is punishable or can be lawfully made to suffer in body or goods except for a distinct breach of law established in the ordinary legal manner before the ordinary courts of the land'.[1] And the learned author then contrasted this with 'every system of government based on the exercise by persons in authority of wide, arbitrary, or discretionary powers of constraint'.[2] This conception is related principally, though not entirely, to the criminal field and its substance lies in the exclusion of *arbitrariness*. The reference to the ordinary courts of the land would now require expansion to embrace various tribunals and other bodies, clothed by law with special powers, that have since come into existence. And Dicey's fear of what might be done under the guise of discretion can hardly have been aimed at either (a) the exercise of a judicial discretion in the course of the judicial process as, for example, in excluding unfair evidence or deciding upon an appropriate sanction; or (b) the exercise by the law officers, or those appointed as public prosecutors, of a just discretion in the prosecution of offences. These are essential discretions which must, of course, be exercised fairly and independently of the executive if they are not to run the risk of becoming arbitrary. But they have a long history and a strong tradition behind them and normally offer no threat to the Rule.

Yet these points, though important in themselves, are of relatively minor significance; the core of the matter is that the decision which punishes or prejudices a person must be founded in law and not reached by *arbitrary* methods.

The second of the conceptions mentioned by Dicey emphasizes *equality* before the law. With very few exceptions (such as the Sovereign and those accorded diplomatic immunity) all are subject to the ordinary law of the land. The way Dicey summarized this is worth recalling, though it must, of course, be read in the light of his complete text. He said: 'We mean in the second place, when we speak of the "rule of law" as a characteristic of our country, not only that with us no man is above the law, but (what is a different thing) that here every man, whatever be his rank or condition, is subject to the ordinary law of the realm and amenable to the jurisdiction of the ordinary tribunals.'[3] These words convey what they proclaim sufficiently for most purposes, provided it is understood that they do not mean that the law is or ought to be identical for all the Queen's subjects. The circumstances affecting different classes and kinds of people may well justify rules of law applicable to some but not to all. The statute book contains numerous instances of this. For example, it makes special provision (involving both obligations and rights) for those in the armed forces, for medical doctors, for the legal professions, and for those engaged in factories and workshops. I do not think Dicey ever intended to suggest that 'every man' was subject to special laws of that kind as part of 'the ordinary law of the realm'. On the other hand, it seems no less clear that he regarded the fundamental human rights (some of which he proceeds to discuss) and their relative obligations as a part, and a very important part, of the ordinary law. For this reason I believe it is safe to say that he would not have considered any country accepting slavery or some other form of apartheid as honouring the Rule of Law in its constitutional meaning. Such a country might well have achieved an ordered society and might indeed have reached a notably high standard of judicial and administrative competence, but it would not have become a free society. The line between what is and what is not part of the 'ordinary law of the realm' in this context is not always easy to trace, but Dicey's exposition and the weight of public opinion may be said to make the field of doubt comparatively small.

As a general, if imperfect description of the Rule of Law in its constitutional meaning I venture to repeat the following passage from a lecture I gave in this University some years ago when discussing the requirements of sound law-making. It runs:

> The law should also enshrine the 'rule of law'. This is the badge of a free people. The full significance of the expression is hard to catch accurately in words: but it stands for equality (or at least a very high degree of equality) before the law, for the independence of the courts, for the absence of arbitrary government and for established sources of law. It prefers the individual to the state and suffers whenever the normal freedoms and liberties of the former are curtailed without just cause.[4]

I believe that accords with the gist of what Dicey wrote or implied respecting the Rule of Law as a feature of the British constitution. And that, of course, is the constitution we are now considering. But we should remember that other countries – and not all of them common law countries either – have been seeking to formulate a Rule of Law on similar though not identical lines. In 1957, for instance, in the University of Chicago a five day conference was held on *The Rule of Law as understood in the West*, and in one of the general summaries issued thereafter there appears this passage: '... the rule of law does not depend only upon contemporary positive law ... it may be expressed in positive law but essentially it consists of values and not of institutions; it connotes a climate of legality and of legal order in which the nations of the West live and in which they wish to continue to live.'[5] That, I believe, is true of the constitutional meaning which I have been discussing. It is, above all else, a matter of values and a way of life.

Two further points must be noted before we come to the worth of the Rule of Law. The first is that the Rule, as described by Dicey, does not diminish the authority and duty of the government of the day to maintain law and order. Dicey himself has made this abundantly clear. In *The Law of the Constitution* he is at pains to point out that in its proper sense 'martial law' means the suspension of ordinary law and the temporary government of a country or parts of it by military tribunals, and that this is unknown to English law. But he then adds that the same expression is sometimes used as describing some of the emergency powers which the common law does recognize. And this is how he puts the matter:

> Martial law is sometimes employed as a name for the common law right of the Crown and its servants to repel force by force in the case of invasion, insurrection, riot, or generally of any violent

resistance to the law. This right, or power, is essential to the very existence of orderly government, and is most assuredly recognized in the most ample manner by the law of England. It is a power which has in itself no special connection with the existence of an armed force.[6]

The second point to be noted is this. The Rule of Law of which I am speaking falls to be considered and weighed as a whole and not as a divided thing. It has been appropriate to refer to its two meanings because most people are aware of the primary meaning while relatively few appreciate the nature or even the existence of the constitutional meaning; and it will be convenient to continue to refer from time to time hereafter to these meanings in this way. But both are aspects of the same entirety, with the primary meaning a manifestation of the constitutional meaning, and the constitutional meaning dominant in the sense that it provides the broad guiding principles, the philosophy and the atmosphere by which much of our positive law (including that covered by the primary meaning) has been shaped and informed in the course of its gradual development over the centuries.

THE WORTH OF THE RULE OF LAW

With these prefatory remarks I turn to consider the value of the Rule as it is known and still honoured within this Kingdom. I have already described it in terms which are sufficient, I think, to justify the assertion that as a concept it has the virtues of being fundamental, liberal and conducive to the dignity and freedom of mankind. Let us, however, now go a little further and subject this general proposition to a couple of more specific tests by asking – First, how has the Rule influenced the everyday maintenance of law and order, particularly in relation to the judicial process in criminal matters? And secondly, what has the Rule accomplished respecting the individual's relationship to the state?

As to the first of these tests, let it be said at once that all progressive societies have placed a high value on the Rule in its primary sense. Until men learn to live together in a state of grace, it is necessary to save the strong as well as the weak and the affluent as well as the poor from those who would wrongfully act to their detriment; and this means that there must be a system of law, duly enforced, to deter the lawless from injuring the persons and property of their fellows, and from seeking to overthrow or undermine the state by force or other unlawful means. Without some such system, society will grind to a halt as anarchy gets the upper hand. The change may be sudden or slow according to the strength, determination and endurance of the opposing forces, but in the absence of some over-riding intervention (such as plague, famine or conquest) it will continue until law and order are otherwise restored. The British, as a people, have got so used to a trained and organized police force and to its keeping of the Queen's Peace that they take this important function very much for granted, with some prepared to assume that all would go on happily as before if the entire constabulary were given permanent leave. I believe that view to be profoundly mistaken. In such an event the predatory classes might take a few weeks to realize their opportunities, but after that few would be safe in the streets of our big cities at night, and looting and burning and murder would get out of control. The veneer of civilization is thicker in some places than others, but, by and large, it is still woefully thin. And modern life has brought with it much to increase the dangers. It is a sobering thought, of which this City of Belfast needs no reminder, that, given a reasonably safe base, some elementary scientific knowledge and the capacity to steal and drive a motor vehicle, a relatively small body of people can maintain a long series of bombing attacks causing heavy loss of life and the widespread destruction of millions of pounds worth of property; and that despite the deployment of strong and alert security forces. Planned violence like this makes it encumbent on the executive government, as the authority primarily responsible for law and order, to have done with wishful thinking and to ensure that their security forces lack for nothing in training, equipment, numbers, conditions of service and leadership. This would mean more spending on a programme of preparedness; but I think it may be said quite generally, and without special reference to this or some other specific region or regions, that that would be an excellent investment. It would deter the criminal, whatever his motives, and thus reduce the growing volume of offences; it would help to forearm the peace-keeping authorities with appropriate counter-measures and techniques; and, above all, it would enable them to keep subversive and other forms of criminality from attaining dangerous proportions. I would lay particular emphasis on that last point, for experience shows that prompt and effectual action against an outbreak of lawlessness may avoid a rising tide of trouble and the demands on manpower and the economy which that would entail. I remember the late Viscount Simon once saying that, in 1915, when Mr Asquith appointed him Home Secretary his briefing was as short as it was sagacious. 'Don't forget,' said the Prime Minister, 'that your chief function as Home Secretary is to prevent small rows becoming big ones.'

So far, then, as the Rule in its primary meaning is concerned, there can be little doubt that it confers a benefit on the community it serves and therefore on its individual members. But the value of the benefit is another matter. A country may maintain law and order successfully, yet in a manner which is harsh and unjust and obstructive of a proper recognition of the dignity of man, for it may have no complementary Rule of Law corresponding to that covered by what I have called the constitutional meaning. Law and order are certainly essentials well worth striving for, but the price may be higher than is wholesome. In this Kingdom, as it seems to me, that danger is avoided or kept at bay by the impact of the Rule in its constitutional sense. This impact makes itself felt at various points, but I must content myself with one instance drawn from the criminal law. The Rule is emphatic against adjudication and punishment of an *arbitrary* kind and equally against procedures that may open the door to that sort of thing. And so the law today surrounds the criminal trial with a whole series of protective rules attuned to this fundamental consideration. For example, in normal times the prosecutor must be independent of the executive; the charge must be for an offence known to the law and must be proved by sufficient evidence if not admitted; the court must also be independent both of the executive and the parties; and the judge must follow the law as it has been laid down whether he likes it or not. The whole procedure of the criminal trial has shed many defects in past years and has not yet attained perfection. But I think the only reasonable conclusion on this test is that in this sphere the Rule has made a contribution of outstanding merit.

The second test concerns the relationship between the citizen and the state. This is a subject all in itself and I cannot attempt to explore it fully in the time at my disposal. At present the multifarious activities upon which this state is engaged – I refer to the United Kingdom – show no signs of abating and its power has grown as its domain has widened. This may have added to the worries and complications of life for the average individual, but I think it can be said that his status *vis-à-vis* the state – and therein lies much of his freedom – has been maintained with the aid of the Rule and the traditions which have gone to form it. Indeed it is, I believe, rather higher today than it was before the passing of the Crown Proceedings Act of 1947 which made the Crown and its subjects more equal before the law than previously. What the Rule emphasizes in this connection is the supremacy of the law over all. The Minister, his officers and the citizen are alike subject to the law of the land, and the powers of the state over the citizen are those given by an elected Parliament, with the exception of some remaining prerogative rights which are of small consequence in time of peace. This aspect of the Rule remains in theory at the mercy of Parliament; but as long as the Rule is allowed to retain its present virtues this second test goes in its favour and confirms its worth.

In the result, we find the Rule of Law still difficult to describe exactly and still exhibiting the blurred edges that, while producing some degree of uncertainty, are growing points which allow of adaptation and improvement as conditions change. But we are also, I would suggest, still driven to conclude that it stands today as a well rooted conception, apt to nurture freedom and promote justice, which should be preserved and strengthened in the interests of all.

THE DECLINE OF THE RULE OF LAW

Having reached that conclusion we have next to ask if the Rule is in decline – in decline, that is, in its salutary effects, whether by reason of neglect, or inadequacy to meet current trends; or for some other cause. Here, again, it will be convenient to regard both meanings, bearing in mind that they are parts of the same body and that a decline in the influence of one aspect of the Rule can hardly fail to have a prejudicial effect on the other. Assuming, as we may, that the first meaning is focussed on order and the second on freedom, our hopes and expectations, *if all is well*, should be for a continuing ordered freedom, with order guarding freedom and freedom pervasive and strong because it respects and is supported by a regime of order founded on law. But is all well? And are such hopes presently justified?

We must not forget that hope makes its noblest contribution to human society in times of adversity, and that to dim its kindly light when confusion abounds makes it all the harder to find and follow the right road. But that is no reason for putting our heads in the sand and not attempting to assess the position and see where we are. Such an attitude would weaken the national will and substitute for hope a complacency which might very well become despair.

The most obvious way of gauging the effect of the Rule on law and order is to examine the criminal statistics which are published officially every year for each of the Kingdom's jurisdictions – England and Wales, Scotland and Northern Ireland. These are elaborate documents compiled with care and containing a wealth of information. For example, that for 1971 for England and Wales (Cmnd. 5020) contains 214 pages and costs £2.05. I wish, however, that they could also be issued in a simpler edition which would be more readable and more easily understood by the general public. My impression is that most ordinary people like reading about lurid crimes and trials, but have little interest in the subject as a whole. A small annual booklet showing the main trends with the help of graphs, describing the various punishments and penal establishments, the housing of the prison population and its cost to the taxpayer would, I think, help to stimulate anxiety as well as interest on a matter which poses many problems and should concern us all. But I must return to what we have. The details I leave to your private study rather than encumber this paper with a multitude of figures. I must, however, emphasize that for present purposes the survey should be selective. It would, for instance, be better to discard summary offences entirely, for many of these are trivial and the volume of particular categories may be related to little more than the changes following on a more sophisticated way of life, such as the growing density of road traffic. In 1971, in England and Wales, for example, out of 1,366,144 convictions for non-indictable offences, 987,538 were for motoring offences. I therefore turn to the figures known to the police for indictable – that is to say for the more serious – offences. In mercy to all present I have committed these to an appendix showing for each of the United Kingdom's jurisdictions the position for the last 11 years. But having done this, you must allow me to give a brief summary. In 1961 for the whole United Kingdom there were 924,250 offences known to the police of an indictable or similar nature. Each year since this total has mounted with long strides until, in 1971, it had become 1,857,632, an increase over the period of just above 100 per cent. And to make the picture even darker the figures for violence to the person in 1971 continued to rise in all jurisdictions.

This persistent rising tide of criminality presents a situation of the utmost gravity. Its due significance cannot be explained away by a state of regional emergency, such as we are experiencing in Northern Ireland. And I can find no other factor sufficient to avoid the conclusion that this nation has become more given to violence and more dishonest than it used to be. The Criminal Law Revision Committee, under the chairmanship of Lord Justice Edmund Davies, has recently put forward a number of recommendations (Cmnd. 4991) aimed at a more efficient administration of justice, and it may be that these will lead to legislation with a deterrent effect that will reduce the volume of crime eventually. But the specific causes of this malignant disease remain difficult to ascertain and isolate, and remedial measures may have to take various forms. It is to be remarked, moreover, that it has spread during a period of affluence and of educational facilities available on a greater scale than ever before. Poverty and ignorance would not, therefore, appear to be major contributory factors; but it seems likely that at any rate a partial explanation of the phenomenon is to be found in a loss of moral values in an increasingly permissive society, the break up of family life and a lack of national purpose. Yet, whatever the causes, there can be little doubt that the general attitude to the law and law breaking has altered for many. I remember when to be 'summoned' by the police was widely regarded as a family disgrace. Now it is different and repentance is often more related to the error of being caught than to the commission of the offence. The idea that the law is the bond of the community and that the community suffers when it is broken seems to be on the way out. I say that in relation to the whole Kingdom but, sad to state, its most cogent illustration lies in the events of the last four years in this jurisdiction of Northern Ireland. We have all seen the growth of violence and hatred during this unhappy period and there is no need to rehearse the shameful tale on this occasion: but two comments are relevant.

Each of the numerous groups and factions in Ulster that are presently involved in the struggle for power makes its own vociferous claim for justice; but each means something different by the word, which as often as not is a short way of describing what the particular group or faction demands. The Rule of Law lies here in pieces before our eyes, and its unifying influence has for the time departed.

And now for my second comment. It would be rash to think that the other parts of the Kingdom stand immune in this respect. Four years ago the crime rate in Northern Ireland, particularly that for crimes of violence, and the detection rate also, compared favourably with the corresponding rates in Great Britain; and that was so even for the City of Londonderry despite its long and heavy burden of male unemployment. The change we have witnessed could happen elsewhere: more slowly perhaps than here because the Rule of Law is more deeply entrenched in England and Wales and Scotland; but those jurisdictions are also vulnerable to violence, as their statistics show, and it could grow to graver proportions with them should divisions on issues of moment become deep and bitter.

So far, then, as law and order are concerned, I see no escape from the conclusion that the Rule of Law is in decline. The Rule retains its qualities and is not in itself the source of what is occurring. But it has declined because, along with the virtues that support it, it is falling out of respect and has shed much of the influence it once had.

The waning of the Rule's influence can also be seen in other aspects of our national life. Here the evidence is not as direct as that relating to public order, but the factors I mention – I have only time for a few – are, I think, rather more than straws in the wind.

I would refer first to the impact of numbers on the administration of the law, particularly in times of political controversy with the main political parties so balanced as to give neither a wide margin of power. In such a setting the force of numbers can be a potent weapon in the hands of those who unite to flout or ignore the law of the land. The industrial strife of this year, especially that centring upon trade union opposition to the passing of the Industrial Relations Act of 1971, makes it plain, despite the restraint and respect for the Rule shown by many union leaders, that this is not an idle fear. The ordinary processes of law cannot be evoked effectively against large masses of individuals, and proceedings against a selected few, such as a strike committee, are apt to produce a technique of 'facelessness' which ultimately increases the dilemma of enforcement. Trade unionism naturally relies upon the movement's solidarity and capacity for exerting economic and social pressures, but recent events have shown how strong the temptation to tilt at the law of the land can become, and this of itself marks a weakening of respect for the Rule of Law. I do not suggest that the Trade Union Council has any desire or ambition to constitute, as it were, a third estate. Nonetheless, I think it would be true to say that today more people than formerly – and I speak generally and not just of the industrial sphere – are prepared to relate their observance of some item of established law to their view that it is a bad law or unfair or unsuited to their own aims and requirements. It is one thing to criticize and protest about a law in the making or to seek its repeal when made, but quite another to disregard it because of its alleged shortcomings once it has become a part of the law of the land. The Rule of Law cannot support the latter course. To do so would be to create a state of chaotic uncertainty and ultimately to destroy the authority and independence of the courts.

Another relevant factor must be added to that of the weight of numbers. Politics remain the art of the possible, especially in democratic countries, and a policy of expediency and compromise becomes inevitable as complicated issues arise and pressures increase. Within limits that may be a practical and praiseworthy way of getting things done. But it seems fundamental that acting in a manner which is really prejudicial to the Rule of Law should be regarded as well outside those limits. Yet, on occasion, the executive has appeared content to let the Rule look after itself; and during the present emergency in this country the governments at both Stormont and Westminster have been thought to err at times on the side of expediency. The facts and circumstances are still so often too confused and uncertain to permit of a fair conclusion, that I shall confine myself to one example which in its salient features seems beyond doubt.

In August, 1971, a statutory regime of internment was put into force in Northern Ireland in an attempt to curb the growing campaign of terrorism. The resulting period of detention was, as respects a relatively small number of those detained, used to interrogate them 'in depth': that is to say when under the influence of certain forms of ill-treatment (as found by the Compton Committee (Cmnd. 4823)) such as hooding, wall standing, continuous noise, reduced diet and lack of sleep. This treatment was to facilitate a fruitful interrogation and so get information about terrorist activities. When these events were revealed by the Compton Report the Home Secretary, Mr Maudling, appointed a Committee of Privy Counsellors to consider whether 'the procedures currently authorized for the interrogation of persons suspected of terrorism' required amendment and if so in what respects. These procedures were based on methods that had been followed by the Army in dealing with certain earlier terrorist campaigns overseas, and the anxiety to obtain information about terrorist plans were in the circumstances understandable. But whatever the words 'currently authorized' were meant to convey there was no lawful authority for what had been done either under the prerogative, an Act of Parliament or the common law. The Prime Minister, Mr Heath, repudiated the course followed and there is nothing to show that he or Mr Faulkner at Stormont knew what was happening. But it was a matter of deliberate expediency, albeit in a time of stress, and it was allowed, at what must have been a high level, to oust the Rule of Law. It had the most unfortunate results which offset the immediate advantages gained from the information obtained. It not only slighted the Rule, but it did perhaps more than anything else to bring the policy of internment into disrepute. Repugnant though it is, there is a place, compatible with the Rule of Law, for internment, as an instrument of almost last resort, which is authorized by Parliament in times of emergency. But the methods I have described are no part of statutory internment and their use serves to show how the Rule may suffer at the hands of authority.

This example suggests that the Rule in its full sense may not be as well appreciated or recognized in the corridors of power as it once was when the law of the constitution received more attention in educated circles. And whether as a consequence of that or not, it must be admitted that the contemporary state of public opinion shows a widespread disregard for authority which cannot but prejudice the Rule and weaken its influence. Even the courts have not escaped and would have fared worse were it not for the law of contempt which still has a restraining effect. This is not to say that justice should be a cloistered virtue or the work of the courts beyond criticism. Far from it. But trial by the news media, groundless attacks and sub-judice interference trespass against the Rule because they conflict with the independence of the courts and weaken the supremacy of law.

THE WAY TO IMPROVEMENT

So, then, if the Rule of Law is a conception of value and in distress how can the situation be relieved? There is no straight road to a solution, and I have no comprehensive list of remedies. But it is necessary to think constructively on this vexed and vital question and I therefore conclude by enumerating a few suggestions for restoring the Rule to a somewhat better state of health. The earlier of these are addressed for the most part to authority, and the others to the community – and that of Northern Ireland in particular. If some of them reek of hindsight I offer no apology. Matters have reached a pitch when we must be prepared to learn from experience and parti-cularly from that of the recent past.

1. An all-round effort to restore the moral standards of the nation would do much, if successful, to improve the position. Such an effort would be well worth a trial, and the provision (particularly for the young) of more opportunities for community service would add greatly to the chances of success. There is nothing bland or easy about this suggestion. I think it accords with what many people, and most judges, know in their hearts, namely, that permissiveness does not stand for progress and that goodness still exalts a nation.

2. I consider the time has come to promulgate the Rule of Law through the medium of a general education. Instruction in the broad principles of law should no longer be confined to those seeking to become lawyers. It could, I believe with much advantage, be made part of a syllabus on civics in schools; and it should be an essential subject for those entering the civil service. Recently, I read a depart-mental statement which, in describing a major responsibility of certain new boards, referred to the administration and co-ordination of the public services in question 'within the terms of the enabling legislation as interpreted by the Ministry ...'. That, I am certain, was written with the best of intentions, but I think a course on the lines suggested would have avoided imputing such powers to the executive. We cannot, however, expect the Rule of Law to have an honoured place in the community if the rising generation and our administrators have not had a chance of learning about it.

3. The protection of the Rule of Law must be regarded as a cardinal function of government. This leaves it open to Parliament to provide special powers to deal with special situations and so maintain a regime of law and order. But to assume such powers without the authority of law (as in the instance I have cited) demeans the Rule as well as setting a very bad example. And it goes without saying that if the Rule is to flourish it must be kept out of the party arena and beyond mere political expediency. This autumn attacks by so-called loyalists on the security forces in this Province provoked hints of 'withdrawal' and of a policy of 'letting them fight it out' which appeared in the press and in several political utterances. These can be regarded as a natural reaction, and may have been intended simply to produce a constraining effect; but they ignored the plain duty of the government in power to restore law and order and thereby dealt the Rule of Law another blow. Nor did the unfortunate consequences end there: the republican forces gained fresh hope; the silent majority who want nothing to do with the rule of the gun and the apostles of violence were discouraged and bewildered; and once again, the fear spread that history would repeat itself and that armed revolt would succeed, despite military failure, as the forces of law and order were called off for political reasons. Fears of this kind may, indeed, be groundless – even ridiculous; but they have a paralysing effect, and if the Rule is to gain health and strength again in this country it will have to be better understood and cherished in public and private by all who are not in revolt.

4. The campaign against violence in which so much courage and patience have already been shown by the Army, the Royal Ulster Constabulary and the auxiliary security forces, and in which so many have been killed and injured in the course of their duty, must, as I have already indicated, be assisted to maintain an increasing initiative by the best organization, training, equipment and leadership that can be provided. Progress in this direction was delayed after the hurried adoption of the Hunt Report in 1969 (Cmd. 535), which led to changes in the structure and functions of the police and to a divided responsibility for security, on a mistaken prognosis of the position. Much ground then lost has since been regained and the number of those made amenable before the courts for subversive activities has been increasing. *But it cannot be assumed that time is running in favour of law and order*, and there is more to do not only on the lines mentioned but also by the way of clarifying and strengthening the law as respects such matters as emergency legislation, offences relating to explosives and firearms, powers of arrest and the use of force in relation to the prevention of crime, the capture of criminals and the

restoration of order. As I have dealt with this subject earlier this year I shall confine myself to a single specific example, that is to say, the practice of going about masked or otherwise disguised which has got prevalent and which undoubtedly shakes public confidence in the Rule of Law. At present this is only an offence if other conditions (such as a special intent) can be proved,[8] and that is often impossible. If the practice were made an offence irrespective of the existence of other conditions, it, and the schemes lurking behind it, would be easier to stop.

5. I had got to this point in preparing this lecture when Mr Whitelaw, the Secretary of State, published his 'Green Paper' on the future of Northern Ireland. This document contains much food for thought on the institutions and policies to be favoured in relation to our future governance. Its political conditions and choices are beyond the scope of this lecture and I do not comment upon them save to hope that they will be subjected to the careful and critical scrutiny they deserve. But it has several implications with a bearing on the Rule of Law, and these I endeavour to describe in the next paragraph.

6.1. The Green Paper is intended to provide a comprehensive basis for further discussions which are to be put in hand immediately and 'must go ahead with the utmost urgency'. It is to be hoped that this does not mean that the campaign against violence, which I have considered in paragraph 4, is to mark time or be slowed down as a noncomitant of such discussions. They are indeed essential; but winning the battle of law and order merely by a process of debate seems now to be more than remote; and the issues to be discussed are of such grave consequence for the entire community that those taking part should at least have the relief and assurance of knowing that the Rule of Law is well and truly on the way back to its rightful place. At the end of four years of strife the new dispensation has to be founded on the Rule, and a settlement which leaves violence still active as a political weapon is likely to be short lived.

6.2. When in 1969 the disturbances in this Province got beyond the power of the police to control, the Army was asked by the Government of Northern Ireland to come to the aid of the civil power and it has since done so, with numbers mounting as the situation has deteriorated. When soldiers are thus committed to peace-keeping duties it is trite law that they have only such powers, apart from their discipline and skill in arms, as the law of the land gives them; and it is also clear that it is the legal duty of the commander concerned to come to the aid of the civil power when needed and to take all reasonable steps which the law allows to end the disturbances and to protect the lives and property of the civil population. This in broad outline was the law as it had developed in relation to the sporadic and localized outbreaks of earlier periods of disorder in various parts of the Kingdom. But difficulty was soon experienced in applying it to the events of the last few years in this jurisdiction. Lawlessness has become widespread and organized; the Northern Ireland Legislature and Government had no authority over the armed forces of the Crown; there was an absence of complete confidence between that Government and the Government of the United Kingdom; and the underlying political issues of the conflict and its day to day events were being canvassed on press and screen around the world. For these, or some of these reasons, the United Kingdom Government assumed direct responsibility for the armed forces in their peace-keeping role.

I think it may fairly be said that our constitutional law and practice governing the role of the armed forces in time of emergency was insufficiently developed to deal satisfactorily with the position which had thus emerged. But the course taken has undoubtedly led to the executive Government of the United Kingdom exercising a greater degree of control and authority over the armed forces than has previously been countenanced. Just as it is not for the executive to tell the judges how to reach their decisions or to direct the police what breaches of law they are to notice and what breaches they are to ignore, it has been the general practice in times of emergency for the commander on the spot or his military superiors, if in touch with the situation, to determine what the nature of the military intervention should be. No one would want to raise fine points of constitutional law in the face of organized terrorism, and it is not my wish to express a view here as to where, in the future, responsibility for security should lie in relation to this Province. But the Green Paper contemplates that the present method of control by the United Kingdom Government should continue at least for a time and this raises a much broader question than one pertaining to Northern Ireland alone. What authority is the executive to have in the future, either here or elsewhere, over the armed forces when they are called upon to aid the civil power?

That the law should be modernized in this regard, to take note of changing circumstances, must be the opinion of many, and it is idle to suppose that the responsible executive can today stand entirely aloof from the methods and policies to be followed by the armed forces in times of grave emergency. But the degree and extent of the executive's power of control and direction cannot be left at large, and the history and nature of the Rule of Law call for a careful approach to this problem, with the powers of the executive reasonably defined and openly declared. In the interests of the Rule I would suggest that this is a United Kingdom rather than a local problem and that Parliament should take the necessary steps to resolve it in preference to leaving matters as they are. In paragraph 79(c) of the Green Paper there is an admirable plea for clarity in the relationship between national and regional authorities. 'Ambiguity', it is observed, 'in the relationship is a prescription for confusion and misunderstanding.' The same might well be said of the relationship throughout the United Kingdom between the executive in power and the armed forces of the Crown in times of emergency. And –

6.3. The Green Paper stresses the financial inability of Northern Ireland to hold the standard of living it now enjoys without the aid of United Kingdom subventions, and is at pains to emphasize the sovereignty of the United Kingdom Parliament. It also reiterates the specific pledges given by statute and successive United Kingdom Governments that Northern Ireland will remain part of the United Kingdom as long as that is the wish of the majority of the Northern Ireland people. But it is clearly the intention of the Green Paper that the continuation of that status will be the subject of certain terms and conditions to be imposed by the United Kingdom Parliament. Though the nature of these, or some of them, is hinted at rather than specified, there can be little doubt that certain changes are inevitable and that much can be done in this direction which would not result in lowering or prejudicing the status of Northern Ireland and its people as a part of the United Kingdom. But what is to happen if some of the conditions to be imposed would have such a result? The Green Paper does not dwell on this, and as it does not canvass the historical reasons for Northern Ireland's relative poverty and for conferring powers of the nature granted in 1920, it may be that the Paper's true intent is that the status of Northern Ireland and its citizens will not, as long as they wish to remain part of the United Kingdom, be reduced in any significant way below that of the rest of the United Kingdom – as, for example, by being made subject, in some material respect, to some external body which has no similar authority over the Kingdom as a whole.

If such is indeed the intention I would venture to suggest, for two reasons, that it should be made very plain. To do so would, in the first place, help, at a critical period, to banish fears for the future. And secondly, it would mean that the *extent* of the sovereignty of the United Kingdom Parliament would be less likely to become a controversial issue at an inopportune time. That sovereignty may not be so absolute as the Green Paper possibly supposes. The point has never been finally settled, and much can be urged on both sides. But as respects a juristically recognized region of the United Kingdom like Northern Ireland it is at least arguable that, in the absence of duress, or consent on the part of the region concerned, or the wish of its people to secede, the United Kingdom Parliament has no power to alienate the allegiance or reduce the status of the people of that region. British sovereignty sits on a platform which rests firmly on a collection of treaties, acts of conquest, Acts of Parliament and solemn undertakings that have all been cemented together by a wide consensus: and it cannot lightly be taken for granted that the planks of the platform can be removed at pleasure.[9]

7. I end with a word to the community, particularly to those who live in Northern Ireland – the republican terrorists, the unionist extremists and the rest of the population – that patient, suffering majority I have spoken of – who hate violence and want for their posterity as much as for themselves peace and prosperity and a return to the common virtues of kindness and decent behaviour.

The first of these categories, the terrorists, are animated, I understand, by a desire to unify Ireland by force of arms; and to that end they have done their worst by bomb, bullet and fire to kill, injure and impoverish their fellow-men. The excitement of this cruel and heartless campaign seems to have blinded them to the fact that the nature of their efforts has produced a powerful, and now a fruitful, logic against the very purpose they have so wickedly pursued; for the ordinary folk of this Province are coming to say something like this – 'If those are the methods taken to persuade us we must expect worse should those who use them succeed in their object, for if they master one part of Ireland in that way they will seek to do the same for the other.' And a much wider community, those all over the world who are sick and tired of violence in all its forms, from hi-jacking in the skies to mugging on the streets, are slipping back from a traditional sympathy with revolutionaries at a safe distance to ask, with a new fear in their hearts, 'will not things get worse for us all if the gun succeeds in Ulster?' I fear I would be wasting words if I appealed to this republican terrorist category to desist from violence in order to show their humanity – to want to live rather than to die for Ireland. But in the interests of all they should see the signs of the times and stop before the gathering wave gets higher.

8. The unionist extremists are a different species. Their loyalty knows no depth for they have spurned the Rule of Law which it is the duty of the loyal to honour. And in the recent past they have disgraced the name of Protestantism by attacking isolated Roman Catholic homes and driving out their occupants in the most cowardly

and cruel fashion. I do not believe this category to be typical, but they have done more to hurt the cause of the union than they have been able to comprehend. One can only hope that they will learn to comprehend, and that the forces of law and order will assist them to see the error of their ways.

9. Finally, I return to the silent, waiting, majority. They must realize by now that the rift which has redeveloped in the last four years between Roman Catholic and Protestant has produced a lack of consensus that augurs ill for the early establishment of sensible institutions and a return to wholesome and effective government. I have said 'redeveloped' for a reason which casts a ray of light on this sad picture. Only five years ago signs were not lacking that the sectarian divide was being bridged at various levels and that there was a new ferment of goodwill at work. Perhaps things then went too fast to last. But I believe the ferment has not gone beyond recall and that most of us can help best by seeking to bring it back and trying humbly and without ostentation to heal the wound by relearning the Golden Rule. The Rule of Law is far nearer to that than most imagine, but it does not tell us how to engender brotherly love afresh. At this late hour it is not for me to depart from my subject in an attempt to answer that vital question fully. But, greatly daring, I would venture to look ahead and suggest a way of getting an answer some day. It is that the time has come to reconsider, on a basis of tolerance and consent, the opening of all our schools to the children of all religions. I know that it is a controversial subject and I would compel nobody. But I believe it is worth further thought and that, at no risk to Faith, it would in time substitute friendship and respect for hate and suspicion.

APPENDIX

Offences known to the police for 1961–1971 which are indictable or of a similar nature.

		England and Wales	Scotland	Northern Ireland	Total
1961	...	806,900	107,500	9,850	924,250
1962	...	896,424	115,000	10,286	1,021,710
1963	...	978,076	128,399	10,859	1,117,334
1964	...	1,067,963	133,654	10,428	1,212,045
1965	...	1,133,882	140,141	12,846	1,286,869
1966	...	1,199,859	147,749	14,673	1,362,281
1967	...	1,207,354	153,213	15,404	1,375,971
1968	...	1,399,799	152,242	16,294	1,568,335
1969	...	1,488,638	155,970	20,303	1,664,911
1970	...	1,555,995	167,223	24,810	1,748,028
1971	...	1,646,081	180,723	30,828	1,857,632
TOTAL	...	13,380,971	1,581,814	176,581	15,139,366

NOTES

1. *Law of the Constitution* (10th ed. 1965), 188.
2. *Law of the Constitution* (10th ed. 1965), 188.
3. *Law of the Constitution* (10th ed. 1965), 193.
4. *Protection from Power under English Law* (1957), 7.
5. See pp. cviii–cx in Professor Wade's Introduction to Dicey's *Law of the Constitution* (10th ed. 1965).
6. *Law of the Constitution* (10th ed. 1965), 288.
7. See 'Law and Order in Times of Emergency' (1972) *Jur. Rev.* 1.
8. See, for example, Reg. 24 made under the Civil Authorities (Special Powers) Act (Northern Ireland) 1922; and s. 73 of the Customs and Excise Act, 1952.
9. The effect of the United Kingdom entry into Europe, and whether such statutes as The Act of Union (Ireland), 1800, The Government of Ireland Act, 1920, and The Ireland Act, 1949, together constitute a fundamental law, are also matters calling for consideration. See Lord Cooper on the nature and effect of the Union between England and Scotland legislation in *MacCormick* v. *Lord Advocate*, 1953 S.C. 396 at 411; and Professor Calvert's commentary in his *Constitutional Law in Northern Ireland* (1968), 10 *et seq.*

Stanley Alderson

The Referendum under
the British Constitution

Northern Ireland is to hold periodical referenda on the
Border. The Labour Party, when returned to power, may put renego-
tiated terms on the Common Market to a referendum. This country
already has significant experience on local referenda. The Public
Libraries Act of 1850 provided for local authorities to hold referenda
among ratepayers before establishing public libraries. Scotland has had
'local option' on the abolition and reduction of pubs since 1920. Wales
has had local option on the Sunday opening of pubs since 1961. The
Sunday opening of cinemas has also been the subject of local referenda,
under the 1932 Sunday Entertainments Act. A borough or an urban
district has to hold a town meeting before it may promote a Private
Bill and in certain circumstances (usually if it is demanded by 100
electors) must hold a referendum as well. The provisions for this in
the 1933 Local Government Act have not, however, been re-enacted
in the 1972 Local Government Act. These are the only local referenda
for which express statutory provision has been made. Others have
been held on the initiative of local authority themselves. Because it
was instigated by the State, the railwaymen's ballot, though on an
occupational instead of a geographical basis, was in the nature of a
limited referendum.

The effect of the new local-government reorganization on local
option is already an issue in Wales, where the next polls are due in
1975. The Government has decided to hold the next polls on the basis
of the 37 new small districts rather than of the eight new counties.
Small units favour the 'dries' and large the 'wets'.

The case for the referendum under the British Constitution was
strengthened in 1911, when the Parliament Act deprived the House of
Lords of the power to veto most legislation, giving it instead only the
power to delay its enactment for two years. This left the Commons
all but absolute during the lifetime of a Parliament.

When in possible conflict with the Commons, the people should

Reprinted from *Contemporary Review*, vol. 223, no. 1294 (November 1973),
pp. 247–250. By permission of the author and the publisher.

ideally be represented by the Lords and the Sovereign. George V fulfilled this ideal of the Sovereign's role over the Parliament Act itself. He agreed that if necessary he would create enough new Liberal peers to pass the Bill, but only after a second general election (in a year) had enabled the electorate to make its support clear beyond doubt. In effect, George V put the Parliament Bill to a poll of the people.

The House of Lords retains the power to veto a Bill prolonging the lifetime of a Parliament beyond five years, thus preventing a tyrannical House of Commons from ruling indefinitely. The Queen might refuse the Royal Assent to any other Bill manifestly against democratic principle or the Rule of Law. But there remains a mass of legislation over which the Lords has only a delaying action (reduced from two years to one by the Parliament Act of 1949) and the Queen has conventionally no power whatever.

The referendum was originally regarded by the Swiss (who did most to develop it, though Massachusetts can claim to have initiated it in 1778) as a means whereby democratic representatives, seen as agents of the majority, could seek fresh instructions when matters arose which had not been envisaged before their election. We might express this view in modern times by saying there should be referenda on measures for which the Government has no mandate.

Referenda could never be held on all such measures. Some are too urgent, others too trivial. Nor is it possible to define satisfactorily in advance those measures meriting referenda. The measure most meriting a referendum is likely to be unforeseeable. We could take a proposal from Lord Balfour of Burleigh's Reference to the People Bill, which was debated at some length in the Lords in March, 1911, before the passing of the Parliament Act: that, when the Lords rejected a Bill, either the Lords itself or the Commons should be able to put it to an immediate referendum. If the electorate rejected a Bill, the Government should not be free to proceed with it during the current Parliament. If the electorate supported it, it should be passed forthwith.

In putting a Bill to a referendum, the Lords would give up its right to delay its enactment for a year. It would not therefore put a Bill to a referendum frivolously, for, if the electorate supported it, it would be passed a year earlier. The Lords would in any case lose dignity if it put to referenda Bills which received overwhelming popular support – as the Government lost dignity when the railwaymen supported their leaders by six to one. Even less would the Commons put a Bill to a referendum frivolously: if the electorate supported it, it would be passed only a year earlier, whereas if the electorate rejected it, it could not be passed during the current Parliament.

The right of the Commons to put a Bill to a referendum would serve to deter the Lords from using its delaying power frivolously. In practice, however, the Lords has been reluctant to use its delaying power. It has been on the defensive, conscious of itself as undemocratic, frightened of being abolished if it did not remain docile. It would be readier to reject a Bill in a good cause if it could seek the endorsement of the electorate. The Constitution of the Weimar Republic provided for the House of States to ask the President to submit a constitutional matter to a referendum against the wishes of the *Reichstag* (which would be automatically dissolved). The power was never invoked. 'Having neither the weight and tradition of the British House of Lords nor the constitutional powers of the American Senate, the House of States found little favour with the German people, who thought of it merely as a formal and mechanical part of the legislature.'[1] If the House of Lords were given the power to refer Bills to referenda, its weight could and should be increased by reforming its membership.

Those mistrustful of Rousseau-esque democracy should be reassured that the electorate would be able to reject a Bill only when one of the Houses of Parliament also believed it should be rejected.

It might be possible to exploit that strength of the British Constitution, its reliance on convention, by having an understanding that the power to put to referendum would be invoked only for a Bill passed with the Government Whips on (or for a Bill for which the Government Whips might be expected to be on). This would exclude Bills such as that abolishing capital punishment – Bills traditionally passed on free votes and dealing with subjects which are not made national election issues.

Public-opinion polls have shown a consistent majority in favour of capital punishment. But it does not follow that an unrestricted power of the House of Lords to refer Bills to referenda would have perpetuated capital punishment. It is precisely because referenda are unfamiliar in this country that politicians have developed the tradition of doing good in defiance of public opinion, if possible by stealth. Sir Ernest Gowers, the chairman of the Royal Commission which recommended the abolition of capital punishment, revealed that he believed in it at the time he took up his appointment – before, that is, he examined the evidence. If the Lords had referred the abolition of capital punishment to a referendum, the penal reformers would have done what they have never yet done and made a concerted attempt to gain support among voters by presenting to them the kind of evidence which converted Sir Ernest. The actual Campaign for the Abolition of Capital Punishment was directed essentially at MPs and the minority of intellectuals capable of putting moral pressure on them, not at the electorate.

Although the abolition of capital punishment must be acknowledged an absolute good, the fact that it was passed in the face of the known opposition of the electorate has created bewilderment and resentment which have diminished respect for democracy and increased resistance to other measures of penal reform – which have indeed brought periodical demands for the restoration of capital punishment. Britain's role as a member of the EEC looks like being restricted by a similar bewilderment and resentment. If the House of Lords had already possessed the power we are proposing, the European Communities Bill would have been an obvious subject for a referendum.

An important objection to referenda is that different results can be obtained by phrasing questions differently. Under our proposal the question would always take the form: 'Are you in favour of such and such a Bill which has been passed by the House of Commons but rejected by the House of Lords?' That is as neutral as can be. Since the parliamentary debates on the Bill would have been widely reported, and the press and television would also have provided other views, the electorate would be as informed as we can ever expect it to be.

The Constitution of the Fifth Republic of France (Articles 11 and 89) provides for referenda only on Bills. Five referenda have been held so far (there having also been one on the Constitution itself). The first two dealt with Independence for Algeria; the third with the election of the President by universal suffrage; the fourth with the creation of regions and the renovation of the Senate; and the fifth, last year, with the extension of the EEC (to include, among others, Britain). It is generally accepted that the French people have understood what they were voting about. There has, however, been a tendency for referenda to be regarded as votes of confidence in the President.

This is the obvious danger of what we are proposing: that the electorate will vote according to party allegiance rather than on the merits of the case. But this danger is inherent in party politics. At least the electorate is more likely to vote on the merits of a case in a referendum than in a general election – it being possible to oppose the Government without putting it out of office or to support it without confirming it in office. Even if voting were entirely according to party allegiance, a referendum would serve a function in allowing an issue to be resolved without the disruption of a general election.

As a safeguard against apathy, it might be provided that the rejection of a Bill in a referendum would be valid only if the negative votes constituted 35 per cent. of the registered voters. The 1913 Temperance (Scotland) Act established a precedent in laying down that pubs in a local-authority area should be abolished or reduced only when majorities were achieved with 35 per cent. of the registered voters voting in favour.

Referenda not only resolve disputes without the disruption of general elections; they may be literally the only means of resolving certain electoral disputes: the next election provides no redress for a gerrymandering Act.

Our proposal is experimentally modest. Hence it has limitations. A Government may on occasion be able to gerrymander by failing to implement proposals of the Boundary Commission. There is then no Bill for the Lords to reject and to put to a referendum. To deal with this eventuality, the Lords would need the power to put to a referendum a Bill of its own rejected by the Commons.

NOTE

1. Sir Stephen King-Hall and Richard K. Ullmann, *German Parliaments: A study of the development of representative institutions in Germany* (London 1954), p. 86.

O. Hood Phillips, QC

Need for a Written Constitution

CONSTITUTION AT THE MERCY OF PARTY MAJORITY IN THE COMMONS

The British Constitution is found to be largely at the mercy of a small, temporary party majority in the House of Commons. This situation has arisen as a result of unplanned historical development. Why has it been allowed to remain? Because it has suited the leaders of both sides in the political 'game', giving inordinate power to the Prime Minister of the day, which will be inherited by the Leader of the Opposition in due course, while the general public are apathetic or unaware.

... a written Constitution with judicial review is desirable for this country. There are no legal limits to what Parliament can do by ordinary legislation, that the Government virtually controls the activities of Parliament, that the maximum duration of a Parliament is too long, that the existence of a (reformed) Second Chamber with some power of rejection or delay is essential, that important areas of law and practice are uncertain, that the 'Parliament Act 1949' is of doubtful force, that too much power is concentrated in the hands of the Prime Minister, that the dissolution of Parliament needs to be regulated, that the law relating to judicial tenure should be improved, and that there is a call for a new Bill of Rights. In our system, or lack of system, all exists on sufferance, depending on the legislative supremacy of Parliament. There are permanent, or at least abiding, principles of constitutional government in the national interest as against the sectional interest of a temporary and perhaps small party majority; but the former can only be secured against the latter by limiting the power of Parliament, which in effect means placing restrictions on the Government of the day.

Reprinted with additional notes from O. Hood Phillips, *Reform of the Constitution* (Chatto & Windus, London 1970), pp. 144–162. By permission of the author and Chatto & Windus Ltd.

PURPOSE OF ENACTING A CONSTITUTION

The purpose of enacting a Constitution – the institutional laws, the main conventions relating to the Executive, and the fundamental individual rights – would be partly to clarify the principles, but mainly to entrench the most important provisions against repeal or amendment except by some specially prescribed procedure. At present it is possible for constitutional changes to be brought about by a majority of one in the elected Chamber. A Government elected with a small majority may not be truly representative of the people after its first year of office. The strength of party discipline means that the Government controls the Legislature. Restrictions on the Legislature would therefore in practice be restrictions on the Government. In the recent proposals of the Canadian Government for a new written Constitution it was argued that the mechanism for ensuring democratic government should be the subject of constitutional guarantees, and that the institutions of government and individual rights are fundamental to the whole Constitution.

The function of a written Constitution, then, would be to entrench the main institutions of government, the relations among themselves and between them and the private citizen. Foremost among these provisions – apart from matters on which there has been no conflict since 1688, such as the Monarchy and succession to the throne, and taxation – would be the following:

National rights of England, Scotland, Northern Ireland and Wales as members of the Union.

Regional rights, if there is a further measure of devolution.

The status of the Channel Islands and the Isle of Man.

The Second Chamber, its composition and numbers, and its powers in relation to legislation. Disputes between the two Houses might be settled differently according to whether the matter was general Government policy, such as economic policy, or Fundamental Rights.

Provisions relating to Parliamentary government, in particular, the reduction in the maximum life of Parliament to four (or perhaps three) years; annual meeting of Parliament; the Electoral laws, including Boundary Commissions.

Common Market membership and obligations (if we join).*

Formulation of certain constitutional conventions, to protect the Queen as ultimate guardian of the Constitution as far as possible from involvement in politics, and to reduce the power of the Prime

* The UK has now joined the Common Market.

Minister. Such formulations would include the choice of Prime Minister, and the dissolution of Parliament, when and by whom advised.

The appointment, tenure and independence of the Judiciary – a reformed judicial tenure, substituting the advice of the Judicial Committee of the Privy Council for an address from both Houses in the removal of Judges, and perhaps establishing a Judicial Services Commission.

A new Bill of Rights, preserving notably *habeas corpus* and the free expression of opinion, and taking account of the European Convention.

Emergency powers and their limits; entrenchment to prevent government by decree or the establishment of extreme one-party rule.

The Constitution would be declared to be the supreme law of the land. Jurisdiction in constitutional questions (judicial review) would be conferred on the superior Courts, with appeal to the Judicial Committee of the Privy Council or a Special Constitutional Court.

Procedure for constitutional amendment, e.g. a two-thirds majority in each House for a Bill describing itself as a Constitutional Amendment Bill.

A written Constitution in itself would not clear up uncertainties in the law; indeed, a cynic might argue that it would increase them; but the exercise of drafting one would provide a unique opportunity for a wide and thorough overhaul of both the laws and the conventions. Further, its enactment – even apart from entrenchment sanctioned by judicial review – would fit in with our current phase of codifying various branches of English law, in particular, the proposal for a Criminal Code.

ARGUMENTS AGAINST A WRITTEN CONSTITUTION WITH JUDICIAL REVIEW

The general arguments used by lawyers against the adoption by this country of a written Constitution with judicial review are that it would lead to rigidity, that it would increase the volume of litigation, and that interpretation of the Constitution would involve the Courts in the decision of political questions. Rigidity, however, is a matter of degree, depending on the method prescribed for constitutional amendment. It need not be excessive, nor need the enactment of a Constitution prevent the growth of new conventions. In a unitary State or Union it is unlikely that there would be a great increase in litigation. Nor is it likely that many of the questions of construction that came before the Courts would be policy questions. The main objection hitherto has arisen from the innate conservatism of the common lawyer, his attachment to judge-made law and his dislike of statute law. He is not accustomed to a category of cases called 'constitutional'.

With regard to constitutional conventions there are legitimate queries. Are some of the conventions sufficiently definite to be capable of formulation in a statute? Are there some conventions that it would be undesirable to crystallize in statutory form? Are the Courts a suitable forum for adjudicating upon the proper observance of conventions? It is undoubtedly difficult to formulate conventions, though in a number of the newer Commonwealth Constitutions it has been attempted. They have incorporated the most important conventions relating to the exercise of governmental powers, either specifically or by reference to the British practice. The kind of problem that may arise is illustrated by the case of *Adegbenro* v. *Akintola* (1963). Under the 1960 Constitution of the Western Region of Nigeria the Governor had power to dismiss the Premier if it appeared to him that the Premier no longer commanded the support of a majority of members of the House of Assembly. The Governor dismissed the Premier, Chief Akintola, on the strength of a letter signed by a majority of members of the House, and appointed Adegbenro in his place. A political emergency arose during which the matter was taken to the Courts. The majority of the Federal Supreme Court of Nigeria, following what they understood to be the constitutional convention in Britain, held that the dismissal of Chief Akintola was invalid, as the Governor's power to dismiss the Premier was exercisable only when the House of Assembly itself had formally signified its lack of confidence in him. This decision was reversed on appeal by the Judicial Committee of the Privy Council, who came to the conclusion that the Governor was entitled to obtain his information as to whether the Premier had lost the confidence of the House from any apparently reliable source. A somewhat similar case arose in Sarawak in 1966 with the opposite result, when the High Court of Malaysia in Borneo held that the Governor of Sarawak (if he had power to dismiss his Chief Minister) could dismiss him only following the unfavourable vote of the Legislature, and that a letter of no confidence was insufficient. In each country a constitutional amendment later nullified the judicial decision.

Factors to be taken into consideration are that the making of declarations by the Court is discretionary; that the Courts are reluctant to make decisions that will be ineffective; and that matters of this kind, such as whether a Prime Minister ought to resign or whether the Head of State may dismiss him, are usually decided by political methods and procedures, depending ultimately on public opinion. Lord Radcliffe, in the Privy Council case cited, referred to the lack of judicially discoverable and manageable standards for resolving such disputes, and thought that Courts were hardly suitable bodies to answer such questions.

We would not propose the formulation of constitutional conventions except as part of the exercise of enacting the Constitution as a whole, although the conventions relating to the exercise of the powers of the Governor-General of New Zealand did have to be formulated without enacting the rest of that country's Constitution as it appeared that his Letters Patent needed to be redrafted. On the other hand, if we find it desirable on other grounds to enact a Constitution we could not leave out the Executive altogether, while to incorporate the laws relating to the Executive without referring to the conventions would be equally impracticable. Mr Trudeau thinks that in the new Canadian Constitution conventions should be formulated in a general way, and his draft includes outline provisions relating to the government and covering the Head of State, the Executive, the Privy Council, the Prime Minister, the Cabinet, and the Ministers. The solution to this problem may be to provide that such existing conventions as are enacted shall not be justiciable. We have some rules that are expressly non-justiciable, for example, the functions of the Speaker under the Parliament Acts. It has been held by the Court of Appeal of New Zealand in *Simpson* v. *Attorney-General* (1955) that the Governor-General's statutory obligation to issue writs for a general election is not justiciable. Although the Courts may find in such cases that the exercise of statutory discretions is impliedly not justiciable, it would be preferable in the Executive part of the proposed Constitution to specify any particular provisions that are to be non-justiciable.

RIGHTS OF THE INDIVIDUAL

The first problem in framing a declaration of rights is that of selection. Most of the 'rights' of the individual that would be contained in a declaration of rights would be liberties, involving restrictions on the Legislature and enforceable against members of the Executive, such as personal liberty, freedom of speech, association, assembly and worship. In some instances, for example, non-discrimination, there might be redress against private persons. Some, such as the franchise, would be political in the strict sense. This and a few others would be available to citizens only: most would be available to all persons lawfully present in this country. The inclusion of general duties of the State or Government to provide welfare benefits, education, health services and so on, is not suggested. Such economic or social rights find a place in some Constitutions as 'Directive Principles of State (or Social) Policy', and are expressly declared to be not judicially enforceable. They are rather ideals or guides to Legislatures and Governments, and at most might have some slight effect on the construction of ambiguous statutes.

The next major problem is that of drafting. One has to consider in each case both the proposition and the exceptions. Should the language be general like the American Bill of Rights, or should it be detailed, specifying the various limitations and exceptions like the Fundamental Rights in the Indian or Nigerian Constitution? On the one hand, the First Amendment to the United States Constitution provides simply that 'Congress shall make no law ... abridging the freedom of speech or of the press', an impossibly general statement that has caused endless difficulty for the Supreme Court. On the other hand, section 24 of the Federal Constitution of Nigeria (1960) read as follows: '(1) Every person shall be entitled to freedom of expression, including freedom to hold opinions and to receive and impart ideas and information without interference. (2) Nothing in this section shall invalidate any law that is reasonably justifiable in a democratic society – (a) in the interest of defence, public safety, public order, public morality or public health; (b) for the purpose of protecting the rights, reputations and freedom of other persons, preventing the disclosure of information received in confidence, maintaining the authority and independence of the courts or regulating telephony, wireless broadcasting, television, or the exhibition of cinematograph films; or (c) imposing restrictions upon persons holding office under the Crown, members of the armed forces of the Crown or members of a police force.' Expressions like 'reasonably justifiable' and 'democratic society' would provide many pitfalls for judges faced with the task of construing them; but prominence would rightly be given to 'protecting the rights, reputations and freedom of other persons' at a time of increasing licence on the part of the press, and growing intolerance on the part of noisy minorities who try to break up meetings held by speakers with whose opinions (if they listen to them) they do not agree.

Critics of a Bill of Rights raise the question, what would be the effect on existing legislation? The exceptions, they argue, might nullify the propositions. The Constitution would have to state, if that is the intention, that the declaration of Rights was not to have retrospective effect, though it would raise presumptions of interpretation. But if no change in the existing law is intended, why go through the trials and tribulations of drafting a Bill of Rights? As far as criminal or civil liability is concerned, the principle would remain that people may do what they like unless forbidden by law. Some changes might be made in the existing law, such as the recognition or extension of the right of privacy. What would be the effect of a declaration of the invalidity of a subsequent statute on those who have *bona fide* acted under it? There would be uncertainty and much litigation, it is said, and the Courts would be required to decide policy questions. These questions reveal fears that in this country might well prove unfounded. The answer may lie partly in the device of prospective overruling, which is discussed later.

CAN PARLIAMENT BIND ITSELF?

'If an Act of Parliament had a clause in it that it should never be repealed,' said Chief Justice Herbert in the celebrated case of *Godden* v. *Hales* (1686), 'yet without question, the same power that made it may repeal it.' The proposition that Parliament cannot bind itself or its successors appears to some people to express a paradox. If there is something Parliament cannot do, they ask, how can we speak of its legislative supremacy? But the paradox is verbal only. If the proposition is put in the form, 'Parliament is not bound by its predecessors', the difficulty vanishes. There is no judicial authority for the power of *express* repeal or amendment: it is so well established that it has not been raised in the Courts. If Parliament intends to repeal or amend a previous statute it usually does so expressly; but through oversight this may not be done, in which case the Courts will try to reconcile the two statutes as far as they reasonably can. Otherwise, a later Act or section supersedes an earlier Act or section with which it is inconsistent; in other words, it impliedly repeals or amends the earlier. So in *Ellen Street Estates Ltd.* v. *Minister of Health* (1934), where there was a discrepancy in the methods of assessing compensation prescribed by the Acquisition of Land (Assessment of Compensation) Act 1919 and the Housing Acts 1925 and 1930, the Court of Appeal held that the Housing Acts impliedly repealed the Act of 1919 in so far as they were inconsistent. 'If in a subsequent Act', said Lord Justice Maugham, 'Parliament chooses to make it plain that the earlier statute is being to some extent repealed, effect must be given to that intention just because it is the will of the Legislature.'

Special considerations may apply where the earlier Act is part of an arrangement of an international character, such as the Statute of Westminster, Independence Acts and perhaps the Act of Union with Scotland, though even there it is likely that British Courts would regard themselves as bound by the later Act, regardless of any political or international repercussions.

The advocacy by the Constitutional Society of New Zealand of a written and entrenched Constitution for that country, including a Bill of Rights, has not so far been successful. Meanwhile the New Zealand Legislature, suffering perhaps from a guilty conscience in having abolished the Second Chamber in 1950 and been unable to devise a substitute, included in the revised Electoral Act of 1956 a section (s. 189) stating that certain provisions relating to such matters as the life of Parliament (consisting now only of the House of Representatives and the Governor-General), the franchise and secret ballot, should not be repealed or amended except by a majority of 75 per cent. of all the members of the House or by a simple majority of votes at a referendum. Section 189 was not itself one of the provisions requiring this special procedure for repeal or amendment. There are three views as to the effect of a provision such as this. The first is that it is binding on the Legislature as providing a new definition of 'Parliament' for this particular purpose: this is an adoption of the 'manner and form' argument discussed below. The second view is that the special amending procedure could be evaded, but that it would have to be done in two stages: the New Zealand Parliament could (and would need to) repeal section 189 first, and then it could proceed to amend the reserved provisions. This seems to be rather a pointless technical distinction, as the two things could be done in two consecutive sections of the same statute. The third view, which we think is the correct one, is that section 189 constitutes merely a moral sanction, albeit a strong moral sanction amounting to a constitutional convention. The reason why the Legislature did not try to 'entrench' section 189 itself is that it appreciated that a double pseudo entrenchment would be no stronger than a single pseudo-entrenchment, and so *ad infinitum*. As Bacon said in his *Maxims of the Law*: 'Acts which are in their nature revocable, cannot by strength of words be fixed or perpetuated.'

Jurists tell us that there must be some 'rules of recognition' (Hart) or 'rules of competence' (Alf Ross) by which we may know what Parliament is and what is an Act of Parliament. From this some constitutional writers draw the conclusion that Parliament can bind itself as to the *manner and form* of legislation, and that therefore if it prescribed a special procedure for the alteration of particular laws, such as electoral laws or fundamental rights, the Courts would not uphold amendments to such laws unless they were made by the special procedure laid down. They follow the late Sir Ivor Jennings in citing the case of *Attorney-General for New South Wales* v. *Trethowan* (1932), in which the Judicial Committee of the Privy Council held that the New South Wales Legislature had no power by a statute passed in 1930 (after a change of Government) to abolish the Second Chamber without a referendum, because that Legislature had passed an Act in 1929 providing that the abolition of the Second Chamber would require approval at a referendum. But the reason for that decision was that the State of New South Wales was subject to the Colonial Laws Validity Act 1865, which declared that a representative colonial Legislature had wide powers of lawmaking so long as its laws did not conflict with statutes of the United Kingdom Parliament applying thereto, and provided that its laws were passed 'in such manner and form as may from time to time be required' by any law (including a Colonial law) for the time being in force in the territory. Clearly the decision was based on the fact that the New South Wales Legislature was a *subordinate* legislature, bound by the 'higher law' laid down by the United Kingdom Parliament. The analogy from a subordinate to an autonomous Legislature is false.

Then they cite the famous 'Cape Coloured Voters case' (*Harris* v. *Minister of the Interior*, or *Harris* v. *Dönges*, 1952), in which the Appellate Division of the Supreme Court of South Africa rightly held invalid a statute passed by the South African Parliament purporting to place the Cape Coloured voters on a separate electoral roll, because it had not been passed in accordance with the special procedure (a two-thirds majority in both Houses sitting together) prescribed for this kind of constitutional amendment by section 152 of the South Africa Act 1909. Now the South Africa Act was the Constitution of South Africa, which created the South African Parliament itself. But because it happened for historical reasons to be an Act of the United Kingdom Parliament and South Africa had since the Statute of Westminster 1931 been recognized as an independent sovereign State, there was a good deal of confusion between State sovereignty and the 'sovereignty' of Parliament, although it was pointed out that Congress is limited by the American Constitution but no one would deny that the United States is a sovereign State. Partly to avoid the supposed difficulty of ascribing limits to a 'sovereign' Parliament, an ingenious formula propounded by Professor D. V. Cowen was adopted, which involved a quibble with the word 'Parliament'. Although for general purposes the bicameral 'Parliament' of South Africa was sovereign, the 'Parliament' for the purpose of amending section 152 of the South Africa Act was a two-thirds majority of a unicameral body. *Dicta* were thrown out to the effect that a similar line of reasoning might be applied to the United Kingdom Parliament, which could thus bind itself. Again, the *Harris* case is a false analogy, for the South African Parliament was bound by a higher law, namely, the South African Constitution.

The same applies to two recent appeals in the Privy Council from Ceylon. In *Bribery Commissioner* v. *Ranasinghe* (1965) it was held that the Bribery Tribunal by which the respondent had been convicted was not lawfully appointed; and in *Liyanage* v. *R.* (1967) it was held that a court of three Judges (without a jury) nominated for the particular case, by which the accused were convicted of offences arising out of an abortive *coup d'état*, was not lawfully appointed. In both cases the reason for the decision was that the statute under which the tribunal or Court was set up involved a constitutional amendment requiring a special legislative procedure which had not been complied with. Ceylon is an independent sovereign State by virtue of the Ceylon Independence Act 1947, but its Legislature is bound by a higher law, the Constitution of Ceylon, which is contained in an Order in Council of 1946.*

One cannot be dogmatic on this matter, but the view put forward here is that a legislature cannot bind itself, whether as to subject-matter or the manner and form of legislation, unless it is authorized (directed or empowered) to do so by some 'higher law', that is, by some prior law *not laid down by itself*. Our test is the probable attitude of the Courts. Suppose Parliament passed an Act this year providing that the voting age should not be raised except with the approval of a majority of 75 per cent. in the House of Commons. It is submitted that if Parliament passed another Act next year raising the voting age and approved by a bare majority in the House of Commons, British Courts would not hold the second Act void. As Lord Pearce said in *Bribery Commissioner* v. *Ranasinghe*, lawmaking powers in all countries with written Constitutions must be exercised in accordance with the terms of the Constitution from which the power is derived. His Lordship added that any analogy to the unwritten British Constitution 'must be very indirect, and provides no helpful guidance'. The reason why the New South Wales Legislature in *Trethowan's* case had to follow the procedure of a referendum prescribed by its own previous statute, was that it was directed to do so by the Colonial Laws Validity Act 1865 ('in such manner and form as may from time to time be required by any

* Ceylon is now the Republic of Sri Lanka with a new Constitution, and appeals from it to the Privy Council have been abolished.

Act of Parliament, Letters Patent, Order in Council, or *Colonial Law* for the time being in force in the said Colony').

If there must be some rule logically prior to Parliament by which an act can be recognized as an Act of Parliament, this identifies Parliament: it does not limit its powers. Since the early middle ages (except during the revolutionary Commonwealth period in the seventeenth century) 'Parliament' has meant the Sovereign, the Lords and Commons in Parliament assembled. An Act assented to by the Queen by and with the consent of the Lords and Commons in Parliament assembled could abolish the monarchy or the House of Lords. P1 would not have bound itself as to the laws it can pass: it would have been replaced by P2. But to say that the prescription of some special legislative procedure for certain Bills is to alter the meaning of 'Parliament' for those purposes is a play upon words.

It would probably not be effective to try to *prevent* the passing of a Bill that infringed an enactment corresponding to the Canadian Bill of Rights or section 189 of the New Zealand Electoral Act. The case of *Harper* v. *Home Secretary* (1955), where an injunction was refused to restrain the Home Secretary from presenting a draft Order (approved by both Houses) relating to electoral boundaries to Her Majesty in Council, is an illustration of the unwillingness of the British Courts in our present system to interfere with the Parliamentary process, apart from the fact that by the Crown Proceedings Act no injunction (as distinct from a declaration of private rights) may be issued against a Minister in his official capacity.

HOW A NEW BRITISH CONSTITUTION MIGHT BE ENTRENCHED

The solution is to bring into being a 'New' Parliament which would owe its existence to a Constitution *not enacted by itself*, from which it would derive both its powers and its limitations. When the possibility of Great Britain and Ireland forming a federation with a rigid Constitution was discussed in the 1880s, Bryce expressed the opinion that Parliament could extinguish itself and a new Federal Legislature could be established following this *breach of continuity*. Then the new Constitution could only be altered in accordance with its own terms. Dicey thought Parliament could *transfer* its powers to another Legislature, but it seems that the *extinction* of the existing or 'Old' Parliament and the creation of a new Parliament would be the more effective method. A Constitution limiting the powers of the 'New' Parliament, in the manner suggested earlier in this chapter, would be adopted by the 'Old' Parliament, and then submitted for adoption by the people in a referendum. The Old (unlimited) Parliament would be abolished, and it would be superseded by the New (limited) Parliament.

Alternatively, it might be preferable for Parliament first to transfer its powers to a *Constituent Assembly*, and at the same time to abolish itself. The Constituent Assembly would then draft a Constitution creating a Parliament with limited powers. Again, the New Parliament would have only such powers as the Constitution gave it. That raises the question of how the Constituent Assembly would be appointed. In some countries the existing Legislature has functioned as a Constituent Assembly, but we can hardly envisage the present Parliament acting in this capacity until the composition of the House of Lords has been reformed. It is probable that a specially appointed Constituent Assembly, if one could be devised, would be the most influential.

The statute adopting the Constitution, or setting up the Constituent Assembly, as well as the Constitution itself, would require the Judges (existing as well as future) to take an oath of loyalty to the new Constitution.

We have suggested that the new Constitution should be submitted for adoption by the people at a referendum. This is because the establishment of a new Constitution is the most solemn and fundamental of all constitutional acts: its approval at a referendum, by putting the new Constitution in a special category, would confer on it the highest possible prestige. Elsewhere we have expressed objections to the general or frequent use of the referendum as a constitutional process, and we do not suggest that this 'unEnglish' device should be employed for subsequent constitutional amendments. Our proposal is for an initial or fundamental referendum only.

CONSTITUTIONAL AMENDMENT

The argument from inflexibility would be largely met, first, by ensuring that all provisions of the Constitution would be amendable in one way or another, and, secondly, by providing that entrenchment need not be total. There would be no parts of the Constitution like the basic articles of the Cyprus Constitution or (according to the recent *Golak Nath Case*) the fundamental rights in the Indian Constitution, that could not be amended at all. Some special procedure for amendment would be required for such parts as the Monarchy, the Unions with Scotland and Northern Ireland, the Islands, the Regions, the Second Chamber, the life and frequency of Parliament, the franchise, the Boundary Commissions, judicial tenure, fundamental rights, emergency powers, judicial review of legislation, and the procedure for constitutional amendment itself. Parts that need not be entrenched, but could be amended by the ordinary legislative procedure, could include details such as the number of seats in the House of Commons, and non-justiciable provisions covering what are now conventions.

An Amendment Bill should be so specified, for this draws the attention of members of Parliament and the public to its significance. The Lord Chancellor or Minister of Justice would be required to examine all Bills with reference to their compatibility with the Constitution and to report. In difficult cases an advisory opinion could be sought from the Judicial Committee of the Privy Council under the Judicial Committee Act 1833, which provides that the Crown may refer any question of law to the Committee for an advisory opinion. The opinion of the Judicial Committee may already be required on the validity of legislation of the Northern Ireland Parliament under the Government of Ireland Act 1920. This procedure would not be appropriate, however, if the Judicial Committee were to be given jurisdiction to decide cases arising out of the interpretation of the Constitution.

A referendum, we have already suggested, would not be desirable as part of the process of constitutional amendment. It is difficult to frame a complex technical question in a way suitable to be answered 'yes' or 'no' by large numbers of people who have not the necessary background and have not followed all the previous discussions. A joint sitting of the two Houses is a doubtful device, at least until we know what sort of Second Chamber we shall have and how its members will be chosen. The most satisfactory method for amending the entrenched clauses would therefore appear to be a Constitution Amendment Bill passed by a special majority of (say) two-thirds in each House. It would be necessary to state whether this was to be a two-thirds majority of members present and voting, or two-thirds of all the members of each House.

JUDICIAL REVIEW OF LEGISLATION

Judicial review is the traditional method of testing the validity of legislation in the United States and Commonwealth countries. A body of judicial precedents of constitutional interpretation is then gradually built up. Certain provisions could, as we have said, be expressly made non-justiciable, such as those relating to the Sovereign's exercise of the prerogative, the functions of the Speaker in the House, and existing conventions relating to the Cabinet system. It would not be necessary for the judges themselves to invent, as the American Supreme Court has done, a loosely defined class of 'political questions' which are not suitable for judicial decision.

The objection that difficulty would be created where acts have been *bona fide* performed under legislation later declared void by the Courts might be met, at least in some cases, by the doctrine of 'prospective invalidation' or (where a precedent of interpretation is being reversed) 'prospective overruling'. This means that the Court could declare, in cases where it thought there were compelling reasons for doing so, that the statute concerned would be invalid in future, but without prejudice to things *bona fide* done in reliance on it down to the time of the judgement. This device has been occasionally used by the American Supreme Court during the last forty years. Thus, previous cases having decided that the conviction of a person on the strength of evidence seized by the police in a manner contrary to the Constitution was void, the question arose in *Linkletter* v. *Walker* (1965) whether all prisoners convicted on evidence unlawfully obtained ought to be released and retried. The Supreme Court held that this drastic action was not necessary, but that the Court could deliver judgement with prospective effect. Again, in *Golak Nath* v. *State of Punjab* (1967) the Indian Supreme Court holding (probably wrongly) that the Indian Parliament had no power to amend any of the fundamental rights declared in the Constitution, even by the special amending process, overruled previous decisions of its own over a number of years upholding several amendments to the fundamental rights: but having regard to the history of the amendments (relating to such matters as agrarian reform), their impact on the social and economic affairs of the country and the chaotic situation that might be brought about by the sudden withdrawal of the constitutional amendments at that stage, the Court, borrowing the idea from its American counterpart, confined the operation of the decision to the future. On the other hand, the doctrine of 'prospective' overruling or invalidation has met with criticism from both American and Indian lawyers as being a repudiation of the principle that the function of judicial review is to declare unconstitutional laws to be *void*; that Courts which invalidate laws for the future are acting as legislators altering the law, although the Constitution is supposed to be supreme.

Ultimate appellate jurisdiction would be conferred by the new Constitution on some Court in any cases in which a constitutional issue is raised. Some countries have special Constitutional Courts with exclusive jurisdiction in constitutional cases, but it would be preferable for us to integrate this jurisdiction with the general jurisdiction of the superior Courts. Constitutional questions could then be dealt with in the normal course of litigation, and in relation to other legal questions that are usually involved in such cases. The House of Lords in its judicial capacity, being technically part of the Legislature, would not be an appropriate appellate Court for this purpose. This points to the Judicial Committee of the Privy Council as the most suitable choice. It already hears appeals from some Courts and tribunals in this country as well as from Courts overseas, and the judicial strength of these two bodies is much the same. It could hardly be objected that the Judicial Committee is in form a committee of the Executive.

The choice of the Judicial Committee would also fit in with the prospect that, as a result of a radical reform of the Second Chamber, the Judicial Committee might become the ultimate court of appeal for *all* kinds of cases, an idea that has been mooted from time to time during the last hundred years.

MORAL AND EDUCATIONAL VALUE OF A WRITTEN CONSTITUTION

Finally, there is the moral and educational value of introducing a written Constitution enunciating in a systematic and inspiring way a set of principles by which people may be guided, and embodying the concepts of legality, stability and permanent values. It is not valid to compare the United Kingdom with other countries that have written Constitutions entrenching fundamental rights and judicial review, and to point to the present political chaos in some of these countries and the plethora of judicial precedents in the United States. There are political and social factors at work in some of the new Commonwealth countries that fortunately do not obtain here, while the American judicial experience is largely due to the manner in which the American Federal Constitution was originally drafted at a time when judicial review seems not to have been intended, and also to the exceptional difficulty of amending that Constitution. In view of the law-abiding tradition and political maturity of this country on the one hand, and the relative flexibility of our proposed new Constitution on the other, the only valid comparison is between the present lack of system in this country and the situation it is hoped would obtain if we had a written Constitution of the kind suggested. In other words, the comparison is between the United Kingdom before and after.

It may be that the leading politicians of the two main parties would at first be hesitant to adopt such a basic and comprehensive reform. The essence of the British constitutional system has been described as two alternating and self-perpetuating oligarchies with supporting retinues, who are capable of collusion when it suits them. Many lawyers would be sceptical, having a romantic attachment to 'judge-made' law and a prejudice against legislation. The initiative for such an ambitious but worthwhile project is therefore likely to depend for its support on the formation of a sufficiently strong body of informed public opinion.

Quintin Hogg

The Constitution: The Right Road to Reform

When I made my speech to a PEST meeting at last year's Conservative conference about constitutional reform I had hardly expected a friendly response from the Government. Yet the proposal for a royal commission in the Queen's Speech so closely resembles my own for a constitutional conference that I was tempted, at least at first, to suspect that there was a causal connection.

As a means, the royal commission is, on the whole, less satisfactory than a constitutional conference. Nobody is impartial on these subjects, least of all those best equipped to express an opinion. A conference under royal patronage and organized by the mean parties would have been less formal, and more flexible, than a commission, with its predetermined membership and rather rigid methods of taking evidence. Still, the thing has got off the ground. Constitutional reform is now open for discussion, and something ultimately must emerge.

It is difficult to see what the Prime Minister thought he would gain by adding the Channel Isles, Man, and Northern Ireland to the menu. The object of constitutional reform is to create a new, and more viable, structure for our own island. No doubt important constitutional issues have arisen in relation to the other island, Man, and the rump of the Normandy Duchy, but they can only obscure the issues at present facing us. The inclusion of the Channel Islands and Man (where constitutional talks already in being were broken off to make way for the commission) has aroused deep resentment. The question of Northern Ireland does not raise purely domestic issues and runs the risk of casting doubt on repeated assurances from Prime Ministers of both parties.

Also controversial is the omission from the agenda of at least two items which are closely connected with regionalism, a Bill of Rights, involving judicial discussion of the validity of Acts of Parliament, and fixed-term Parliaments. The latter is a more important issue than appears at first sight, since the real influence of the public opinion

Reprinted from *The Spectator* (10 January 1969), pp. 39–40. By permission of the author and the publisher.

polls is to give greater power of self-perpetuation to the reigning government, possessing, as it does under present arrangements, virtual control of the prerogative of dissolution.

With its present terms of reference, therefore, the commission is an incomplete and imperfect instrument. But more dangerous than the weakness in its form and agenda are the scepticism and apathy with which proposals for constitutional reform seem to be greeted in academic circles.

I have been myself the recipient of many of these criticisms since I made my PEST speech. Most of them can be grouped under three heads. The first group of critics is composed of those who ask a number of questions perfectly reasonable in themselves, but asked on the assumption that, unless a final answer to them can be given in advance, the case for constitutional reform must fall by the wayside. In this respect, both the Government and I have a ready answer. No one can, and no one should, predict with certainty what particular solutions of known problems will emerge after discussion. That would be to prejudge the outcome of conference or commission. The only circumstances in which the existence of these known difficulties should be a bar to discussion would be if it could be shown that the present constitutional framework is working perfectly (which manifestly it is not) or if it could be shown that the difficulties were of a class intrinsically incapable of solution. This, too, is clearly not so, since the principal difficulties have been solved in one way or another in every developed country except our own.

The second group of critics concentrate on the difficulties, financial and constitutional, of regionalism. What powers do you devolve? How do you create financial independence? By devolving powers do you not give rise to a situation in which different standards of education, pensions, transport, housing and other services exist in different parts of the country? By creating regions are you not destroying patriotism?

These are legitimate questions, and, of course, they are not wholly answered by pointing out that all have been solved elsewhere. The question of financial autonomy is particularly difficult, but in Northern Ireland it has already been solved in principle in this kingdom. No one would pretend that any solution is permanent or perfect. But to remove the shackles of Treasury control without diminishing financial responsibility would, in itself, be the removal of a great burden. Of course, people do underestimate the extent to which differing standards of education and housing apply in different regions already. In fact, the requirements of different regions are not identical and there are many matters in which they can differ without altering standards.

The fact is that standards can adequately be safeguarded by a federal law, and greater financial autonomy between departments and within departments is desirable even if the present system is maintained. Obviously the Northern Ireland formula cannot be transferred bodily across St George's Channel. But to claim the difficulties of financial autonomy as an insuperable bar to regionalism here is surely to overstate the case altogether. There are in truth whole ranges of policy (hospitals and, perhaps, police and probably recreation) where regionalism is the condition of further advance. A slow move towards financial devolution to local authorities already took place when the general grant was introduced. The only trouble was that local authorities were, and are, too small in size to gain the full advantages of such a system.

The third group of critics raise questions about the feasibility of a Bill of Rights, and the right of the judiciary to question the validity of Acts of Parliament. This is, indeed, a doctrine unheard of in Britain for more than 200 years, and it does, at least in theory, conflict with some of the fundamental assumptions of our present constitution. But it is at least noteworthy that almost every country to which we have given independence in the past quarter of a century has had at its own request engrafted into its constitution some safeguards for the individual, and, though their legal effectiveness may be questioned, the rights of the individual, and of minorities, given legal sanction by the European Convention, and by a growing number of United Nations conventions, are slowly becoming embedded in our municipal law by a series of ratifications and Acts of Parliament, gradually but continuously growing. Almost every other country has some such safeguards for individuals and minority groups. There can, therefore, be no difficulty in principle in drafting something, and the days when individual governments could be trusted without judicial surveillance to observe the fairly simple rules of decency are, regrettably, at an end. The Statute of Westminster provides at least one example of Parliament formally, and effectively, fettering its successors. We should not be too timid in supposing that we can do the same again – this time internally.

All the critics really underestimate the extent to which the present dispensation with its highly centralized administration and legislature in Whitehall and Westminster is actually breaking down. I have never thought that the outbreak of nationalism in Scotland and Wales is an isolated phenomenon. But what is clear is that the grievances of Birmingham, Manchester and Bristol are as acute as those of Edinburgh or Merioneth What is lacking is the nationalist spark to give these grievances a mythology, incidentally a largely bogus mythology. Nor have I ever understood what gremlin of perversity leads my colleagues to provide a remedy for Edinburgh not equally available to Newcastle (or, incidentally, Inverness).

The current abuse of politics and politicians is not, I believe, due to an extra dose of original sin in this generation of Members of Parliament. We may be rather less imposing, and even possibly less eloquent, than our predecessors, portentous in their whiskers, top hats and frock coats. But the real truth is that we are trying to force a mass of work through a machine not designed to take a tenth of the pressure. The question is not whether we reform, but how. Recent developments, under the auspices of Mr Crossman, have the effect of making the path of government smoother at the expense of debates on the floor and the power of opposition to hold up business. It is sometimes argued that further reforms in this direction would give the House a renewed opportunity to discuss general issues. To this there is a short answer. It has simply not happened. As committees proliferate, debates on the floor become less and less significant. The real pioneer of this line of thinking was, as he claims in his autography, the Mosley of the New Party. But you do not restore life to Parliament by reducing it to a shareholders' meeting, assembled at respectful intervals to hear the report of the chairman of directors commanding enough proxy votes to be sure of a majority.

If we wish to save parliamentary democracy it is necessary to explore another line of development altogether. This would revive the realities of parliamentary debate in Westminster by devolving much of the administrative, and some of the legislative, work to subordinate, but essentially similar, regional bodies. No doubt each of the two preoccupations will work after its own fashion and dynamic. But the Crossman model, carried to its logical conclusion, would destroy parliamentary government as we know it. The latter at least would preserve the reality by altering the form. The existence of the royal commission at least ensures that reform of this character will be discussed.

Part Two
The Electoral System

Enid Lakeman

A Case for Electoral Reform

Britain's 1970 general election was the surprise one – surprising to most people in its date, and in its result. Both were bound up with the public opinion polls. In the spring these showed a sudden and large movement in favour of the previously unpopular Labour Government (a trend confirmed by local council elections), and Mr Wilson understandably chose to make hay while the sun shone in June, rather than wait for a possible return of frost in October. During the election campaign, polls continued to show a Labour lead, often large, and a third term for Mr Wilson's government was widely taken for granted.

The polls, however, varied in a most unusual manner, from one investigator to another and from time to time, and those taken as late as five days before the real election differed from the actual result far more than is normal. It seems probable that large numbers of electors remained undecided until the last moment, and that a swing back to the Conservatives (of which there were signs in the final polls) gathered momentum during the last few days.

All this illustrates the exaggerated importance that small movements of public opinion assume under the British electoral system, and hence also the great advantage conferred on a Prime Minister by his power to choose the date of the general election. Had Labour's few per cent. lead over the Conservatives continued until the actual vote, that party would have triumphed; at 2.6 per cent. behind, it suffered disaster. Omitting Northern Ireland, which is a very special case and will be considered separately, the Conservatives increased their poll by 4.8 per cent., from 41.4 to 46.2, but their seats by 12.6 per cent., from 242 to 321 – giving us, as usual, a government backed by substantially less than half of those who voted. Labour's vote fell by 4.8 per cent., from 48.5 to 43.7; its seats by 12.2 per cent., from 363 to 287. Those exaggerations, however, are trifling compared with the fate of the Liberals. In terms of parliamentary seats, they suffered the

Reprinted from *Contemporary Review*, vol. 217, no. 1255 (August 1970), pp. 57–62. By permission of the author and the publisher.

catastrophic loss of just half of those they obtained in 1966, but in votes they nearly held their own, falling only from 8.6 to 7.6 per cent.

The handicapping of the parties is seen most clearly in the average number of votes each needed to elect one MP. For the Conservatives, in Great Britain, this was 39,400, for Labour 41,800, and for the Liberals no less than 349,600; moreover, this last is an under-estimate, since they fought only half the seats and their actual support must therefore be substantially greater. The two nationalist parties were similar victims. Taking Wales, where Plaid Cymru fought every seat, it got no seats for 174,916 votes (losing the one seat it had gained in a by-election), while Conservatives got one seat per 60,000 votes and Labour one per 28,000 votes.

Before and during the election, there were many protests from the Opposition because, on the plea of a pending reconstruction of local government, the Government refused to carry out the recommendations of the boundary commissions to remedy large differences which had grown up between the electorates of different constituencies. At the extremes, 18,884 people living in the Ladywood division of Birmingham had the same representation as 124,215 people living in Billericay. The one-to-six-and-a-half difference is, however, considerably less than the nearly one-to-nine difference between the votes needed to elect a Conservative MP and those needed to elect a Liberal, and it is hard to see why people who think it right to take pains to makes votes equal as between people living in different places are unwilling to do anything to make votes equal as between people who vote for different parties.

Boundary revision – however desirable – would do nothing to achieve that; indeed, in the present instance, it would have increased the inequality between Conservative and Labour voters. If the Conservatives are right in their estimate that boundary revision before this election would have given them fifteen extra seats, that would have meant one MP for every 37,400 Conservative votes and one for every 44,200 Labour votes, instead of the actual 39,400 and 41,800 respectively.

There were also complaints that the June election robbed many people of the opportunity to vote because they were on holiday and were not allowed postal votes. But the number thus disfranchised is tiny compared with the 14 million or so who did vote but who had no more effect on the result than if they had all been on holiday. These included, of course, the bulk of those supporting the smaller parties – all the Welsh Nationalists, all but 6,568 of the Scottish Nationalists, and 95.6 per cent. of the Liberal voters; of the 2,090,541 who voted Liberal in Great Britain, only 91,430 contributed to the election of a representative they wanted. But there were also – as always – millions of Conservative and Labour supporters who might as well have been left off the register for all the difference they made, and for many thousands of them this remains true in every election throughout their lives. It has been said that, however low the unemployment figures, for any unemployed individual unemployment is total. For any individual Conservative voter in South Shields, his vote has been totally unemployed in every election, not only for him but for all his ancestors, right back to the creation of that constituency by the first Reform Act in 1832, and all Labour supporters in the 'stockbroker belt' have been in that same position ever since their party was founded.

Moreover, even those who vote on the winning side contribute much less than they should to the democratic process; they get an MP of the party they prefer, but he may not be at all the kind of person they would choose to represent them. In this election, for instance, there was a sharp division among Conservatives over the personalities and policies of Enoch Powell, but anyone who lived in Wolverhampton SW and who wished to elect a Conservative government had no means of promoting that, other than to vote for Mr Powell, however much he might dislike that candidate's ideas, while a Conservative in my own home town had no option but to vote for a man of diametrically opposed views, even if that voter was a Powellite. Only those prepared to vote for a different party because of the candidate's views on, say, immigration or the Common Market had any possibility of using their votes to make known their opinions on such matters, and in many cases not even that possibility existed, since all the candidates might be agreed on that subject. Variations in the 'swing' from one constituency to another suggest that such considerations may have influenced voters rather more than in most elections, but interpretation of the results is very much a matter of speculation; they give no clear verdict.

In some places, indeed, there was a choice between different candidates supporting the same party. For instance, in Surbiton a Conservative supporting Mr Powell stood as an Independent against the anti-Powellite Nigel Fisher who was the official Conservative candidate. The Independent polled only 1,706 votes, compared with Mr Fisher's 17,359, but that is no reliable measure of the Conservative voters' opinions of the two men. For all we know, there may have been many thousands who preferred the Independent but who thought that, having no party organization to back him, he stood no chance of election and who therefore voted for the official Conservative to avoid any risk of 'letting the Socialist in'. This handicap applies to all candidates outside the largest parties. In this election there was, indeed, one successful revolt against the choice of the local party organization – Mr S. O. Davies, refused re-nomination by Labour in Merthyr Tydfil on account of his advanced age, insisted on standing as an Independent and was triumphantly re-elected with 16,701 votes, the official Labour candidate coming second with 9,234. But that was possibly only because the Labour majority there is so huge that no one could imagine the seat would be endangered by splitting the vote; voting for Mr Davies involved no risk of letting in any other party.

Thus, this general election, like any other in Britain, illustrates the two great objections to the system under which it is held: the choice put before the voter is extremely restricted, and the composition of the House of Commons bears little relation to the choice that is expressed. These things very likely have something to do with falling polls and with the tendency to resort to demonstrations of one kind or another to express opinions that cannot be expressed through the ballot box. The low turnout this time may have been due partly to the newly-enfranchised 18- to 20-year-olds, of whom some have not yet developed an interest in politics and others feel they know too little about it to vote, but the poll also fell in the two previous elections, although that of 1966 was on a very new register. Turnout is also very obviously related (though not exclusively) to expectation that the vote will make a difference to the result: the very high polls (headed by North Cornwall's 85 per cent.) are all found in marginal constituencies, the very low ones (down to Stepney's 44 per cent.) where the result is a foregone conclusion. There is a feeling that the act of voting gives the voter too little choice in the running of his country (or of his town), but most voters have no idea what, if anything, can be done to make it more effective.

The need is for a much wider and freer choice for the voter, not limited to one nominee from each of two or three parties, and for much greater assurance that the choice expressed will affect the result in the way the voter wishes.

To illustrate how this can be done, let us consider two areas in this election. First, four constituencies which cover rather more than the Greater London borough of Bromley: Beckenham, Bromley, Chislehurst and Orpington. The Conservatives polled 53 per cent. of the votes (102,162 against Labour 47,744 and Liberal 42,717) and won all four seats. Moreover, one of the defeated candidates was Eric Lubbock, who is widely considered by people of all parties to be a serious loss to the Commons. Such losses are frequent; in this election they have included George Brown and Jennie Lee, and if the Conservatives had been defeated as was expected, Mr Heath himself would very likely have been a casualty. Then, the six constituencies of west London, covering the boroughs of Hammersmith and Kensington and Chelsea. Here, the Conservatives again had just over half the votes, but instead of winning all the seats they got only two; Labour, with 71,671 votes against the Conservatives' 81,926, got the other four. This has been the pattern in nearly every election since the war.

To secure a consistent relation between a party's support and its representation, it is necessary to treat each of those areas as one constituency – electing four and six MPs respectively. So long as they remain divided into single-seat constituencies, it is impossible to avoid either of these anomalous results – even if only two parties are involved. In the first area, the same party is leading by only one vote in each case. The best we can do is to make sure that the winner is acceptable to at least half of those who vote and does not get in, as in Chislehurst and Orpington, with fewer votes than the other two candidates combined; it is not possible to give any effect to the votes of the minority.

Neither, with single-member constituencies, is it possible to give any more effect to a very large majority than to a very small one. In South Kensington, the Conservative had three times as many votes as his one (Labour) opponent, a majority of 14,663, and in Chelsea the position was nearly the same. In North Kensington, on the contrary, the Labour majority over the Conservative was only 3,383, and in Baron's Court 1,105 – four majorities of that order outweighed the two large Conservative ones.

Conservatives in South Kensington, knowing that the seat is safe without their help, commonly put in work for their party in North, or in Baron's Court; if they could transfer to those areas their *votes* as well as their work, they could ensure to their party its fair share of the seats. Similarly, if Labour voters in hopeless Orpington could have moved into Chislehurst, and a few of the Beckenham Liberals into Orpington, their parties would each have won one seat, leaving the Conservatives with two, which is clearly a fair division.

But we can go one better than that – we can allow the Labour or Liberal voters to concentrate, not on the candidate who has had the luck to be adopted by the division where his party is strongest, but on whichever of the candidates the voters consider the best. To do this, we vote in the multi-member constituency by numbering candidates in the order of the voter's preference, and we declare elected any candidate who attains a quota of the votes. (The quota is the smallest number of votes than can be obtained by each of as many candidates as have to be elected, but not by more; in the Bromley area it would be one more than one-fifth of the total valid votes, in West London, one more than one-seventh.) The numbers are an instruction to the returning officer: 'Please give my vote to the candidate I have marked 1. Most likely, it will help to elect him, but if it cannot (either because he has enough votes without mine or because he has so few votes as to be without hope of election), do not waste my vote but give it instead to the candidate I have marked 2. If it cannot help him either, then give it to my 3 – and so on, as far as may be necessary.' (In practice, few votes need to go beyond their second preference.) One immediate effect of this is to give a vote that reflects the voter's real wishes: he need have no hesitation in voting '1' for the candidate he really thinks the best, even if he thinks nobody else will do so (or, for that matter, if he thinks everybody will), for this cannot cause the vote to be wasted, provided only that the voter has marked further preferences. Nor can there be any question of 'splitting the vote'; the voter has a free choice among as many candidates, of all parties and of none, as may like to seek his support.

The voters' wishes, thus expressed, will be reflected in the result. If one quota of electors vote first for all the candidates of one kind (whether that be all of one party, all the anti-Marketeers, all the women, or anything else, according to what the voters think is important), those votes are bound to accumulate on one candidate of that kind, and to elect him. And it will not be just any one of them; it will be whichever most of those voters think is the best. For instance, Liberals in the Bromley area could demonstrate their admiration for Eric Lubbock by voting '1' for him, just as, in Cork last year, five-sixths of the Fianna Fáil voters voted first for Jack Lynch in preference to his party colleague, but if they did not want him they would be equally free to elect another candidate of the same party instead. Two of the four Conservatives now sitting there would not be elected, but they would not necessarily be the two who now hold shaky seats in Orpington and Chislehurst; they would be whichever of the Conservative candidates the Conservative voters considered the most expendable.

It will be seen that this does make possible – without a separate referendum – an expression of public opinion on important questions such as EEC. Any supporter of a major party is sure to have more than one candidate of that party presented to him, and he cannot vote for that party without deciding which of those candidates to put first. He may choose to put first a candidate who wants to join EEC, and if most voters make that same choice, that opinion will predominate in the House. Or, of course, vice versa. That voter may then go on to number other candidates of his own party, or, if he feels very strongly about EEC, to candidates of other parties who share his views on that matter. In any case, when he has come to the end of his own party's candidates, he can do that party no harm by going on to others (since a later preference can never count against an earlier one). His attention is therefore drawn to the fact that, even if he heartily dislikes the other parties in general, there are some among their candidates who have their good points – some, at any rate, who are not so bad as others!

That, perhaps more than any other consideration, makes it highly desirable to re-introduce this system in Northern Ireland. Re-introduce, for it was originally applied to the whole of Ireland, and has been continued in the Republic. To discuss Northern Ireland's internal elections would, however, take me beyond the scope of this article. As far as representation of that province at Westminster is concerned, the single transferable vote has never been applied, but some of its possible advantages can be seen from this election. Though there are only twelve seats, these were contested by no less than eight parties and three different Independents. The ancient division of Unionist and anti-Unionist still dominates the scene, but each side is fragmented; that is indeed natural, for people who agree on wanting (or not wanting) to remain within the United Kingdom do not necessarily agree on anything else. In some constituencies, one side, or both, managed to agree on one candidate – which of course robs the voters of any chance to express their opinion on any other matter, but gives the united side a better chance of winning. In others, there was a wide choice but the winner may well not be wanted by the majority. In North Antrim, there were five candidates, Ian Paisley winning by 2,679 votes over the official Unionist, with three anti-Unionist candidates getting 12,875 votes among them. The supporters of those three almost certainly think the one brand of Unionist preferable to the other, but they have no means of saying so. A system that makes people vote as if they thought one candidate was perfect and there was nothing to be said for any of the others is highly unsuitable.

In my opinion, it is unsuitable for any country, indeed for any kind of election, but the United Kingdom is one of the small minority of states that cling to it. Why? When the Speaker's Conference recommended 'no change', it presumably had its reasons, but what were they? They have never been published – why not? Again, the two big party organizations profess to believe that our existing system is the best and that the change I have discussed would be bad, but they give no reasons and supply their speakers and writers with no material to enable them to argue the case. Why not? The way in which we elect our rulers is important; let us have it properly discussed.

Edward Mortimer

Representing More of the People
Most of the Time

The British electoral system is justified, in the words of Professor W. J. M. Mackenzie, 'by history rather than by logic'. It evolved long before political parties were thought of, as a method by which, in case of dispute, a local community could decide who was to represent it in dealings with the (non-elective) central government. A vote was taken, and the man chosen was the one with most votes. If both seats were contested, each elector voted twice.

Such a system, even as modified by the nineteenth-century reforms of the single-member constituency, secret ballot and manhood suffrage, could never have been devised *a priori* for a nation choosing its sovereign representatives from among candidates proposed by national parties. For its effect in that context is to ensure that at most only one more than one half of the voters in each constituency is effectively represented. The remainder have no effect on the result. Suppose they vote for the winner: they cannot help him win the seat more than he already has, and therefore they cannot help his party. Suppose they vote for the loser they cannot save him from defeat, nor can they help any other member of his party to win any other seat.

Of course, these two phenomena may cancel each other out. But that is a matter of chance. If party support is spread evenly through all the constituencies (which in a modern urban society could easily be the case), a party with a bare majority of votes may win all the seats. If its support is heavily concentrated in certain constituencies, a party with a majority of votes may find itself with a minority of seats.

All this presupposes constituencies of equal size and only two candidates for each seat. The former presupposition is very approximately justified, thanks to the work of the Boundaries Commission. The latter, of course, is very often not – with the result that many British MPs are, in fact, elected by a minority of their constituents. The combined effect of all these phenomena is that every British

Reprinted with some additions from *The Times* (13 September 1973), p. 16. By permission of the author and the publisher.

government since the war has been supported by a majority in the House of Commons representing a minority of the electorate.

Why then have we kept the system so long? Principally, of course, because it suits those in power. An MP who has won his seat under one electoral system is naturally reluctant to vote for its replacement by another system which might prove less favourable to him; and this consideration applies even more strongly to party leaders and party whips. The party in power at any given moment knows that but for the system it would either not have a majority in parliament, or at least not have such a large one; and that the system enables it virtually to dictate to its supporters in each constituency whom they shall elect as their MP. It is, therefore, not surprising that the periods when the government has been willing to consider electoral reform in this century have been periods when no party had undisputed control of the House of Commons, 1917, when a coalition government was in power and the largest Parliamentary party had split; 1930, when a Labour minority government was dependent on Liberal support; and 1965, when the Labour majority was so small that Liberal goodwill was worth cultivating.

On the first occasion a reform proposal was narrowly defeated on a free vote. In the other two cases the discussion was effectively ended by a general election which gave one party a comfortable majority.

If electoral reform is topical again, it is partly because there seems a better-than-average chance that the next general election will again produce a House of Commons with no clear majority for any party; partly because membership of EEC has brought us closer to (and may involve us in joint elections with) countries whose electoral systems are different from ours; partly because the troubles in Northern Ireland have recently led the Government to introduce a form of proportional representation there; partly because both by-elections and opinion polls show growing support for the Liberal Party, which has long advocated the introduction of the same form of proportional representation – the single transferable vote (STV) for parliamentary elections in the United Kingdom; and finally because both this Liberal revival and the success of Mr Taverne at Lincoln have been widely interpreted as expressions of discontent with the two-party system in its present form, for which the method of election is largely responsible.

It therefore seems a good time to review the various systems used for parliamentary elections in different countries, and the advantages and disadvantages which each presents. That is the purpose of this table. I have tried to present it neutrally. But it is based largely on the work of Miss Enid Lakeman and the Electoral Reform Society.

Undoubtedly it does tend to show why that society considers STV superior to other systems, and was able to convince Mr Whitelaw of this when it came to choosing a system for a fresh start in Northern Ireland.

For what are the objections to STV? The view that it necessarily destroys the two-party system – as arguably the List System or the Second Ballot would do – is not borne out by the experience of Tasmania or Malta. It does not *guarantee* the survival of that system, true enough. But then, nor does our present method of election – as Ronald Butt pointed out in a recent article. The difference is that STV would make the number of parties dependent on the will of the electorate, rather than on the chance distribution of party support between constituencies.

Then there is the relative complexity of the procedure for counting votes and attributing seats. But this has not given rise to any serious difficulty in practice, and could certainly be speeded up with the use of computers. For the voter, the procedure is quite simple: he numbers as many candidates as he wishes in order of preference.

It is true that STV does away with single-member constituencies, which are thought to be a valuable bond between people and Parliament. But how much of a bond are they, when only 58 per cent. of voters can remember the name of their MP, and when MPs share with property developers the bottom rung on the popularity scale of professions? Would not voters feel a closer bond with the one out of five or seven members for whom they had themselves voted?

Party discipline might be weakened by STV. This is true, and certainly explains the hostility to it of the leaders and officials of big parties (including Fianna Fail in Ireland). But how much weight does this argument carry with the general public? The choice in the last resort is between parties that are omnipotent and ones over which the voter has some control. Fianna Fail governments have twice tried to abolish STV by referendum. Both times the Irish people refused. The Lincoln by-election results suggests that the British people, if given the choice, might well take the same view.

HOW THE FREE WORLD CHOOSES ITS PARLIAMENTS

A. Majority Systems
Winner takes all in single-member constituency*.
General Advantages: Each constituency has own MP to look after its interests. Very small parties unlikely to win seats. Voting is for man, not party – but party can choose own candidate.

* Larger constituencies can be used, but this makes gross under-representation of the minority virtually certain.

General Disadvantages: No representation for minority in each constituency, or for surplus voters of each winning candidate. This usually means the national minority is under-represented, but can sometimes enable it to get more seats than the majority (e.g. South Africa, 1948 and 1953). Size and shape of constituencies can give rise to 'gerrymandering' charges. Political differences between regions exaggerated.

TYPES

1. *Simple plurality* – or 'First Past the Post' system.
Examples: Britain, United States, Canada, South Africa, New Zealand.
Procedure: One ballot only. Leading candidate elected whether or not he has majority of votes cast.
Advantages: Voting and counting very simple. Favours two-party system; improves chance of one-party parliamentary majority. May give voter clear choice between alternative governments.
Disadvantages: Many MPs elected by minority of their constituents. Government often represents minority of electorate. Local particularisms can be heavily over-represented (e.g. Irish Nationalists before 1918). Result very unpredictable, especially when more than two parties are regarded as serious contenders. 'Wasted vote' bogy: only official candidates of big parties stand real chance.

2. *Absolute majority.* a. *Alternative Vote.*
Example: Australia.
Procedure: Voter numbers candidates in order of preference. Bottom candidate eliminated and his votes redistributed according to next preference. Repeat until top candidate has absolute majority of votes.
Advantages: Each MP has majority support in his constituency. 'Wasted vote' bogy eliminated, so that smaller parties and unofficial candidates have better chance.
Disadvantages: Result decided by 'most worthless votes'—i e. lower preferences of least successful candidates. Chance of one-party majority diminished. Distorted results, e.g. party with fewest first preferences can win all the seats, if it runs second in each constituency and is everyone's second choice.

b. *Second Ballot.*
Example: France. (And many other European countries before World War I.)
Procedure: If no candidate has absolute majority on first ballot, a second is held in which only candidates who obtained at least 10 per cent. of votes are allowed (but not obliged) to stand: the effect in most constituencies, but not all, is to produce a straight fight.

Advantages: Most MPs (but not all) elected with majority of votes cast. 'Wasted vote' bogy partially eliminated (but not completely, since vote can be transferred only once).
Disadvantages: 'Sordid' bargaining between parties for second-ballot withdrawals. Tends to promote multi-party system with weak party discipline.

B. Semi-Proportional Systems

Procedure: Elector either has fewer votes than there are seats to be filled, or can vote more than once for the same candidate. Votes not transferable.
Example: Japan. (Single Non-Transferable Vote.)
Advantage: Ensures some representation for minority in each constituency.
Disadvantage: Premium for parties which can correctly predict their support and can organize supporters into dividing equally among the right number of candidates. A party dividing its votes among too many candidates may cause some or all of them to fail, while one that wins extra votes for too few candidates cannot benefit.

C. Proportional Systems

Seats obtained by quota in multi-member constituencies. (One vote for each elector.)
General Advantage: Natural Justice. Each voter gets as nearly as possible an equal share of representation.
General Disadvantages: Lack of consensus can become more difficult to conceal, and fiction of General Will more difficult to sustain. Each MP does not have a constituency to himself.

TYPES
1. *List System* (Proportional as between parties.)
Procedure: Vote is cast for a list of candidates. Seats distributed among lists in proportion to votes cast for each. Most systems also allow voter to influence order of list by expressing preference for individual candidates.
Examples: (no preference): Israel. (one preference, optional): Belgium, Denmark. (one preference, compulsory): Finland, Netherlands. (four preferences, optional): Italy. (whole list rearrangeable): Norway, Sweden. (preferences shareable between lists): Switzerland, Sweden, Norway.
Advantages: Palpably fair as between parties. Makes for strong party discipline.
Disadvantages: Elector forced to vote for a party whether he wants to or not; even where he puts his cross against an individual candidate,

his vote is bound to help other candidates on the same list.

Very large constituencies make MP remote from individual voter.

One-party majority in parliament is rare. Hence general election is seldom clear choice between two alternative governments.

Parties tend to cultivate support of particular interest groups; they govern in coalition but fight elections as enemies, thereby encouraging public cyncism about parliamentary politics.

Unofficial candidates have no chance. Votes for new or very small parties may still be 'wasted'.

2. *Mixed Systems* (Combination of List System with some aspect of majority system.)
Example: West Germany.
Procedure: Elector votes once for individual candidate in single-member constituency, and once for national party list. Half Bundestag elected by first votes exactly as in United Kingdom, but each party is then topped up to its proportional strength as revealed by second votes —provided that it has secured *either* at least three seats by first votes *or* at least 5 per cent. of second votes.
Advantages: Link between MP and constituency is retained. Small parties eliminated. (Result in practice has been 3-party system, and could in future be 2-party one.)
Disadvantages: Voter has no influence on parties' choice of candidates. Small parties' supporters not represented.

3. *Single Transferable Vote* (Proportional as between candidates.)
Procedure: Voter numbers candidates in order of preference. First preferences are counted first and any candidate obtaining the quota (e.g. in a five-member constituency, one more than one sixth of the total number of votes) is declared elected. Any votes he has over and above this minimum are transferred to the voters' second choice. When no candidate has attained the quota, the bottom candidate is eliminated and all his votes transferred to their next preference. These two procedures are repeated until all the seats are filled.
Examples: Irish Republic, Malta, Tasmania, and now Northern Ireland. (Also senatorial elections in Australia and South Africa; General Synod of the Church of England; and committees of many unofficial bodies.)
Advantages: Reasonably proportional result can be obtained in much smaller constituencies than with List System.

Small parties penalized but views of their supporters not ignored. Need for small parties reduced, since large ones encouraged to offer variety of candidates.

'Wasted vote' bogy eliminated. Voters can pick and choose among party's candidates, and thereby vote on issues which cut across party lines.

Candidate can appeal to voters against non-selection without damaging party's chances.

Two-party system not impossible. (E.g. Tasmania, Malta.)

One-party majority in parliament quite common. (E.g. Fianna Fáil governments in Ireland.)

Parties' election campaigns have to appeal to others' supporters as well as their own. Hence coalitions and compromises in government less shocking to electors.

Voters can endorse or reject proposed coalition by distribution of lower preferences.

Almost every voter has an individual MP whom he helped to elect.

Disadvantages: Procedure seems unduly complex to the uninitiated.

Strict party discipline difficult to enforce.

Danger of emphasizing 'parish-pump' issues and personalities at expense of great national choices.

Encourages in-fighting and back-stabbing between politicians of same party.

Tends to produce very small parliamentary majority requiring very tight parliamentary discipline.

Part Three
Parliament

John Mackintosh, MP

Failure of a Reform: MPs'
Special Committees

In the early 1960s, ideas for parliamentary reform ceased to be mere theoretical proposals. They were worked out in detail by academics and by clerks of the House of Commons in a body called the Study of Parliament Group. Active politicians also realized that the increasing criticism of British institutions had some political force, and felt that this was a time when some changes might be achieved. The two pressures came together when the 1964 and 1966 elections brought a large number of new young MPs into the House of Commons, many of whom had been influenced by academic criticism of the procedure of the House.

The theory underlying this demand for Parliamentary reform was seldom set out in precise terms, the nearest approach being Professor Bernard Crick's book on *The Reform of Parliament*. But the general lines of argument were accepted by most reformers. The central theme was that, with the growth of powerful party loyalties, the Commons' capacity to defeat a government had gone, and with it there had disappeared much of the influence of the House. Britain was acquiring a form of plebiscitary democracy in which there was less and less scope for an intermediary between the people and the executive – i.e. for a House of Commons. The result was cumulative in that poorer candidates stood for parliament; the public's confidence in the old institutions and in the notion of a participatory democracy declined; and all this encouraged the Prime Minister to ignore the Commons and deal directly through the press and television with the electorate.

The second strand in this argument was that the public wanted to choose between the parties. So there could be no return to the old days of independent MPs voting down clauses of a bill, yet leaving the government in power. The only way to revive the influence of the House of Commons was to give it powers, to open up discussion of policy before decisions were taken and the stamp of party approval

Reprinted from *New Society* (28 November 1968), pp. 791–792. By permission of the author and the publisher.

(and therefore the guarantee of passage) was given to one proposal or another.

In order to extract this measure of information and prior discussion, it would be necessary to alter procedure because at present arguments on legislation take place after a bill has been negotiated with outside pressure groups and published. It would also be necessary to break the convention of civil service anonymity and find a means by which MPs could discover what was going on inside the ministries and what was being arranged between officials and the representatives of outside bodies.

The methods by which these reforms were to be achieved were complex. But the vital institution or technique was the 'specialist committee'.

In fact, these committees are Select Committees of the House, but the word 'specialist' was used to show that they were to be different from the Nationalized Industries Select Committee (which moved from one industry to another) and from the sub-committees of the Select Committee on Estimates (which also moved from one topic to another). The word 'specialist' meant that the committees were to attach themselves permanently to one subject or area of work. They were to have powers to call witnesses, ask for papers and have their proceedings televised, and were to continue year by year building up a specialized body of knowledge.

After the 1964 general election the Select Committee on Procedure asked some members of the Study of Parliament Group to give evidence before it. The committee's report for 1964–65 recommended a single Select Committee with powers to conduct investigations. A minority of four members called for a full range of specialist committees. But nothing happened immediately.

Most ministers wished to continue their work unfettered by any such scrutiny and the opposition front bench agreed with them. For many older MPs the House of Commons was not a place for this kind of quasi-governmental activity; it was the theatre in which a part of the struggle for power took place.

The 1966 election brought few positive results (apart from an indication by Harold Wilson that he was prepared to look at two new Select Committees) till Richard Crossman became Leader of the House in late 1966. He and the Chief Whip, John Silkin, were in touch with reforming ideas and Crossman tried to get the cabinet to accept some progress.

He pointed out that parliamentary reform also meant cutting out antiquated methods of procedure, which made it easier to put government business through the House. He evolved a doctrine that if he could get one reform simplifying the work of ministers, the cabinet should concede one which increased the opportunities open to back-benchers.

As a result he was able to propose, in December 1966, the formation of two specialist committees. One was to watch over a department of state and the other to examine a subject which ranged across departments. How the department and the subject were chosen is not absolutely clear, but the Prime Minister appears to have told Crossman that he could go ahead provided he could square the project with the ministers concerned. The department chosen was the Ministry of Agriculture and Fisheries in England and Wales because Fred Peart was willing to allow the experiment. (The Scottish Department of Agriculture was excluded because Willie Ross, the Scottish Secretary of State, did not like the idea.) The subject committee was set to work on science and technology because this was fashionable and Anthony Wedgwood Benn, the minister chiefly concerned, was in favour.

The selection of members to serve on these committees was left to the nomination of the Chief Whips and it is possible that ministers were consulted. Thus, Fred Peart was extremely hostile to British entry to the Common Market and almost all the Labour members originally chosen to serve – including the chairman, Tudor Watkins – shared his view. Scottish MPs were at first excluded on the grounds that Scottish agriculture was not in the terms of reference. But after a row and a threat by the Conservatives to boycott the committee, two Scots MPs (of whom I was one) were added, raising the numbers to 16.

The committee was set up for the session 1966–67 only – and as it began in December, it was left five months to do its work. Much was later made of the 'experimental' nature of the committee, though the members all took this to mean simply that its continued existence depended on the value of the work.

At the first meetings there was a strong impression that Fred Peart had managed to indicate that two subjects of inquiry were unacceptable: the agricultural aspects of the Common Market and the machinery of the annual farm price review. Despite this impression, the topicality of the EEC question was so obvious that members decided to investigate the adequacy of the studies made of the Common Market system by the ministry. Richard Crossman's reactions were not clear but he appeared at times to think that the committee should not have worked on something which involved the merits of civil servants' work but should have sought to study a different kind of topic (such as methods of preserving animal health) and come out with some positive suggestions. Certainly he and other ministers always looked with greater favour on the committee on science and technology because it did just that. It prepared reports on nuclear reactors, coastal pollution and defence research establishments.

Yet, in terms of the original idea of specialist committees, the committee on agriculture was much more what the parliamentary reformers had wanted. And the choice of ministry could not have been better. Since the Agriculture Act, 1947, set up a statutory annual negotiation between the ministry and the National Farmers' Union, all major decisions on agricultural policy had been handled in secret outside the purview of the House of Commons.

On the whole, the ministry tended to bat back parliamentary questions with the minimum information that could be conceded. Debates on agriculture depended on the one or two MPs who did some private research in order to rise above the level of stories about members' farms.

The committee soon ran into a number of problems. The most fundamental difficulty was that the members wanted to find out what arguments had been going on in the ministry about the agricultural effects of joining the EEC, and within Whitehall about the priority to be given to a study of this question. The civil servants were determined never to suggest that they had ever had a doubt or a disagreement.

For instance, the object might be to find out the effect of entry on cereal production. The estimate of the ministry was x and that of the NFU was y. The obvious question was why there was a discrepancy. If this produced no results, the MP might well be driven to ask what study had been made of the matter by the ministry. If, again, the official was unforthcoming, one way out of the impasse was to ask the ministry to submit a paper. The civil servants were annoyed both by the tone of the questioning, and by the extra work involved. But all they need have done was admit a difference in assumptions or whatever else in the weight given to various factors.

Some important specific disputes occurred. The committee wanted to visit Brussels to see if the Ministry of Agriculture's version of EEC policy was accepted there. This request was refused by the Foreign Office on the grounds that this would be misinterpreted as an attempt to open negotiations. After many wrangles with the Foreign Office and with Crossman, the government partly gave way. An equally serious dispute and impasse had been reached over the committee's right to see papers which, in the case of certain letters on staffing, had simply been refused by the Foreign Office.

By the time the committee reported in July 1967 it had achieved a number of the objectives desired by parliamentary reformers. It had extracted a mass of information. The White Paper on the implications of entry, which it obtained from the ministry, had been specifically refused in previous months at question time.

Yet the committee had grated badly both on ministers and on officials, who complained about the work load involved. At first, Crossman had talked of adding two more departmental specialist committees each year. The Labour backbench group on parliamentary reform had asked for committees on Home Office Affairs and on trade and industry.

In 1967 the government reappointed the committee, though only after considerable delay and after increasing the membership from 16 to 25. This was far too large a membership. If everyone had attended, the committee could not have functioned. However, at the first meeting, the new members were asked if they had actively sought to be included. The reply was that the Whips had press-ganged them. So they agreed, with one exception, to stay away, leaving the original group to continue the work.

The committee again went for a central topic: import saving. But parliamentary reform generally was coming under a shadow. The experiment with morning sessions was a failure because only non-controversial business had been put in the mornings. The committee to which the Parliamentary Commissioner (or Ombudsman) reported had a battle with the Foreign Office because the Foreign Secretary, George Brown, had rejected the Commissioner's report on the Sachsenhausen case but would not let the committee review the question.

A deep conflict in the Labour Party over discipline brought the anti-reformers' wrath down on Crossman and John Silkin.

Because of this, and because members' and ministers' minds were turning to the prospect of the next election and to the older forms of cross-Chamber conflict, parliamentary reform became unpopular. It became the hobby horse of a very small group of ideological democrats. The change was confirmed when Crossman gave way to Fred Peart as Leader of the House in mid-1968. Against this background, the agriculture committee sensed that it had no great reserves of strength in standing up to the irritation it had caused in Whitehall. The work it was doing was complex, and it could not complete a report in the 1967–68 session, but the members hoped to be reappointed when parliament resumed in late October. In fact, in November, the government put down an order giving the committee till 31 December to conclude and be closed down.

The members waged a considerable struggle against this decision, and the date was extended to 28 February 1969; but the government won the main point. The committee is to be disbanded.

The specialist committee on science and technology still exists, doing its non-departmental investigations. One may wonder how long even this will go on. In any event, the demise of the agricultural committee is both evidence of the decline in support for parlimentary reform and a further stage in the process. The great prize remains political power. However much individual MPs may be irritated by the demands of party loyalty, the majority respond to this appeal – to the fact that it is 'them or us'. If diversions are required, each MP has his constituency work and the need to make his own mark in his party, none of which is furthered by spending time trying to nibble at the edges of executive power.

J. D. B. Mitchell

Administrative Law and Parliamentary Control

A revolution, if taken seriously, can be helpful. It can compel serious and creative thought on constitutional structures. That process was evident in the French Revolution,[1] it happened (though less obviously) in the French Resistance. It was again evident in postwar Germany, where events forced thought. It does not, of course, follow that the results of the process are necessarily good, but at least there is the possibility of movement, or change, based on coherent thought which has a reasonable chance of being constructive. On the other hand, quiet, or even endemic, revolutions tend not to have the same effect. The stimulus of an element of crisis is lacking and, indeed, the perception of change is often delayed.

INCOHERENCE OF TRADITION

In this country, whatever the benefits we have received from the quietness of our revolutions since 1688, we have lost in this respect. For that there are several reasons. Perhaps above all is the simple fact that it is extremely difficult for a profession to reform itself from within. Medicine is kept alive by the outside pressures of science, but otherwise the closeness of the shop increases the difficulties. Politics and government are relatively closed. The specialty of the House of Commons is known and felt by those who, being Members, are the initiates, but they would assert this mystery is not fully appreciated by outsiders.[2] This is but one example. The Civil Service has also this element of closeness, and the two groups can unconsciously combine. Both know the ways of working the present machine and have a joint interest in keeping that understood machine unchanged. To say that is not, of course, to assert that there are no new ideas, but it is to assert that those ideas emerge and are formulated against a background of the assumed continuance and virtue of the basic structure. They must, whether appropriately or not, be fitted within that

Reprinted from *The Political Quarterly*, vol. XXXVIII, no. 4 (October-December 1967), pp. 360–374. By permission of the author and the publisher.

structure to have any easy chance of acceptance, even though that structure was evolved to meet problems essentially different in size or scale.

Thus, feeling new needs in the immediate post-war years, we created a new system of public Boards. The constitutional difficulty of working these within the framework of our institutional structure was well enough known and in the past had caused the steady submerging of Boards into the departmental pattern.[3] Yet nothing substantial was done to adjust theory or institutions to meet the new conditions, despite the fact that these creations were (and were intended to be) a departure from general constitutional and political theory. Typically, the transplant has not thrived, and the Boards are (whatever the law may appear to say) steadily and effectively reverting to a departmental pattern, or at best living in a curious half world in which none of the traditional constitutional controls work satisfactorily,[4] being ill adapted to new tasks. Yet nothing new is attempted.

PARTIAL SOLUTIONS

Two other things happen in a condition of essential change concealed by an appearance of untroubled continuity. First, we feel too much the weight of chance desires. A sudden unease results from some deep-seated constitutional inconsistency or malfunctioning, and to solve it an easy temporary solution is accepted which does not deal with the essential problem. Typical of this was the adoption of an Ombudsman. The change of name to 'Parliamentary Commissioner for Administration' is chiefly significant as an indication of the desire to disrupt the existing situation as little as possible. (Thus, in the White Paper on 'The Parliamentary Commissioner for Administration' (Cmnd. 2767) one reads: 'We do not want to create any new institution which would erode the functions of Members of Parliament in this respect nor to replace remedies which the British Constitution already provides.') But it was precisely the basic deficiencies of the existing legal remedies and the basic unreality of parliamentary doctrines such as that of ministerial responsibility that lay at the root of the whole problem.[5] The Ombudsman solution had a superficial attraction, for it could serve the purpose of damping down the feeling of dissatisfaction – in much the same way that aspirin may conceivably deal with some of the effects of constant heavy drinking, without ever dealing with the root cause. The second thing is related. Problems are not seen as a whole, and therefore are not dealt with as a whole. The problem of administrative law was thought of both too narrowly and in too fragmented a manner. It was conceived of as a problem of delegated legislation and of administrative tribunals, but both issues were dealt with more or less separately.[6]

Even in so far as the Committee on Ministers' Powers was specifically charged with looking at both problems together, it treated each quite separately; and by reason of the weakness of its approach to the question of administrative tribunals the report at the end of the day only had effect on delegated legislation. It can be regarded as a real cause of the Statutory Instruments Act 1946, but of little else – save muddled thinking, particularly in its attempts to separate judicial, quasi-judicial and administrative functions. Administrative tribunals were left to wait for the Franks Committee and the Tribunals and Inquiries Act. Again, the sequence of events is of interest. The immediate cause of the Franks Committee was the episode of Crichel Down – where the faults lay in acts of general administration. Such acts were beyond the terms of reference of the Committee. Thus, because of the terms of reference, the generality of the problem of the courts in relation to administration could not be looked at, and, perhaps worse, a fallacy arose because of the consequential nature of the report that if only the process of administration could be made more judicial all would be well.

The weakness of the solution, or rather its limitations, soon became apparent. The real problem lay, said the Council on Tribunals, not so much with administrative tribunals – of the type, for example, of those concerned with National Insurance – but with Inquiries.[7] That is to say, with administrative acts. Indeed, it is arguable that the Franks Committee and the resultant Tribunals and Inquiries Act have aggravated the situation in two ways. First, by emphasizing, in effect, a judicial element in the inquiry stage, there was fostered a greater feeling of disappointment when factual arguments which had carried weight at the inquiry were overridden by administrative considerations. Thus the disappointed objector was left thinking that he had won a verdict, but for some outside reason had lost the judgement. Secondly, because of that same emphasis the procedural steps were inevitably complicated, and complication means both expense and delay. Delay can be as important as any other consideration when one is dealing with a road construction programme or a housing programme for a number of sites based on an integrated plan which is vital if machinery is to be efficiently used. A third probable unhappy consequence was the dichotomy created within Ministries of the 'hearing' branches and the general administration. *Imperia* were created within *imperia* and thus the administrative process lost cohesion.

So once again pressures mounted. Partial solutions were seen not to be real solutions and the Parliamentary Commissioner emerged – as yet one more partial solution. That blunt assertion can be made, for still the basic problem remains: the absence of an effective system of public law – that which the Parliamentary Commissioner cannot supply and clearly was not intended to supply. Neither delegated legislation, nor administrative tribunals, were in themselves problems of the first order. They were simply manifestations of a general problem of a modern state, a problem which has grown considerably in the last forty years and which at some time must be faced as a whole.

PARLIAMENTARY CONTROL NOT ENOUGH

The problem has, however, a double aspect. One is Parliamentary, and the other is legal, for the need for a duality of control remains. It is not the object of this article to explore fully the Parliamentary aspect, but something must briefly be said about it. In its essential elements the operation of the Parliamentary system and the ideas upon which it is based are those of the nineteenth century. Its efficacy has therefore been greatly affected by two things in particular: the emergence of parties which are powerful and monolithic, and the fulfilment of Maitland's prophecy, that we were becoming a much-governed nation. The first means that some traditional doctrines like that of ministerial responsibility have to a large extent been emptied of content, while others, like collective responsibility, have become much more rigid. The formal battleground of disciplined armies fighting for power is not an appropriate place for detailed control of administration to be exercised. Administrative errors are not the stuff of real politics, and if they are debated in political terms, as they must be in such an arena, the debate is falsified. The second – the growth of government activity – means that the press of business for which there should be an effective means of redress available exceeds anything which could be dealt with in Parliament, even were that the right forum. Parliament, and the House of Commons in particular, cannot act as a court delivering judgement and having at its disposal a full range of appropriate remedies. (This issue was at the same time admitted and evaded by the White Paper on the Parliamentary Commissioner. In its opening paragraphs it speaks of 'injustices', which traditionally should find redress in the courts, and then speaks of Parliament as the traditional place for ventilating grievances. But the traditional grievances redressed in Parliament were of a general nature; by a longer tradition it was for the courts to do justice to those persons who were specifically aggrieved.) Apart from politics there will always remain an important place for law in government. So while the movements to reform Parliament are welcome and, indeed, overdue, they will not in themselves suffice unless they are accompanied by radical reform in the law.

Such reform is vital since the law has got out of touch with reality and thus has become ineffective. At the same time that a considerable inventiveness was still shown by lawyers in the field of private law, in order to absorb the consequences of the industrial revolution, a parallel inventiveness in the field of public law ceased. Where particular major problems arose, especially in foreign affairs, statutory intervention did happen (though not in any consistent way), as for example, the Foreign Enlistment Act 1870 to prevent a more dangerous Alabama affair. Internally efforts were made by use of prerogative writs or orders to maintain the law in some relationship with the changes in society, but these efforts were bound to have limited results. They were limited because of the checks which the courts imposed upon themselves out of respect for Parliamentary doctrines – which could at the time have some reality, but which admittedly no longer exists. They were limited, too, by reason of the scope of those remedies. By their nature they were inappropriate to the control of general administrative acts and, moreover, were inadequate in the relief which they could offer. The result has been that, for example, Professor Wade, who is far less inclined to a critical view of the law than the present writer, has said that: 'Although the action for damages, therefore, plays a central part, it is incapable of dealing with large classes of administrative acts.'[8] That is to say the law no longer affords fully effective relief.

LITIGATION BETWEEN GOVERNMENT AND CITIZEN

The issues must be seen in their full scope. They extend well beyond those related to controlling what would normally be regarded as an 'administrative act'. In the law of contract it has become apparent that, more often than not, traditional doctrines of contract will not work because of the specific qualities of government contracts. It is easy to cite the two Lang Reports[9] but the difficulties are in truth much more widely felt. They are felt equally in the law of tort or reparation. Administrative law must be thought of in much broader and more general terms than has hitherto been our inclination, and it is because of this failure that we have had only a series of partial measures and are not yet in sight of a proper solution. It is the whole of law in relation to government that must be looked at. Remedies, for example, are at the same time inadequate and too blunt. Their bluntness means that often they cannot be used.

There are real difficulties for both Government and citizen about the present doctrines of Crown privilege, but because of the inappropriate bluntness of rules and procedures it is likely that the protestations in *Re Grosvenor Hotel*[10] are likely to amount to little more than *Vox et praeterea nihil* (and subsequent litigation seems to foreshadow this). Often remedies like injunction, appropriate between individuals whose interests are of the same order, will not be appropriate as against government because of the injury they could do to the public interest. To say that is not to suggest that the individual should be left without remedy – far from it, but the basis on which the remedy must be granted differs from the basis appropriate in litigation between individuals. If an administrator makes a mistaken promise or undertaking, he cannot be held to it as would be an individual as a result of estoppel. Otherwise you have admitted a suspending or dispensing power. A different basis must be found to compensate the individual who has acted to his hurt upon the assertions of a responsible official. Again a different basis is required since, by reason of its purposes as much as by reason of its methods, a government has peculiar strengths and weaknesses not shared by any individual. It alone has the lawful power to change the rules of the game half way through the currency of a contract, and may have an obligation to the generality of its citizens so to do. Equally by the nature of its processes, it may well be in command of information essential to litigation in ways unlike any private party. Yet, on the other hand, it has peculiar weaknesses – again the Lang reports demonstrate that, and the weaknesses are inevitable. Certain forms of expertise will continue to exist outside the Civil Service, which must remain relatively general. Equally the Government may, as a result of social causes, be faced with demands for urgency of a different order from the demands upon business.

Thus two things stand out: one is the need for a different jurisprudence, philosophy is not too grand a word, as the foundation of a proper system of public law; the other is the inevitability of the maxim of Portalis, *'Juger l'administration c'est aussi administrer'* – he who judges the administration must himself be closely aware of both the strengths and weaknesses of the administration and must be aware of the needs of the administration as much as of those of the citizen. He must strike a balance which is a different balance from that struck between private parties in the matters of which account should be taken. The techniques and remedies by which that balance must be struck must differ because of these circumstances from those appropriate as between two private individuals. Not least of our difficulties today is the fact that lawyers and administrators have ceased to talk the same language. They fail to understand each other and without that comprehension the law cannot match the needs of the situation.

NEED FOR A NEW JURISDICTION

We are thus in a position in which the demands of a modern state pose problems for Parliament, they pose even more for lawyers, yet the tradition, rules, and mechanisms of the law have shown our inability to deal with the situation. With the Parliamentary side of the problem reforms are beginning. These reforms will be incomplete and their efficacy reduced unless the side of law is also covered at the same time. A solution is available, which sounds more radical than it is. It is the creation of a distinct administrative jurisdiction.

A new jurisdiction is required in order to free the law from the shackles on thought which are part of the heritage of the past: to free lawyers from thinking in narrow terms about administrative law, and even within those narrow terms of being captivated by the past splendours of the prerogative orders. Above all, new procedures are needed. The extreme orality of existing procedures is an obstacle, and more of an investigatory procedure is needed. New institutions help the evolution of new methods. Again I believe that novelty in composition is necessary. Within limits, the Restrictive Practices Court has shown the way, though it did not go far enough. One of the problems of courts in relation to a modern society is the problem of age. There is with us a tendency for judges to be out of touch, or else to over-correct from a fear lest they be out of touch. Within the Conseil d'État in Paris (which is to some extent the background of this thesis) there is, once its mysteries have been penetrated, a curious blending of youth and age in the whole process of decision-making. It is a process which is more open and more acceptable than the system of clerks to the Justices of the Supreme Court in the USA (and in other courts there), but it has some of the same quality. At all critical stages, youth or intellectually ambitious middle age has a part to play which is serious and formative. When dealing with the law appropriate to the modern state this technique has enormous importance. Equally, the sort of 'seminar' activity built in to the process of judgement there is important, especially when there is the necessity of hammering out a new philosophy of law. That process with us demands more than our traditional forms of advocacy and judgement can supply. This 'seminar' process must be emphasized, simply because the real problems of modern public law are incapable of solution by a nice tidy statute.

What is needed is a jurisdiction which, given an appropriate charter, can itself evolve (by a process familiar to, and accepted by, the common law in its heyday) a new and coherent system of jurisprudence. The selection of such a court itself poses problems. Again the Restrictive Practices Court goes half way, and also shows the danger of stopping half way. The issues that are involved require, without doubt, a sound knowledge of law, but beyond that they demand a sound understanding of the processes of government, of economics, and of social philosophy. All elements must combine: a process of having 'assessors' of this or that qualification, whether they be economists or civil servants, is inadequate. At best, assessors are, in the splendidly descriptive phrase of Kai Lung, 'under-oversmen'. The real oversman remains the lawyer pure and undefiled. At worst they are the advocates for the corps or discipline from which they come. Yet it is essential that they should contribute on equal terms and with equal voice to the decision-making process.

CHARACTER OF A NEW COURT

All these elements combine in one more consideration. The court, the new jurisdiction, must be a collegiate body and should speak with a collegiate voice. Only in that way can it have the strength to match the strength of government. It is not without reason that the Conseil d'État preserves, by convention even more than by law, the secrecy of its final deliberation; and no one with any sensitivity or realization of its tasks would try to break that secrecy. Power must match power. The weakness of the House of Commons will always be that ultimately that power which can match the power of government will not (save in moments of crisis when the fall of a government is generally acceptable) ever be mustered against the power of a government. Below those great occasions there are many instances when the power of the law should correct government action. It is an offence when the whole of the legislative process has become little more than a formality. The legislative history of the installation of the Parliamentary Commissioner is a convenient illustration, though others of wider significance could be chosen. These things are an offence, because they indicate the precariousness of a legal situation, showing the possibilities (happily never yet seriously realized) of abuse. A collegiate decision is one vital element. Cabinet secrecy was and remains one prime cause of Cabinet strength, and thus an illustration of the strength that comes from this type of decision. Perhaps the collegiate idea runs deeper. From young to old, the members of the Conseil d'État are kinsmen, members of the same corps. Some will go away, some will quietly be sent away because they are not up to the strain. Yet all belong. There is within the whole body a devotion to keeping administrative law in touch with the times and yet serving impartially the twin needs of the citizen for protection and the reasonable requirements of efficient administration. Indeed, you can find within the Palais Royal more serious conversation on the reform of administrative law than you will find outside it.

Thus the novelty and distinctiveness of an administrative jurisdiction can be justified. More justification could be produced. In particular there is the need for specialism. The problems of this area of law are acute. They require, if an appropriate coherent system is to emerge, coherent and continuous thought. In one sense the sad history of the Commercial Court demonstrates this need. It has never achieved the results which it could have done, despite some of the great names who have sat within it, because of unevenness and the lack of specialism. The great were often taken away to perform tasks for which they were unfitted. It is, of course, true that distinctiveness can produce all the problems inherent in the duality of jurisdictions, and the shades of pre-1875 Equity and Common Law Courts will be evoked. There are problems; though at the outset it must be said that the flowering of Equity, the inventiveness of Chancery, was due to specialism. The difficulties arose because the two jurisdictions were dealing concurrently with what was essentially an entire situation: a conveyancing transaction, for example, between parties whose interests were of the same legal order. Such a situation finds no parallel in the present context. The duality of jurisdiction poses far fewer problems, because it is a rational dualism: one jurisdiction dealing with conflicts between citizen and government (or intra-governmental conflicts); and the other dealing with the conflicts between private individuals whose interests are of the same legal order. True, there will be grey areas, but with a properly drawn charter these grey areas will be small. Here French parallels are not exact. They, too, can suffer from the history of 150 years, but it is worth having a sound and workable system for 150 years and then carrying out reforms, rather than have inefficiency and the denial of justice for 150 years, as we are likely to have, unless there is some such radical change.

POWERS OF THE NEW COURT

Where and how could such a system be created? It is clear that it must in itself be a United Kingdom system. If ideas which are from time to time floated of some special part of the Queen's Bench Division (aided if need be by assessors) did not fall to be rejected for reasons outlined above (being essentially an inefficient compromise), they fall on this score. To work such a system on a United Kingdom basis while based on the Divisional Court would be difficult to reconcile with the Acts of Union or to make acceptable in Scotland. Moreover, the Divisional Court is too low in the judicial hierarchy. A new jurisdiction needs to be given the conditions in which it can establish itself. A solution, granted our national love of the high-sounding but essentially bogus title, can be easily found.

The new jurisdiction can be located in the Privy Council, recruited initially from judges of existing High Courts, from civil servants and (might one hope) from those who are neither, but yet have studied administrative law seriously. The age span of initial recruits should be such as to cover the possibilities that have been indicated, and be such as would produce an appropriate career structure within the body itself, Thereafter recruitment should be direct to the body itself, wherein the young entrant should, subject to the possibility of detachment, make his life. Certainly it would incorporate the Council on Tribunals, adding enormously to the effectiveness of that body. It is to be hoped that the Parliamentary Commissioner would himself be a member – for there will remain a distinct job of surveying the way in which the administrative machine itself produces unnecessary roughness – a full enough job for any man.[11] The advantage of the Privy Council lies also in the fact that any question of the conflict of jurisdiction could be solved simply in session with the House of Lords as a court without expensive delays of interlocutory proceedings. It can also (because of seniority) surmount the difficulties which may be expected from the ordinary courts, and location there solves the problem of a United Kingdom jurisdiction.

A threefold jurisdiction should be entrusted to the new court: that already exercised over administrative tribunals, etc., through the prerogative orders in England and by equivalent procedures in Scotland; a jurisdiction within a broad definition of the term of review of the legality of general administrative acts; and a jurisdiction in public contracts and in reparation for administrative fault.

It must cover both central and local government to allow for the essential unity of the governmental process. The jurisdiction in reparation is of major importance, for without it a jurisdiction to annul lacks substance. The scope is broad, and capable of frightening simultaneously (though for different reasons) the administration – which will fear too tight a control – and the citizen, who will misunderstand the content of the words 'comprehension of the needs of the administration'. The fears are groundless. First, it must be emphasized that this is an administrative court which is proposed, not a constitutional one like the Supreme Court of the USA. What an administrative court does is to say in effect: 'We care not what policies are adopted – that choice is for the political process; but what we will insist upon is that those policies are carried out with even-handedness and honesty.' Thus immediately it is apparent that this is consistent with, and in no sense opposed to, a true Parliamentary activity. The concern of the court is with administrative morality, and a study of the decisions of the Conseil d'État will show many cases in which it has saved the administration from itself. Indeed there are ways of effectively combining the real needs of the administration and of effective justice to individuals that are entirely closed to our law at present. To that extent it serves the major social purpose of making administration more acceptable. By the evolution of rules and techniques which are both susceptible and penetrative of the administrative process beyond anything that our present law can achieve, it can find solutions to the problems which beset us. It is easy (but false) to say that the Conseil d'État has solved the problem of Crown Privilege by reversing the burden of proof. Certainly it has done that, but the rule as it is there applied and as it has there evolved has within itself that subtlety which is essential to do justice in this difficult situation; that solution seen in its full operation is itself a tribute to what can be achieved by a consistent application of a philosophy by trained body. No longer can the necessary expertise be created or the real problems of government be solved by one of our other traditions – choosing a mixed body of distinguished amateurs. Hard professionalism matters.

ADVANTAGES OF A DUAL SYSTEM

What could be the gains from this? Already it has been said that such a body is consistent, by reason of the limits of its nature, with true Parliamentary activity. There is no need to repeat that the doctrine of ministerial responsibility, in any detailed sense, is a little more than a sham. Mr Crossman has said it firmly. Moreover, the small change of administrative blunders is not the real stuff of politics (or should not be). Indeed, to try to deal with such matters within the House of Commons is wrong. They should not be dealt with in a highly political body, because in that sense they are not political. By excluding these matters from Parliament there should result a concentration by Parliament on matters which are essentially its affairs. Thus full value will be gained from current Parliamentary reforms. On the other hand, by this means a full relief – which certainly cannot be gained from the present law or from the Parliamentary Commissioner

– will be available to the citizen. The denial of a licence, the abuse of power by the Land Commission or by this Ministry or that, cannot be redressed properly by the later retraction of a decision or by the device of confession and avoidance. Compensation is a necessity since meanwhile economic opportunities will have been lost. There is indeed room for all the benefits which can be derived from principles such as that of *'Egalité devant les charges publiques'*, which properly handled can produce a wealth of remedy of which we are not in sight. Nor can we be without this sort of major change.

Beyond these detailed but important gains, there are others of a constitutional order. The unitary nature of our system of public control (which is the result of our necessary reliance on Parliament) means, granted the limitations on judicial controls, a perpetual condemnation to increasing centralization. Without a duality of control the movement to regional government cannot be effective except within narrow limits. If the control is centralized then so, too, must be the administrative process, for it must match the system of control. The degree of centralization, certainly if looked at hard and from outside, is already excessive. And this means that the system of control is itself overloaded, and with the continuing expansion of state activity will become more so. No machine, however excellent, will be efficient if overloaded. The system here advocated can, in operation, be decentralized.

It can, in fact, help many of the sensible reforms now proposed. The proposed new system of decision-taking in Planning appeals would fit admirably and work well within the system here discussed.[12] These would be an effective alternative method of control of the decentralized decisions. Without such a system of law these useful proposals are likely to be frustrated because once again new wine is being poured into old vessels. It is important, too, that such a system can bring sense into our administrative law. The distinction between the activities of a 'servant of the Crown' and of some other governmental agency is in fact often meaningless. Government and administration are whole processes. The law has imposed a dichotomy which is now unreal, and which results from nineteenth-century attempts to resolve certain particular problems.

Local and central government agencies are involved in the same processes for the same ends, even if they operate at different levels, and the law should recognize this unity. Beyond this, there is a place for law in government, if law can have the right shape and the right susceptibility. It is wrong that alongside the Commonwealth Immigrants Act, the real set of rules which actually matter to the immigrant should be the 'Instructions to Immigration Officers' – a White Paper entirely lacking legal force. It is wrong that the foundation of the essential rules for working the doctrine of Crown Privilege should not be legal, but a declaration of the Lord Chancellor in the House of Lords – again entirely without legal force. It is wrong that in the House of Commons a Minister should declare that no matter what forms of contract are evolved the Government would reserve an extra-legal right to demand repayment of profits.[13] These are all only obvious examples. More could be found.

To assert that these things are wrong is not to assert that any of the particular decisions were in themselves wrong. The heart of the matter is that constitutional rules must envisage foul weather as well as fair. It is perhaps true, and this is the real problem, that the administration is forced to those twists and turns because of the shape of the law which takes too little account of real administrative needs. What is needed is a system which can accept those needs and then imagine new remedies which are consistent with them and yet do real justice to individuals. Such a system is by no means impossible and an outline has been sketched here.

ADMINISTRATIVE MORALITY

At the end of the day there remains a problem of administrative morality. One can accept present high standards, yet with the increase in government staffs, the problem of morality must itself grow – as the problem of corruption in police forces grows with the size of the force. Police and government staffs are recruited from human beings. It is at this point that finally the major argument for an administrative jurisdiction emerges. We have in this century tried to deal with past problems as they had emerged. We have never tried to exercise the political imagination which is necessary to create the source of a system of administrative law which will be able to deal, in the future, with the state that we are creating now.

It happens, and everyone recognizes that it is stupid, that from time to time a bridge is created without at the same time dealing with the interlocked road system of which the bridge is an essential part. In relation to our political structures we are constantly doing that. So one returns to the unity of political and constitutional structures. Once one is dealing with the fundamentals of a system – and whether rightly or wrongly the moves for Parliamentary reform are part of a process to enable Parliament to match the needs of a modern state – one should also look to the other related branch of government, the Law, and seek there the same results. The law in the field of Public Law is in even greater need of reform or reconstruction than is Private

Law. The first step to that reform is the creation of an effective Administrative Jurisdiction. Such a new jurisdiction would, it must be emphasized, in no sense operate to derogate from the true functions of Parliament. On the contrary, it would aid Parliament by forcing it to concentrate on the proper business of Parliament: politics. Thus, paradoxically, the establishment of an Administrative Jurisdiction should be looked at as part of the process of Parliamentary reform.

NOTES

1. From the lawyer's point of view this comes out strongly in Sandevoir, *Études sur le Recours de Pleine Juridiction*.
2. The attitude of mystery of which Denman C.J. complained in *Stockdale* v. *Hansard* (1839) 9 A. & E. 1 is emphasized in, for example, Jennings' *Parliament*, and remains too much felt.
3. F. Willson, 'Ministries and Boards' (1955) 33 *Public Administration*, p. 43, shows clearly the correlation between the decline of the Board system and the rise of the doctrine of ministerial responsibility. *The Gilmore Report 1937*, Cmd. 5563, re-emphasized the difficulties of fitting Boards into our constitutional structures just at the time when new Boards were about to be created on the old model.
4. See, for example, Appendix I to the Memorandum submitted by Mr Marking to the Select Committee on Estimates, H.C. (1966–67) 365, and the evidence submitted to Sub-Committee A of the Select Committee on Nationalized Industries, H.C. (1966–67) 440.
5. See Mr Crossman's diagnosis in his Introduction to Bagehot's *English Constitution* on the latter, and see Lord Devlin's *Samples of Law Making* at 104–108 for the former.
6. In particular by the Committee on Ministers' Powers, 1932 (Cmd. 4060) and the Franks Committee, 1957 (Cmnd. 218).
7. See the Report for 1963. Much of the difficulty over Stanstead is caused by the confused impression that exists of the nature of the processes involved and that confusion relates back to the pattern of thought of these two reports.
8. *Administrative Law*, p. 83.
9. Cmnd. 2428, 1965, and Cmnd. 2581, 1965. The point is re-emphasized by *Public Purchasing and Industrial Efficiency* (Cmnd. 3291, 1967), indicating the use of contract as a means to achieve governmental purposes. Such a use is entirely proper, but it means that the contracts in question are quite different from those for which the ordinary law is designed.
10. [1964] Ch. 464; [1965] Ch. 1210.
11. A careful (and it is hoped unbiased) reading of the reports of the New Zealand Ombudsman makes clear that he is tending to do two things: (a) to act as a judge, (b) to survey and improve the general system of administration. Here the P.C.A. could never do the first, but he could do the second.
12. See Town and Country Planning (Cmnd. 3333, 1967). Equally, against such a background the Post Office (Data Processing) Bill would be much more acceptable. The problems of abuse of powers granted would be largely eliminated.
13. 725 H.C.Deb. Col. 1302; and as another example, 686 H.C.Deb. Col. 417 *et seq.*, particularly Col. 423. Examples could be multiplied.

Sir Richard Clarke

Parliament and Public Expenditure

It is sometimes salutary to realize that innovation can take place as rapidly in government and public administration as in technology; and in the last dozen years there have been changes in the system for handling public expenditure which are potentially as far-reaching in the field of government as any of the developments of the same period have been in the field of technology. These changes were initiated by the Plowden Report on the Control of Public Expenditure of July 1961, which itself wove together strands of thought and action that had been developing since the war.

The basic idea was straightforward, that important decisions involving future public expenditure should be taken in the light of regular surveys of public expenditure as a whole, over a period of years ahead, and in relation to prospective resources.[1] But self-evident though this may look, it involves a complete and difficult change from the piece-meal treatment of public expenditure decisions which has been the practice of democratic governments in this country and, as far as I know, everywhere else. Hundreds of important spending decisions are made every year in government, and thousands of people are engaged in making them, and to change the system by which this is done in the Cabinet and throughout the governmental machine is a formidable task. I do not suppose that anyone would claim that this has been done; but great progress has been made, and my own assessment is that after a succession of modifications and growing pains over a period covering four Prime Ministers and five Chancellors of the Exchequer, the point of no return has been passed and the new system is established. Recent public papers[2] are convincing evidence of this, for their depth and comprehensiveness are such that they obviously carry the full endorsement of the Cabinet, describing both the way in which the Government conducts its business and the decisions which it has taken. They demonstrate the existence of a strong and sophisticated technical and administrative apparatus for carrying out the requirements of the PESC[3] system.

Reprinted from *The Political Quarterly*, vol. 44, no. 2 (April-June 1973), pp. 137–153. By permission of the author and the publisher.

THE EFFECT OF PESC

The PESC system enables us for the first time to look at the whole body of public expenditure – Government, local authority, national insurance funds, capital investment of nationalized industries – and see how this is likely to develop over the next five years, a period extending into the next Parliament. This is the summation and the distribution of the whole of Government policy that is expressed in spending – defence, social and environmental services, trade and industry, overseas aid, etc. These are highly 'political' questions: so much so that the Plowden Committee thought it unlikely that[4]

> any Government will feel able to place these surveys before Parliament and the public. To do this would involve disclosing the Government's long-term intentions for a wide range of public expenditure; and also explaining the survey's assumptions about employment, wages, prices and all the other main elements in the national economy. It would be surprising if any Government were prepared to do this.

The Plowden Committee was proved wrong, for Mr Maudling saw advantage in publishing expenditure projections in December 1963, Mr Callaghan in the National Plan in September 1965 and in a special White Paper in February 1966, and the present series of annual White Papers, of which the current one is the fourth, was initiated by Mr Jenkins in 1969 and continued and expanded by Mr Barber. It is now established that the Government publishes yearly its spending policies for five years ahead. Until this year, the debates on the White Papers have attracted little public notice. But the political content is there, although the antiseptic way in which the documents are framed and the unwillingness of MPs (and indeed most journalists) to probe below the surface for the drama on which they thrive mean that the secrets are still kept within the Government. Nevertheless, here is 'open government' over the whole range of the Government's policy, on a scale that leaves few of the options undisclosed.

PUBLIC EXPENDITURE AND RESOURCES

It is easier to deal with small and specific things than with large and comprehensive things; and the aggregates are difficult to handle simply. In the following table, I have taken the figures of public expenditure as defined in PESC, and have compared them for the last twenty years with the simplest measure of resources – the gross domestic product. This is a rough and ready comparison. The coverage of 'public expenditure' is always changing from time to time, e.g. when the steel industry is nationalized or denationalized, or according as the investment incentives to industry are given as investment grants ('public expenditure') or tax relief (not 'expenditure'). Some constituents of 'public expenditure' may be regarded as being on a different plane from GDP: but there are not many of these, for when public money is distributed, whether to people or to companies, it is very likely to be used to buy things and is therefore a charge on the nation's production.[6] The 'ratio' of public expenditure to GDP, which appears on the right of the table, is not suitable for fine economic analysis; but for my purpose here it brings out valid conclusions, which relate not to the question whether the 'ratio' is 40 per cent. or 50 per cent., but to the direction in which the 'ratio' moves over the years. Over periods of years, strictly pragmatically, as this 'ratio' goes, so go the taxes.

Public Expenditure and Gross Domestic Product, 1952-71 (£'000 million)

Year	Public Expenditure (1)	GDP at factor cost (2)	'Ratio' of (1) to (2) %
1952	6.4	13.8	46.6
1953	6.7	14.9	45.1
1954	6.7	15.7	42.4
1955	7.1	16.9	42.0
1956	7.5	18.3	41.2
1957	7.9	19.4	41.0
1958	8.3	20.2	41.2
1959	8.8	21.2	41.3
1960	9.4	22.6	41.5
1961	10.3	24.2	42.6
1962	11.0	25.3	43.5
1963	11.7	26.9	43.3
1964	12.7	29.1	43.8
1965	14.1	31.0	45.5
1966	15.3	32.8	46.7
1967	17.5	34.7	50.5
1968	19.1	36.8	51.9
1969	19.8	38.8	50.9
1970	21.6	42.6	50.7
1971	24.2	47.7	50.8

The 'ratio' column expresses twenty years' history in a nutshell. It starts with the weight of 'Korean war' rearmament, which had split the Labour Government and brought Mr Gaitskell's 1951 Budget, with more new taxation than any Budget since. The Conservative Government rapidly reduced defence expenditure, and with the steady growth of GDP (Mr Butler's 'doubling the standard of living in twenty-five years') achieved the only substantial period in which resources rose faster than public expenditure. In the Budgets from 1952 to 1959, rates of taxation (direct and indirect) were reduced by the equivalent of about 6 per cent. of GDP.[7] As the massive social and environmental programmes of the mid-1950s got under way, however, the 'ratio' began to creep up from the 1957 minimum of 41 per cent. This was a post-war watershed, symbolized by the resignation of Mr Thorneycroft and his two Treasury colleagues in January 1958 on a public expenditure issue (Mr Macmillan's 'little local difficulty'); and followed by the adoption of interventionist policies, including incomes policy (1961), the creation of 'Neddy' (1962) and 'indicative planning'. The spending momentum grew, with the social programmes reinforced by increased defence. The 'ratio' rose to 43.8 per cent. (1964); and these Budgets were an uneasy sequence of tax rises and falls.

Mr Wilson's Government was the first to experience a new law of public expenditure, that each Government in its first two years has the public expenditure bequeathed by its predecessor – in this case, a fast rising one, to which the new Government, imprudently but irrevocably committed to further expansions, was bound to add. With rapid growth in public expenditure and little growth in the national economy, the Government was in trouble. By 1966, the 'ratio' was back to the Korean war level; and in the next years to 1968, nearly all the growth in GDP was bespoken for public expenditure, with the 'ratio' at 51.9 per cent. Determined efforts were then made to check the growth of public expenditure, and these had some success. But in the whole period from 1964 to 1970, tax rates rose by the equivalent of about 6 per cent. of GDP – very much the same as the reductions which had been made in 1952–59.

It is too early to evaluate the experience of Mr Heath's Government. It benefited from the Labour Government's attempts to curb the momentum of public expenditure: it made heavy tax reductions to stimulate the economy, seeking to reduce the expenditure/resources 'ratio' by increasing resources. The unfavourable course of employment, however, and the consequent U-turns in the Government's policy called for new increases in public expenditure. For 1972–73 an increase of 6.2 per cent. at constant prices is envisaged,[8] and for 1973–74 a further 5.3 per cent. Even if the GDP rose by 5 per cent. in each of these two years, the 'ratio' would be moving back to the peak reached in 1968. When we look forward to the next three years, 1974–75–76–77, the expenditure is planned to increase by only 5 per cent. in three years, and if the economy could grow at 5 per cent. a year, the situation would ease very fast. But the Government would have to hold to this plan very firmly if it was not to become, like some others before it, a 'false dawn'; and to sustain for several years growth of GDP at 5 per cent. a year is a formidable task. So the situation confronting the next Parliament is likely to be a challenging one: and it is too early to predict which way the relationship between public expenditure and resources (and over the long period, the taxes) will move.

AGREEMENT ON MORE SPENDING

Two political factors emerge strongly from this twenty years' experience. First is the force of the momentum that drives public expenditure forward. One can identify some slowing-down and acceleration (in addition to the rising cost from pay increases, etc.), but it is difficult in retrospect to link these with specific Government actions, such as 'stop-and-go'. Secondly, one cannot deduce from the figures the existence of a 'high-spending' party and a 'low-spending' party: one cannot even identify party differences on questions of priorities between, e.g. defence and social services, or between one service and another.

The first turning-point in this story was the decision by Sir Winston Churchill's Government to abandon 'Korea' rearmament and drastically curtail defence spending; by 1959 this had gone so far that it had to be reversed. The second turning-point was in the late 1950s, when Mr Macmillan's Government decided implicitly that the expansion of social and environmental programmes then being launched was more important than the desirability of reducing taxation: 'implicitly', for without PESC, government cannot consider such strategic issues with any knowledge of the numbers at stake and thus of the practical implications.[9] The third came in the middle period of Mr Wilson's Government, when the fact had to be faced that this great complex of programmes was hypothecated upon an assumed rate of economic growth that would not happen. This illustrates the darker face of PESC, which is self-destructive if actual spending plans are related to 'targets' or 'objectives' for the rate of growth of resources. In this case, the original growth rate of 4 per cent. a year used as the basis for 'Neddy' studies in May 1962, and endorsed as an 'objective' by the 'Neddy' Council in February 1963, was politically inevitably endorsed by Mr Maudling as the basis for the Government's medium-term planning (and of course tacitly by the Labour Opposition also). None of these three turning-points were related to political party issues.

Over the whole twenty years there has been deeply fundamental agreement between the parties that the social and environmental services should be pressed forward hard, with not very much regard for the implications for the national economy (and other widely held political objectives) of the rate of their development. This is not a British phenomenon alone: it has been common to all the advanced democratic countries in the period since Europe's recovery from the war, and it has been one of the powerful pressures making for inflation everywhere. It is nevertheless remarkable that something so huge both in economic terms (now over £16,000 million a year) and in terms of social policy should have advanced over so many years with so little political controversy except on details which over quite short periods show themselves to be unimportant.

THE ATTITUDE OF PARLIAMENT

The control of Government expenditure and Parliament's unique right to levy taxes have been a continuing theme throughout Parliament's history, from 'no Supply before redress of grievances' to the debates on entry into EEC. But the distant past shows, like the recent past, that when its authority is secure, Parliament never shows much zeal for the details of expenditure control. From the time of Queen Anne to the 1780s, the House of Commons 'made no effective attempt to enforce the responsibility of the Executive for efficient economical government';[10] and it took several decades for the reforming Governments of the nineteenth century to introduce a new system of estimates, accounts and audits, including the establishment of the Comptroller and Auditor-General and the Public Accounts Committee, in the Exchequer and Audit Departments Act of 1866, which is still the basis of Parliament's control. It is not known whether senior officials then had to spend more time than now in the corridors of Westminster waiting for a quorum of MPs to assemble. But Government and Parliament were agreed, however, upon the doctrine of retrenchment and free trade; and an 'economist' was then a man who believed in economy;[11] and MPs tended to leave the gritty detailed task to a combination of the Treasury and the C. and A.-G.

In the last decades of the century, public expenditure began its 100-year growth, fast outstripping the growth of resources,[12] pushed on by the widening of the franchise in the 1867 and 1884 Reform Acts; and the role of backbenchers as independent critics of the Executive gradually faded as the party system took firmer shape.[13] It would be interesting to know whether at any time from the 1870s to 1914 Ministers were ever under serious restraint from Parliament on public expenditure questions. The doctrines of the 1860s were still there, though progressively weakened; but I doubt whether backbenchers held them more strongly than Ministers. Immediately after the First World War there was strong pressure from Parliament to cut expenditure and lower taxes; and the 1931 crisis was presented to Parliament and the public as a public expenditure crisis. But the erosion of the doctrinal and political hostility to public expenditure, in which majorities of MPs saw the national interest in the protection of the interests of the taxpayers more than in the development of social services, had gone far by 1939.

It could not in the 1930s be foreseen that a time would come when the pressures exerted by successive Parliaments on all Governments would be to expand the spending programmes faster. But the trend was there; and the point came, no doubt under the combined impact of the Second World War and the Keynesian revolution, in which the balance tilted over, and the interests of the public as consumers of public services became regarded as politically more important than their interests as taxpayers. My figures for the last twenty years show how dominant this view has become, certainly since the middle 1950s; and there is no sign that this situation is changing.

The social and political forces at work in this field are deep-rooted in our national life, and in those of all advanced countries; and Parliament in the last century has consistently reflected them.

THE TASK FOR THE HOUSE

The path-breaking report of the Select Committee on Procedure, under Mr Donald Chapman's chairmanship,[14] said that the House should establish a system of expenditure scrutiny, with three tasks closely related to one another:

(i) discussion of the Government's expenditure strategy and policies, as set out in projections of public expenditure several years ahead;
(ii) examination of the means (including new methods of management) being adopted to implement strategy and to execute policies, as reflected in annual estimates of expenditure;

(iii) retrospective scrutiny of the results achieved and the value for money obtained....

This work is the business of Select Committees, rather than of debate on the floor of the House. This part of the parliamentary process is sometimes thought to be more difficult now than it was previously, because of the growing complexity of the Government's activity; but I believe that the problems are inherent in the institution.

It is not easy to find MPs who are prepared to devote the amount of time and continuous effort to the work of a Select Committee to make it effective: this is always regarded as secondary to the action on the floor of the House; and the possibility of either favourable publicity or party preferment arising from good performance in the Committee is remote. This could be changed overnight if the political importance of Select Committee work changed; and to the eyes of an outsider this could look sensible, for experience on a Select Committee is potentially good training for Ministerial timber, and its substance can add much to the quality and effectiveness of debate: but this is not universally agreed. Some criticize the insufficiency of staff: this is less convincing to the outsider, for more staff would undoubtedly increase the workload on the Committee members, not reduce it, because unless they apply themselves industriously to the papers produced by the staff, and so generate their own ideas, the staff is just another bureaucracy and the Committee are cyphers.

The problems flow from the fact that the members of a Select Committee are not really responsible for anything. One cannot readily see, however, in our system of government, with Ministers (not MPs) responsible for governing the country, how more responsibility could be given to Select Committees. The combination of an integrated Executive and Legislature and a rigid and all-embracing party system is unpromising ground for all-party committees of backbenchers. Unless one is going to change this – and there is no obvious tide of opinion in Parliament or out of it in favour of such a change – the question is whether some lines of development of the Select Committees' work and structure would be more promising than others. It would be valuable to all our governmental institutions if we could make Select Committees more effective in the expenditure field; but it is necessary to be selective and realistic to achieve this.

EXPENDITURE AND ESTIMATES COMMITTEES

The Expenditure Committee was set up early in 1971, under Mr du Cann's chairmanship, to carry out the Procedure Committee's proposal.

In my opinion it has made a good start. The General Sub-committee under Mr Taverne produced some authoritative and influential reports describing and examining the PESC system, and making proposals about how the PESC material should be published in order to enable Parliament and the public to consider it effectively. The Trade and Industry Sub-committee under Mr Rodgers produced a comprehensive and effective report on *Public Money in the Private Sector* (H.C. 347, 1971–72). Other Sub-committees' reports dealing with more specific fields are listed below.[15] My purpose here is not to discuss these reports, which would require lengthy treatment, but to see how the Expenditure Committee, following its experience in its first two Sessions, can, with the other Select Committees in the expenditure field, be developed most effectively.

The Expenditure Committee replaced the Estimates Committee, a Select Committee which had been started in 1912, with the original purpose of applying to the Estimates – i.e. the expenditures before they happened – the same kind of scrutiny that the Public Accounts Committee devoted to the Accounts. This was never achieved; and the Committee after the Second World War settled down to examine in sub-committees a series of selected subjects. There was a continuing problem about whether the Committee could discuss 'policy' as distinct from 'administration'. Successive Governments refused to agree to this, and there was a periodic argument resulting in compromise. The Committee did always discuss policy, for the only purpose of administration is to carry out policy; and on many occasions chairmen and members of sub-committees used the reports as a vehicle for advocating changes in policy, usually involving increased expenditure. The sub-committees rarely reached the point at which the permanent officials under examination had to refuse to answer the questions posed. The proceedings of the Committee over the years were somewhat ambivalent; and its operations were subject to the customary difficulties to which I have referred. Nevertheless, there were reports of permanent importance, e.g. *Treasury Control of Expenditure* (H.C. 254, 1957–58, Sir Godfrey Nicholson), as a result of which the Plowden Committee was appointed; *Treasury Control of Establishments* (H.C. 228, 1963–64, Sir Eric Errington) and *Recruitment to Civil Service* (H.C. 308, 1964–65, Dr Jeremy Bray).

Taking the whole experience since the war, however, it must be doubted whether the contribution was commensurate with the amount of effort of the members concerned and of the officials who were its main witnesses. Not very many of the reports had much impact on Ministers and Whitehall, and influenced what actually happened: nor did they always perform the other equally important role of Select

Committee reports, to inform Parliament and public opinion and create better public knowledge and improve the quality of the public debate.

To the extent that the weakness was one of inadequate authority, this has now been overcome; and the Expenditure Committee's right to examine policy and to question Ministers was stated firmly by Mr Whitelaw in the debate on the Green Paper on Procedure.[16] But those of the problems which are typical of Select Committees are still there to be solved.

EXPENDITURE AND TAXATION

There was a long dialogue between Mr Taverne's Sub-committee and the Treasury, which can be regarded as having ended in a draw. The Sub-committee, with the help of its adviser, Mr Wynne Godley, made many good proposals, which the Treasury have incorporated in the latest five-year White Paper (Cmnd. 5178). These reports – based on 1,373 questions, twenty sessions with witnesses, and 483 pages of evidence, the whole comprising one of the deepest examinations in parliamentary history, distinguished by the high intellectual level and good temper throughout – were designed to get the information in the form in which the Sub-committee wanted it. The question is then whether the Expenditure Committee could use the information to clarify for Parliament and public opinion the issues embodied in the White Paper. The Fifth Report, 1972–73 Session (Mr Sheldon), issued just before the Budget, which made unanimous and pertinent criticisms of the Government's expenditure planning, was an encouraging first result.

On the main point of disagreement – the request that the Treasury should publish its medium-term economic assessment, a point which must be regarded as having been tolerably met by the Treasury – the Sub-committee may have proved too much. It became clear that one could not think sensibly about the aggregate of public expenditure without at the same time bringing in the aggregate of taxation and the relation of all this to the future development of the economy. Mr Peter Jay, who has made a unique contribution to the public explanation of this series of problems, drew the logical conclusion; i.e. that there should be a Select Committee concerned with the whole range of central economic subjects. This goes far beyond 'expenditure' in the sense of the Select Committee on Procedure. I do not personally think that this central nexus of macro concepts is yet sufficiently developed; or that Governments move in it readily enough, on principles which are well enough established, to make it suitable for

Select Committee treatment. The concept of long-term budgeting which I saw as the objective ten years ago[17] seems now to be about where the present practice of short-term budgeting was fifteen years ago – a useful light for the Chancellor of the Exchequer who had to take a decision, for which one candle was better than nothing, but not yet an apparatus of facts and thought which carried the decisions and their justification along with it. In my opinion, this is unlikely for some time yet to be a fruitful area for the Expenditure Committee.

OTHER SELECT COMMITTEES

The Select Committee on Nationalized Industries was set up in 1957 to apply a regular process of review to the nationalized industries: each year it conducted a full examination of one of the nationalized industries, and in the process it played an important role in sorting out the criteria for these industries' performance and the relations between them and the government. The individual members were important, as always in Select Committees, and whether the Committee would have made such a contribution without Sir Toby Low (now Lord Aldington) and Mr Austen Albu could be debated. After the first round of the industries had been completed, which took ten years, it decided to review some general problems affecting the industries as a whole – Ministerial Control (H.C. 371, 1967–68) and Relations with the Public (H.C. 514, 1970–71) – which were perhaps less successful as reports.[18] However, this Committee has certainly maintained a high level of contribution over fifteen years.

The specialist Select Committees arose from the previous review by the Select Committee on Procedure (H.C. 303, 1964–65), and were started experimentally in the following year. The Select Committee on Science and Technology would be generally regarded as having successfully entered new territory by interrogating Ministers and by encouraging publicity, and by contributing to current policy-making. Whereas the old Estimates Committee discussed 'administrative policy' and the Expenditure Committee discuss 'policy', the Science and Technology Committee has from the start tried to influence the Government's current decisions. For example, the report on the Nuclear Power Industry (H.C. 401, 1968–69, Mr Arthur Palmer) described the collection of evidence from all the nationalized and private industries involved, and Mr Wedgwood Benn, the Minister responsible, and thence proposed a specific (though not unanimous) 'solution' to the problem before the Government. Ministers did not accept the Committee's recommendations on this or other subjects, for those who have the responsibiilty for taking decisions must take many other considerations into account than can a Committee who can make a recommendation and then go home. But the process is no less useful for that.[19]

Government intervention in industry creates problems *vis-à-vis* Parliament. There are many charlatans in science and technology and many people who will use the members of Select Committees or anyone else to further their own interests. Again, when the Government is helping British industry to fight foreign competition, it is rarely desirable for the arrangements to be shouted from the housetops – in Germany or France or Japan this is inconceivable. Officials can resist, perhaps with some unfavourable headlines that are part of the day's work: but heads of companies summoned to give evidence before a Select Committee may fear that they will be sent to the Tower if they refuse to answer questions. Again, men who have been asked to make confidential reports to a Minister are rightly aggrieved if such reports are then published.

The appearance of Ministers before Select Committees requires comment. A Minister may attend to explain a particular decision about the Committee's business.[20] The proceedings may not always attain the summit of non-party behaviour, which happened in 1970,[21] when Mr Taverne, then Financial Secretary to the Treasury, attended the Public Accounts Committee (of which he was an *ex officio* member) to explain a point of propriety on which the Government disagreed with the chairman, Mr Boyd-Carpenter: in the end, the chairman with Labour members of the Committee outvoted Conservative members by 5–4 with Mr Taverne abstaining! In such specific cases there is no problem, but it is likely that if Ministers attend regularly to expound party-political policies, the Select Committee will increasingly divide on party lines (and the Whips will ensure that they do). If the Select Committees become a microcosm of the floor of the House, they lose their purpose; and it is probably best for officials to be the regular witnesses.

These are general points arising from these Committees' experience. But the important one is that the specialist committee's subject-matter is the same as the Expenditure Committee's. There is no separate subject of 'finance' or 'expenditure': the problem is how the department uses its resources, its priorities, its means of getting efficiency and value for money. So there is a real duplication and co-ordination problem; and in my opinion there is no place for the specialist committees if the Expenditure Committee is effective. The same subjects will be dealt with, but in a more articulated way.

PUBLIC ACCOUNTS COMMITTEE

This is the *doyen*, born in 1866; with its ex-Ministerial Opposition chairmen (Mr Lever, Mr (now Lord) Boyd-Carpenter, Mr Harold Wilson); the assistance of the Comptroller and Auditor-General and the Exchequer and Audit staff; its world-wide prestige and its reputation of being the terror of the departments. No other Select Committee has the same authority, clarity of remit, and breadth of depth of advice available to it. It has always refused to consider Westminster mergers or takeovers, fearing that its own special functions could be diluted. Nevertheless, if Parliamentary control of public expenditure is to become something real, the PAC's position needs to be considered.

Its first function is to audit the accounts and to guard the procedures and proprieties of control by Parliament. The archaic elements are being gradually cut away. Not much is lost directly by having them, for no C. and A.-G. or Permanent Secretary has any illusion about them. The cost is in people's minds throughout the departments, for it makes people think of financial control (and indeed of Parliamentary control) as an arcane and irrational process: and sensible moves for the management of departments must not be made to appear inconsistent with 'financial control'. There must be sharp rules, endorsed by Parliament, but they should be contemporary rules.

Secondly, there must be an outside audit on the propriety and honesty of departments' operations. Is a Minister using the taxpayers' money to pay for his political publicity or his personal image? In the rapidly extending business relations between the Government, industry, the City and the professions, can we be satisfied that no corruption is creeping in? We are happily freer from this than most advanced countries, but the pressures are growing. Again, are the persons and institutions who receive Government money, directly or indirectly, using it in accordance with the rules laid down? This is the initial purpose of the C. and A.-G., going back to 1866 and to Burke's Economical Reform Act of 1782. It requires an arm's length relationship between the department and the auditor, and a very sharp confrontation in the occasional cases when there may be trouble.

For checking the efficiency of departments and the avoidance of waste, however, the present machinery is less clearly appropriate. The responsibility for this must be riveted on the departments, and audit is one of the Permanent Secretary's main arms for this purpose. The auditor should be his ally, and not his arraigner and inquisitor in public when some weakness is discovered: the higher management should be trying to find weaknesses, not being criticized in public when weaknesses are found. It is the Treasury's (or the Civil Service

Department's – their roles are inextricably mixed) duty to satisfy itself that the departments are doing this job.

There is overlap here between the Public Accounts Committee and the Expenditure Committee; and the distinction between what has happened in the past, and what the departments are doing now, and what they are intending to do in the future is difficult to draw. The Expenditure Committee's report, *Public Money in the Private Sector*, covered much of the same ground as was examined in the PAC's Third Report 1971–72. The more the PAC applies itself to picking out general problems of efficiency and value for money, and using particular past cases to illustrate them – as it has been doing increasingly in the last decade or more – the more difficult it becomes to distinguish its function from that of the Expenditure Committee.

PUBLIC EXPENDITURE AND ACCOUNTS COMMITTEE

Starting from scratch to devise the best system for carrying out the Select Committee on Procedure's requirements, I would consolidate it all into one powerful Public Expenditure and Accounts Committee (PEAC), with one General Sub-committee and a number of other sub-committees to take on particular tasks: the Select Committee on Nationalized Industries and the specialized Select Committees would disappear. Whether there should be a Select Committee on Taxation is a separate question: the task of examining taxes and tax structures is different from that of examining departments' expenditures and policies; and if there were such a Select Committee I would not include it within this group.

The PEAC would be the successor of the PAC, with its ex-Minister chairman, and with the advice of the Comptroller and Auditor-General and his department. It would be a Select Committee of great power and prestige and tradition. The best guarantee of good and responsible work from MPs is the Select Committee's standing; and this takes time to build up. The consolidation would enable Parliament to make the best possible use of the limited number of MPs who are capable of and devoted to this kind of work; and membership of the Committee could become a mark of status in Parliament. The Committee would act as a steering committee for the whole complex, perhaps with a somewhat more positive co-ordination than the present practice; and it would be the C. and A.-G.'s point of reference on questions of accounts and estimates and on any cases that he brought to light involving propriety and personal behaviour.

The consolidation would provide in effect a collective service for the whole complex; and changes would take place in the C. and A.-G.'s staff to fit into the new tasks. These would be helped by a further change of balance from Exchequer and Audit to internal audit; so that the role of C. and A.-G. and his department would fit in better with the requirements of modern management in the departments while maintaining a sharp scrutiny of personal propriety and focusing the Sub-committees' critical attention on what is done in the departments and why and how.

The General Sub-committee would examine the Public Expenditure White Papers and similar data primarily in order to bring out the essential points for Parliament and the public. There is a precedent in 1960–61, when the Plowden Committee concepts were taking shape: a Sub-committee of the Estimates Committee was set up to do this for the Estimates as a whole (i.e. the Supply element in public expenditure). It made improvements in the annual Financial Secretary's memorandum on the Estimates, just as Mr Taverne's Sub-committee has done in the annual Public Expenditure White Paper; but never developed this. It still produces a valuable annual report on the Supplementary Estimates as a whole. The General Sub-committee might also report on across-the-board issues, e.g. the public sector's demand for highly educated manpower (a dynamic subject, relevant to the formation of opinion about public expenditure) or the impact of public expenditure on the distribution of income.

In the interests of effective Select Committee operation, it would be wise to limit the number of sub-Committees to what could be manned by MPs with a real competence and determination to do a good job. They should be divided flexibly between broad areas, and not be confined to specific departments or groups of departments. The areas of government on the borderline between the natural divisions are frequently those that require closest examination. A Sub-committee in a small field, moreover, always risks being dominated by the department or by MPs with a special interest in this field (e.g. in agriculture and sometimes in science and technology); and it is too cosy when one set of MPs is too long associated with one set of officials. I would favour a mix of rather wide issues (e.g. 'Public Money in the Private Sector' or, say, 'The Government's Influence on Local Authorities' Spending'), together with solid examinations in depth of public organizations (every year one large nationalized industry, one public service like the hospitals, and the efficiency of one department), and then the kind of sharp and varied questions about proved performance unearthed by the G. and A.-G. The witnesses would be normally officials (and of course outsiders) with Ministers in reserve. There would be co-ordination from the main Committee in the selection of subjects and sometimes in discussion of treatment, and if this was effective the Sub-committees could stand on their own, and report directly to Parliament.

CONCLUSION

In order to provide an effective scrutiny of public expenditure by Parliament, as proposed by the 1968–69 Select Committee on Procedure, I think that a new momentum is likely to be needed. There are great forces of inertia on all matters involving Parliament's control of expenditure; and one can easily imagine that in spite of a promising start the Expenditure Committee could become no more than a glorified (perhaps not very much glorified) Estimates Committee by the end of this Parliament or the middle of next. It is indeed the scale of the task and the scarcity of resources to do it that leads me to favour a radical consolidation of Parliament's efforts as the next step.

NOTES

1. Cmnd. 1432, para. 12.
2. *Public Expenditure to 1976–77* (Cmnd. 5178 of December 1972). *Public Expenditure White Papers: Handbook on Methodology* (H.M. Treasury, 1972). *Reports* from the Expenditure Committee: Command Papers on Public Expenditure, H.C. 549 of 1970–71; Changes in Public Expenditure, H.C. 62 of 1971–72; Public Expenditure and Economic Management, H.C. 450 of 1971–72; Relation of Expenditure to Needs, H.C. 515 of 1971–72; Fifth Report, 1972–73 Session, in Cmnd. 5178.
3. So described from the initials of the Public Expenditure Survey Committee which is the central official element in the system.
4. Cmnd. 1432, para. 17.
5. *Hansard*, 7th February 1973. Cols. 458–590.
6. See *Handbook on Methodology*, paras. 80–87.
7. *Cf.* my chapter, 'The Long-Term Planning of Taxation', in *Taxation Policy* (Harmondsworth 1973).
8. Cmnd. 5178, para. 5.
9. Mr Selwyn Lloyd was the first Chancellor of the Exchequer to have discerned, before coming into office, the existence of this staring gap in the government apparatus.
10. Rosevcare, *The Treasury* (London 1969), p. 86.
11. 'He was a rigid economist,' Mr Gladstone would recall of Peel with relish, 'Oh, he was a most rigid economist!' Rosevcare, *The Treasury*, p. 192.
12. *The Plowden Report*, para. 10, gave the proportion of Supply expenditure to GNP as rising from 4 per cent. in 1870 to 6 per cent. in 1910, to 12 per cent. in 1930 and 22 per cent. in 1960.
13. The percentage of 'party' divisions (i.e where 90 per cent. of voting MPS

voted in their own party lobbies) rose from 35 per cent. in 1871 to 76 per cent. in 1894, and built up from there in the twentieth century to virtually 100 per cent. Lord Campion, *Encyclopedia Britannica*, 1963 edition, on Parliament.

4. H.C. 410, 1968–69, *Scrutiny of Public Expenditure and Administration*, para. 12. See *The Political Quarterly*, Vol. 41, No. 1, p. 115.

5. 1970–71: Education and Arts (H.C. 545). 1971–72: Probation and After-Care (H.C. 47), Private Practice in the National Health Service (H.C. 172), Diplomatic Staff (H.C. 344), Defence (H.C. 147 and H.C. 516). 1972–73: Further and Higher Education (H.C. 48), Urban Transport Planning (H.C. 57).

6. *Hansard*, November 12 1970, Col. 620.

7. *Stamp Memorial Lecture* 1964, Athlone Press, p. 24, quoted on p 93 of H.C. 549 of 1970–71: and my chapter in Taxation Policy, ed. Bernard Crick and W. A. Robson (Harmondsworth 1973).

8. *The Political Quarterly*, Vol. 40, pp. 103 and 494, and Vol. 43, p. 229.

9. In the particular question of nuclear plant, however, waiting for the Select Committee lost the Government a year.

20. For example, Mr Jenkin's appearance at the Expenditure (General) Sub-Committee to explain why the Government could not publish the Treasury's medium-term assessments, H.C. 450, 1971–72, Q. 345–397.

21. *Third Report from the Committee on Public Accounts, 1969–70*, p. lxxi.

Parliament and the Pressure Groups

It has often been said that while the executive arm of government has grown out of all recognition, compared with what it was a century ago, the mechanism of democratic control has failed to show a similar extension of its powers. But the contrast is more glaring and more complex than is indicated by this analogy of rapid growth as compared with stagnation or even a degree of atrophy. A hundred years ago Parliament included representatives of the most powerful interests in the country. It is true that the landowners had been defeated by the Anti-Corn Law League in 1846 but they were still present in the House of Commons in large numbers. So were the railway company directors, who needed an Act of Parliament in lieu of the modern planning permission and compulsory purchase orders to build their lines. The old West India interest had given up trying to buy seats after the 1830s as this became too difficult and they had lost their sugar monopoly, in part owing to the strength of the East India company in politics, which lasted till it was discredited by the Indian Mutiny. But all these forces wishing to influence the government focused their attention on the two Houses of Parliament. The corollary was a convention which held that it was quite improper for civil servants to see pressure group spokesmen; any communications between officials and such people should be by correspondence only. When the unions combined to form the TUC to put their case for certain legal changes, the executive was named 'the Parliamentary Committee' because its chief job was to lobby Parliament, and if a deputation wanted to see the government, they always called on the appropriate minister and not on the officials of the Board of Trade.

The changes that have occurred have not merely been the vast extension of the numbers in Whitehall and of its responsibilities and

Reprinted from PEP (Political and Economic Planning) The Social Science Institute, *Reshaping Britain: A Programme of Economic and Social Reform*, Vol. XL, Broadsheet No. 548, December 1974, pp. 79–98. By permission of the publisher.
Although the report *Reshaping Britain* is a collective work, the author who had primary responsibility for the paper reprinted here is John Mackintosh, MP.

activities, in addition, as Parliament's capacity to amend and reject laws and to influence policy has declined, the powerful groups in society have shown less interest or have even opposed the election of their leading members to the House of Commons. They prefer to send them to deal directly with the civil servants, which increases the latter's power and further diminishes that of Parliament.

It is well known that this process started between the wars, grew rapidly under the pressure of the wartime emergency and became established after 1945. The official guide to civil servants' duties came to include a section on their obligation to consult all recognized interest groups. The criteria by which a group became accepted and put on the list of bodies to be consulted were fairly simple. The group had to represent the bulk of the persons or companies or organizations in the area of activity and had to accept that all negotiations were to be kept confidential, even from its own members. In return, the leaders of these interest groups were consulted before any government plans were published and they could thus make their representations at a formative stage when plans were still open to argument and when no loss of face was involved in making changes. Those groups which wanted new laws (which had been the usual objective in the nineteenth century) would go to Whitehall if what was wanted arose out of existing policies: that is if the matter was not highly controversial. On the other hand, if the proposal was in this category, then the pressure group could not deal directly with government departments. It had to turn to open advocacy of its case through the media, trying to reach the public and MPs. Those groups whose sole or main objective was a 'cause' requiring legislation clearly still had to try and influence Parliament, particularly if it was an issue on which the parties were not committed, such as penal reform or the abortion laws. But these groups constitute a small minority. The majority are interested in the development and execution of accepted policies and they are on the consultation list and deal directly with government.

In one case, the form and propriety of these dealings was laid down in an actual law. The 1947 Agriculture Act prescribes an annual meeting between the government and the National Farmers' Union at which the prices for the coming year are to be determined. Other bodies, such as the British Medical Association and the National Union of Teachers, do not have quite such a legal right to consultation, though it is unthinkable that anything should be done about the Health Service or about Education without the views of the BMA or the NUT being obtained. The same is true of the representatives of industry and the TUC.

There are two consequences of these developments. One is the diminution of the influence of Parliament, which has already been noted. It would now be hard to find in the House of Commons men sufficiently prominent in industry, either on the management or on the union side, to be accepted as the spokesmen or as the mouthpieces of these interests. In any case, because MPs' votes can usually be taken for granted, an MP who had such a connection would not be seen as the kind of representative who could speak for an outside group. As a result, ministers wanting some evidence of the views of an organized section of the community consider that they are obliged to look outside the House. Pressure group leaders, for their part, will not seek membership of the Commons, partly because of the diminished influence of backbenchers, but largely because they do not wish to face conflicts of loyalty when party discipline pulls one way and the demands of their organization another.

The second consequence follows naturally from the practice of regular consultations between pressure groups and government departments. If there has been an interruption of the process, it is regarded as something highly abnormal and means that the legislation concerned has not been through the usual procedure taken to be necessary when policy decisions are being made. If this happens, it may be an indication that the government expects serious opposition from the group and has decided either that there is no point in meeting just to register disagreement or that there is no time for a prolonged conflict. The other situation, which will cause less anxiety and friction, but which is nevertheless undesirable, is when consultation does take place but the government ultimately decides to turn down all or most of the advice of the pressure group. In these cases, what can a pressure group do to indicate to its members that on this occasion it either was not consulted or had its advice rejected? Pressure groups are not allowed, by the convention of consultation, to reveal the precise points put to the government or its responses. Yet, somehow, pressure group leaders will want to indicate either that they were not consulted or that part or all of their advice was rejected and that they object strongly to what the government has done.

The National Farmers' Union solved the problem after each annual determination of agricultural prices by announcing that the outcome was 'agreed' with the government or that it was 'not agreed' and, in one case, they would not say either that they agreed or did not agree; they simply reserved their position. It seems that governments going through these negotiations with the farmers hold a certain sum (reputedly about £2 million) in reserve and offer it as an additional bonus if the NFU is prepared to say the final outcome is 'agreed'. Similarly, the TUC has objected in the strongest terms on the very rare occasions when it was not consulted (as over the 1972 Industrial Relations Act) while the CBI has indicated reservations on Fair Trading Bills and on legislation on monopolies.

If the pressure groups act in this way, there are two consequences. On the one hand, it releases MPs associated with that interest from any restraint and they can attack the government. While negotiations are proceeding, the MPs are told nothing. They are in total ignorance as to what is happening and if they know that consultations are taking place and if they press ministers to reveal some details, they are at once asked not to 'rock the boat' by both the government and the pressure group. At a crucial stage in negotiations between the National Union of Mineworkers and the Department of Employment in late 1973 Mr Roy Mason, then chairman of the group of miners' MPs in the House of Commons and an *ex officio* member of the NUM executive, asked if he could attend a meeting and was told to stay away; interventions by MPs were not helpful. But once negotiations have broken down, the pressure groups may ask or encourage MPs to make some trouble for the government, usually simply on the grounds that important considerations advanced by the pressure group have been neglected. The NFU will ask MPs from agricultural constituencies to stress certain points in their questioning of the minister but not to push too hard or in a way which would damage the relations between the union and the department.

The second consequence is that if there is a major breach between the pressure group and the government and if there has been either an avoidance of the normal processes of consultation or a breakdown, the leaders of the pressure group may claim that they are under no obligation to recommend their members to co-operate with the government. They may go further and say that members need not obey the law as, in some sense, it is not legitimate. The denial of legitimacy is a clear consequence of two concepts, first that passage by the House of Commons is not, of itself, an adequate indication of the consent of the community and second that prior consultation with recognized groups has become an essential part of the legitimizing process.

Several other developments have added force to these concepts. The old assumption that passage by the House of Commons was adequate evidence of public consent has been seriously damaged during the controversy over British membership of the Common Market. When Mr Heath said that he would not consider it proper to take this country into the EEC without 'the full-hearted consent of the British people', he was apparently suggesting that passage by the House of Commons was not enough. The Labour Party then carried this downgrading of Parliament much further by proclaiming the necessity for a referendum. Yet if ever there was a free and deliberate expression of opinion by MPs it was on this occasion. Party lines were broken, 69 Labour MPs voting with the Conservatives and 20 more abstaining, so that entry was endorsed by a majority of 112, yet this was not taken as 'full-hearted consent'. The evidence of opinion polls showed that a majority of the British people was opposed to entry and that, in consequence, the verdict of Parliament was inadequate. Usually, those who argue that Parliament's consent is not enough point to the strength of the party hold on MPs so that the verdict of Parliament can be taken for granted. If this is a weakness, it has been intensified in recent years with the increasing tendency for party conferences (which are, in practice, much less representative than the House of Commons) to set out detailed programmes which are held to be binding on MPs, whose task is simply to push these policies through. It seems as though the unfortunate MPs lose both ways. When they assert themselves, break party ranks and vote according to deeply held convictions, as they did over the Common Market, they are asked 'whom do you represent? You are simply asserting your own personal opinion.' When they enact the points in their party programme endorsed by the party conferences they are told 'your vote meant nothing; you were committed to this by the party manifesto'.

This devaluation of the process of parliamentary democracy has been carried further by many well-meaning people who have advocated greater public participation in decision-making, since one of the implications of their case is that the traditional and normal channels of representation are inadequate. If there are strong objections to a third London airport, the arguments ought to be pressed on MPs as they have to reconcile the conflict of interests between airline passengers and local residents, between London's development as a world commercial centre and the demand for peace and quiet in nearby villages. Yet the current tendency for those who feel strongly on such matters is not just to lobby MPs, the assumption being that if the party whips are put on, there is little the MPs can do. In such cases, an 'action committee' is formed and while it will seek the support of local MPs, it will also appeal to the public, press the government directly and possibly even contemplate some kind of 'direct action'.

In addition to these doubts about Parliament, there is a disenchantment with the political driving force which operates through the House of Commons: the political parties. In recent years, the membership of the two main parties has declined and the same accusations of being rigid and unrepresentative are levelled against these bodies. Thus active citizens who wish to further certain public causes may feel it is more effective and appropriate to join pressure groups such as Shelter to get something done about housing and the homeless; they may join the Child Poverty Action Group or Amnesty rather than belong to a political party. While these bodies, like local amenity societies and consumers' protection groups, will seek the support of particular local or well-disposed MPs, they will also use many of the methods of the economic and professional pressure groups in attracting attention, spreading information and pressing for action in specific situations.

While the position of Parliament and the political parties has declined for all these reasons, the significance of the major pressure groups has become evident and their reputation for getting what they want has grown. Anyone with a knowledge of these bodies, from the Confederation of British Industry to the National Union of Teachers, may know that they are cumbrous and have internal problems of organization. Their full-time officers may be accused of being 'out out of touch' and they may often guess at, rather than have accurate methods of ascertaining, their members' views. Yet their standing has improved as their capacity to command their members' loyalty has been demonstrated and as their record of success has become more evident. Thus, members may have doubts about a pressure group's course of action but the key economic and professional groups can usually command more loyalty than the government of the day. There were many miners, for example, who were opposed to the overtime ban called by the National Union of Mineworkers in the autumn of 1973 but by the time the situation had deteriorated and a full strike was called, almost all were behind the NUM executive. Many non-militants in bodies as diverse as the Association of University Teachers, the Local Authority Associations and the British Medical Association may disagree with particular points pressed by their representatives but they appreciate the need to retain a united front and not to discredit the spokesmen of their interest.

Such groups have, therefore, been able to insist that the citizen's first loyalty is to them rather than to any concept of the national well-being as enunciated by the government. Also, the high degree of interdependence in the economy means that if such groups act together, they can inflict much greater damage on the society at large than their members may suffer. Indeed, the members may endure only mild discomfort as a result of pressure group action which, nevertheless, may have a serious effect on the economy, on fuel supplies or the provision of essential services.

Two further factors have aided pressure groups in asserting their case in this way. One is the nature of the laws or instructions they are asking their members to defy. In many cases, no laws may be broken. The actions may be refusals to perform rather than acts that defy the law. For instance, teachers may refuse extra but essential tasks, doctors may refuse to take on extra duties to let colleagues go on holiday, businessmen may refuse to invest more or train drivers may work to rule. None of these activities on its own is illegal. They are certainly not illegal if done by a single person so there is a reluctance to regard them as wrong when done by a large number of people belonging to a pressure group. For instance, any doctor may contract out of the Health Service. It is not illegal for all in an area to do so. But if the objective of a mass resignation is to force up salaries by more than a norm laid down by statute, then those giving and those receiving the higher pay may be acting in a manner forbidden by anti-inflationary legislation. For the public at large, to break the kind of laws enforced by the police where the individual act is morally wrong and socially destructive is clearly reprehensible. But it is less obviously wrong to act in a manner which is legitimate if done by an individual and is socially reprehensible only if committed simultaneously by a mass of people and even then is wrong only if the analysis of the situation and the remedial measures of the government are accepted as fair and appropriate. Increasingly, governments have been drawn into legislating and target-setting in areas of social policy, to try and secure stable prices or full employment or regional development, where defiance or refusal to co-operate may be due to disagreement with the objectives or the mechanism of the policy and where it is arguable whether the government is on the right track.

Even when there is a measure of agreement, breaking such laws is less shocking because there is less insistence on the sanctity of law, on its special character; the distinction between law and policy is less clearcut. For instance, Sir William Armstrong, head of the civil service till 1974, said that when he was a young official in the 1930s and had to advise a minister that the legal authority to enforce a given policy did not exist, it was axiomatic that nothing could be done till a new statute conferred the appropriate powers on the government. But Sir William noted that by the mid 1960s and early 1970s, if a minister lacked the powers, there was a tendency to announce the new policy and start to enforce it directly, a later bill being used to confer retrospective legality on what had been done.

All these points have to be put together – the changed nature of much legislation, the diminished conviction that a law is a special kind of command, the increased power and capacity of pressure groups and the lower standing of Parliament – in order to appreciate the situation which has arisen in the last decade where the will of the government, as expressed in laws or explicit policies, has been successfully disregarded or defied by powerful pressure groups. This has happened both over things the government wanted done and over actions it had intended to prohibit, though clearly the effect is more startling if the conflict is over a refusal to obey a law or over a demand for its repeal than if the conflict arises over a failure to comply with certain policies. Thus, the 1970–74 Heath government and, to some extent, the previous Labour government called on industrialists to invest more. Mr Heath was particularly bitter when the investment upsurge he had hoped for in 1971 did not take place, but this was a failure to respond and was the result of a number of individual decisions rather than of any concerted policy by the CBI.

Much more startling was the way the trade unions were able, through their direct contracts and through trade union sponsored MPs, to persuade a majority of the Labour cabinet to desert Mr Wilson and Mrs Castle and thus force them to abandon their proposed legislation on industrial relations in 1969. The TUC then went on to show such opposition to the Labour government's incomes policy that it, too, was abandoned in the winter of 1969–70. The next June, the Conservatives were elected and among their policies a central place was given to a new law on industrial relations. This had been elaborately prepared while the party was in opposition and once Mr Heath came to power, it was rapidly introduced without the normal careful consultation with the TUC. From the start, the unions declared their adamant opposition. The vast majority obeyed a TUC recommendation to refuse to register, thus placing their organizations outside the legal protections the Act still conferred on unions. They refused to register, in part because they would not let the agencies set up by the government examine and approve their rule books. A minority refused to appear before the Industrial Relations Court or to defend themselves, the Engineering Workers thus incurring a number of fines. The unions also encouraged individual workers to refuse to obey injunctions issued by the Industrial Court. As a result of all this opposition, by the end of 1973 large sections of the Act were rendered inoperative while the Court and the government tacitly allowed other sections to lie unused rather than face renewed industrial conflict. At the same time the unions, with no real difficulty, had the total repeal of the Act given pride of place in the Labour Party's election manifesto and the Act was repealed by the minority Wilson government in the summer of 1974. By then, the Conservatives had come to accept that though they still wanted to achieve the Act's objectives, legislation so totally unacceptable to the section of the community it was designed to regulate either could not be enforced or the effort caused more disruption than it was worth; and the Conservatives therefore did not oppose the repeal of the bulk of the Act.

In 1972, the Conservative government turned away from its previous objection to statutory incomes policies and this time, after elaborate consultation with industry and the unions, it set up a system of controls with a Pay Board and a Prices Commission. By the autumn of 1973, the policy had moved into what was called Stage III and six million workers accepted wage settlements within the formula set out by the orders made under the Act. But the National Union of Mine-workers demanded an increase well above this limit – having defeated the government and obtained a high award only eighteen months earlier. Mr Heath and his government set their faces against any concessions, announced fuel economies and then put industry on a three-day week to conserve coal stocks. The miners moved towards and then called a full scale strike while the Prime Minister decided to hold a general election on the question of whether a pressure group should be permitted to defy the government in this way. After a confused and mixed campaign neither of the major parties had a clear majority but the result was manifestly a defeat for the Conservatives and Mr Wilson took over with a minority government. Immediately, the miners' pay rise was conceded and the Labour administration began the dismantling of the incomes policy and the repeal of the Industrial Relations Act, both so disliked by the trade unions.

For its part, the Labour Party announced that it had reached 'a social contract' with the unions whereby they would voluntarily limit wage increases to a level which did not exacerbate inflation. The government, in return, promised the abandonment of the two policies mentioned, a rent freeze and an immediate rise in pensions. All these policies were enacted or adopted by the Labour government and it, in turn, called on the unions to fulfil their side of the contract by limiting wage demands to a level which would maintain but not increase real wages. At the same time, Mr Wedgwood Benn sought an arrangement by which industry would inform the government of its investment plans, respond to pressures to increase or alter these plans and obtain extra money from (or face purchase by) a National Enterprise Board.

A final, and perhaps the sharpest, experience any government has had with a pressure group came in the early summer of 1974 when Protestant workers in Northern Ireland organized by the Ulster Workers' Council staged a quite overt political strike to force the Faulkner coalition government out of office and succeeded. It seems to be the case that the Labour Government considered asking the Army to break the strike but either there was reluctance on the part of the Army or senior officers dissuaded the government or it changed its mind. Whatever the explanation, the Ulster Workers' Council won and the Faulkner government resigned.

TRIPARTITISM AND THE NEDC

In all these cases, except the last, where there was a direct challenge to the existence of the Northern Irish government, pressure groups were, in fact, asking or forcing the British government to change its policies or to legislate in a certain way. It was assumed that once industry and the unions had agreed on the form of an incomes policy or on a social contract or on changes in laws dealing with industrial relations, these changes would be obediently and speedily enacted by the House of Commons. The interesting development in this process of consultation as compared with the kinds of dealings with pressure groups that have already been described is two-fold. First, the discussions often included both sides of industry. Second, they took into consideration matters such as the level of pensions, rents and the incidence of taxation which were strictly outside the immediate concern of the pressure groups involved. In fact, in every case, attempts were being made to reach some kind of 'contract' between the groups concerned, a 'contract' which recognized that these groups do have considerable power – if largely a veto power – and which assumed that Parliament had no effective role to play except to register and enact the contents of any contract.

This approach, to draw in the most powerful pressure groups on both sides of industry, has sometimes been called 'tripartitism'. It has a respectable history in this country and has been developed quite extensively elsewhere. It began in Britain as an attempt to work out joint plans between government, industry and the unions in a manner which would encourage mutual confidence, show up weak areas and commit all participants to a common objective of faster growth. The National Economic Development Council was set up in 1962 with a representative tripartite council to bring in the constituent elements and an economic staff to contribute professional expertise. It was made clear that the NEDC was an independent body and that its role was purely advisory; there were no sanctions to enforce its conclusions. But the idea was that as all the three constituent parts shared the common objective of faster growth, if there was a general agreement that certain steps were necessary to further this objective, then all three elements would seek to take these steps or to aid in their achievement.

Early in its existence, the Council looked at growth targets, picked 4 per cent. per annum and asked its office to work out the implications. The result was a report on the targets[1] and a study on *Conditions Favourable to Faster Growth*.[2] This study indicated actions needed to back up the growth programme in such fields as education and training, labour mobility, regional development, the balance of payments, taxation and prices and incomes policy. The contribution government, industry and the unions could make in these various fields was indicated in rather general terms. The 4 per cent. target was accepted as official government policy and the 1963 Budget was framed in order to achieve this objective. The Chancellor of the Exchequer said he did so in 'the confident belief that as the government set the lead so management and unions as well will join in a national drive to achieve a national objective'. Economic Development Committees (little Neddies) were set up for particular industries.

When the Department of Economic Affairs was created in October, 1964, some of the NEDC planning staff were moved to that Department but the NEDC Council was enlarged and in August, 1965, the Prime Minister became Chairman. When the NEDC Plan was brought up to date and reissued in September 1965 as *The National Plan*[3] it had become a 'commitment and blueprint for action' on the part of the government. The NEDC was asked 'to review regularly the progress being made in each field, to see whether the various policies are proving effective ... and whether further action is required'. When the NEDC drew so close to the government and the DEA absorbed so much of its staff, the original concept of an independent body 'under the aegis of but not in' the administration, as Mr Maudling had put it, could have been lost. But this was a time when George Brown had extracted the 'Declaration of Intent' from the TUC that they would keep incomes in line with the growth of productivity and when industry was still prepared to co-operate with the Labour government. This atmosphere came to an end with the financial crisis of July 1966 when the National Plan targets were abandoned, the DEA lost the main reason for its existence and the government began to move from co-operation in reasonable growth of incomes to positive restraint and an incomes policy.

The impressive feature of the NEDC experiment was that the Council, the top-level meetings of the three constituents, survived these set-backs and the growing tension between the government and both sides of industry. From January 1969 to the June 1970 election, the NEDC again looked at the conditions for overall growth though the resulting document, *The Task Ahead*, was much more tentative.[4] Then the Conservative government elected in June, 1970, wondered whether the whole institution should be abandoned, but soon decided to leave it in existence. It slipped, in practice, into the void left by the government's early dislike of any prices and incomes policy. Sir Frank Figgures, the third Director-General, got the three 'parties', government, CBI and TUC to talk about the problems of inflation, employment levels and the rate of investment. In August, 1971, the need for these three estates of the realm to work together became so pressing – with inflation increasing, no investment revival and unemployment rising towards one million – that a 'Group of Four' was set up. They were the Permanent Secretary of the Treasury, the General Secretary of the TUC, the Director-General of NEDC and the Director-General of the CBI. Their task was to prepare an agenda for full Council meetings but not merely in the sense of listing points for discussion. *The Times* said their activity 'consists of that delicate therapy ... whereby a conception develops into a considered consensus ready to be embodied in a visible contract'.[5]

As part of this therapy, the TUC brought forward the idea of cost-of-living threshold clauses in pay settlements. The CBI contributed a self-denying ordinance for the top two hundred firms, which were voluntarily to limit price increases to 5 per cent. a year. It was on this basis that the Chancellor of the Exchequer, Mr Barber, set off on his dash for 5 per cent. growth per annum. As a result of the discussions and the problems, the government, though at loggerheads with the TUC over the Industrial Relations Act and disenchanted with industry because of its failure to raise the rate of investment, felt it had to keep in close touch. The Group of Four was supposed to go over the issues so that when the pressures on the three parties rendered them willing to consider a social contract (these words were used at that time) on pay, prices, employment and growth, all misunderstandings and obstacles to agreement would have been cleared away.

In a curious way, the participants managed to operate in a very different fashion at two distinct levels. On the top political level, the government was in conflict with the unions over wage increases and industrial relations legislation and with industry over its reluctance to invest. At a different, broader level, there was a recognition of the need for collaboration in isolating the problems and narrowing the areas of disagreement. Thus, the NEDC provided the forum in which extensive consultations took place as the government turned back to an incomes policy. There were meetings of the Group of Four and then a Co-ordinating Committee which paved the way for meetings with the Prime Minister at Chequers or 10 Downing Street. There the incomes policy was hammered out with its Stages one, two and three, the government offering certain formulae in return for non-enforcement of sections of the Industrial Relations Act and controls over prices on the part of industry. It is often forgotten that much of this was successful and that six million workers did settle under Stage III of the Conservative prices and incomes policy. However closely the unions allied themselves to the Labour Party during its seven months of minority government in 1974, many union leaders were willing to reach a kind of social contract with the Conservatives before the February 1974 election and were clear in their minds that they would have to try again if and when the Conservatives returned to power.

At the same time, on the more political level, the government and the unions clashed over wages and industrial relations policy till the National Union of Mineworkers decided to press its demand for a claim far in excess of the norm permitted under the prices and incomes policy. The NUM held out for this despite all the pressure the government could muster, including a three-day working week, and finally a general election in February 1974. Much to the surprise of most politicians, the voters refused to rally to Mr Heath's cry of 'who governs the country?'. In a curious way, the result reinforced the deeper level of activity in the NEDC and the tripartite discussions in that it showed that neither industry, the government nor the unions could easily over-rule the others; they had to work together if the country was to make reasonable progress.

INSTITUTIONAL CHANGES TO BRING IN THE PRESSURE GROUPS

So, in mid-1974, there has been the experience of two British governments, one Labour and one Conservative, each failing to get British industry to respond in the way they wanted and each taking on the unions over industrial relations policy and incomes policy and losing. On the other hand, neither of these pressure groups can operate without an effective government and both struggled at one political level to get the kind of government they wanted while at another level they sought to maintain good communications with whoever was the government.

Because of this, when any academics or commentators concerned about British problems have propounded solutions, they inevitably include these power blocs. Some of those writing on an incomes policy have wanted the share-out of wages determined by a kind of industrial parliament,[6] while others have advocated restoring industry by a £20 billion investment programme to be pushed through by a board representing unions, industry and the government.[7] These comments all recognize that in policy-making and legislation, those with power in the community have to be consulted and to concede a measure of agreement or the policy will not work.

The way the government approached this task in the 1960s and early 1970s meant that it descended into the ring and fought out a series of duels single-handed with these pressure groups. In the course of these bouts, the government had no method of rallying the other groups who had accepted its policies to its side. It was the government versus the miners while the six million workers who had accepted the policy and who had, therefore, a vested interest in seeing that the miners secured no special advantage over them were unable to bring their influence to bear. The public sometimes sympathized with the group which had taken on the government because they were unable to see what would happen if all unions (or industrialists) behaved in the same way. Once the government committed itself to a trial of strength with the pressure group, it was in difficulties as the political leaders felt they would lose support if they were too adamant or 'abrasive' while the pressure group leaders knew they would be sacked by their members if they were not tough and did not insist on fighting to the last ditch.

Yet everyone knows that a country cannot be run in this way and the willingness of the pressure groups to go on talking through such bodies as the NEDC shows that they understand that such conduct ultimately harms everyone. So what can be done about this situation? How can the realities of policy and rule making in our society be incorporated in the machinery of government so as to recognize the legitimate interests of the various parties and, at the same time, restore the position of the government; that is restore it as a party above the battle, as the representative of the broader national interest, and give it a degree of authority different in kind from that of the pressure groups?

There are two areas in which it is possible to look for help. The one is previous attempts to solve this problem, for there have often been periods when governments have had to struggle to assert themselves against power blocs in the community. The second is to consider attempts made by other nations to tackle this same problem. On the first, the history of mediaeval parliaments is helpful. The problem for mediaeval monarchs was that the barons often had all the attributes of monarchs within their own areas. Indeed, as with the modern pressure group, some barons could obtain the prior allegiance of their tenants in any dispute with the Crown. If there was a dispute between the Crown and some powerful baron, the Crown would not wish to take on such an overmighty subject single-handed while the barons watched to see if it would be worth their while to engage in similar confrontations. So it was in the Crown's interest to draw these tenants-in-chief into a constant consultation on national policy. If this was achieved, the barons went on record in front of their peers and any subsequent refusals to observe laws that had been agreed were defiance not merely of the Crown but also of the other tenants-in-chief. This meant that the King could expect the other barons to join in putting pressure on any recalcitrant individual. It was this desire to legitimize policies and laws by getting the prior consent of the most powerful men in the country that led to the creation of Houses of Lords which were, in practice, the most important chambers in mediaeval parliaments.

The chief difficulty the Crown faced was to persuade the more powerful barons to attend as they knew that in doing so, they accepted the sovereignty of the King and the practical fact that if they agreed to policies, they had to help carry them out. If, afterwards, they went their own way, they were defying rules or requirements whose legitimacy they had explicitly accepted. Because the King wanted to establish this kind of social contract with all the powerful elements in the country, bishops and abbots were also included, sometimes in a separate house, while in a lower chamber, there were representatives of the Commons who were expected to indicate what their counterparts at home would accept. If any group of representatives objected, they had to be won over or be made to feel that they were in too small a minority to maintain an opposition. Once they had agreed, they had to explain the policies to which they had consented to their constituents.

All this is useful because it points to the fact that one reason why the Commons has lost power is because its members are party nominees rather than the actual representatives of an area or a group. Few now think the votes of MPs indicate the positive assent of those they are held to represent, which is why the acceptance of a law by the House of Commons is not now regarded as conveying sufficient legitimacy by itself. But it is of considerable help to the government if the contemporary equivalent of the barons give their assent – if the CBI, the unions or professional associations indicate their agreement – since they can then be held to account and can be expected to secure the co-operation of their members. And if, in the process of consultation, some of the power blocks agree but others do not, then the minority is struggling not merely with the governments but with the rest of its peers who are prepared to agree. The importance of this kind of pressure was seen when Mr Scanlon's AUEW did not wish to endorse the 'social contract' with the Labour government at the TUC conference in September 1974. Probably no government could have forced the AUEW to give its official consent but the other unions were able to make the Engineers feel so isolated that they decided to conform. And once they have conformed, though this may not guarantee observance of the contract by subordinate branches of the union (just as mediaeval barons could not always ensure good conduct by all the minor lords in their territory), at least there can be no argument about the legitimacy of the contract and it is much harder for the union itself to countenance or promote blatant breaches.

Mediaeval parliaments were based on the sensible assumption that if there were powerful elements in the country whose understanding and agreement had to be obtained for any common policy to be enforced (and taxes raised), then it was far easier if these groups could be gathered together, the common problems examined, a certain because the other powerful groups without land sought representation unity obtained and then these elements could not avoid some responsibility for the rules and for their enforcement. In the late nineteenth partly because landed magnates wielded much less power, partly century, the remnants of these Houses of Lords declined in importance in the lower or elected houses. Now that power groups are not territorial and so do not fit a constituency pattern and since these groups also tend to neglect the elected houses and deal directly with the governments, it may make sense to try and bring those with power together in a chamber like the old upper houses of mediaeval parliaments. The object would be to obtain greater mutual understanding, to get in consequence some pressure by peer groups on recalcitrant authorities, to have an open record of any support that is conceded and to accord greater legitimacy to any rules or policies which have been endorsed by such a body.

It is for this reason that various modern countries have set up a range of bodies varying from advisory planning organizations of the NEDC type to virtual third chambers like the French Economic and Social Council whose composition and powers are set out in the

Constitution. The latter consists of 200 (originally 205) members chosen for five years by the appropriate organizations. There are forty-five representatives of manual and black-coated workers, forty-one from the managerial side of private and nationalized industry, forty from agriculture and forty government nominees, with smaller numbers of representatives of social and cultural organizations. The Council is restricted to matters on which it is consulted by the government except for any suggestions it may make about social or economic reforms necessitated by technical changes. Its object is to bring together the representatives of the major social and economic pressure groups who either would not normally meet or would be summoned only at a time of crisis when their interests had come into sharp conflict. The Council breaks into 'sections' to study economic problems and to put forward reports to the government, but its success should be measured more in terms of the understanding that has developed among the leaders of interest groups, whose members' general ignorance of each other and mutual hostility is still very marked. It is difficult to be precise about the impact of the Council because so much of its work is in secret and it is essentially a consultative body. The French government itself stated in 1960 that 'in the field of agricultural policy the advice of the ESC on the agricultural bills has been substantially utilized by the government in the preparation of the legislation submitted to Parliament.'[8] In 1961, General de Gaulle congratulated the Council on its work over the Fourth Plan: 'Your participation in this vital matter ... has been both skilled and objective.' Then the Council wanted to go further than consultation and the proposal of amendments. Over the Fifth Plan, it wanted to set out a series of alternatives from which Parliament could choose, while the government decided to make its own proposals without first submitting them to the ESC. As a result, the Council's reactions to the Plan were extremely critical and Parliament drew heavily on its report when criticizing the Plan. In 1963 and 1964, the Council turned to an examination of the prerequisites of an incomes policy and one of the trade union representatives said, 'Of all the institutions in which the social partners at present meet, we prefer the ESC to serve as the framework for an incomes policy', but in early 1965 the draft proposals were defeated by 93 to 29 as the interest groups did not have enough confidence in the government to entrust it with the task of carrying through an incomes policy.

Although the ESC thus, in rejecting an incomes policy, ranged itself along with other 'factious obstructors' of Gaullist policy, the General said there was a larger role for the Council to fulfil and in 1964 he talked of merging it with the Senate or of the Council acquiring legislative powers. In France, the Senate embodies the old republican elite, the representatives of the many town councils throughout France, while the ESC represents the more recent pressure group leaders. There was therefore nothing very strange in suggesting that the latter might more appropriately exercise the legislative powers of the Senate. M. Mendès-France[9] pointed out that this would stop the groups merely presenting their own grievances. If they had to share responsibility for making the rules, they would have to consider the broader national interest. Others who have considered the role and composition of the Council have discussed whether interest group representatives should be elected or nominated by the groups, whether the weak or un-organized should be represented and whether consultation by the government on all economic questions should be made compulsory. The farmers' organizations have been most enthusiastic about the work of the Council, the businessmen somewhat reticent, while the trade unions are torn between a desire to influence decisions and a refusal to accept any responsibility for the working of 'the system'. The history of the Council certainly confirms Professor A. Sauvy's claim that it 'is a more or less conscious attempt to legalize the powers that be, the only serious attempt to modernize our political system'.

In Belgium, a Central Economic Council was created in 1948 and a National Council of Labour in 1952. The former has fifty members, twenty-two being nominated by the 'most representative organizations' of industry, agriculture, commerce and small business while the two largest trade union organizations have eight each, five come from consumer co-operatives, one from a small labour organization, and the remaining six are chosen by the government on a three pro-labour, three pro-management basis. Below this, there are the equivalent of 'little Neddies' for the various industries. The Council prepares reports on economic questions, particularly in the period each year before the government produces its budget and then afterwards comments on the results. There is also the National Council of Labour, which deals with 'social objectives' and which has been kept as a separate body to overcome Labour's fear that if there was an economic council only, economic efficiency would take priority over all other con-siderations.

One of the first issues in which the Central Economic Council played a decisive role was in persuading the government to set up a planning department in 1959, the Office for Economic Programming. This Office consults the Council when preparing plans and, when agreed, these become laws as far as the government is concerned. The plans or laws do not set out objectives for the private sector but there is an implicit obligation on employers' and union representatives to help the government carry out the plan, to sell its objectives to their members and to direct their organizations in a manner which fits in with the plan.

In the Netherlands, a Social and Economic Council consisting of employers, employees and public representatives was set up in 1950 and has proved useful. When relations broke down between government and the two sides of industry over a wages pause in 1971, the only way consultations could be resumed was by asking the Council for its opinion. When it unanimously recommended a restriction of government intervention in overall wage and price policies, the government agreed and turned instead to regular tripartite consultations over wage and price policies. It was because three of the original members of the European Community had bodies of this kind that the Treaty of Rome established an Economic and Social Committee of 121 members, appointed by the Council of Ministers as 'representatives of the various categories of economic and social life'. One third came from employers' organizations, one third from the unions, while the remainder represented 'the general interest'. In certain cases, the Council of Ministers has to seek the advice of this body while in others, consultation is optional. The advice does not have to be taken but some important interests (particularly in agriculture) are represented and their views are given due weight.

THE SOLUTION IN BRITAIN

The question is, first, whether it would be useful to bring the pressure groups into an institution which emphasizes the legislative character of the decisions that they and the government take. If so, the second question is: What would be the best form of institution?

On point one, part of the answer is evident. The relations between the major economic groups and the government are already arranged in and through the NEDC, while the other pressure groups have their conventional arrangements with Whitehall. If no more is needed, then all that is necessary is to develop these institutions and processes. During the October general election, Mr Heath addressed himself to this problem and wanted the NEDC arrangements to be extended, formalized and conducted before the media so that those participating could subsequently be held to what they had said and undertaken at the Council.

But this points to a feeling that the NEDC approach has not so far been entirely satisfactory. First, it has failed to put participants 'on the record'. The main decisions have still been taken at smaller, informal and totally private meetings. Secondly, the system excludes other, often equally important pressure groups. Thirdly, it still down-grades Parliament and encourages the pressure groups to look only to Whitehall. Fourthly, it fails to force the representatives of special interests to explain their case in front of other pressure groups competing for the same scarce resources. Finally, for the same reasons, public opinion is inadequately informed and roused about decisions which often seriously affect people as consumers, citizens and tax-payers.

If these disadvantages suggest that something more than an expanded or strengthened NEDC is necessary, should Britain contemplate the creation of a third chamber, an economic and social council? This would meet some of the deficiencies listed above in that it would include the other important groups and would be a chamber where discussions could be in public and cover broader issues than the bilateral relations between a single pressure group and the government. The weakness of the proposal is that it must be open to doubt whether such a chamber would ever be accepted as an integral part of Parliament, in the sense that the Lords and Commons are parts of Parliament. And part of the objective is to restore the position and prestige of Parliament and to restore a proper sense of legitimacy to its legislation.

As a result, it might be simpler to combine the creation of a new institution with the reform or transformation of the existing House of Lords. Some might feel diffident about calling pressure group leaders 'Lords' (though some strange creations have appeared in that Chamber). In this case, all existing peers could keep their titles but would no longer be members of parliament. The new members could be called 'Members of the Upper House'. A total of, say, 200 Members would be appointed for the duration of each Parliament, the trades unions and industry being asked to nominate forty each; the government would appoint perhaps twenty ministers, officials and experts to put its case and the remaining 100 would be allocated among the existing pressure groups 'recognized' by Whitehall.

One convenient aspect of this solution is that the existing powers of the Upper House would be entirely suitable for the new chamber. It would continue to exercise the present very restricted powers to review legislation and to hold up measures for a maximum of six months but it would have no power over financial legislation. Also, it would have nothing to do with the political complexion of the government as the Prime Minister would still owe his position to his control of a majority in the House of Commons. In order to retain the consultative and fact-finding role of the NEDC and of the present secret negotiations between pressure groups and Whitehall, provision would have to be made for a select committee system in the Lords. Select committees on economic policy, agriculture, transport, trade and industry and so on, could continue to bring the various interests together, produce reports, find out government thinking on new legislation, put the pressure groups' case and prepare members for the broader debates in the House itself on policy matters.

There are many objections to such a radical proposal, but the issues are the same whether a third chamber is established or use is made of a reformed Upper House. It is perhaps better to consider these objections in sequence, first dealing with the 'will it work?' questions, then turning to possible dangers and finally to the advantages.

The first question is: Why should the pressure groups agree to take part? Almost all of them will feel it is better to negotiate on their own with the government; they can always make their special case look convincing if it is simply set against a very amorphous 'national interest' represented by the government. It is quite different and much harder for them (if they are, say, farmers) to convince the representatives of the consumers or, if they are miners, to convince postmen and dustmen or, if they are trade associations, to put their case across to a variety of other interests. Moreover, much or all of the discussions will be in public and the pressure group members will know what their spokesmen are saying. The answer is that the inducement to participate will be the same inducement that has kept both sides of industry going to the NEDC despite public confrontations, showdowns and the periodic collapse of communications; it is the desire to be consulted, to be in on the framing of policy. This is the desire that has kept the NFU going constantly to the Ministry of Agriculture whatever the level of disagreement the farmers and the government have had about particular policies. The government would simply need to insist that all consultation takes place through the committee system of the House of Lords so that those who do not come are excluded. This would, judging by the experience of all the countries that have adopted any system of consultation, ensure full participation.

The second objection concerns the numbers and method of selection of members. If the reconstituted Upper Chamber is to vote on issues, there could be serious disputes about the numbers. Why should 'Labour' have only forty (or whatever) out of 200? But the other interest group representatives would not all fall on the other side in straight class divisions; the agricultural vote would include representatives of the agricultural workers and the teachers and other white collar professional groups might well join with the trade union representatives. Yet the real answer is that in a House of this kind, for a government to press on with a labour relations policy against the advice of the labour members or with an investment policy against the express wishes of the business interests would be to court defeat. Also, much more attention would have to be paid to the committees and an agricultural bill which was unanimously rejected by the agricultural committee or a health measure objected to by all the representatives of the Health Service would clearly be difficult to operate. Moreover, the objections of the interest groups would be seized on by the opposition in the House of Commons and it would be hard for a government to proceed unless it was prepared for a confrontation.

There might be some argument as to whether the representatives of the groups should be directly elected by the members. How far, it could be asked, are the existing pressure group leaders really representative of their members? But there would be great resentment if the government tried to intervene in or lay down rules for the internal arrangements of the pressure groups. The value of the system being proposed depends very much on the participation of the recognized spokesmen for the interests and therefore it seems better to leave them to arrange the method of nomination. If all other modes of consultation were banned, then it is virtually certain that the existing office-bearers would nominate themselves or arrange for an election of the kind which chooses the members of the TUC from among the various unions.

Turning to the dangers which some might detect in such a system, there might be worries about the effect on the normal working of Parliament and whether the creation of a new chamber described as 'the Upper House' would in fact place it in a position superior to the Commons. There might even be suggestions that this would be a step towards a 'corporate state'. On the first, it might be thought that any such chamber should be purely consultative, but if so there is the danger that when proposals were really tendentious, the government would cease to consult (as the Conservatives did over the Industrial Relations Bill). Also, this kind of second or upper chamber would have a role to play in all forms of legislation except taxation and if it is thought that this would mean that many bills would pass without much discussion, it should be remembered that this is the situation now in the House of Lords. What matters is that issues closely affecting the powerful groups in the community would be properly studied in committee by all those affected and then their views would have to be taken into account in the actual legislative process. And as one of the objectives is to gain greater legitimacy for laws, there is no substitute for involving the groups who can confer such legitimacy not only, as at present, in the informal preparatory stages but also later in the formal legalizing stage.

As to dangers to the House of Commons, these must be considered against the present reduced power and prestige of that body. The Commons would keep the existing chief source of its remaining authority: that it is out of the Commons majority that the government is formed and it is to the Commons that the government would remain responsible. At the moment, the most serious challenge to the authority of the House lies in the periodic quasi-legislative yet informal meetings held between the government and the major pressure groups and it would help Parliament as a whole if this process was brought back within the Palace of Westminster.

Finally, some may look back to theories of the corporate state current in the 1930s and ask how far the recognition of the power of such groups is a denial of democracy. Clearly, in the sense that these proposals recognize that legislative chambers based on 'one person one vote' are not enough in themselves either to contain all the necessary parties to negotiations or to legitimize all laws, this is true. But if power in a society is 'lumpy', then the lumps will remain and the only question is whether their position is to be regularized and institutionalized or left on an informal basis. There might be a claim that the representation of such groups should be counterbalanced in the Upper House by the inclusion of representatives of the public, of the weaker sections of society or of the unorganized. But this would really be open to serious objections as it would suggest that a genuine numerical balance could be achieved between the pressure groups and the public at large in one chamber. It is better to recognize that the upper house would be a rough and ready way of gathering the voices of the powerful and that precise numbers did not matter while the Commons remained the true voice of the people, the consumers and the taxpayers.

Lastly, some will say that this is all constitutional tinkering beloved of political scientists and of academic reformers steeped in the nineteenth-century liberal tradition. But such a criticism neglects the crucial fact that in society, modern or ancient, only two ways have been found of getting people to work together. One is force. The other is the observance of laws based on consent. Recently, the British system of government has failed to generate an adequate sense of consent and powerful pressure groups have successfully defied successive governments. As a result, if the system of government is not to degenerate into chaos, either force must be applied or a new and better method of producing legitimacy must be evolved. Many people, because they have no idea how to produce the last of these situations and they shrink from physical force, are turning to the idea of non-physical force: the fear and weakness caused by mass unemployment. Yet this solution brings as many or more problems than those it sets out to cure. So there is nothing cranky or academic in pointing out that there is a method of obtaining greater consent which has worked in previous historical periods and has begun to be tried in other countries: that is to draw the elements whose consent is required into institutionalized processes which encourage co-operation and help confer legitimacy on what is decided.

Nor are these proposals long term. They could be started at once with one simple Bill which would alter the composition of the present House of Lords and bring the bargaining process between the pressure groups and the government back inside Parliament. This new method of decision-making could be in operation within a reasonably short period. The only thing required is an agreement that it is better to try the institutional alternative rather than wait till the position deteriorates to a level where force becomes not merely the idle daydream of retired colonels but the preferred solution for influential sections of the community.

NOTES

1. *Growth of the UK Economy to 1966*, NEDC, 1963.
2. NEDC, 1963.
3. Department of Economic Affairs, Cmnd. 2764, September 1965.
4. Department of Economic Affairs, *The Task Ahead*, HMSO, 1969.
5. *The Times*, 9 August 1971.
6. See for example E. H. Phelps Brown, *Collective Bargaining Reconsidered*, Stamp Memorial Lecture, London School of Economics, 1971.
7. *The Times*, 19 December 1973.
8. This and the subsequent quotations on the French Economic and Social Council are taken from J. E. S. Hayward's *Private Interests and Public Policy: The Experience of the French Economic and Social Council* (London 1966).
9. *La République Moderne* (Paris 1962).

Bernard Crick

Whither Parliamentary Reform?

I believe that there are three questions by which the working of the House of Commons can be tested, both today and for future change: First, is the legislative process designed to enable policies to be translated into law at the speed required by the tempo of modern industrial change? Secondly, can our time-table ... leave room for debating the great issues and especially for the topical debates on matters of current controversy which provide the main political education of a democracy? Thirdly, while accepting that legislation and administration must be firmly in the hands of the Government, does the House of Commons provide a continuous and detailed check on the work of the Executive and an effective defence of the individual against bureaucratic injustice and incompetence? It is by these three tests, I suggest, that we should try out both our existing procedures and the proposals for modifying them put forward by the various schools of parliamentary reform.

R. H. S. Crossman in the debate on procedure of 14 December 1966

If one accepts these three tests, let it be clear that one may have sensible criteria to judge how well the House of Commons is working, but not to judge how important is the House, indeed Parliament as a whole, in the whole pattern of British government and politics. Sometimes both reformers and House-traditionalists have claimed too much for the power or influence of Parliament.

THE WIDER CONTEXT

Take Mr Crossman's criteria in turn. The speed of legislation, on even the most superficial level, is as much a product of the organization, attitudes and behaviour of Whitehall as of Westminster –

Reprinted from A. H. Hanson and Bernard Crick (eds.), *The Commons in Transition* (Fontana/Collins, London 1970), pp. 249–276. Copyright 1970 by A. H. Hanson and Bernard Crick. By permission of the author and the publishers.

and to speak of 'the executive' is only to provide a verbal link between two machines and cultures which at times have remarkably little mutual knowledge and interaction; and, on a more profound level, we are still on very dark and slippery ground, on the evidence of the Five Year Plan and the annual economic forecasts, in thinking that 'the tempo of modern industrial change' can be speedily 'translated into law'. Rarely are we sure which is cause and which is effect. So much basic statistical knowledge is still lacking that much legislation is still a stab in the dark – and hence so much amendment.[1] But we should have learned at least that many such laws depend far more on their acceptance and on the way in which they are administered than on their hatching in 'the Cabinet', their drafting in Whitehall and their promulgation in Westminster – to allude delicately to incomes policy and the aborted Industrial Relations Bill. The question should at least arise of what do we mean by legislation? The intention, the statutes, or the effect?

Take Crossman's second point too. It is at least plain that Parliament has effective rivals in the business of raising 'current controversy' as 'the main political education of democracy'. When Bagehot used the terse phrase 'political education' to describe the main function of Parliament, which Crossman eloquently echoed, he was writing before the cheap popular press, radio and television and a universal educational system up to the threshold of manhood. All these now have their place, and it is extremely hard – no political scientists have even attempted to measure it – to see the precise nature of the primacy that Parliament may have among them either in shaping or in expressing public opinion, let alone public behaviour. It is not so long ago that Parliament attempted to insist that radio and television should not discuss matters of current controversy while they were before the House. And when a 'Politics Association' was recently formed by teachers, at a large conference in London, to raise the standard of civic education, which was generally agreed to mean getting more realism and somewhat less 'constitution' into syllabuses, *The Times* did not think it worthy of mention nor the Ministry of support. Changes in the press and changes in schools could well have more effect on the general 'political education' of the public than any changes that are likely to come out of Parliament, but they are perhaps even more difficult to realize than changes in Parliament.

And for the former Leader of the House's third point, it is all too obvious that it both is and should be the case that press, radio and television can both rival and complement Parliament's activities in 'defending the individual against bureaucracy'. How well either do it is a different question; but neither could do it alone. Politician and journalists quarrel like husband and wife.

Now I am not criticizing Mr Crossman. I doubt if he would disagree I only wish to point to the general context of politics in which Parliament may, perhaps, play the dominant or the primary part, but not the omnipotent or the only part. The greatest importance of Parliament is as a centre of political communication, and a two-way process. Thus while Mr Crossman's criteria should give a sense of direction to the methods of the House, they do not define its scope or relative importance. The inference I wish to draw is simply that the House should act with an outward-looking rather than an inward-looking eye. The future of parliamentary reform lies in such a direction. Many things can be done, as Crossman pointed out in the same speech quoted above, to modernize the House and to increase the ease and conveniences of Members, which may have little to do with enabling Parliament to have any great influence on the social and economic problems of British society.

So here I am primarily concerned with the role of Parliament as an agent of reform or, in Crossman's words, as 'an effective institution for furthering and criticizing Government policy and the conduct of public affairs', not with its own internal modernization. There are obvious connections between the two: an inefficient Parliament can delay and frustrate policy, above all it can fail to act as an important device for actually changing public opinion on particular issues;[2] but the most streamlined and well-equipped assembly in the world cannot rise above an ineffective Government or an inert or hostile population. Someone who believes somewhat less than I do in the need for basic economic and social reforms has put the essential matter well:

No constitution, written or unwritten, is worth more than the political temper of the community allows it to be worth. The best of paper constitutions is worthless if applied to an unstable, divided or intolerant community. The worst of paper constitutions can evolve into something better in the right political atmosphere ... a narrow institutional view of Parliament can be a distorted one. It can give the impression that our political attitudes have been entirely created by Parliament whereas (although Parliament has fostered their growth) it might be equally true to say that our political attitudes have created Parliament.[3]

And Mr Butt goes on to quote the doleful remark of Sir Kenneth Pickthorn that 'procedure is all the Constitution the poor Briton has'. Above all, parliamentary reform should not seek to 'take the politics out of politics' or to leave it elsewhere, but to make Parliament a more effective political forum. Parliamentary reform is itself a political issue, albeit one that cuts right across party lines. Some resist it because they see it as a threat to their Government – even to all government; some applaud it because they see it as a way of limiting all Governments and parties; while some see it as the need to assert something like Crossman's three criteria in a particular epoch when too many of the cards are in the hands of Governments. There is never a 'balance', but there can come about a gross inequality in the fight. This does not mean, however, that parliamentary reform automatically favours the Opposition over the Government; it can well strengthen opposition within the governing party (which is what many Ministers have against it: they can look after the Opposition, it is their own friends who worry them); and it can, on occasion, strengthen the collective ability of the House to influence, not just weakly mirror, public opinion. There is at times a terrible shyness in admitting that communication is a two-way process, and that politics is much more lumpy a business than pure smooth government or pure smooth democracy – if ever either existed alone.

WHERE DO WE STAND TODAY?

Certainly some progress has been made during the period of the two Labour Governments since 1964, and stirrings were abroad before that – as in the late 1950s when many began to consider the problems of Parliament under a long period of one-party rule and as, surprisingly quickly afterwards, some Conservatives came to consider – a little more pressingly – the problems of opposition.[4] But when anything in politics gets even mildly near to improvement, it becomes a bore to the press and the public. The press was full of parliamentary reform from 1964–67, but when 'the Crossman reforms' went through in the winter of 1967–68 there was little notice taken and less enthusiasm; the Bill to reform the Lords of 1969 was almost universally unpopular in the press, being actually attacked for its 'political' character (in that it represented an agreed compromise between the two front benches), and all sorts of politically unrealistic, constitutional bright-ideas were peddled in editorials; and, recently, the most important report for many years of the Select Committee on Procedure, on 'Scrutiny of Public Expenditure and Administration', got extraordinary little coverage in the press, and it appeared to defeat television altogether. Perhaps basic political issues have reasserted themselves over exaggerated hopes for reforms of procedure? Somehow one doubts. Perhaps these matters are just too difficult and given to the press with too little time to digest (forty-eight hours to be precise) before they become yesterday's – the great god – 'news'. Or perhaps Parliament simply has to be judged by results, not by good intentions? And it can hardly grumble at that. For we are all, after all – and politicians must forgive us for it – usually more worried at being misgoverned than grateful for being governed so relatively well. Only in autocracies do people celebrate the routine competence of their rulers. In political democracies, as the great Mr Dooley, the Aristotle of the Chicago Irish, once remarked, we build our triumphal arches of bricks, not of stones, so they can be quickly torn down and hurled after the departing heroes – even a Churchill. The chairman of the Select Committee on Procedure is as inherently unlikely to be hoisted on the shoulders of the workers and the students as he is to be stoned. Most people have not heard of him – which is the position, if he is wise, that he should prefer.

Perhaps it is a good sign that parliamentary reform has become a bore; but then bores must justify themselves by looking backwards. It amounts to this: since 1964, when a really effective and continuing Select Committee on Procedure was set up on the somewhat tentative 1962 model and since the heady two years when Mr Crossman was Leader of the House, more deliberate changes in parliamentary procedure have taken place than at any recent period of the House's history – for anything like it one must go back to Balfour's reforms of the 1900s or Gladstone's of the 1870s. And if they have contained large elements of streamlining the business for the good of the Government (like the Morrison 'reforms' of 1945–46), yet they have also been deliberately balanced (unlike the Morrison 'reforms') with reforms in the interest of Parliament as a whole to improve the quality and relevance of debate or of the critical scrutiny of the administration.

The continued reappointment each session of the Procedure Committee is no small innovation and achievement. From being an occasional and spasmodic *ad hoc* creation (there were only three important reports of such a committee between 1918 and 1964, those of 1932, 1946 and 1959), it has become in the last six or eight years firmly established as a senior committee of the House and seemingly now almost as much a permanent and prestigious institution as the Public Accounts, the Estimates and the Nationalized Industries Committees. This alone is no small change. At least Westminster, if not Whitehall, is now under a continuous scrutiny and investigation. The Committee has done much good work, perhaps not enough, but certainly it has changed much of the familiar geography of parliamentary procedure. A lot of the 'parliamentary mumbo-jumbo' has gone: notably the end of pretending to debate Supply on Supply days so that they are now quite simply Opposition Days, and will be so called; and the Mace will remain steady on the table, as will the Speaker in the chair (or as a school essay I have just been shown puts it – 'Black Bob now only comes knocking at the door when sent for at the end of each term').

At least the textbooks are now out of date, and they will have to remain so. There is now obviously going to be continual change, adjustment and experiment in details of procedure: accounts of the House, even or particularly for school children, can now no longer be sensibly written in terms of 'good old traditional procedure', but rather in terms of the basic political forces and parliamentary needs which give rise to changes of procedure – and policy! They will now be driven to explain the 'why?' and the 'what for?', not just the 'how?' of Parliament. The bulk of the Finance Bill will now probably settle down upstairs, for instance, but it would be ludicrous to write even the most simple account of Parliament which did not attempt to show what kind of items from the Bill the Opposition now pick for the three days on the Floor. The famous Three Readings *tout simple* of a Bill can now no longer be taught; the greater use of Second Reading Committees will have to be mentioned, but it is still not clear how the moving pattern will settle down, if ever it settles down like before. The Report Stage, for instance, plainly needs tidying up: it tends to be a regurgitation of the Committee Stage by the same Members who spoke at that stage, but now addressing a largely empty House. But, anyway, clear knowledge of this kind of detail never mattered as much as the textbooks implied, so it is as well that their authors may be driven to look at the contents a bit more than the vessel and to see them both as parts of a political process. The sweet fixity of procedure, which enabled so many school-teachers and a good many Members to take refuge from policy in procedure, has now gone forever.

On the other hand, there is room for genuine disappointment. Some of it, of course, arises because all this procedural change (dare one say 'superficial'?), all the brave and vague words spoken by Ministers (of which the Prime Minister's Stowmarket speech of 3 July 1964 was the classic example) and the gentle rain of reports from the Procedure Committee itself, have all aroused quite false expectations. And on top of this must be mentioned, once again, the more professional attitudes of the new intake of Members on both sides in 1964 and 1966, their undoubted commitment to free politics, but their lesser respect for the traditions of the House and their, at times, not very great understanding of its difficulties. But some of the disappointment is more genuine. When the first round of new specialized committees were set up in 1967, it was assumed that they would be reappointed annually. But after the Select Committee on Agriculture had had its famous dispute with the Foreign Office over visiting Brussels, Crossman tolerantly announced that it would be allowed one more session, since its work had been somewhat delayed, but that 'our original intention was that a departmental committee should spend one Session on each department and then move on'. As has been unkindly said, this 'original intention' was one of the best kept secrets with which the then Leader of the House was ever associated.

Mr John Mackintosh, himself a member of the Procedure Committee as well as the Agriculture Committee, did not share the evident satisfaction of some of his colleagues with, as it were, 'steady progress made' and 'the new status of the committee itself'. He wrote a *Times* turnover article in angry or exasperated vein:

> In a special report published yesterday the (now defunct) House of Commons Select Committee on Agriculture forcefully criticizes the Government's decision to end its existence. A few weeks ago the Committee on Education formally protested against the announcement that it too will be closed down at the end of the Session, while on February 11, the protracted struggle by the Nationalized Industries Committee to extend its terms of reference was finally lost. These events show that while the committees wish to continue with and even expand their work, the Government has lost any enthusiasm for this experiment....
>
> The Agriculture Committee has been replaced by a committee on the Scottish Office, which is simply to give the Government something to point to when attacked by the Nationalists; while Education is to be replaced by a committee on Overseas Aid – in Whitehall terms a peripheral and quite unimportant department. There remain committees watching over certain Acts (race relations) and institutions (the Parliamentary Commissioner) but they are not performing the main task of scrutinizing sections of Whitehall. Thus instead of ending this Parliament with an established range of investigatory committees covering the key sectors on internal administration and with a solid body of Labour and Conservative MPs convinced by experience of the value of this work, an incoming government will inherit a run-down experiment which, if its leaders desire, can be quietly dropped.[5]

And one must remember that Mackintosh must have been writing this with at least the broad outlines in mind of the radical proposals (as we shall see) of the Procedure Committee for expanding the

Estimates Committee to obtain a *general and comprehensive* scrutiny of the effectiveness and efficiency of administration.[6] But all that could be seen as pie in the sky. So opinions obviously vary both as to the value of what has been done and as to the probable consequences.

WHAT HAS BEEN DONE?

So let me try to survey briefly what has been done since 1964 either by way of changes in procedure or changes in the practices of Parliament which affect the way procedure is used,[7] limiting myself in both cases to changes which could have some real affect on the products of the whole parliamentary process.

(i) *Salaries*. The increase of basic salary from £1,750 to £3,250 which followed the Lawrence Committee Report of November 1964 for the first time put salaries on a half-way decent level, which was an essential condition for enabling more 'young professionals' to stay in politics and for replacing a fair number of old lay-abouts (who all, of course, admirably represented the average citizen). But the basic nonsense remained that MPs had to meet most of the expenses of their job from their own basic salary – thus penalizing the active and over-rewarding the idle.[8] Only last year did a committee of the House firmly insist on linking the question of salary to that of services and facilities available.

(ii) *Services*. The *Sixth Report* from the Select Committee on House of Commons (Services)[9] began: 'Many Members have made representations to Your Committee that their present salaries are not sufficient to enable them, in addition to paying their living costs, to meet out of their own pockets expenses necessarily incurred in the discharge of their duties.' The most important of their recommendations (on which no decision has yet been made) is that 'provision should be made at public expense for secretarial assistance or an allowance to meet the cost up to a maximum of one full-time secretary per Member'. Free trunk calls were also proposed, a more generous photocopying service and free postage on all official business both in Session and in the recess (that is to include correspondence between Members and on all parliamentary business, not just letters to Government Departments and other official bodies).[10] And they kept up their by now often repeated demand for an office for each Member and his secretary – which everyone recognizes to entail a new building. Their only omission was not to link the question of increasing the staff of the Commons, both on the Clerks and the Library side, to services and facilities. But quite apart from specific reports, the very existence of this committee, first set up in 1965, has given the House much more initiative and control over its own facilities than ever in the ramshackle division of authorities in the past. Perhaps quite as important as the Services Committee's advocacy on accommodation and individual facilities[11] has been the work of its sub-committee on the Library – particularly in relation to the expansion of the Research Division.

(iii) *The Library*. The Research Division in particular and the information services of the Library in general have been considerably expanded, adding scientists and more statisticians to their staff (the first statistician arrived in 1946). The House has now, in fact (although I am not sure if Mr Geoffrey Lock would agree with this description), a Legislative Reference Service such as would grace an average size American State Legislature.[12] I do not mean this ironically, for the comparison with the Legislative Reference Service of the Library of Congress (itself the national library) would be absurdly out of scale. But the Library is now just about coping with a greatly increased demand from Members, is beginning to anticipate demand (perhaps even, dangerous to say, to create it in small ways) and is plainly going to be a key institution in a reformed or still reforming Parliament. It stands at the heart of the whole communications process. And in theory there is no reason (if not in immediate practice because of staff and cost) why many of the background papers, reference sheets and bibliographies it provides for Members should not reach the public.[13]

(iv) *The Ombudsman*. If his powers and his facilities are not enough, at least the foot is in the door. And it is worth remembering that the existence of the office is the result of a timely bright idea, a press campaign, and pressure from lawyers outside the House.[14] It is now only amusing to remember all those metaphysical objections about 'ministerial responsibility' and the like which evidently so worried such intensely practical men as Mr Harold MacMillan as Prime Minister and Lord Dilhorne as Lord Chancellor. Perhaps it has not really made all that much difference, but that was not what these weighty opponents prognosticated: their fears were greater than the hopes of the reformers. And the institution has been sensibly linked, after some initial fears to the contrary, to a Select Committee of the House who consider the Parliamentary Commissioner's reports and make recommendations (a linkage much on the lines that the Study of Parliament Group proposed in a privately circulated but widely reported memorandum at a time when the matter was in doubt).[15]

(v) *The New Committees.* Again, a mixed record both of creation and achievement, but a foot in the door: a general acceptance of their benefits even if continued scepticism by many MPs about their extent. Agriculture was shut down after considering horticulture, fisheries, the formation of agricultural policy generally and the sensitive question of agricultural prices in relation to possible entry into the Common Market; and Education was put in jeopardy after considering the school inspectorate and staff–student relations. Here the myth was born and sustained that the object of the 'Crossman reforms' of the committee system was to have departmental committees, usually no more than two, tackling one department a session but then moving on; but that there were also to be 'across-the-board' or functional committees which might enjoy a longer life – a sort of 'Ulster right' tenancy based on custom but no legal right, and the real risk of being expropriated if they improved the property. So Science and Technology continues from 1967, and in 1968 a Select Committee on Race Relations and Immigration was set up with a wide and potentially powerful remit – powerful in the sense that it is operating in a field where the leaders of both major parties will, for political reasons all too obvious, welcome not merely cross-bench support but also cross-bench initiative.[16] Perhaps the new and permanent Welsh Grand Committee comes into this category too, although at the moment it is only a debating and not a report-producing committee. And in place of axed Agriculture and Education, committees on the Ministry of Overseas Development and on Scottish Affairs – on which John Mackintosh's sardonic comments seem fully justified.

(vi) *New Developments in Committees.* The Nationalized Industries was the first since the 1930s to meet in public[17] and was the second (after the Estimates sub-committee on Government Services) since the 1920s to be allowed to employ a temporary but expert outside consultant. Generally since 1964 slow but steady progress has been made in allowing Select Committees to hear evidence but not to deliberate in public, to recruit specialist assistance up to two days a week and to meet in the field and even to travel abroad; but staffing on an adequate scale could soon become a problem, and in some ways a more acute one than that of finding enough Members to man an expanded committee system: for the House has learned that far smaller committees than in the past can be trusted and can do the work well or even better. The Nationalized Industries Committee did not fight shy of issues of major policy, as its First Report of the Session 1967–68 showed on Ministerial Control of Nationalized Industries which followed long hearings, mostly in public, of evidence from heads of the Nationalized Boards as well as Ministers, senior officials and independent experts. It has moved a long way from its early reluctance to get involved in issues of major policy even when those issues were not partisan. But, on the negative side, its wish to do a broad study of the Bank of England was disallowed,[18] after an extraordinary delay the following Session in setting up the committee at all, a delay due to civil service opposition and dispute about its proposals for new terms of reference.[19] Also on the negative side was the brief experiment in 1965–67 of allowing the sub-committees of the Estimates Committee to specialize – following the famous Fourth Report of the Select Committee on Procedure, 1964–65 (H.C. 303).[20] But in November 1967 the size of the committee was cut down, and with the appointment of the first two specialized committees they were persuaded to give up specialization,[21] and in the next session they suffered still further cuts in size. The new committees were won at perhaps too great a price, particularly when some of them proved so transitory – as the Procedure Committee has now come to see.[22]

(vii) *Privilege.* A Select Committee reported that much archaic matter should be swept away, that reporting of Parliament should be not even technically a breach of privilege and generally that the House should take a more pragmatic view of alleged 'contempts'.[23] But as yet the Government has taken no action on the report – it rests in limbo. The reason for including it in this list, however, is that one suspects that its logic will prove irresistible and that it will have to be acted upon if MPs do not abide by its advice or ever come again to embroil themselves and the press in any new round of technical, touchy and factious privilege cases – such as led to the setting up of this select committee in the first place. While the committee did not consider that the House should surrender its penal jurisdiction to the courts, it did argue that: 'In the future exercise of its penal jurisdiction the House should follow the general rule that it should be exercised (a) in any event as sparingly as possible and (b) only when the House is satisfied that to exercise it is essential in order to provide reasonable protection for the House, its Members or officers, from such improper obstruction ... as is causing, or is likely to cause, substantial interference with their respective functions.'

(viii) *Discipline in the Governing Party.* Procedure has to be seen, as we have said, in a wide and ultimately political context. Therefore, quite as important as many of the strictly procedural reforms has been the greater easing of discipline within the Parliamentary Labour

Party than in the Attlee administration. Amid trials and tribulations, mistakes and provocations from high as well as from the depths, Crossman and Silkin, while Leader of the House and Chief Whip, went far to establish a new style of 'firm but tolerant' leadership which has allowed far more open opposition from within the governing party itself. The dropping of the proposed Industrial Relations Bill in 1969 and of the Parliament (No. 2) Bill showed the strength of the backbenchers and, for once, of the Parliamentary Labour Party, particularly when its chairman read the balance and intensity of opinion somewhat differently from the Prime Minister. And Mr Douglas Houghton has claimed that a new, or greatly revived and expanded, pattern of consultation between the Government and its backbenchers has emerged in the last two years, born of political necessity but admirably conformable with reason.[24]

(ix) *Lords Reform.* The great frustration? A sensible and extremely well presented compromise, agreed by both front-benches, thrown out by a strange alliance of those who thought it went too far and those who thought it stopped too short of the knife. But if the dropping of the Bill, to clear the decks for the Industrial Relations Bill, also withdrawn, was either a first-class piece of mis-management by the Government or a rather second-class vindication of the power of the backbenches, depending on how one chooses to look at it, the logic of the White Paper and the Bill can hardly be avoided whenever the matter comes up again: a nominated chamber still but with a not-too-gradual weeding out of hereditary right; and with a strong and independent committee to review the kind of nominations made.[25] And one most important note for the future was struck in Appendix II of the White Paper on 'Possible Changes in Functions and Procedure': 'The proposed reform of the composition and powers of the House of Lords would open the way to a review of the functions and procedure of the two Houses of Parliament.'

(x) *The Finance Bill.* The 'Mumbo-Jumbo' has been taken out of Supply procedure for the voting of money and the Supply days are now in effect 29 Opposition Days which can be scattered more widely throughout the Session, taken in half-days even and, of considerable importance, subjects can be raised at forty-eight hours' notice – a formidable potential increase in the topicality of major debates in the House. As for the Finance Bill itself, it was eventually decided, after successive Procedure Committees had almost despaired of the Government and the House ever making up their minds,[26] that the committee stage should be taken upstairs rather than on the Floor. In the memorable committee stage of 1967–68 the Opposition made its dislike effective, proving by deliberate obstruction that it is politically impossible to thrust on the House major changes in procedure with which substantial numbers of Members simply will not co-operate. So in 1968–69 a compromise was struck which shows signs of sticking: that the Bulk of the Bill goes upstairs, but that the Opposition select two or three juicy issues and can hold the floor on them for three days. The Government gets its business through more quickly, the House is less cluttered with detail, but the Opposition get the best lines and the largest audience – which is about as it should be.[27]

(xi) *Streamlining the Legislative Process.* The phrase was Mr Crossman's and this streamlining was supposed to be part of the famous 'package deal' of 1967 by which the House allowed the Government to get major legislation through with greater speed and control of the time-table in return for some concessions to the Opposition in particular and Private Members in general. Its main features were a simplification of the stages of most Bills – the Third Reading is now ordinarily taken without debate (S.O. 55, 14 Nov. 1967), some Bills can now be taken in committee for their Second Reading (S.O. 60, 14 Nov. 1967) and even on Report (S.O. 62, 14 Nov. 1967). Also the Guillotine can now be put after only two hours' debate. And, of course, the new arrangements for the Finance Bill. One part of the alleged streamlining broke down completely – morning sessions. These had been authorized in December 1966[28] but were soon abandoned since they provoked determined obstruction from the Opposition and had little support from the Government's backbenchers. All that was left was a provision to suspend debates until the following morning if the 'midnight hags' attempted to ride too often – which has been useful and apparently successful.[29] The concessions for this streamlining were, specifically, the changing of S.O. No. 9 to allow more urgent and topical debates,[30] the widening of the Statutory Instruments Committee's terms of reference, and the granting of half-days and motions at forty-eight hours' notice for Supply (now Opposition) Days; and, more generally, a noticeably more relaxed attitude by the business managers of the House towards Private Members' rights – so as not to put the new arrangements under strain.[31] But procedure on legislation is still a patch-work quilt with remarkably little shape or pattern. No such conceptual breakthrough has been made as, even on the level of reports if not of implementation, appears to be the case for financial control. The House is still hypnotized by legislation actually before it, and spends far too much time on Bills that are going to pass anyway, but too little time (and what time there is, far too haphazardly) on the 'pre-legislative' stage of legislation and on subsequent detailed and systematic scrutiny of what happens to the law-as-voted-upon when it becomes the law-as-acted-upon – or not, as the case may be.

(xii) *Estimates and Public Expenditure.* Most radical of all have been proposals by the Procedure Committee to gain greater 'control' or influence over public expenditure by devising procedure to look at public expenditure as a whole – not just of individual services on an unreal year to year basis, but the implications of each authorization for future expenditure over several years, and also whether it is giving value for money or proving cost-effective. The committee made two main recommendations: (1) That the proposed new annual White Paper on Expenditure should be the occasion of a major debate on the Floor, and that it should both furnish detailed reasons for variations in estimates and make a five-year projection, based on the first three years for which the Government will have taken decisions, of the whole pattern of public expenditure and income.[32] (2) That the Estimates Committee should be reconstituted as the Select Committee on Expenditure. It would then divide into eight sub-committees each specializing in a broad field in such a way as to cover all activities of government and the nationalized industries and public corporations. Each of these sub-committees would have a three-fold task:

(a) It should, first, study the expenditure projections for the Department or Departments in its field, compare them with those of previous years, and report on any major variations or important changes of policy and on the progress made by the Departments towards clarifying their general objectives and priorities. (b) It should examine in as much detail as possible the implications in terms of public expenditure of the policy objectives chosen by Ministers and assess the success of Departments in attaining them. (c) It should enquire, on the lines of the present Estimates Sub-Committees, into Departmental administration, including effectiveness of management.[33]

In other words, that the House should shift from its attempts at querying changes in Estimates, on the one hand, and piece-meal and sporadic investigations of particular subjects, on the other, into attempting to discover the assumptions on which policies and economic projections are made; and generally to see financial control as concerned with the whole efficiency of a department, with getting value for money, in relation to the policies of a department. And the committee's proposals would involve winding up the ad hoc new specialized committees, but putting all hands and extra staff into a greatly expanded and specialized Estimates or Expenditure Committee.[34] For once it is not misleading to report good intentions as progress: to establish the correct concepts is more than half the battle. For the first time a senior committee of the House has grasped fully the indissoluble link between public administration and public finance (not helped by the almost complete divorce of these two activities when taught as subjects in the academic syllabuses and textbooks).

If one thinks, as I do, that the whole parliamentary reform movement of the last six years has been concerned simply to match the new machinery of the executive with new machinery in Parliament, the responses have been piece-meal and opportunistic, assessable and even mildly heartening in quantity rather than in quality, until this last report of the Procedure Committee. But this last report attempts to match qualitatively the stress on accountable-management and cost-efficiency analysis that runs all through the Plowden Report on Control of Public Expenditure and the Fulton Report. The new Estimates sub-committee would be equipped to follow these developments, to scrutinize them intelligently, even to stimulate them further. At last it has been seen that financial control is meaningless in terms of book-keeping and pounds, shillings and pence unless it can comprehend and control the efficiency or inefficiency of the management of resources. Expenditure is a function of management. The only doubt, however, is that beyond management there is still policy. In government, management is ultimately a function of policy; what different patterns of expenditure can be created and rendered more compatible, self and mutually sustaining; but also, far beyond and above that, what patterns of priorities *should* be instituted? Political ends need better technical means, and Whitehall is now reaching and Westminster could reach far in those directions; but techniques do not determine ends, or if they do then 'we', in any possible sense (politicians, voters or simply mankind) have lost control indeed or, more likely, cannot understand the unconscious assumptions and moral goals on which we are in fact basing our techniques.

WHAT STILL NEEDS TO BE DONE?

To be brief and not to repeat what is elsewhere.[35] Oh like Bentham that one could go on for ever plagiarizing oneself in ever new words, sometimes jargon and sometimes sprightly, all as if newly invented!

Parliament should not and does not threaten the ability of a Government to govern. But it still needs, in the most general terms, to make sure that more and more of that government is 'opened up' to the light of publicity and that controversies can take place at a time early enough to affect a Government's thinking, not when matters are cut and dried into the Bill as printed for the First Reading or the

Order in Council or other Statutory Instrument. This should be done, briefly, for three reasons: because it ought to be done as a matter of principle (democracy has far more to do with openness, communication and publicity than it has to do with direct participation);[36] because it is likely to prove educative to the public if it is so done; and because if so done it is likely (or more likely than any other way) both to mobilize more energy and support behind the Government's economic policies and to stop a Government in time before it attempts the impossible in terms of public opinion or expert support. The functions of Parliament in 'mobilizing consent' (in Professor Samuel Beer's phrase) and in 'mirroring opinion' (John Stuart Mill's) are equally important and are a fully complementary relationship. Where major Bills have had to be withdrawn, as in the salutary lesson of Lords reform and industrial relations in 1969, it has been precisely because of a double failure of the Government to build up support in public opinion first and among its own backbenchers – themselves usually the best missionaries.

Perhaps we can now begin to apply, in this light, Mr Crossman's three tests[37] quoted at the head of this essay: the efficiency of the legislative process, the effectiveness of the House in airing great issues topically, and the quality of its defence of the individual against the bureaucracy. And to see them in the light of four likely tendencies of future development. I see as overwhelmingly likely that (i) the House of Commons will spend less time in consideration of legislation already before the House (which is going to pass anyway, by virtue of parties fighting elections with programmes) and more time in looking at the before and after of legislation thus narrowly conceived: it will both 'get into the act earlier' and stay with it longer. (ii) The House will create more facilities to enable individual MPs and committees to participate in these processes more fully and to be more fully informed – a general increase in staff, particularly in the Research division of the Library, but also a general application of Fulton doctrines on the Clerks' side too. (iii) The eventual reform of the House of Lords will lead to a rationalization of functions between it and the Commons, so that it will develop more into an Upper Chamber of committees to the Commons, a House of Scrutiny which will do those things which the busy Commons leave undone rather than to presume to censure those things which it ought not to have done. And (iv) the way of working of Parliament will be profoundly affected by both the opening-up and the greater degree of professionalism in the new Civil Service and by the increasing degree of occupational mobility in British professional life as a whole – there will be more people around with experience of different sectors of the economy and the national life as a whole, and this will help to take away the mystery from each: the precise political effect will be more resignations among senior MPs and Ministers and fewer slavishly loyal and over-reliable hangers-on.

These things will emerge as a consequence both of decisions already taken in the narrow field of parliamentary procedure and of changes more basic by far in British society, particularly in the social structure and educational experience of the professions. But how well will they work is quite another matter. Here certain things need to be done or to be seen correctly which are by no means as highly probable.

The Legislative Process. It may seem odd to say, but the primacy of the political needs to be asserted if we are not to turn into an unreflective technocracy only concerned with identifying trends and delaying them or accelerating them. Consider again the Procedure Committee's excellent report on 'the Scrutiny of Public Expenditure and Administration'. It moves the House forward into the post-Fulton world of accountable management. But, as we have said, the management function cannot provide goals any more than the accountancy function can, and if the goals are wrong or self-contradictory, neither the economy nor the quality of life can be rewarding. To come down to brass tacks: would the proposed net-work of sub-committees of the Expenditure Committee sweep away the existing and hard-won specialized committees? Their report leaves this profoundly unclear. Several of these committees have, quite apart from financial control, raised issues of policy, not always but often, well. This should not be lost. Policy cannot simply be reduced to cost-effectiveness. Cost effectiveness of what and for what? The House must do both tasks: scrutinize the real effectiveness of the administration and question the assumptions behind its policies, but also float new policies, form an alternative source of policy advice and influence to ... one wonders what even to name? Both tasks need doing. If the objection is numbers, the answer is simple: the kind of things the Procedure Committee wishes a new Expenditure Committee to do can be done, in the sub-committees, by very few people indeed *if* they have sufficient clerical, administrative and expert help. But select committees like the Race Relations Committee and the Education Committee need more members, adequately to mirror sections of opinion within the House, because they are – and should be – dabbling in policy.

The Sixth Report of the Procedure Committee for 1966–67, on Public Bill Procedure, needs to be kept in mind: their argument for pre-legislative committees. The danger of this is, of course, that it would simply add another stage: the pretence of consultation at 'an early stage' can be more galling than the cut and dried commands. The idea is right, but the means are far less likely to be yet new committees, than the uncovering of areas of administration or public concern which need new legislation or amendments to statutes as a result of increased select committee activity. The House will get in first by getting in first, helping to create the climate of opinion which makes legislation appear necessary – not by asking to be told a little earlier what the Government intends to do. There may be a case for both, but the latter without the former would be a Pyrrhic victory.

The traditional concept of control of legislation is that the House is primarily concerned only with the stages of a Bill before it, but this concept is really relevant only to those Bills which emerge directly from the party programmes. But there are at least two other major sources of legislation: inconsistencies and contradictions between previous laws discovered in administrative practice, or else quite simply the lack of powers to carry out already agreed public policy or the plain public interest; and the need to react to unexpected events. The committees of the House are wise to keep clear of the first, but with the other two they should reach a point where they discover the administrative problems at about the same time as the department does (if all functions were covered by permanent and specialized committees), and can speedily hold inquiries into the nature of unexpected events which affect the public interest.

In general on legislation I cannot do better than to quote the words of my colleague, Mr Stuart Walkland:

> The legislative process in Britain is first and foremost an executive process, and this it will, and should, remain. Parliament has many virtues and many capacities, particularly those associated with a wide and varied membership, an ability to reflect electoral fears and wishes, and to represent to a government 'the state of the nation'. Its capacity for detailed work of a specialist kind is, however, necessarily limited by the capacity and experience of its members; it is far greater than most Ministers and civil servants would credit it with, and rather less than some parliamentary reformers wish to believe. But policy needs to be developed and legitimized by the activity of an informed and representative assembly. To advocate changes that would ensure this is not to advocate parliamentary dominance of what is and should be an executive function. It is, however, an attempt to add a realistic and powerful political dimension to the work of government. That is what Parliament exists for; that is what it often finds difficult to do at present.[38]

We are getting nearer the time when backbench MPs will realize that what is actually in the Bill as it advances to the Second Reading, whether upstairs, downstairs or in my lady's chamber, can often be very much a product of the degree of scrutiny that a department has been subject to and to the evaluation that has been put, by both Westminster and Whitehall, on how the previous legislation in the particular field worked out in practice.

Airing the Great Matters. Again, no wish to underestimate the importance of procedure – providing more time for Opposition Days, adjournment debates and emergency debates etcetera; but these must be seen in the whole context of communications. No one has even begun to study the actual effectiveness of Parliament as a communicating device with the public, nor yet how well the Press does this part of its job. The working of the lobby and lobby correspondents are, unfortunately, arcane if fascinating trivialities compared with gaining a better knowledge of how much opinion filters up, and how much filters down. Two things are fairly clear: that the House still has many absurd restrictions on the working of journalists, but also that few, if any, papers have staff remotely large enough to cover properly and to digest adequately either parliamentary proceedings or parliamentary and government publications. The Press is very touchy on this score. The meanness of proprietors goes hand-in-glove with an ingrained and rather charming old-fashioned amateurism in the style of operation of most political and lobby correspondents.

Debates are vitally important, but they are only one part of a total flow of information – a flow so great that it threatens at times to defeat its own objects and to drown us in milk and honey. Digesting becomes of vital importance. And still more so journals or periodicals of record – which would simply record what has been done in Westminster and Whitehall, knowledge which otherwise vanishes in the day to day reporting and the worship of the great Moloch, 'Instant News'. As many people feel that the future of the Press, if it is to resist television as news, lies in developing better features and background material, so the effectiveness of Parliament in the future may lie less in picking out and sharpening 'great debates', but in continuing to develop – and to release to others, above all to journalists – digests of what has happened over reasonably long periods of time. If the Library of the House of Commons moves this way, there is no real reason – and there would be much public benefit – why it should not ultimately become a centre of service not merely to Members, but to journalists and academics as well: part always, of course, for the urgent needs of Members; but a new and larger part as a centre that studied and disseminated information about what has happened in

Parliament to all who need to know. It is an odd thought that 'the Mother of Parliaments' has no publication like *The Congressional Quarterly* – and a still odder thought that few readers will know what I am talking about. Look and see. Trivial or academic? I think not. The character of any organization is much affected by reading well-informed and intelligently critical accounts of what it has been doing – far more so than by the always expected, hence always discountable, brick-bats, laurel wreaths and ordinary wreaths of the daily press.

Individual Rights. Again the importance of the House cannot be underestimated. But alone it is not enough. It is beginning, ever so slowly, to sink in that even Parliament plus Parliamentary Commissioner and our good old courts still leave some odd gaps. It is now over forty years since William Robson published his *Justice and Administrative Law*. Rumours are rife, among a few, that Ministers have actually asked for and read papers arguing the case for a new administrative jurisdiction, and that some civil servants now have a fairly clear idea that countries can be governed which have a Conseil d'État.[39] Again, this idea is not opposed to the growth of specialized committees, but rather complements it; and perhaps a direction in which a section, at least, of a reformed and de-politicized Upper Chamber might move.

Above all, however, a point not covered in Mr Crossman's three tests: the degree to which Parliament is the centre of our national life. After all these criticisms, I hold to a somewhat old-fashioned but true view of things: that as much as one needs to specialize and distinguish, something has to pull all threads together and look at all things that affect each other as part of one system. And in our national life that is Parliament. Ultimately knowledge and information, to be used as well as gained, depend upon the contact of acting and thinking men in different fields, professions, vocations – classes and regions even. Anything that is important, and anyone who has anything to say that is important, should somehow pass before or through Parliament at some time.[40] MPs can sometimes be as strangely isolated on an island as can civil servants in a ministry or the management or workers of a great industry – not to mention Fleet Street, despite its pride to the contrary. This is the ultimate point and test of select committee procedure and 'opening up' the civil service; that all those who have problems in common should meet, and that meeting place is Parliament. When people of real or believed importance think that Parliament can be by-passed, be they Ministers, industrialists, trade union leaders, it is up to Parliament to prove that they are wrong. The power of Parliament was never great, so cannot be restored; but its authority influence and prestige was once greater, and should be greater again – but in a very different manner.

NOTES

1. See Malcolm Joel Barnett, *The Politics of Legislation: the Rent Act 1957* (London 1969) for a rare case-study which shows how an important change of law intended to achieve certain precise targets of decontrol, drew these targets from ministerial speeches based on no real feasibility studies; and how, stuck with these targets, the Ministry made no attempt to predict the consequences of varying levels of decontrol. Such things never happen now, of course.

2. As I argue at length in Chapter 11, 'Parliament and the Matter of Britain', of my *The Reform of Parliament* (2nd edn, London 1968).

3. Ronald Butt, *The Power of Parliament* (London 1967), p. 2.

4. I do not imply that nothing happened under the Conservative Government. If the Report of the Select Committee on Procedure, 1959 was largely ignored, the debate began and the Procedure Committee was established as a hardy annual in April 1962 – though mostly dealing with small things. Selwyn Lloyd was the most forthcoming Chancellor of recent years, starting the White Papers on Public Investment and on Government Lending to Public Bodies, and Maudling published the first 'forward look' on public expenditure in 1963. Many Conservatives, like Selwyn Lloyd, became highly interested in Parliamentary reform, like Airey Neave's *Change or Decay* (London 1963) group of MPs. But by then political change was in the air.

5. John P. Mackintosh, 'Dwindling Hopes of Commons Reforms', *The Times*, 13 March 1969.

6. 'Scrutiny of Public Expenditure and Administration': First Report from the Select Committee on Procedure, 1968–69, H.C. 410, published in July.

7. A very useful more detailed and deliberately less interpretative account of the former is Clifford Boulton's 'Recent Developments in House of Commons Procedure', *Parliamentary Affairs*, Winter 1970, pp. 61–71.

8. See my *Reform of Parliament*, pp. 62–6 for an account of the disputes about money.

9. 'Services and Facilities for Members'. Sixth Report from the Select Committee on House of Commons (Services), 1968–69. H.C. 374.

10. The kind of thing they are up against can be seen by the following paragraph from their Report:

'14. Your Committee recommend two other small concessions which have been agreed to by the Treasury [i.e. that's as far as the Treasury would go]. These are: (i) That Members should be allowed a free supply of stationery up to the value of £25 instead of £20. (ii) That Members should be entitled to a free supply of 100 file pockets for their filing-cabinets instead of the existing 25.'

Quis custodiet custodes?, indeed. While as a tax-payer I am, of course, delighted at such strict Treasury control of the watchdogs themselves, yet as a man of average common sense I find it hard to believe that without such tight restrictions MPs would start to use official stationery on a vast scale for commercial, literary, social or amatory purposes, or would start selling file pockets for filing cabinets.

11. Strange to relate there is no clear and definitive account of what facilities MPs can use and are entitled to in all aspects of their work; a sub-committee of the Study of Parliament Group hopes shortly to remedy this odd omission.

12. As well as G. F. Lock, 'The Role of the Library with a note on official publications' in *The Commons in Transition*, ed. A. H. Hanson and Bernard Crick (London 1970), pp. 130–151, see David Menhennet, 'The Library of the House of Commons', *Political Quarterly*, July–Sept. 1965, and David Menhennet and J. B. Poole, 'The Information Services of the Commons Library', *New Scientist*, 7 Sept. 1967.

13. See J. B. Poole, 'Information Services for the Commons: A Computer Experiment', *Parliamentary Affairs*, Spring 1969, which described the Library's role in the experimental *Current Literature Bulletin* sponsored by the Office for Scientific and Technical Information (O.S.T.I.) – aimed at extending to civil servants, Local Government officers, libraries and social scientists bibliographical references already available to MPs.

Also see Antony Barker and Michael Rush, *The MP and His Information* (London 1970), the result of research jointly sponsored by Political and Economic Planning (PEP) and the Study of Parliament Group.

14. For which Mr Louis Blom-Cooper may first claim credit, in an article in the *Observer* of 31 May 1959, which newspaper then kept up the advocacy and discussion on many occasions – notably 7 June 1959; 10 and 31 January and 11 December 1960, and 12 June 1961. Other notable blows were *The Citizen and the Administration*, the unofficial report published by the lawyers' organization, Justice (usually known as the 'Whyatt Report'); John Griffith, 'The Council and the Chalk Pit Case', *Public Administration*, Winter 1961, and the three articles he published and his own editorial in *Public Law*, Spring 1962; and Geoffrey Marshall's influential, 'Should Britain Have an Ombudsman?', *The Times*, 23 April 1963.

15. See *Guardian* report under Home News, 6 Dec. 1965.

16. Their remit is 'to review policies but not individual cases in relation to – (a) the operation of the Race Relations Act 1968 with particular reference to the work of the Race Relations Board and the Community Relations Commission, and (b) the admission into the United Kingdom of Commonwealth citizens and foreign nationals for settlement'.

Their first report was on 'The Problems of Coloured School Leavers' 1968–69, II.C. 413 – thus playing themselves in gently, avoiding for the beginning the most contentious issues, but a report, none the less, of first class importance and at the heart of the matter of race relations.

17. And I was the first – and very lonely – member of the public, other than officials and journalists, to attend.

18. Select Committee on Nationalized Industries, Special Report, 1967–68, H.C. 298, proposed to widen their scope to cover the Bank of England, British Petroleum, Cable and Wireless, the Independent Television Authority and some smaller bodies. It was reappointed only in February of the following Session with terms of reference allowing them to look at I.T.A., Cable and Wireless, and activities of the Bank *other than* monetary policy, management of the money market and exchange control etc. – Hamlet without the King and the Queen at least. (See H.C. Debates, 777, cols. 1181–1274, 11 Feb. 1969).

19. See Early Day Motion 81, 1968–69, tabled in December 1968 by Mr Ian Mikardo and others protesting at the delay in setting up the committee.

20. Select Committee on Estimates, First Special Report, 1965–66. H.C. 21.

21. Select Committee on Estimates, First Special Report, 1967–68. H.C. 28.

22. See below, (xii) *Estimates and Public Expenditure.*

23. Report from the Select Committee on Parliamentary Privilege, 1967–68. H.C. 34.

24. See Douglas Houghton, 'The Labour Back-Bencher', *Political Quarterly*, Oct.–Dec. 1969, pp. 454–63.

25. House of Lords Reform. Cmnd. 3799.

26. The Select Committee on Procedure's Fourth Report, 1966–67, H.C. 283, had set out all possible alternatives and told the House to make up its mind.

27. Although some backbenchers with specialized or particular constituency points now count themselves losers that they cannot bring them to a standing committee which has more time than the Floor.

28. See the motion moved and the debate, H.C. Debates, 738, 14 Dec. 1966, cols. 70–610.

29. See Sessional Order of 12 Dec. 1967 and S.O. of 12 Nov. 1968.

30. Select Committee on Procedure, Second Report, 1966–67. H.C. 282. This could become important and perhaps deserves singling out. For about five debates a Session of this kind have taken place since all the old precedents were swept away and the Speaker given complete discretion. They take place the day after being raised and at 3.30 p.m. – hence they get great publicity.

31. Mr Douglas Houghton has recently argued that backbench pressure 'has persuaded the Labour Government to end the hypocrisies and the frustrations of the traditional procedure on Private Members' Bills'. With some obvious pride and justification he points to the number of important Bills on moral issues which have passed in recent Sessions – the Government no longer allowing any small group of Members to filibuster them out of existence. See his 'The Labour Back-Bencher', *Political Quarterly*, Oct.–Dec. 1969, pp. 454–63.

32. Which proposals were foreshadowed in Michael Ryle's 'Parliamentary Control of Expenditure and Taxation', *Political Quarterly*, Oct.–Dec. 1967. But Ryle put the case for a new Economic Affairs Committee to prepare the ground and to look in detail at the assumptions made in such projections. To follow his argument would suggest that the proposed new committee structure might have too many disparate tasks foisted upon it.

33. First Report from the Select Committee on Procedure, 1968–69, 'Scrutiny of Public Expenditure and Administration'. H.C. 410.

34. As was generally argued for in the Study of Parliament Group's evidence to the Select Committee on Procedure of 1964–65, republished in *Reforming the Commons*, the Oct. 1965 issue of P.E.P.'s serial, *Planning.*

35. See Chapters 10 and 11 of my *Reform of Parliament.*

36. See my ' "Them and Us": Public Impotence and Government Power', being the University of Nottingham's Gaitskell Memorial Lecture for 1967, *Public Law*, Spring 1968.

37. Just to pause to say, 'Damn all those authors and MPs who deliberately or in unguarded moments talk (*o mea culpa!*) about "*the* function of Parliament", and then worry, as does Mr Michael Foot, for instance, that "the vital function of debate" gets neglected if everyone runs to earth in committees. Parliament does and should fulfil many functions and, with all those MPs can give a fair crack of the whip to them all if it thinks in relative and proportional, rather than absolute, terms.'

38. S. A. Walkland, *The Legislative Process in Great Britain* (London 1968), pp. 103–4.

39. See especially J. D. B. Mitchell, 'Administrative Law and Parliamentary Control', *Political Quarterly*, Oct.–Dec. 1967 (pp. 360–374).
40. But this is not to imply that Parliament need be in one place all the time. I see no overwhelming reason against, and much advantage for, those aspects of parliamentary control which affect Scotland and Wales, particularly or peculiarly, being exercised in Scotland and Wales. The devolution of Parliament is a more realistic speculation than the setting up of new parliaments.

The Rt Hon. Michael Stewart, CH, MP

The Power of Parliament

It is fashionable today to talk of the decline of Parliament and to suggest that it is undignified, ineffective and ill-informed, and to argue that the real power of decision lies elsewhere. But was this ever unfashionable? Dickens, once a parliamentary correspondent, called its proceedings 'theatricals', and the MPs who appear in his novels are stuffed shirts. Thomas Hughes called it, contemptuously, the 'Palaver' and represented it as a snobbish club. Bernard Shaw's contempt was unbounded ('The British people have always elected a Parliament of lunatics'). Even the gentler Tawney was once heard to describe it as a 'damned monkey-house'. All these were men who passionately desired reforms, the virtue of which is now universally admitted; the reforms were brought about by legislation passed by Parliament. No reform, however, is so virtuous that it does not excite hostile prejudices or give, to some groups, legitimate anxieties about their livelihoods. It is in Parliament that the reformer's zeal meets its enemies and critics, and the patient engineering has to be performed which will produce as much reform as can be made acceptable to the public opinion of the day. This is a laborious process, and the reformer, exasperated by the complexities of Parliamentary procedure, projects upon Parliament the resentment he rightly feels against those who, for more or less creditable reasons, oppose his reform.

There is a further reason why publicists, whether of press, radio or television, resent Parliament. People in this position like to feel that they sway opinion, and, through opinion, the course of events. 'The Times', wrote Bagehot, 'has unmade many Ministries.' Would he say so today? It is naturally vexatious to those who thus seek to influence affairs to find that what really happens will in the end be determined at Westminster, and that the individual MP, though concerned about press comment, is quite prepared to resist it.

Events in the present and the last Parliament have made it plain enough where lies the final repository of power. If, as now seems

Reprinted from *Contemporary Review*, vol. 220, no. 1275 (April 1972), pp. 174–78. By permission of the author and the publisher.

well-nigh certain, Britain enters the EEC, it will be because on October 28 1971, and subsequent occasions, individual MPs weighed the matter up and cast their votes this way or that according to their judgement, the majority being in favour. In the last Parliament, the British Government was under great pressure from many quarters, with very different motives, to prevent the Nigerian Government from buying arms in Britain to combat Ojukwu's rebellion. The matter was often debated in Parliament, and the argument cut across parties, but on every occasion Parliament supported the Government's policy. Without that support the policy could not have been continued; equipped with that support the Government could resist its critics. Conversely, the failure of the Labour Government to pass its Industrial Relations Bill and its plan for reform of the House of Lords was due to lack of Parliamentary support. The Conservative Opposition refused to support either of these measures, and the defection of a number of Labour MPs was sufficient to ensure their defeat.

It would be absurd to suggest that outside influences have no effect. The original proposal in the London Government Act to cut the London County Council's education services into twelve pieces was defeated by a combination of party opposition and an uprising of London parents. The essential point, however, is that all propaganda – meetings, press articles, television programmes – fails of its purpose unless it can influence votes in the House of Commons. Perhaps one should add, Commons or Lords; for it was the Lords, acting in one of the few fields where their powers are still comparable to those of the Commons, who prevented the establishment of the international airport at Stansted.

The critic may reply that all this is but a truism. Admitted that we are ruled by the law, and that the consent of MPs is necessary to the making of law: but are they in fact free to give or withhold their consent, or are they the creatures of someone or something else? The Royal Assent is necessary to the making of a law; but the monarch is not free to give or refuse it at will. Is the power of Parliament no more than this? This seems to be Richard Crossman's argument. He takes the distinction which Bagehot drew between the 'dignified' parts of government (e.g. the Crown) and the parts which really did the work; following-up this distinction, Crossman argues that Parliament is now no more than one of the 'dignified' parts of the apparatus.

If this argument is sound, it must mean that MPs are either subject to outside constraints which they cannot resist, or that they lack the will or the knowledge to make decisions of their own. Who, if this be true, does decide? We have to examine the various answers given to this question.

Shaw found the answer in Big Business. 'I am the government of your country,' says the armaments manufacturer, Undershaft, in *Major Barbara*. Time has put this contention on the shelf. It is true that leading industrialists, and Trade Union leaders, influence governments. Yet compare any statement of aspirations by the CBI or by the TUC with what actually happens and it will be apparent that a third, and independent, force is at work; and this force is Parliament, knowing that it has to answer to the whole people and judging for itself how the gratification of sectional interests can be accommodated to the general welfare and the state of public opinion. If 'Big Business' really had its way, the Welfare State would become a wraith, and Ian Smith's Rhodesia would have been approved at once, before even Sir Alec Douglas-Home could have enunciated his Five Principles for a settlement. Powerful groupings will always press their claims; but it does not lie with them to decide how much of their own way they will get.

Can this contention be maintained in the light of the recent victory – for it would be mealy-mouthed to call it anything else – by the National Union of Mineworkers? I believe it can. At first, the Government was resolved on a straightforward confrontation with the NUM: but they were careful not to embroil Parliament. On those occasions when the matter was raised in the House it was apparent that one side was entirely opposed to the Government and that many of the other side were deeply unhappy. In face of this situation, the Government appointed Lord Wilberforce and, with his help, extricated themselves from an impossible situation. The miners won because a decisive majority of the community thought they were right; and this feeling reflected itself in Parliament. If on some future occasion a trade union or professional organization, or group of business men, chose to assert a sectional interest, they could not hope for victory unless they could be certain of the same degree of public and Parliamentary support as the miners enjoyed on this occasion. A Government which can rely on Parliament to provide it with all the necessary powers to meet an emergency can stand and resist; without that support it must come to terms.

A more recent answer is that the Government, with the help of the Whips, really bosses Parliament and that the individual MP must toe the Party line. Most of the time he does vote for the Party line, but this is because most of the time he believes in it. The test will be, how does he behave on the few occasions when he does not? The answer, from experience, appears to be that on very great matters he will use his own judgement, as many MPs on both sides have done over entry into Europe: on lesser matters he will usually agree with the Whips that he ought not to endanger the survival of a Government with which, in general, he agrees. The late Sir Beverley Baxter, a Conservative MP strongly opposed to commercial television, was reproached for being about to vote in favour of it at the request of the Whips. He replied, straightforwardly, 'I think commercial television is bad; I think a Labour Government would be worse.'

This reply illustrates the power of the Government to present its supporters with a package-deal of policy. The Government must take care that the package as a whole is attractive to a majority of the Commons: this is the tribute the Government must pay to Parliament's supremacy. The MP must, with a few exceptions, take or reject the package as a whole; that is the tribute Parliament must pay to the Government's leadership.

At this point we must examine more closely what kind of creature is this Parliament whose power we are discussing. Unlike the Congress of the USA it is not merely a legislature. It is the body which contains the members of the Government, the body from which members of the Government are drawn and the body which can, in the last resort, sack the Government. The pivot of our constitution is the nexus of the Government and its supporters in Parliament. If this tie is seriously weakened the Government is in peril and a General Election is at hand, so that the nexus can be re-created. This is why the lawyers tell us that we should not say 'Parliament' but 'the Queen in Parliament' – that is to say the executive working in, through and with the ultimate consent of the legislature. The Government and its supporters are different persons, but must be thought of as composing a whole. As Saint Athanasius might have put it, we must think rightly of this matter, neither confusing the persons nor dividing the substance. If we can think thus, we see that Parliament, rightly interpreted as the Queen in Parliament, is the effective sovereign.

A more sophisticated contention is that although MPs try hard they cannot have, in our complex society, the necessary knowledge to form independent judgement. Richard Crossman supports this with the striking statement that the senior members of the Attlee Government concealed from the Cabinet as a whole and from Parliament the fact that they had authorized the construction of atom bombs. It is a statement that has often been made, and it is entirely untrue. This decision was recorded in Cabinet minutes and made known to Parliament in answer to a question. It is surprising that it did not evoke comment at the time; but the charge of concealment will not stand. The fact is that MPs are deluged with information – books blue and red, papers white and green; their real problem is to find their way through it. The MP finds that he can only do this by specializing in a few subjects and has to give time to reading about them rather than listening to debates on other, perhaps more exciting, topics. This is why, except on great occasions, debates in the House are becoming more well-informed and less well-attended.

The limited staff of the Commons library do their valiant best to help MPs amid the jungle of documents; but there is still need for a real Parliamentary research staff at the service of all MPs.

There remains a cruder attack on Parliament. This is to say that the Members are, in the main, second-raters; that powerful Trade Unions and businesses will want people in the House to express their views, but do not wish to spare their ablest people for this purpose; and that the resultant assembly can easily be dominated by the few people of real ability who are there. It is difficult for someone who is himself a Member to give an impartial account of the qualities of himself and his colleagues, but some comments may be made in answer to this charge. The first thing that those who make this charge should do is to read Hansard – all the more necessary since press reports of debates are, in comparison with the past, skimpy. They will find the occasional episodes of rowdyism and obstruction, but beyond that they will find a high level of informed argument. Nor should the rowdyism and obstruction be set wholly on the debit side of the ledger. Parliament is not a debating society: it can determine what will happen about issues on which people are deeply and sincerely divided: an assembly which did this in an atmosphere of unbroken decorum would not be human. We find, moreover, from the lists of applicants to local party organizations, that there is no lack of able people of all kinds who want to get into Parliament. Indeed, some of our critics in the press are people who have tried to get in, and failed. One recalls, from *The Importance of Being Earnest*, Lady Bracknell's rebuke to her nephew: 'Never speak slightingly of society, Algernon, only people who cannot get into it do that.'

Will this sovereignty of Parliament be swept away by entry to the EEC? Surely not. A future British Government could if it wished and had the support of Parliament, announce its withdrawal from the Community – unwise as that would be. The final word, then, lies at Westminster. Meanwhile, it is true, Parliament will be creating an important form of 'subordinate legislation' – the decisions of the Community, to which force will be given in Britain by virtue of a British statute. Parliament has often done this kind of thing – it has, as it were, leased out its sovereignty to Ministers, corporations, etc.; but it has always – to change the metaphor – kept one end of the rope in its own hand. This time the rope is longer and the lease of power greater than before; but the end of the rope remains where it was.

It may well be that in time no member of the EEC will want to think of leaving, any more than we should wish, by Act of Parliament, to re-create the Heptarchy in England. The fact that we do not do so is not a limitation of sovereignty; it is a recognition of reality.

The European debates have thrown light on the relationship of the MP to his party, and help us to assess the claim that Parliament is a sham because MPs are the creatures of the party machine. There are, of course, some in whose eyes the MP is always wrong: if he follows the party line he is a stooge, if he deserts it he is disloyal: if he does what most of his constituents would like him to do he is a vote-catcher; if he disagrees with them he is arrogant. A study of the relation between MPs and their local parties and constituents over the European question may help us to a more balanced judgement. An MP will normally want to be in agreement with those who have in the past voted for him, and those who have worked to get him into Parliament, because they are people with whom he has a mutual relationship of trust and affection; what has been demonstrated recently is that this relationship will, in most instances, stand the strain of a particular disagreement. An MP wants to give loyal service to his party; he is not prepared to be enslaved to it.

The ancient structure of Queen-in-Parliament remains. It is surrounded, like a mediaeval King by his barons, by their modern equivalent – industrialists, trade unions, press, etc. It cannot govern in disregard of them, but it is more successful than many mediaeval Kings in remaining the final arbiter of what can and ought to be done. Into this ancient structure a democratic electorate and the political parties have injected the modern idea of popular sovereignty – not in the sense that the people give month-to-month instructions, but that the people in the end decide who shall be Members of Parliament. In speech and writing one can distinguish Government, Parliament and People: one cannot understand what is happening unless one perceives them as a whole, acting and reacting on each other. In this complex, it is Parliament's position as the central link which gives it its importance and explains its survival.

Part Four
Government and the Administration

Patrick Cosgrave

The Weakness of the Prime Minister

Issues in British politics nowadays have a way of appearing and disappearing. And this is disturbing, because it suggests a certain frivolity in the approach to politics of our most learned and informed critics. One of the most notable examples of this frivolity has been discussed in one way or another for some years now; and was, indeed, picked up again by the newspapers a week or so ago. It is the question of what kind of organization the Prime Minister – any Prime Minister – ought to have backing him up at No. 10 Downing Street. Should it be a super-charged personal secretariat? Should it be a special Department of State, responsible only to the Prime Minister himself? The frivolity lies in the endless discussion of means of providing the PM with machinery for overcoming the immense amount of inertia, most of it Civil-Service-generated – if generated is not too forceful a word to use in conjunction with inertia – without any suggested resolution to that discussion. Thus we see that our critics are both disturbed by the forces of inertia in British society; and perturbed by the danger of giving any Prime Minister too much capacity to overcome those forces. In the eager search for reformist compromise we lose radical direction.

So, too, in recent years we have heard a great deal about presidential government, as embodied in the office of Prime Minister; and we have debated whether or not it is true that the Prime Minister is becoming so powerful as to undermine our system of cabinet and parliamentary government. All this conveys our national awareness of something wrong at the very heart and centre of our politics; and it also suggests that we feel it too dangerous to do anything about that wrong. We feel that the centre does not function; and we fear that the steps we can take to make it function will imperil the fabric which the centre exists to serve. In this state of mingled fear and analysis we brood. The only refuge is in truth.

The truth is this. In the last decade we have seen an exaltation

Reprinted from *The Spectator* (2 September 1972), p. 357. By permission of the author and the publisher.

of the style of the Prime Ministership which does not correspond to any increase in prime ministerial power. The fact of the matter is that of all members of the Cabinet the Prime Minister is the weakest not the strongest. He is weakest because of that peculiarly British characteristic of government, the power of the negative. The strength of the Civil Service, of individual Departments of State, of the establishment itself, are all mobilized behind the desire to do nothing; or to do something only in frivolous and unimportant areas like the reform of censorship; or of laws about homosexuals; or of laws relating to what may be performed on the stage. On anything of real and fundamental importance, power is mobilized to do nothing.

And Prime Ministers dislike this. They do so because of their character. All Prime Ministers of this century have been initially men of radical bent. They have all seen that something must be done – usually something in the field of financial or economic re-organization – to re-structure and re-direct the national effort. But, though it is possible for a given Prime Minister to have his way on a given subject, even one of very great importance – as Mr Heath has had his way on the European Communities Bill – it has rarely been possible for any Prime Minister to exercise that broad, continuous and effective power over the government machine which alone can lead to the efficient and successful implementation of desired reforms. The only genuine exception to this was the wartime government of Churchill; here the combination of an exceptional secretariat, and an exceptional personal metabolism – and, of course, an exceptional situation – led to detailed and effective supervision over and stimulation of the national effort and the machinery of government alike. What other exceptions there have been are more apparent than real. Reforming governments like those of Asquith and Attlee had, initially, such wide support as to overcome inertia: they did so not so much through Prime Ministerial effort as through consensus for action. In the case of the Heath government, while much has been done that the Civil Service would have preferred left undone, in large areas – and notably the economic and industrial areas – policies have been reversed without trial, and the very consideration of a Prime Ministerial Department, however tentative that suggestion may be, demonstrates widespread unease in the ranks of the Prime Minister's closest associates about his effectiveness in gaining control over the gigantic apparatus which runs the modern state.

We must grasp, too, that a Cabinet cannot control or exercise its collective power over the bureaucracy. Eustace Percy once wrote of the First World War that, in 1916, the co-ordination of the war effort had been left to the Cabinet, which was the least effective body imaginable for that task. It is the function of the Cabinet, acting collectively, to support or oppose policies put before it; and, again collectively, to be responsible to Parliament for those policies. It is not the Cabinet's function actually to run the country: that is the job of individual ministers and departments, presided over in the executive field by the Prime Minister himself. We know that, as time passes, ministers tend to identify more with their departments, tend to come to represent more readily the departmental point of view. It is the Prime Minister's task, in part, to prevent this happening. Sometimes he discharges this task by means of reshuffles, for, though it is commonly supposed to be a good idea for ministers to stay in their departments for a long time, thus becoming experts on the department's work, in truth it might be said that a short tenure, during which a minister loses neither his edge nor his enthusiasm, is better for government, for party, and for country.

More often, in his day to day work, the Prime Minister chivvies and stimulates departments and ministers alike to get on with the task of implementing a party manifesto. One junior minister in the present government told me recently that nothing seemed to happen in his own section of a great Department of State unless the Prime Minister himself was known to be interested, and willing to put his shoulder to the wheel. And, while I was considering the toll this must take of any man, even one as physically fit and sensible about expenditure of energy as Edward Heath, a senior Minister told me he thought the Prime Minister's job impossible. It could not, he said, be done by any one man, however loyal and devoted his ministerial colleagues. The Prime Minister needed, this man believed, at least a very high-powered executive chief of staff, a political rather than a civil service figure, to assist him. We know, of course, that Mr Terry Pitt, of the Labour Party's research department, has long been convinced that the programme of a radical party can be implemented only if each minister is assisted by such a chief of staff: otherwise, Mr Pitt thinks, little or nothing will ever be done.

Labour Party commentators speak with particular authority on this subject because of the high hopes and daring schemes with which their party entered office in 1964; and the low spirits and chastened imaginations with which they left it in 1970. To be sure, some of the Labour failure was to be attributed to loss of nerve, incompetence, and lack of realism in the schemes of their manifesto. But something was also due to the resistance of the government machine to the plans of the democratically elected government. And while few of us would like to see the British Civil Service in any way politicized, the fact of the matter remains that, for the health of our democracy, it is far more important that governments should be able to get through those fundamental points of policy on which they are elected than that the Civil Service should be able to continue to run the country in the manner it thinks fit.

Nonetheless, it is clear that there are many gaps in this government's control over the administration of the country; and the continued existence of these gaps is largely to be put down to the weakness of the Prime Ministerial office. Whether in recent years the Prime Minister's ascendancy in Cabinet has or has not grown is very nearly an irrelevant question; his power certainly has not grown in relation to the machine of government. If anything it has declined, through the punishing routine of his office, which drains even the strongest men of energy and purpose. A method must therefore be found for making the Prime Minister's office more powerful in relation to the rest of the Civil Service, and the great departments in particular.

Brian C. Smith

Reform and Change in British Central Administration[*]

It is generally accepted that Britain is passing through a period of reform in its political and administrative institutions. Practically no government organization has escaped this phase, at least to the extent of being subject to critical scrutiny by specially selected advisory bodies in an atmosphere charged with assumptions about the desirability of externally induced changed. Administrative reform is perhaps the most important part of this, at any rate in terms of the resources which have been devoted to the reformist effort. This paper examines the source of such assumptions and the methods employed to bring about reform within the administrative sector of central government.

Reform in public administration obviously implies organizational change, but of a special kind. Although we tend to speak of 'reform' in the public sector and in particular in relation to the Civil Service, whereas administrative theorists tend to talk of 'change' in relation to private organizations, the two terms are by no means synonymous. Administration or organizational change can and does take place without reform. In fact administrative reform is a response to political decisions about certain kinds of organizational change in the public sector.

No organization is static and this is particularly true of British central administration. It is an error to present Civil Service organizations as still cast in the nineteenth-century Northcote–Trevelyan mould. The Service may not have been *reformed* since 1854 (and this is probably not true) but it has certainly changed. To confuse reform and change is to ignore that the former relates primarily to personnel and the latter to managerial structures and practices.

The object of this paper is to show the way in which the two

[*] Paper delivered to the annual Conference of the Political Studies Association at Birmingham, March 1971.

Reprinted from *Political Studies*, vol. XIX, no. 2 (June 1971), pp. 213–226. By permission of the author and the publisher.

organizational phenomena of reform and change are related. It is necessary firstly to explain what is meant by change in central government administration as a background to the current reformist movement. Some historical material will be introduced where relevant to support the argument.

CHANGE

Organizational change entails the adaptation of existing structures, expressed in terms of functions and responsibilities, to new objectives, technology, resources and environmental factors. Such adaptation alters the allocation of work within the organization, the size of managerial units and the methods of planning, co-ordination and review. It is a process of clarifying organizational goals and adjusting procedures for the allocation, control and co-ordination of administrative responsibilities to meet new standards of efficiency.

The most familiar type of organizational change originates in the setting of new goals in terms of policy objectives by successive governments. The familiar Ministerial 're-shuffles' are outward manifestations of changes which penetrate far deeper into the organization. Organizational structures must respond to changes in policy goals. A recent example is the October 1970 White Paper on *The Reorganization of Central Government*. The re-grouping of functions, particularly in the Department of the Environment and the Department of Trade and Industry, was justified both in terms of creating an administrative machine which reflected the government's strategic policy objectives, and of administrative advantages, such as economies of scale, increased managerial responsibility, more effective delegation, a better application of 'analytic' techniques, improved communications and a greater capacity for strategic policy formulation. The pressures for internal reorganization which such policy and administrative objectives will generate are obvious.

Even without specific expressions of policy reorientations accompanying changes of Government and Ministerial re-shuffles, organizational change is a continuous process. The hidden dynamic of government organization is a spontaneous response to feed-back from and reviews of the administrative process, the introduction of new management techniques and supporting services and the development of administrative responsibilities which gradually attract ancillary functions. An example, which could be multiplied endlessly, is the experiments of the Ministry of Housing and Local Government in deciding how to combine functional expertise within housing and planning with knowledge of the specific problems of geographical areas.[1] A further example is the reorganization of the management structure of the Prison Department following the identification of organizational malfunctions by a management review team.[2] Organizational change in central administration reflects an on-going search for improved performance which is almost totally undocumented.

The introduction of new techniques for the management of resources within government has had a profound effect on organizational structures. The growing consciousness of the importance of management skills to public administration reflects an awareness of the qualitative changes which the vast expansion of government functions has introduced into the public sector. It has changed not only in terms of the numbers of public servants involved, but also in the complexity of administrative arrangements for executing a wide variety of government functions and powers. The striking feature of this growth in government in the last fifty years is not just that vast new functions of direct management, regulation and control, involving the deployment of technical and scientific expertise, have been added to the traditional functions of defence, law and order and the conduct of foreign affairs. It is also that the administrative machine has evolved in an extraordinarily complex and unsystematic way. The problems of size, in terms of manpower and cost, and the complex relations between the parts of the machinery of government have greatly contributed to the attraction which management science currently exerts over central administration.

As a result, new techniques of controlling resources in the public sector are being developed, both within its operational units and for the system as a whole. In the context of the overall deployment of resources among the parts of the government machine, the development since 1961 of public expenditure planning is of paramount importance.[3] The improvement of quantitative techniques for forward-looks at public expenditure on a programme basis has important implications for organizational structures and methods within central administration. The search for greater rationality in determining priorities in policy objectives and the inter-relationships between public expenditure decisions is an important source of organizational change. Considerable effort is being put into the development of information systems and techniques for relating the 'output' of Departments and other agencies to 'inputs' in terms of resources.

Such organizational changes are reflected in the creation, in 1961, of the interdepartmental Public Expenditure Survey Committee, composed of the Principal Finance Officers of the Central Departments, and the Treasury reorganization of 1962. PESC is responsible for the preparation of annual public expenditure surveys on a functional and economic category basis assuming the continuation of present policies at constant prices. The Treasury reorganization placed Treasury control of expenditure on a functional basis, cutting across Departmental boundaries, making it easier to 'look, as a whole, at important aspects government policy which affect several departments'.[4] Further reorganization followed the creation and then disbandment of the Department of Economic Affairs, as responsibility for long-term strategic economic planning moved between the two Departments.

The decision to plan total expenditure within a long-term framework on the basis of planned estimates of the costs of alternative policies inevitably places new responsibilities on the spending Departments, involving organizational change.

Firstly, Departments are now required to carry out a detailed costing of their policies on a five-year basis. Functional costings systems are being developed in defence planning, the road programme, the educational programme and the health service. 'The shift of emphasis to the evaluation and appraisal of long-term programmes and the long-term allocation of resources to them is leading to the development of better methods to measure and compare the cost-effectiveness of alternative courses of action.'[5] Secondly, the spending Departments are required to prepare their estimates in a manner consistent with the long-term allocation of resources to each of the main public services. Finally, the Departments are committed to a 'strict review of individual programmes' to introduce flexibility. These developments include the improvement of techniques and criteria for investment appraisal in the nationalized industries. The central Departments are thus under growing pressure to introduce more cost-conscious and rational methods of decision making. The application of output-budgeting to government operations is being experimented with to clarify Departmental aims in terms of policy programmes and to relate the use of resources to the achievement of objectives. New control systems, such as management by objectives, are also being introduced and adapted from the private sector for the systematic comparison of performance with organizational goals. Such developments inevitably lead to the review of management structures and the reallocation of responsibilities within the organization. Despite the considerable difficulties in applying techniques initally devised for tests of profitability to the public sector where equity and impartiality are part of the overall objectives, efforts are being made to define Departmental aims more clearly, to measure 'costs' and evaluate 'output'.[6] Any movement towards identifying the responsibilities of line managers for performance (i.e. budgetary control) and away from the centralized financial and personnel controls of traditional Civil Service methods involves the introduction of different organizational arrangements.

The increasing intervention of government in areas requiring technological and scientific expertise has led to numerous organizational experiments to integrate the work of administrators and specialists in the interest of efficiency. New organizational units have been created for the administration of education, defence, planning, transport and public works. Considerable departures have been made from the traditional separation of administrators and profressionals, with administrative responsibility allocated according to the nature of the task. One observer has commented that, given the unique features of each Department, all 'which contain a large body of professional civil servants are likely to find it difficult to resist pressure to introduce some form of integrated structure'.[7] Further extensions of accountable management and management by objectives will have implications for organizations where administrators and specialists are jointly responsible for an area of the Department's work.

REFORM

Administrative reform is an entirely different phenomenon. It is political rather than organizational. It has a moral content, in that it seeks to remedy an abuse or a wrong, to create a 'better' system by removing faults and imperfections. 'It is undertaken in the belief that the end results will always be better than the *status quo*, and so worth the effort to overcome resistance.'[8] Change is incremental, whereas reform entails comprehensive reorganization, although in a specific part of the administrative system. Caiden's definition of administrative reform as 'the artificial inducement of administrative transformation, against resistance'[9] identifies three distinguishing features — 'moral purpose, artificial transformation and administrative resistance'. This blurs the distinction between organizational change and administrative reform which recent British experience so well exemplifies. It ignores the relationship between reform and personnel, and exaggerates the conflict between the reformers and the public service.

The history of administrative reform in this country suggests that reform originates in a belief that organizational change needed in government cannot take place given existing methods of recruiting, training, deploying and managing the organization's human resource. Reform is designed to make change possible by injecting, through the reorganization of the public service, or part of it, new and different blood into the organization.

Reform also appears to be associated with other external political values which the artificially induced change is designed to serve. In addition to facilitating organizational change, reform aims to make administrative structures and practices compatible with broader political goals. Reform has a moral purpose not only in the way in which it compares existing public personnel unfavourably with a set of organizational values, but also in that additional political values are used as yardsticks against which to judge administrative performance. New demands are made on administrative organizations by reformers, who, at the same time, see administration as inadequately meeting existing demands. A distinction between this and organizational change can be summed up by an adaptation of Downs' notion of performance gaps. Change has its source in a recognition by the members of an organization that a 'significant discrepancy' exists between actual and desired performance.[10] Reform follows from a similar decision, but one made externally, ultimately by political leaders. Reform is politicized change.

Reform thus occurs when two conditions are present: a set of political values with which existing Civil Service arrangements are seen as being in conflict; and public concern that the existing personnel in the public sector cannot achieve the new goals being set for it. This pattern of political circumstances can be observed during the periods of administrative reform in the modern history of the British Civil Service.

THE NORTHCOTE–TREVELYAN REFORMS

The background to the Civil Service reforms of the second half of the nineteenth century may be viewed in the context of political concern about governmental efficiency, and a growing hostility towards patronage as a method of selection for professional life generally. Alarm at the inefficiency of government had been growing since the War of American Independence. As government activity expanded the need to check corruption became increasingly apparent. Gradually the importance of relevant qualifications came to be recognized; 'as a result patronage was regulated in the interests of efficiency'.[11] The reform of the Indian Civil Service was followed by university reform and the Civil Service had to be brought into line. Some sinecures were abolished, a superannuation scheme was devised and appointment on the basis of qualification began to reduce the detrimental effects of patronage in some Departments.

The political origins of these reforms were very closely related. The growing criticism of patronage was not derived from any notion of social equality but from its evident inefficiency as a method of recruitment. 'The impetus behind these changes was not so much an attack on privilege as a desire to achieve economy and efficiency and the belief, following the ideas of Bentham, that the utility of administrative practices and procedures should be openly examined and adjustments made as necessary.'[12] Frequent Parliamentary expressions of dissatisfaction with the rising cost of administration led in 1848 to the appointment of a Select Committee on Miscellaneous Expenditure to seek economies. Before it, Sir Charles Trevelyan, Assistant Secretary to the Treasury, demonstrated how inefficiency and waste followed from a system of recruitment based on patronage. The principles of division of labour and appointment and promotion by merit, together with other rational methods of organization, were advocated for central government by a growing number of reformers.

The reformist movement was strengthened, after the publication of the Northcote–Trevelyan report, by public dissatisfaction with the mismanagement of the Crimean War. The administrative Reform Association was established in 1855, and the Civil Service Commission was appointed in the same year. The reports of the Commission publicized the damaging effects of patronage on administrative efficiency. Parliament set up a Select Committee on Civil Service Appointments in 1860, to enquire into the possibility of expanding the recruitment of 'properly qualified persons', and gave a hesitant though significant impetus to the principle of competition.

It is important to recognize that the implementation of the North-cote–Trevelyan reforms did not follow automatically and immediately upon the publication of recommendations by official investigators. The introduction of the reforms associated with the Northcote–Trevelyan report only really began when strong political pressure was exerted on the government, as a result of publicity given to mismanagement within the Civil Departments. Government action necessary to bring about fundamental changes in the structure and organization of the Civil Service depended on the political opportunities provided by public pressure, rather than on acceptance in principle of the arguments produced by reformers, to which there was initially considerable hostility from those whose interests lay with the preservation of political patronage.

Similar political pressures were associated with subsequent reforms. Despite the emergence of staff organizations and further enquiries into the service, notably by a Selection Committee of 1873 and the Playfair Committee of 1874–75, the two decades following the reforms of 1870 were a period of consolidation during which 'the Service was left to digest the reforms already initiated'. Playfair led to nothing more than the creation of a common Civil Service grade at the lowest level.[13] The Ridley Royal Commission 1886–1890 was mainly a response to internal Civil Service pressures for better opportunities for promotion and led to an extension of by now widely accepted practices. The Royal Commission of 1912–1915 under the chairmanship of Lord MacDonnell again simply applied the principle of division of labour to the Civil Service structure. Subsequent official enquiries dealt with problems arising from the application of these basic principles formulated in the 1840s and 1850s, culminating in the 1920 report of the Reorganization Committee of the newly established Civil Service National Whitley Council which produced a Civil Service structure that lasted until the post-Fulton reforms. The Royal Commission of 1929–31 (the Tomlin Commission) 'marked and recorded the culmination of the changes that were recommended by Northcote and Trevelyan'[14] on recruitment, work classification, promotion and Civil Service unity. Specific groups of Civil Servants (e.g. accountants, medical staff and the works group) and particular aspects of the Service such as training (Assheton, 1944) and pay (Priestley, 1953–55) were subject to official review, but these dealt essentially with matters of detail. The general reorganization of the British Civil Service on the principles of Northcote–Trevelyan was complete by 1930.[15]

THE FULTON REFORMS

The current wave of reform is equally motivated by strong political pressures derived from a belief that the Civil Service as constituted was inadequate to cope with the tasks of a modern administration in an efficient way.

Since 1960 the Civil Service has been presented in many circles as, in Professor Robson's words, 'a scapegoat for real or imaginary ills'.[16] Criticisms of the Service focused on its structure and the damaging effect of this on efficiency. The amateurism and lack of professional managerial skill was seen as characterizing the Service, which was consequently compared unfavourably with the equivalent personnel of the private sector.

This view was represented in its most outspoken form in 1963 in Professor Chapman's book, *British Government Observed*, which reduced the qualities of the Service to 'simple diligence' and 'native wit'.[17] In 1967 E. M. Nicholson compared the poor results of British amateur sportsmen with the consequences of amateurism in government in his book *The System*. Nicholson regarded the Civil Service as a surviving Victorian anachronism.[18] Again the Service was blamed for 'assisting to make Britain itself extinct as a great force in world affairs'. Its 'morbid mistrust' of knowledge, expertise and research was related to a selection procedure which recruited cadets for the higher Civil Service from 'the picked products of Victorian approach (*sic*) to life'.[19] The Service was 'at our expense, the last and most obsessive stronghold of amateurism', filled in its highest ranks with 'the completely untrained administrator, who is only a professional in the sense that he is permanently and highly paid as if he were one'.[20]

The more positive aspects of this doctrine were beginning to infiltrate the ranks of the Civil Service itself by 1964. P. D. Nairne, then Assistant Secretary at the Ministry of Defence, wrote in *Public Administration* that the Service should recognize that 'management is not merely a function of establishment divisions, nor the property of the big spending and economic departments'.[21] Its relevancy extends beyond personnel matters and the application of management techniques. 'It is something more fundamental – a more positive approach to the planning and administration of policy in all spheres of government'. It should be extended to the executive and professional classes and within the administrative class it was 'important that all its members should recognize their responsibilities as managers'.[22]

In 1964, coinciding with the return of a Labour Government, the Fabian Society published a pamphlet[23] which clearly had a considerable influence on Government thinking about Civil Service reform, influence which was transmitted to the official committee later to be appointed under the Chairmanship of Lord Fulton.

The existing Civil Service 'system' was described as 'dating back' to the mid-nineteenth century and notably the Northcote–Trevelyan report of 1854. It had not changed to meet new responsibilities in economic and social policy. The isolation of the administrator from other fields of society, the notion of the 'omniscient all-rounder' and the inferior status of the professional were identified as particular weaknesses. The system was judged as 'out of touch with the times' and as having an adverse effect on post-War economic policy. The Fabian Society's criticism of amateurism, the negative approach of civil servants and their secretiveness was a remarkable premonition of the subsequent findings of the Fulton Committee. So were the proposals of the Society, which included wider graduate recruitment, better training, the fuller use of experts, more movement in and out of the Service, and the reform of its structure and organization. In fact the Fulton Committee's report looks remarkably like an expanded version of *The Administrators*.

By 1966 the framework for a political view on the Service was firmly established and 'reform' became an issue. The final impetus came from the Estimates Committee, which in 1964–65 examined Votes relating to Civil Service recruitment.[24] The Committee typically did not restrict itself to administrative arrangements for recruitment to the existing Service, but extended its enquiry to the policies governing the division of functions within the Service and the choice of people for different kinds of work. Although primarily concerned with Civil Service Commission recruitment methods, the Committee, under the influence of the pervading reformist atmosphere, drew attention to the policies underlying recruitment, such as the structure of the Service, the task of Government and the need for expertise and specialized skills. Three areas were identified as requiring further investigation which 'might be expected to lead to proposals for change'.[25] These were mobility within the Service and between it and other occupations; the need for professional training particularly in specialist techniques; and the effect of recruiting policies on the supply of qualified manpower. Finally, a further official investigation by the Government into the structure of the Service was recommended.

Although the Labour Party's 1964 manifesto mentioned only briefly and in passing the need for a review of the practices of the Departments of State, the Government decided in February 1966 to set up a Committee to examine the structure, recruitment and management, including training, of the Home Civil Service. In his statement to the House of Commons the Prime Minister referred to the need to ensure that the Service is properly equipped to meet the changing demands placed on it by the modern State and the changing educational organization of the country. Thus a 'fundamental and wide-ranging enquiry' was commissioned from an official Committee.[26] The Fulton Committee began its work in a climate of hostility towards the existing organization of the Civil Service based on a number of inter-related assumptions about the managerial defects of the Service as compared with foreign and industrial systems of administration. Further publicity was given to the reformist case after the Fulton Committee began their work by a re-issue in 1966 of the Fabian pamphlet and the reprinting in 1967 of Thomas Balogh's essay on 'The Apotheosis of the Dilettante' which protested that it had 'no connection whatever with the author's subsequent official assignment' as Economic Adviser to the Cabinet from 1964 to 1967.

METHODS OF REFORM

Administrative reform is usually associated with an investigation, report and recommendation by some type of public enquiry. Since 1850 there have been no fewer than fourteen major official investigations into the organization of the Civil Service, leaving aside Parliamentary Select Committees and including Northcote–Trevelyan and Fulton. Most of the important ones have already been mentioned.

It is extremely difficult to generalize about relationships between the composition of such investigatory bodies, the recommendations which they made and the results of their efforts. As John Bourn has shown, the more significant results seem to follow from the reports of committees with a high proportion of officials among their members.[27] It is perhaps more important to remember that the implementation of reform has never followed automatically from the recommendations of a public enquiry or a Royal Commission. Reform seems to be much more a function of Government policy decisions, which themselves are motivated by other factors. It is clear that the committees which have from time to time enquired into administrative reform fall into one or other of Wheare's[28] categories of committees to 'camouflage' a decision that has already been taken, or committees to pacify certain sectors of public opinion when the government has no intention of taking a decision (or, it should be added, no power to act).

Thus the report commissioned from Sir Stafford Northcote and Sir Charles Trevelyan by the Chancellor of the Exchequer, Gladstone, in 1853 was met with such hostility that no immediate action was taken. It was not until after the fall of Aberdeen's Ministry that the Government felt powerful enough to begin the implementation of Civil Service reform. The most important decision in this phase of reform was the Order in Council of 1870 which established the practice of recruitment by open competitive examination. This decision was taken at a moment that was politically expedient, without a further committee of enquiry.

The Playfair Commission of 1874–75 followed agitation by an association of Writers who felt aggrieved at the Order in Council of 1871 which defined unattractive terms of employment for temporary and unestablished clerks. The Commission had very little effect because Gladstone's Government fell before it reported and the Conservative successor was not prepared to implement its recommendations in full. Staff agitation also led to the appointment of the Ridley Royal Commission, which was not concerned with reform so much as with extending the application of accepted principles, and then most of its recommendations were rejected by the Government. The culmination of this phase of Civil Service reform came with the Reorganization Committee of the National Whitley Council which represented in its report the implementation of Government decisions following the Gladstone Committee's reports of 1918–19.

The idea that administrative reform is concerned with the quality of personnel, and follows from political decision-making, to which various kinds of committees to enquire are marginally related, should shed some light on the current phase of reform associated with the report of the Fulton Committee.

In the first place the terms of reference of the committee were limited to personnel matters and were not extended to include the machinery of government. The committee included a brief section on 'hiving-off' and an important chapter on the structure of Departments in relation to the promotion of efficiency. But its consideration of these matters stemmed from a conception of Departmental personnel. Almost everything the committee said appeared to be 'derived from the simple premise that the present faults of the Civil Service arise from the amateurism of its members'.[29] The Committee's report also reflects in its criticisms of the Service the prevailing conventional wisdom, outlined above, much more than the conclusions of its own research and evidence. As Professor Robson said, the committee 'undoubtedly succumbed to the climate of opinion' created by the critiques published in the previous five years. The Committee's criticisms of amateurism, ignorance of managerial skills, class barriers to promotion by merit and inefficient personnel management will be too familiar to require documentation. The point is, they follow slavishly the political view which had developed and on which the Government was determined to act.

The eagerness to say what the Government wanted to hear led the committee into some obvious traps. One was fundamental to its reasoning. In ramming home the need for a greater orientation towards management in the higher ranks of the Service, the committee ignored its own definition of administrative work which it set out in non-managerial terms: advising on policy, preparing legislation, assisting ministers with Parliamentary business, producing briefs for debates, appearing before Parliamentary Committees, drafting regulations and answers to Parliamentary Questions – work with 'no counterpart in business or, indeed, anywhere outside the government service'.[30]

This is not the place to set out a detailed critique of the Fulton Committee's report, although it probably deserves more critical review than it has received so far. But in view of the closeness with which the report follows the study of Civil Service work by a group of management consultants, the conflict between some of its own research and the report's conclusions, and its readiness to overlook the political factors which make the Civil Service what it is, in favour of a managerial approach to government organizations, one cannot help but conclude that some fairly basic decisions about the organization of the Civil Service were taken before Fulton began work, with the Fulton exercise designed to support them.

In the Fulton report a new yardstick of achievement was imported from private enterprise as a measure of Civil Service efficiency. A second underlying assumption was that performance could only be improved in order to meet these new standards by means of personnel reforms. These two hidden premises can only be explained in terms of the political pressures for reform which had built up to a climax in 1966.

The real test of whether administrative reform is desirable must be a two-stage one. It is firstly necessary to see whether the impediments to organizational change have been correctly diagnosed. Secondly, it must be asked whether the measures designed to remove such impediments have been correctly deduced from the initial diagnosis. It is inappropriate to pre-judge the issue by formulating a theory of Civil Service behaviour and then constructing a concept of administrative objectives to square with this theory. In the case of the Fulton reforms, for example, one must ask whether the introduction of output budgeting, accountable management, management by objectives, the improvement in Vote accounting, the measurement of performance, 'hiving-off' and so on, depend on the reform and restructuring of the Civil Service.[31]

THE IMPLEMENTATION OF REFORM

A decision to reform needs to be followed by two sets of organizational change. One implements the changes affecting the organization of personnel and follows directly from, and is part of, reform itself. The other is an indirect result of reform and entails the introduction of organizational changes which administrative reform is designed to make possible. The distinction is important to further understanding the difference between reform and change in public administration, and to the question of whether specific reforms are necessary to the introduction of specific changes. The post-Fulton phase illustrates the distinction.

Some of the decisions linked with reform can be implemented without further deliberation. In the case of Fulton, for example, the creation of a new Department to take over the Treasury's functions in respect of establishments into which the Civil Service Commission was integrated and the expansion of the Centre for Administrative Studies into the Civil Service College were among such decisions.

Other reforms on the personnel side have to await further investigations and consultations. Since 1968 the most important decisions affecting the structure and organization of the Civil Service have been taken within the Service itself. In order to plan the implementation of the new Civil Service structure and to consider other Fulton recommendations a Joint Committee of the National Whitley Council was set up to ensure consultation with all affected interests. Management consultants have been brought in to help with the introduction of a new 'open' structure at top levels of the Service and the Civil Service Department has carried out investigations into occupational groups and grading levels. But the planning of the new unified grading scheme was wholly the responsibility of the Joint Committee. Consultation with the National Staff Side has been extended over the 'whole range of the post-Fulton programme'.[32]

In addition, inter-departmental consultation had to be instituted for the implementation of other Fulton proposals, particularly in relation to recruitment, structure, personnel management and training. For this purpose inter-departmental committees of senior officials, both administrators and 'professionals', were set up for each of these major areas of work, under the general guidance of a Steering Committee chaired by the Head of the Civil Service.

The bureaucratization of the post-Fulton reforms is further illustrated by the recent work of the Civil Service Department, into which the work of implementing reform has been absorbed. Reform has very quickly become internalized with the important decisions being taken by the Civil Service itself. 'The job of the Civil Service Department is the reform of the Civil Service.'[33] The aim of the Department apparently is 'not to push Fulton through. It is to make the Civil Service a more effective, economical and humane instrument of government.'[34] In very broad terms the Department's responsibilities divide into two: personnel management and the organization of work. Thus, the initiative in the implementation of reform and the introduction of change has passed to this central establishment's organization. The Department's responsibility is 'to take the lead in reconstructing the Civil Service taking into account the report of the Committee on the Civil Service'.[35] It is significant that the language of 'reconstruction' has replaced the language of 'reform' in official circles.

Such developments as these perhaps help to explain why it appears from the history of administrative reform since 1850 that many more permanent changes have been associated with the recommendations of official enquiries carried out by committees composed predominantly of civil servants.[36] The influence of the 1920 Reorganization Committee, when seen in its historical context, represents the final stage of a lengthy process during which the principles of Civil Service structure had been absorbed by the administration and endorsed by the Service. The final organization, which lasted nearly half a century, was 'worked out largely by the Civil Service itself'.[37] In fact, as the post-Fulton experience shows, the procedures used in the implementation of reforms follow very closely the methods by which organizational change is introduced into central administration, with or without a reforming impetus.

ADMINISTRATIVE CHANGE SINCE FULTON

A number of changes in organizational structures and methods have been considered, planned or introduced since 1968. They are widely regarded as following naturally from the Fulton Committee's enquiry and as part of the change which had to be preceded by the reform of the Civil Service. Many of them involve further detailed investigations, sometimes by committees bringing in non-civil servants. Much of the subsequent investigation and experiment takes the Fulton Report as its point of departure.

There have been many developments at the level of the overall strategic planning of central government resources. In the machinery for personnel recruitment, firstly, management consultants were employed by the Civil Service Commission to suggest ways of speeding up central recruitment processes and the Commission was reorganized as a result. The Method I system of recruitment of graduates to the Administrative Class has been abolished and Method II was the subject of an official enquiry by four outsiders and one Establishments Officer. A number of changes have followed their report.

Management training has been expanded considerably as a direct response to the Fulton Committee's findings on the subject. Further extensive investigations are being carried out into techniques of career planning, the development of pay systems to increase incentive and reward merit, the management of specialist staff and the definition of administrative specialisms. A greater interchange of staff with industry, commerce and professional services is being organized.

An investigation into particular areas of work in the non-Civil Service has been conducted by a panel of business men, under the chairmanship of Sir Robert Bellinger, in order to find savings in manpower by looking at the tasks which are carried out within government Departments.

At the Departmental level studies and experiments in new methods of management are being conducted into the use of planning machinery and the hierarchical structure of Departments, with special reference to the use of specialists in integrated hierarchies. 'Hiving off' was made the subject of a confidential internal investigation, although with the option of using outside experts held open. Government activities which might be appropriate for hiving-off as a means to accountable management, such as the commercial and quasi-commercial operations of some Departments, have been reviewed.

Individual Departments have been surveying their work to identify the areas to which the Fulton concept of accountable management might be applied. Pilot schemes have been initiated and work has been done in developing techniques for the measurement of costs and output.

It can be seen that the two sets of changes following from administrative reform, namely reorganization of the Civil Service and the introduction of organizational change for which reform is said to be a necessary condition, are the responsibility of public bodies, the personnel of which have been the subject of reforms. The final product is more a result of decisions taken at the political level, combined with detailed planning by those most affected by reform and interested in change, than of the deliberations and recommendations of official committees of enquiry. The use of official committees and consultants as part of the follow-up stage of reform is not evidence of further external pressure and influence on an administration unwilling to change but is perfectly consistent with the methods employed by the government organizations as part of the logistics of structural re-organization. Departmental and advisory committees from Assheton, through Plowden and Osmond, to Davies and 'the team of businessmen' constitute a familiar part of the process of administrative change in which authoritative views are collected and a disinterested decision arrived at.

CONCLUSION

Despite the passion for reform by committee of enquiry, noted by a recent editorial in *Public Administration*, such investigatory bodies are but trimmings to the main business of producing change as a result of political dissatisfaction with administrative performance. The historical and contemporary evidence suggests not only that such investigatory committees should not be regarded as a 'substitute for critical reflection and constructive action by those who actually have public responsibilities',[38] but also that they are in fact no substitutes for political decisions.

Decisions to reform are taken by the relevant ministers largely independently of any specially appointed investigatory body. The implementation of reform falls to the public organizations themselves to plan and execute. It is not surprising that some of the most enthusiastic reformers are to be found in the ranks of the reformed. And it is a matter of practical administration that this should be so, particularly if the proposed reforms originate from political pressures for irrelevant organizational change.

The distinction between reform and change in government organizations corresponds to the broader distinction between synoptic, rational planning in administration generally and the marginal decision-making of 'disjointed incrementalism'.[39] Both the implementation of reform decisions and the introduction of administrative change with or without reform produce fragmented decision-making and change at the margin rather than total reorganization according to a rational model of reform. The comprehensiveness implied by reform is quickly reduced by the implementing agencies – Departments and committees – within the administrative apparatus itself to relatively small and incremental changes in personnel management and organizational structure at the margin of existing policies.

Administrative reform is designed to facilitate organizational change by equipping the administrative apparatus with a new component which is regarded as a necessary condition of improved performance, both in terms of the identification of objectives and the creation of administrative structures and processes for achieving them. Reform is a response to political pressure for change and its effectiveness as regards the quality of administration depends on how far those pressures correctly identify the causes of weakness in the administrative system. If the defects in administration are misunderstood it may be that reform, concerned as it is with personnel, will be irrelevant to the problem of change.

NOTES

1. Evelyn Sharp, *The Ministry of Housing and Local Government* (London 1969), p. 212.
2. J. Garrett and S. D. Walker, 'Management Review—a Case Study from the Prison Department of the Home Office', *O and M Bulletin*, Vol. 25, No. 3, 1970.
3. Green Paper *Public Expenditure: A New Presentation*, Cmnd. 4017, 1969. Sir Samuel Goldman, 'The Presentation of Public Expenditure Proposals to Parliament', *Public Administration* (Autumn 1970).
4. Lord Bridges, *The Treasury* (London 1966), p. 143.
5. White Paper *Public Expenditure: Planning and Control*, Cmnd. 2915, p. 8.
6. J. Garrett and S. D. Walker, *Management by Objectives in the Civil Service*, CAS Occasional Paper No. 10 (HMSO, 1969).

7. D. E. Regan, 'The Expert and the Administrator: Recent Changes at the Ministry of Transport', *Public Administration* (Summer 1966), p. 164.
8. G. E. Caiden, *Administrative Reform* (London 1969), p. 65.
9. Caiden, *Administrative Reform*, p. 65.
10. A. Downs, *Inside Bureaucracy* (Boston 1967), p. 191.
11. E. W. Cohen, *The Growth of the British Civil Service, 1780–1939* (London 1965), p. 85.
12. J. B. Bourn, 'The Main Reports on the British Civil Service since the Northcote–Trevelyan Report', Memo. No. 10, *The Civil Service*, Vol. 3(2), Surveys and Investigations (HMSO, 1968), p. 424. See also M. Wright, *Treasury Control of the Civil Service, 1854–1974* (Oxford 1969), p. 352.
13. Cohen, *British Civil Service*, p. 135.
14. Bourn, 'Main Reports', p. 457.
15. Bourn, 'Main Reports', p. 458.
16. W. A. Robson, 'The Fulton Report on the Civil Service', *Political Quarterly*, No. 4, 1968.
17. B. Chapman, *British Government Observed* (London 1963).
18. E. M. Nicholson, *The System* (1967), p. 467.
19. Nicholson, *The System*, p. 468.
20. Nicholson, *The System*, p. 472.
21. P. D. Nairne, 'Management and the Administrative Class', *Public Administration* (Summer 1964), p. 122.
22. Nairne, 'Management', p. 122.
23. *The Administrators, The Reform of the Civil Service* (Fabian Society, 1964).
24. Sixth Report from the Estimates Committee, Session 1964–65, *Recruitment to the Civil Service*, H.C. 308 (1965).
25. Sixth Report, p. 105.
26. See 'Quarterly Notes', *Public Administration* (Summer 1966), pp. 231–232.
27. Bourn, 'Main Reports', p. 464.
28. K. C. Wheare, *Government by Committee* (Oxford 1955), pp. 83–93.
29. A. Grey and A. Simon, 'People, Structure and Civil Service Reform', *The Journal of Management Studies* (October 1970), p. 288.
30. *The Civil Service*, Vol. 1, Report of the Committee 1966–68, Cmnd. 3638, para. 27.
31. In this context it has been argued that the real defects of administrative organization in central government 'derive from the system of procedures under which activities are allocated, co-ordinated and controlled within the organization', i.e. the organization's structure, which in turn follows from the peculiar working environment, the nature of political responsibility and the realities of the political process. Grey and Simon, 'Civil Service Reform'. It is also significant that the former secretary to the Fulton Committee talked, in a lecture to the RIPA, about the organization of government work in terms quite distinct from those relating to Civil Service structure. Not only was the Government said to have been 'quite good' in the past at organizing work effectively, but it was admitted that even with the Fulton reforms 'we have a very long way to go in this field before it can be claimed that the organization of government is equal to the tasks that it has to perform', R. W. L. Wilding, 'The Post-Fulton Programme: Strategy and Tactics', *Public Administration* (Winter 1970), p. 395.
32. R. W. L. Wilding, 'The Post-Fulton Programme: Strategy and Tactics', *Public Administration* (Winter 1970), p. 397.

33. Wilding, 'Post-Fulton Programme', p. 391.
34. Wilding, 'Post-Fulton Programme', p. 391.
35. First Report of the Civil Service Department, *CSD Report 1969* (HMSO, 1970).
36. Bourn, 'Main Reports', p. 464.
37. Bourn, 'Main Reports', p. 450.
38. 'Reforming the Bureaucracy', *Public Administration* (Winter 1968), p. 367.
39. Charles E. Lindblom and D. Braybrooke, *A Strategy of Decision* (1963).

Sir Richard Clarke

The Number and Size of
Government Departments*

One of the most striking recent developments in government has been the emergence of 'giant' departments, of a size never before seen in peacetime. At the beginning of the First World War there were eighteen main departments; twenty-one years later, in 1935, there were twenty-three; twenty-one years later again, in 1956, there were twenty-six; now there are seventeen; with civil service staff of 700,000. Foreign affairs, which only twenty-five years ago occupied four major departments, each with its own Secretary of State – the Foreign, Dominions, Colonial and India Offices – are now managed by one Foreign and Commonwealth Office (FCO) with its appended Overseas Development Administration. There is one giant Ministry of Defence, employing nearly 300,000 people (apart from military personnel and locally engaged staff overseas), which has absorbed the three Service Departments and has also now assumed responsibility for aviation research and development and military procurement, formerly a large part of the successive Ministries of Supply, Aviation, and Technology. The Government's relations with industry and commerce, apart from labour questions and agriculture, and including the nationalized energy and steel industries, the aircraft industry, shipping and civil aviation, are concentrated in a giant Department of Trade and Industry (DTI). The departments formerly responsible for housing and local government, transport and works, which have themselves gone through great changes in past years, have been replaced by a giant Department of the Environment (DOE). The old social service departments are in the Department of Health and Social Security (DHSS); and education and the Research Councils are in the

---

* This article is based on a lecture at a seminar at All Souls College, Oxford, on October 15 1971. It develops further the analysis in a series of lectures in Spring 1971, under the auspices of the Civil Service College, published in December 1971 by HMSO under the title 'New Trends in Government'.

Reprinted from *The Political Quarterly*, vol. 43, no. 2 (April–June 1972), pp. 169–186. By permission of the author and the publisher.

Table I. Major Government Departments: 1914[1] to 1972

1914 (18 depts.)	1935 (23 depts.)	1956 (26 depts.)	Jan. 1972 (17 depts.)
Treasury	Treasury	Treasury	Treasury Civil Service
Inland Revenue Customs & Excise	Inland Revenue Customs & Excise	Inland Revenue Customs & Excise	Inland Revenue Customs & Excise
Foreign Colonies India	Foreign Dominions Colonies India	Foreign Commonwealth Relations Colonies	Foreign & Commonwealth
Admiralty War	Admiralty War Air	Defence Admiralty War Air Supply	Defence
Home Scotland Ireland	Home Scotland	Home Scotland	Home Scotland Wales
Lord Chancellor's	Lord Chancellor's	Lord Chancellor's	Lord Chancellor's
Trade Agriculture	Trade Agriculture Labour	Trade Fuel & Power Agriculture & Food Labour	Trade & Industry Agriculture & Food Employment
	Transport	Transport & Civil Aviation	
Works	Works	Works	Environment
Local Government	Health	Housing & Local Government	
	Pensions (War)	Health Pensions & National Insurance	Health & Social Security
Education	Education DSIR	Education DSIR	Education & Science
Post Office	Post Office	Post Office	Posts and Tele-communications

[1] 1914, 1935, 1956, from *Organisation of British Cabinet Government 1914–1956*; Royal Institute of Public Administration.

Department of Education and Science (DES). Table I shows the changes in major departments over sixty years.

A DECADE OF INSTABILITY

There is no moment in the last decade at which the course changed. At the beginning of Mr Wilson's Government in October 1964, one could have been excused for thinking that the trend was going the other way with the new Department of Economic Affairs and the new Ministries of Technology, Land and Natural Resources, Overseas Development, none of which survived seven years later. In retrospect one sees that the movement to consolidate departments in foreign affairs and defence had been going steadily forward since the early 1960s; but there has been a continuous splitting-up and regrouping of the department in the economic and financial, industrial, environmental, scientific and technological fields, and it is only in the last three years (under both Mr Wilson and Mr Heath) that the outcome has been established as the emergence of 'giant' departments, with a smaller number of major departments even than there were in 1914 (though with over ten times as many civil servants). These rapid changes in machinery of government and departmental structures reflected the changing concepts of the role of the State from the latter part of the 1950s onwards and the continuous attempts by successive Prime Ministers from Mr Macmillan onwards to find the best apparatus for doing the new tasks which confronted government. It is still not certain that stability has been reached, for the process of change of concepts has not reached its end, and the entry into the European Economic Community will bring with it new duties for central government which have hardly yet been surveyed. Moreover, the 'giants' are bound to be regarded as experimental. Nevertheless, in my opinion the new structure looks more stable than any for many years.

The real quesiton is whether a small number of large departments is better or worse for the efficiency of government than a large number of small departments. The issue is not whether large departments are better than small departments, but whether a few large ones are better than a lot of small ones. It is the management of central government as a whole that must be optimized, and not the management of any single part of it.

SCALE OF CENTRAL GOVERNMENT

We must therefore start from the size of the work of central government. There is wide agreement that central government, as we now have it in Britain, is too big a unit for efficient operation. To have one group of people, the Cabinet, responsible for the day-to-day conduct of the whole overseas and defence policy of the country, the course of the national economy including employment, growth, balance of payments, etc., and the situation and prospects of particular industries, the overseas economic and commercial policy, the expenditures of the public sector and the taxation required to pay for them, the provisions of the social services and the educational system, law and order, etc., presents them with too heavy a task, especially as their work in carrying out their collective Cabinet functions and their individual departmental duties is only a part of their daily responsibilities and preoccupations.

Can this load of decision-making at the centre be reduced? I can see no practical answer. It has been suggested that the Government should 'hive off' certain tasks to other public bodies or to the private sector; but virtually no progress has been made, for good reasons. Both parties accepted at the end of the Second World War far-reaching responsibilities for the course of the national economy; and they have since made their criticism of their opponents' performance and their own promises the centre of their electoral appeal. They could not now convince the public that the ability of government to carry out these responsibilities is not nearly as sure as the claims of twenty-five years ago required. Given the responsibility that they have assumed for the course of economic events, governments cannot devolve the work of running the public sector to independent bodies (so avoiding being continuously concerned with these problems in Cabinet) for they will always feel that they must be able to intervene in the nationalized industries and other public agencies in order to carry out policies for keeping the economy under control.

The pressure on the centre could be much reduced by handing over responsibility for education and the social services to elected regional bodies with the power to raise money by taxation; and having no 'national' policies for education, health and housing. The central government would then provide only the underlying legislative framework, and provide grants to the regional governments for them to spend as they thought best. But the experience of the last twenty-five years is that there is no regional consciousness upon which such a decentralized system could be based. Differences between standards provided by local authorities are regarded by the public and the experts in these fields as 'anomalies' which should be 'put right' by national measures, and not an expression of local choice and independence.

To make a large enough move to make any noticeable difference to the load on the Cabinet and the central machinery of government would require a revolution in public opinion. Entry into Europe will not help: it will introduce a new dimension of central government responsibility into the consideration of most questions, and will for the first ten years or so increase the load on central government and not reduce it. So we must assume that the load on central government is more likely to increase than to diminish. The answer must be found, therefore, in equipping the central machinery of government to do its work better. The argument starts here between a central government machinery consisting of a few large departments and one of more and smaller departments.

SIZE OF DEPARTMENTS

Table II sets out figures about the size of departments, for which I am indebted to the Civil Service Department. They show the number of Ministers, the number of top-level staff, and the total staff, distinguishing between those engaged in central administration and those engaged in the provision of public services or the provision of services to other departments. The best indication of the size of the load and the burden on Ministers (which is the crucial question) is the number of Under-Secretaries and above, which is closely correlated with the number of staff engaged in central administration. These columns in Table II illustrate the difference of scale between the 'giant' departments and the 'conventional' departments. Note that the provision of large nation-wide services, such as the collection of direct taxes (60,000 Inland Revenue staff), the social security benefit regional organization (51,000), employment and training services (16,000), or indeed the maintenance, repair, storage and supply organizations for the Services (110,000) do not present the kind of problems that limit the viable size of a department. Policy formulation and all that goes with it in the Cabinet, in Parliament and in the country, rather than executive action, is what creates the problems of scale.

Classification by expenditure which at first sight is a natural indication of load, is a misleading guide. Public expenditure in the only meaningful sense includes direct expenditure by departments (e.g. defence), expenditures from national insurance funds, expenditures by local authorities and other public bodies and certain expenditures by nationalized industries (all controlled to a varying extent by departments). The aggregate of expenditure coming within one department's purview does not determine the scale of the departmental effort required to handle it: public expenditure on education is greater than that on defence, but it needs only a very small central government machine to deal with it.

	MINISTERS		SENIOR STAFF			TOTAL STAFF (thousands)	
	Ministers	Parly. Secs.	Permanent and Second Perm. Secs.	Deputy Secs. and above	Under Secs. and above	Total Staff	of which Central Administration
Giant Departments							
Foreign & Commonwealth	4	3	16	51	183	13	4.9
Defence	3	3	6	23	125	281	(19.0)
Trade & Industry	4	3	3	20	95	28	6.5
Environment	4	4	3	20	86	76	6.2
Social Services	2	2	3	12	57	76	7.4
Conventional Departments							
Scotland	2	3	1	6	33	11	4.0
Agriculture, Fisheries & Food	1	1	1	8	33	16	3.7
Home Office	3	1	1	5	32	26	3.3
Employment	2	2	1	6	28	33	1.7
Education & Science	2	2	2	9	27	4	2.2
Very Small Departments							
Lord Chancellor's Department	1	0	1	4	13	13	0.2
Wales	2	0	0	1	7	1	0.8
Posts & Telecommunications	1	0	0	1	4	½	0.3
Centre Departments							
Chancellor of the Exchequer's (Treasury, Inland Revenue, Customs & Excise, etc.)	4	0	7	26	86	116	6.4
Civil Service Department	1	1	3	8	28	2	1.2
Cabinet Office	0	0	5	12	24	½	0.6

NOTE.—Includes only Ministers with responsibilities within Departments. Staffs divided according to Ministerial responsibility (e.g. DOE includes Ordnance Survey). Senior staffs, classified by salary (and ambassadors by grade), as of 1 October 1971. Staff figures exclude military staff and overseas locally-engaged staff. Central administration column is from new presentation given by Mr Howell on 9 November 1971 (*Hansard*, cols. 130 to 140): it includes HQ staff concerned with policy and central services, e.g. personnel, finance.

INTERNAL AND EXTERNAL ECONOMIES

We look at the optimal size of departments in two ways. First, there are the internal economies and diseconomies, the comparison between having a large department or a number of small departments to handle a set of problems. Where are the limits of size of one department under one Minister and one Permanent Secretary; and what is gained or lost by pushing up the size of the department to this limit? Is a large department a good thing in itself, and how large should it be? Second, there are the external economies and diseconomies: from the point of view of the problems of running the whole Government, is it better to have large or small departments? Should one, in order to simplify the relations between the departments and make the system easier to run from the centre, reduce the number of departments to the lowest possible figure; or should one take as the main criterion the size of unit which is best for carrying out the tasks at the periphery? It is not unlike the problem of a large holding company in deciding whether to have a few large and powerful subsidiaries or a larger number of small subsidiaries, in a business in which all the activities are interlocked, and in which the holding company management will be held personally and publicly accountable for the subsidiaries' actions.

COHERENCE OF A DEPARTMENT

There is one definite limit to the size of a department under one Cabinet Minister and one Permanent Secretary. This is the coherence of the subject-matter of the department, for which the Minister is responsible to Parliament. The task of a Minister in charge of a department, whatever its size, is to formulate and express a political concept covering the department's entire field of responsibility. This concept determines his handling of the department's business in Cabinet and in Parliament, and informs all the department's activity. There is no place for a 'conglomerate'. Disparate subjects may be brought under one Minister, simply because none is important enough to justify having a Minister to itself. But the great Departments of State should be set up to deal with great subjects of State, with a Minister with a philosophy and a policy which embraces all his subjects and relates them together. There should be only one Minister in charge of each great subject of State, for if one tries to divide one great subject between two Ministers each with his own philosophy and policy, it is most unlikely that coherent government will result: it is probable, indeed, that some other Minister, or the Cabinet itself, will have to spend time mediating and adjudicating between them.

Judged by this criterion, FCO and the Ministry of Defence must be viable units, for their subject-matter is unquestionably coherent and best handled according to one Minister's concept. DTI is likewise coherent in this sense: there is no part of it which is not 'trade and industry' and which involves different basic concepts from the rest. The coherence of all parts of DOE is less obvious: the integration of housing and transport and local government is excellent, but the link with the provision and upkeep of Government buildings is more tenuous. In practice, there is little administratively in common between the health and national insurance sides of DHSS, but there is a useful 'social services' concept. The department which is most 'conglomerate' is one of the oldest of all, the Home Office. Taking the departments as a whole, however, it could not reasonably be argued that the present structure breaches the principle that each department should have coherent subject-matter.

SECTIONAL INTERESTS

At the other end of the spectrum is the question whether the scope of some departments is too narrow. The danger of excessive narrowness is as great as that of excessive width. If the activities of a Minister and his department are focused on one small sector of the national life, the interests of that small sector will get too much weight in the Cabinet and in government generally. This is not a question of 'vested interests' in the pejorative sense of the term, although these are always there, and are more difficult to deal with when the purpose of the department and the purpose of the 'vested interests' run closely together. The essence of good government is to appraise all sectional interests against the Government's concept of the national interest; and this cannot happen if some sectional interests are given too large a voice. This is not a matter of the size of the department. The dangerous combination is that of a powerful department with a narrow scope. A small department with a narrow scope is unlikely to be strong enough in the Cabinet and in Whitehall: the greater danger is that it will be ineffective.

The balance between size and scope is fundamental. In defence, for example, the three old Service Departments were all substantial in size, but each dedicated to the interest of its own Service – a very narrow scope, even within the subject of defence. The giant Ministry of Defence is of tremendous size and manageable scope, much more sensible for defence than the old system. The foreign affairs illustration shows the point well also. Throughout the process of formulating economic policy towards Europe and through the successive negotiations from the early 1950s onwards, the separate Commonwealth Relations Office, responsible for the relations between Britain and the independent Commonwealth countries, was inevitably in effect a spokesman for the commercial interests of the Commonwealth countries (particularly, given the trade network, for the old Dominions). Many people thought that we could have got into the Common Market ten to fifteen years earlier and on better terms both for Britain and for the Commonwealth countries, and in a much more favourable and expansive economic background, if our Governments had decided earlier where our interests lay, and had negotiated more flexibly. If this is true, then the cost of having this representation in the Government of one sectional interest (admittedly very important) which was always a brake on policy decisions and on manoeuvre in negotiation may have been very great.

The Ministry of Agriculture and Fisheries was another spokesman for a sectional interest which was naturally opposed to a policy of economic union with Europe, and here too was another built-in brake on Governments' movement towards the Common Market. The Department's sectional character was to some extent mitigated in the years following its merging with the Ministry of Food in 1955, and its assumption of the responsibility for the Government's relations with the food industries and trades and for consumer protection in food; and of course in European policy the sectional interest of our agricultural industry changed as it began to appear that entry into the Common Market was likely in general to benefit the interests of British farmers rather than damage them. The position of the Secretary of State for Commonwealth Relations and the Minister of Agriculture and their Departments illustrates the impact that representation of sectional interests by Cabinet Ministers with strong departments behind them can have on the course of Government policy.

Similarly, on the industrial side, would the Government in 1962 have embarked upon the Concorde project if the responsibility for civil aircraft development and the support of the aircraft industry had been within a department with wide responsibilities for industry and transport (and which therefore had to weigh its choices between a score of competing projects for resources) instead of being in a Ministry of Aviation specifically created only two or three years before in order to foster aviation? Again, was it sensible in the interests of the application of science and scientific research to industry to have the Department of Scientific and Industrial Research as a scientific enclave, entirely separate from the departments concerned with industry? One can well argue that it both led the scientists into an 'ivory tower' instead of the market place and also left the industrial departments immured in the non-scientific politicians' and administrators' 'ivory tower'.

SPREAD AND SCOPE

The spread and scope of a department appear as the fundamental criteria which determine the limits of size. If the spread and scope are too big, the department becomes a conglomerate, which cannot work effectively in government. If the spread and scope are too small, the department either becomes an enclave carrying on its work in a backwater of public affairs or becomes the voice of a sectional interest, distorting the use of national resources and frustrating the sensible development of national policy.

In the present departmental structure, provided that one assumes that the Ministry of Agriculture, Fisheries and Food has a sufficiently balanced series of responsibilities to be no longer regarded as a solely sectional interest – which I would personally consider to be a legitimate view – there are only two points which might be criticized on these criteria. One is the Welsh Office, and the presence of a Secretary of State for Wales in the Cabinet. This now seems to be established practice, which can be justified on the widest political grounds whatever may be the merits of conducting a separate public administration for about 5 per cent. of England and Wales: the political advantage for the cohesion of the whole community which results from the specific representation of this particular section of the community may be regarded as outweighing the economic loss to the whole community from the failure to get the economies of scale in the administration of the various services and from whatever misdirection of resources may occur. The other anomaly is the Ministry of Posts and Telecommunications, which will probably be absorbed into one or more of the main departments sooner or later: the responsibility for supervising a nationalized industry should never be carried by a department with no wider functions, for such department has no wider experience to contribute; and the responsibility for the control of broadcasting, although a very important one, manifestly does not require a special department. However, these are not easy functions to allocate to the existing departments, and this is not a case in which the Ministry represents a damaging sectional interest.

MINISTERIAL HANDLING

Of equal importance to 'spread' and 'scope' is the problem of handling by Ministers. The new giant departments have teams of Ministers, at the head of which is THE MINISTER, responsible to the Cabinet and to Parliament for the whole department – Mr Davies for DTI and Mr Walker for DOE. It is possible to have two Cabinet Ministers in one department. In the last ten years this has often been so in the Treasury and the Foreign Office, for good reasons; and in the 1969 Ministry of Technology there were Mr Benn and Mr Lever, and it worked well. But for giant departments generally it is in my view right to have one and only one; and if one Minister cannot cover the whole of the department's Cabinet business, I would say that this proved that the department was too large. In DTI and DOE there are three Ministers below THE MINISTER, all Ministers with the rank and standing of men and women who are capable of dealing with the department's business, both in Parliament and with the customers outside. Below them again are Parliamentary Secretaries, bringing the numbers in each department up to seven or eight.

THE MINISTER must clearly be able to handle the department's business in Cabinet; and he must be able to lead his team, guiding them on policy, supporting them when they run into difficulty, and knowing about the subjects with which they are dealing to handle them at a moment's notice in Cabinet, but in no circumstances superseding them in their negotiations with industries or local authorities or whoever the customers may be. This requires a somewhat different mix of qualities from those which top-ranking Ministers have usually needed in the past. The three subsidiary Ministers also have a difficult task, for they must both behave as responsible Ministers and cede the ultimate responsibility to THE MINISTER. Formerly, men of this level would often have smaller departments of their own, which is a different kind of experience. The Minister in charge of a small department who was outside the Cabinet would try to distinguish himself by his conduct of his department and by pressing the department's sectional interests. In the new system, the subsidiary Minister must distinguish himself as a member of a team working over a large area, which is much more difficult. Rising politicians will certainly adjust themselves rapidly to this change in the requirements for promotion. This could lead eventually to better professionalism and teamwork in the Cabinet and fewer buccaneers; and for a country which can no longer determine the course of world events and must live by adapting itself quickly and easily to them, this may be a change for the better.

These problems on the Ministerial plane depend partly upon formal structure and partly upon the qualities of the individuals who are available and the Prime Minister's skill in deploying them. If one had to make an argument against the giant department it would be based on this kind of consideration, not unlike the corresponding argument in industry, that it may be easier to find and deploy twenty capable men and women than to find and deploy ten men and women of the highest capacity. This will probably sort itself out in time, but I stress it here because in this as in all questions of management the decisive considerations relate to people and not to analysis.

CIVIL SERVICE PROBLEMS

There are problems of civil service organization and people at the top of the giant departments which are similar to those of Ministers. There will be fewer full Permanent Secretaries and more Second Permanent Secretaries, men of marginally lower rank and standing. The tasks of Permanent Secretaries change, with more emphasis on management and less on the details of policy, with more emphasis on the strategy of the whole department and Ministerial team and less on the day-to-day tactics. I do not believe that these considerations are limiting factors in their own right, as distinct from the limiting factors of scope and Ministerial handling. Nobody can survive in the top echelons of the civil service nowadays without great adaptability and ability to work in teams; and compared with Ministers, civil servants have the advantage of continuity and of not being in the firing line, which makes it easier to see the changing situations objectively and adapt to them.

Managing giant departments presents problems, but I do not believe them to be significantly greater than those of managing the conventional departments of the past. The intractable problems are those of communication within the department, and of knowing what is going on and of influencing the thought and attitudes throughout the entire structure. But the conventional departments have been large enough for twenty-five years past to present these problems acutely, and the manifest need in a giant department to think and organize about this may lead to better results than were achieved previously when less attention was paid to this at the top. Similarly, the handling of staff – promotion machinery, training, career development, management services – may be better done in a giant department, where it obviously must be organized, than in a department of conventional size which tries to use the traditional informal methods which are excellent in a small organization where the men at the top can have personal knowledge of everyone in the department but which are inadequate as soon as the department reaches what might be regarded as the 'normal' size in the 1950s and 1960s.

RESOURCE ALLOCATION

The giant department must have an apparatus and procedure to determine its strategy and to allocate its resources. In a small department with only a few tasks, the Minister and the top officials can carry the strategy and priorities in their own heads. But sorting out the priorities of a giant department is very different; and one of the main reasons for having a giant department is to enable the Government's choices to be properly made. By joining the old Ministries of Transport and Housing and Local Government into one DOE, the Government could bring the decisions on housing, roads and other public infrastructure into one system, and bind these into an articulated programme. The 1972 DTI is responsible, like the 1969 Ministry of Technology, for a wide range of public expenditures for the support of industry and for industrial investment – civil aircraft projects, shipbuilding, nationalized industries' investment, nuclear reactor development, regional assistance and so on. Bringing these together in one department makes it possible to try to apply the same criteria and policy throughout, so that the prospective return to the national economy from the investment of £10 million of public resources in each of them is reasonably similar. Only in departments of this size is it practicable to employ the special skills which are needed to make such comparisons.

Such criteria can be developed only when there are different kinds of things to be compared. For civil aircraft projects, highly sophisticated appraisal techniques were introduced, which led the Government, for example, to decide against Government participation in the European airbus. Similarly for appraisal of nuclear reactors. In the industrial and even in the advanced technology fields, the process of creating an appraisal system is more straightforward than the appraisal of environmental investment, as was shown by the fate of the Roskill Commission's analysis about the third London airport – by far the most comprehensive and sophisticated cost-benefit analysis ever made in this country, and probably anywhere. Nevertheless, wherever choices are made for the allocation of resources and priority between projects, a system of appraisal must be developed, for otherwise the Government have no objective guidelines at all. The last word throughout the public sector must always be with the political judgement, which embraces all the considerations which cannot be measured by the tools of the social sciences. It is sometimes argued that because the decision in the last resort is always a political one it is silly to spend a lot of resources and effort on serious appraisal. This view is in my opinion wholly mistaken. The point of the economic or social/economic appraisal is to get the considerations clear from the point of view of the national economy (i.e. the national economic interest), so that if the Government wish to bring other arguments to bear, the cost of doing so is definitely known; and to stop people from using wrong and untrue economic arguments to justify what they want to do (maybe on entirely legitimate grounds).

I emphasize this because it is in my opinion right for public expenditure decisions to be taken on political grounds, for that is what public affairs are about; and there are no 'correct' and 'non-political' methods of deciding how public money should be spent. What is wrong is to take public expenditure decisions without a clear understanding of the objective economic and social considerations as far as these can be determined, and of the cost of disregarding them. The more each department is required to set up the apparatus and procedures to sort out its own decisions and priorities in this way, and the more firmly it is laid down at the centre of government that the Cabinet will not agree to expenditure proposals unless this is done, the more likely it is that the political judgements will be made wisely and realistically. There will always be opposition to this in any Government, for there will always be some Ministers who will prefer catch-as-catch-can and will expect to get more from their colleagues by political short cuts. This is where the role of the Prime Minister, and indeed of successive Prime Ministers, is of decisive importance.

TREASURY CONTROL

With few and large departments, each capable of working out its own strategy, allocating its own resources, and settling its own problems within itself, the way is cleared for substantial external economies. The functions of the Treasury for financial control and of the Civil Service Department for civil service manpower control can be radically changed. These cease to be detailed day-to-day controls, and become much wider – allocation of resources between departments, examination of departments' own control and decision-making systems, laying down the groundrules for departments' operations, receiving regular performance and progress reports. In these questions of finance and manpower, the relationship between the Treasury and the Civil Service Department on the one hand and the giant department on the other becomes much more like that between a holding company and a powerful subsidiary.

In the last ten years, this relationship has changed greatly, following the Plowden Report on Control of Public Expenditure of 1961, but it is still a mixture between the 'holding company' concept and the old-fashioned detailed day-to-day control. The full change cannot come until there are only a few main departments, each with its own effective organization. But when this happens, it will greatly improve the machinery of government, for the Treasury and the Civil Service Department will then be able to concentrate on the proper work of the centre, instead of acting as censors and trying to do what the departments should do for themselves.

LESS CO-ORDINATION

Another great improvement from the point of view of the centre happens because giant departments can solve their problems themselves without the need for co-ordination from the centre and without the need for an immense apparatus of Cabinet committees. Moreover, this should provide better answers, for the process of co-ordination and adjudication at the centre is essentially one of bringing in people who know nothing of a problem in order to get it solved; and the verdict may go in favour of the strongest Minister rather than the Minister who is right, and may indeed be decided according to fortuitous circumstances on the day on which the Ministerial argument takes place – what other questions are up for decision at the same time (and the possibility of package compromise), which Minister is momentarily in the ascendant and which in the dog-house, whether the co-ordinating Minister is tired or fresh and who has briefed him, etc.

Again, with small departments, there is a tendency for polarization to take place: the protagonists, instead of genuinely seeking a sensible solution, take extreme positions in order to gain in a compromise settlement. For example, there may be a controversy between a nationalized industry and its suppliers of equipment: before the creation of giant departments, the former would be under the Minister of Power, the latter under the Ministry of Technology or the Board of Trade. Each industry would rely upon its own department and its own Minister to fight its case, if necessary to the Cabinet; and in practice the problem might never be solved at all. But when both are within the scope of DTI, they know that one Minister must take the decision; and both industries are then under pressure to seek solutions themselves.

Even when the number of departments has been reduced to the practical minimum there will be overlappings of interests. But in general there will be two or perhaps three giant departments involved instead of five or six, and this immensely simplifies the task of discussion and settlement, and avoids the burden upon the centre of having to organize an endless series of meetings. In such discussion, moreover, the protagonists are more equal. Instead of the Treasury towering over several weaker departments in the economic field, it is confronted by a powerful DTI. Regional industrial policy involves DOE and DTI (with the Scots and the Welsh). Defence and overseas policy are concentrated on Defence and FCO (with of course the Treasury). This should all lead to faster and better government, and better-informed and less arbitrary decisions, and less load on the desperately overloaded centre. It takes time to make this effective, for in each department a new integrated structure must replace the structures of the original constituent departments. But this is not inherently difficult.

GAINS AT THE CENTRE

Seen from the very centre of government, the gains from all these factors are great. It becomes possible to have a smaller Cabinet, a perennial preoccupation of Prime Ministers. It avoids the awkwardness of having some departments with a Minister not in the Cabinet, an anomaly which is bad for their work (at the moment, the Ministry of Posts and Telecommunications is the only one). It avoids having some Cabinet Ministers who are always concerned to defend sectional interests; and it provides some large and exacting Ministerial jobs. It also reduces the load on the Cabinet by having fewer problems which engage the interests of many departments and thus occupy senior Ministers and the central machine; and therefore it enables the Cabinet to devote more time to its true (but often ignored) function of determining the strategy of the Government.

ADVANTAGE OF GIANT DEPARTMENTS

My conclusion is that the external economies from having a few giant departments instead of a large number of conventional departments are substantial if they can be attained. But this cannot be done by stealth. The improvements will not happen unless they are made to happen – the changed role of the Treasury and the Civil Service Department, the willingness of the Cabinet to allow the Ministers in charge of giant departments to settle issues within their

own department and in consultation with each other instead of bringing them to Cabinet committees, the introduction to the Cabinet
of systematic discussion of the Government's strategy. I have pointed
out that these changes are not necessarily in the interests of all
Ministers, for they introduce the concept of a deliberately thought
out long-term Government policy and strategy and allocation of
resources between departments to carry it out, which will by no
means suit all Ministers.

The internal economies are less decisive, but my own opinion,
which is backed by some experience, is that the giant departments
can be run effectively, provided that the two basic conditions are
met, viz. that the scope and subject-matter of the department's work
makes a coherent whole, and that the scale and complexity of the
work is within the capability of the department's team of Ministers
to handle. My own impression is that DTI and DOE are, so to speak,
bumping up against the ceiling in these respects; but it is early days
to judge. The potential gains at the centre seem to me so great that
if one had to choose whether to run risks with the size of the giant
departments or to retreat from the concept of giant departments, I
would unhesitatingly recommend the former.

TIME AND STABILITY

Finally, the dimension of time. In all changes of machinery of government there is a heavy disturbance cost. Few people welcome change
for its own sake, for it alters everyone's working relations, concentration on the job, career expectations. It occupies the time and thought
and energy of the people at the top of the department, at the expense
of their proper work. It may at one stroke destroy many years of
constructive organizing effort. In the Ministry of Technology we
had four years of mergers involving five important departments. To
carry out these mergers and create an integrated department, we did
immense operations in creating promotion machinery, training, career
development, the building of new administrative structures, all necessarily tailored to the new department's needs. We did this three
times – once when the original Ministry was formed in November
1964; once when it was merged with the Ministry of Aviation in
February 1967; once when it was merged with the Ministry of Power
and large chunks of the Board of Trade and the Department of
Economic Affairs in October 1969. When the department was split
up again in October 1970 all this work inevitably vanished.

My own opinion, which I have never heard challenged by anyone
with experience of this kind of operation, is that it takes about two

years to get a merged department into working shape, and probably twice as long to begin to secure the real benefits which the merger is designed to achieve. So the case for change must be very powerful if it is to be justified and if it is to be a worthwhile investment of administrative effort.

Of course there may be times when the departments have got into a rut and a shock is needed. But after the experience of the last ten years, this is not the situation in Whitehall. The overriding need is now a stability of structure for at least ten years, to let the new departments settle down and to enable the changes at the centre to be made gradually but steadily in order to realize the potential gains which are the justification for the change of system. This should not be contentious between the political parties. The idea that seems to have developed in the last ten years that a new Administration should change the machinery of government, which gives a party-political content to these changes and tends to make further changes inevitable at the next swing of the political pendulum, is unlikely to help any political party. Both parties gain equally from improvements in the machinery of government, and there is nothing in the present structure that is more appropriate to a Conservative Government than to a Labour Government. For both parties, as we have seen, changing the machinery of government is an expensive investment, the benefits from which can accrue only after several years of stability; and to regard such changes as a means of tangibly improving a Government's performance within the lifetime of one Parliament is likely to prove itself to be a mirage. It is greatly to be hoped, therefore, that the increasing academic and political interest in the machinery of government will not create a political atmosphere which makes this subject a field for political controversy and thus usher in a further era of continuous change.

C. H. Sisson

The Civil Service after Fulton

Whether or not new wine is being poured into the Civil Service these days – and it has been habitual ever since the Fulton Report to assert that there is some heady liquor about – it is certain that the old bottles are there to receive it. They stand in rows, many decorated, and those of the largest sizes have never been so numerous. Or perhaps not since the war. The Civil Service waxes and wanes – but on the whole waxes – and it is a curious consequence of the fact that it is *permanent* that the top posts are always manned, disproportionately, by those who have found favour during an expansive epoch. An administration which has in view even a gentle repression of this buoyant corps therefore starts with a disadvantage. It takes several years of attrition even to arrive at a point from which they would wish to have started. By then another election is in sight, and that in itself sometimes has liberating consequences, if you regard White-hall as a genius to be liberated.

The business of filling senior posts is one of the more mysterious processes in this strange world. It centres around what is best conceived of as a sort of Renaissance court maintained by a functionary known as the Head of the Civil Service. It was formerly kept in the Treasury, by Sir Lawrence (now Lord) Helsby. Now it is kept in the Civil Service Department, which of course is half of the Treasury under another name, by Sir William Armstrong who has given it the decency of certain constitutional proprieties – in the form of an advisory committee – without, it may be conjectured, very much changing the nature of the processes which lead to one of the more august appointments. Renaissance courts are best left to the imagination. If there are vials of poison as well as more pleasant potions in circulation the prince, although immensely powerful, has to watch the game around him, though it would be a clumsy player indeed who was more than occasionally found on the wrong side.

Reprinted from *The Spectator* (20 February 1971), p. 250; (27 February 1971), p. 282; (6 March 1971), p. 314. By permission of the author and the publisher.

But this court is, of course, encircled by a huge congeries of lesser courts, kept by the Permanent Secretaries of the respective Departments. Each of these – only relatively, of course – petty princelings has his own game to play, and his own domestic set of vials and daggers. There are courtiers everywhere who, in good times, think up their own combinations. A Deputy Secretary who is able to fix his own Minister may be able to make sure of his next step, and a knighthood, and if he can also fix the Head of the Civil Service he can probably leave his own Permanent Secretary standing. Ability to catch the eye of a Minister is something the Head of the Civil Service will, in any case, properly not ignore, and if the eye caught is exalted enough a very slight thrill of pleasure on both sides may be enough to achieve remarkable results in the way of a career. Generally, however, it may be said that the game, played with immense discretion as one would expect from so judicious a body of men, is one in which both the Head of the Civil Service and the Departmental Permanent Secretaries have things as much their own way as anyone is likely to, in this hard world.

The characteristics of the higher reaches of the Civil Service are, however, mainly determined by the prevalent forces which mould what used to be called the Administrative Class at large. There is a soggy responsiveness to public opinion which over the long years produces, in a typical member of that former class, a compulsive shrinking from any fact not recognized by the fashion of the moment. It is not that these men are unintelligent; rather the reverse. They lucidly understand the rules of the milieu in which they are allowed to operate, and do not let their understanding interfere with the serious business of earning their livelihoods. The universe of discourse in which a modern government operates is a very restricted one. There are many subjects in which government meddles, and much is made of that by those who like to dwell on the complexity of affairs – real enough in its kind – but the manner of dealing with them has a certain monotony. It is this which accounts for the famous – and now somewhat denigrated – versatility of the late Administrative Class, and enabled, say, a backroom Treasury man suddenly to appear before the world in the role of the manager of a vast organization. The secret is such that it is hardly possible to state it without appearing to be touched by cynicism. It is that, in spite of the importance of facts, and the collection of facts, in the Whitehall milieu, it is not directly they which, in the end, determine the outcome of any crisis. It is what the public most immediately concerned will stand for, at the moment. The art of the administrator in Whitehall, therefore, is to make sure that facts do not get the upper hand. He has to learn to use them in a way which will produce answers which are right by quite different criteria, without in the process getting so confused that the actual mechanics of the conjuring trick come to light, for that too would produce a bad effect on opinion and, by the rules of the game, he would be disqualified. There is no doubt that the pressure of what are called – I suppose jokingly – the public media of communication has immensely increased the part played by opinion in the solution of the administrator's problems. Reality can no longer hope to keep up with what is said to be going on. It takes a long time actually to *do* anything, in a large organization. The best official, therefore, would be one who could shuffle policies a dozen times while ensuring that reality was left quite intact.

While the Fulton Committee could hardly be expected to make revolutionary suggestions which would prove, in execution, absolutely anodyne, certain of their recommendations are models in this kind. They proposed, for example, that 'all classes should be abolished and replaced by a single, unified grading structure covering all civil servants from top to bottom in the non-industrial part of the Service'. One can see at once the appeal of that 'all classes should be abolished', which for emotive effect hardly needs the rest of the sentence. This happy revolution is already on the way. From 1 January this year the Administrative, Executive and Clerical Classes disappeared into one huge pot. What a casting down of barriers! What new flexibility! In making this recommendation the Fulton Committee were following the lead given in the evidence of the Treasury, who knew that the barriers had been down effectively for some years so that one might safely speculate that the real changes in the five years after Fulton, in this respect, will be no greater than in the five years before. There must be some prominent demonstrations, in accordance with the rules, to show that reality is indeed following policy. The staff associations will naturally watch closely and will have fulfilled their mission when they have made the Service more expensive for the change. Such exercises are not new and some horse-trading, the consequence of which will take some years to work out, is inevitable. The comedy of pseudo-egalitarianism goes so far, in the current exercise, that in order to do away with the shocking associations of the word Administrative the new-style graduate entrants are to be called – illiterately – *administration* trainees. There is a big move indeed. There is invention for you. The best one can say of the new arrangement – apart from the fact that it won't make much difference, if that is a good point – is that no young graduate will be sure, when he comes in, that it is a career in Whitehall that he is coming for, for he may find himself not less usefully employed in Wigan. Whether that wholesome deprivation will in fact help to man up the crowded corridors of Whitehall – which after all have to be manned, if not necessarily crowded to the extent they now are – is another matter.

The pseudo-revolution of abolishing classes is of interest as exhibiting a response, infinitely devious in its course through the staff associations, the Treasury, the Fulton Committee and at last through the Civil Service Department, not merely to the opinion of an outside public but to the seething forces of democracy within, which certainly have not less to do with the changes than have the objective needs of the Service. This is an influence which could get out of hand, for the aims of staff associations are not those of management, and should not be, though these enterprising bodies are always ready to take over where they find an inertia or complacency that will allow it. The right tension between management and associations can – the interests of the staff apart – be instructive to the management; indeed, it is the indispensable mark of taut control, and the moment too bland a smile of co-operation appears on the faces of the two sides you may be sure that they are up to no good. Naturally, the larger the scale of the co-operation the more inane the smile. The phenomenon is something that the public should watch for, though it is not very well placed to watch. And the larger the Civil Service is, the nearer it approaches to being an electoral interest in its own right. The simultaneous impingement of mass opinion from outside and inside would make – the use of the conditional implies a hope that we have not yet reached this fatal point, though assuredly it is not far off – would, then, leave the Civil Service unmanaged and finally unmanageable.

THE GREAT MANAGEMENT HOAX

It is the pretension, precisely, of the elements now most influential in the Civil Service that that body is being managed with closeness and efficiency as never before. This pretension is quite without foundation though it has, certainly, superstructure. The suggestion is that a new managerial approach, instigated of course from the top, shows itself in the furthest reaches of employment exchanges and typing pools, as if local offices and other places where the more useful work is done were now for the first time sensible of the need for such control. The exact opposite is in fact the case. Employment exchanges were producing, long before the war, a race of civil servants as tough and as aware as any now to be found in Whitehall – I understate the case – of the need to pack work into procedures and to see that it is done. The characteristic of the last few years is a growth of the *mythology* of management. There has been a deliberate and persistent propagation of the idea that management is a new conception in the Civil Service, and an attempt to persuade people, in and outside the service, that analytical procedures of a kind which have always held an important place at middle executive levels have now been introduced as a startling novelty from the top, and that this is about to produce a new golden age of efficiency. One can only compare the untiring vein of talk on these lines which emerges from influential quarters with the effusions of those, in other fields, whose pronouncements seem to suggest that sex is a novelty or that fornication has just been discovered. In both worlds, of course, there are some queer habits about and there has even been some technical change.

If there has been a new emphasis on management, as opposed to the more political side of Civil Service activity, it may be traced to a realization by some of the more astute persons among those on whom falls the duty of justifying the Civil Service to Ministers that their own role as policymakers was a somewhat elusive and suspect one and that a publicly-acceptable alibi had better be found. The transition is not as difficult as you might think, for these men are, by profession, the pickers-up of second-hand ideas whose careers have been spent in selecting from the garbage heap what they think might be acceptable to their masters of the moment or, more accurately expressed, the masters on whom for the moment the future of their careers largely depends. It is, of course, not necessary for these men to practise management, in any serious way, in order to acquire the reputation of people who care for such things. All they have to do is to persuade politicians and public – who are of course gasping to be persuaded of exactly that – that this is what is mainly on their minds. The actual work they need not touch; and certainly they touch it no more than their predecessors – some of them much less so, for the business of apologetics is apt to become a full-time job. It is possible to occupy a top position in a major department in Whitehall without having the capacity to run a tobacco shop, whatever skills of a political and apologetic kind one may have acquired in thirty years in the service, or been born with.

The sleight of hand has undoubtedly been made the easier by the prevalence, since Keynes, of the notion that the primary duty of governments is the management of the economy, and it is easy to confuse this wider sense of management – what the government does, or purports to do, to the economy as a whole – with the specific control of the operations of its own staff and the execution of functions which it has precise and explicit responsibilities for carrying out. The more tangible functions are no doubt, in some respects, simpler, but they have one great drawback. Their success or unsuccess can often be plainly seen, while the management of the economy gives almost unlimited play to the arts of apologetics in which the best civil servants are most highly trained, and prizes are likely to go to the quickest seekers after alibis, always able to move to the next point at the first sight of a crack in the current theory. It is at what pass for the most crucial points of the Whitehall control system that the development of apologetics is fastest and where, in any case, the chronic pressure for the urgent, as against the important, is most acutely felt.

Nowhere has the overlaying of the Civil Service with talk of management, for reasons of public relations rather than out of regard for efficiency, been more evident than in the field of staff training. The Treasury evidence to Fulton included the report of a committee, among the members of which were experts of a fashionable kind, to give it a respectability which a mere Civil Service committee would not have had. The committee was supposed to study the place of management training in the Service. In fact it did not concern itself with such trivia as whether management training, 'as ordinarily understood in business schools and elsewhere', was what the Service most needed, and it is enigmatically reported that 'not all members of the working party would regard the term' as covering what was wanted. The committee did not examine the relevance of the training to be given to the work actually done; the object was to give the impression that the Treasury was in accord with fashion rather than to improve efficiency. A great superstructure was built on this nonfoundation, and this in turn was used to justify the setting up of the Civil Service College, the opening of which was the first public engagement of the Prime Minister, who had inherited it from his predecessor. It is not that the training given in business schools is not appropriate for some people in the service, or that there is not a case for a Civil Service College. But there is no doubt that a less hasty and dogmatic approach would not only have been very much cheaper to the taxpayer but would have helped more people to do their work better. It need hardly be said that, in this hasty escalation, the numerate techniques which were to save the Service in the future played virtually no part. Cost benefit, ha! ha!

It is of course a consequence of centralization, in so huge an organization as the Civil Service, that it enables mistakes to be perpetrated on an immense scale. The Fulton Committee, some at least of the members of which should have known better, encouraged the notion of a managerial brain which would operate in disjunction from the main policy departments. The second recommendation of the committee ran: 'The extended and unified central management of the Service should be made the responsibility of a new department created specifically for that purpose.' Creation is a strong expression for what actually happened. 'The role of the central management of the Service needs to be enlarged' – that was the Fulton doctrine, and with it went a desire, which cannot be said yet to have been realized, of imparting new hope to civil servants. 'There is today,' the report says, 'a lack of confidence in the Treasury as the centre of Civil Service management.' The Civil Service Department was intended to inspire that confidence, no doubt. 'In our judgement the Treasury has contributed' to this lack of confidence 'by employing too few staff on this work.' That at least has been put right.

Of course the Fulton Committee was not unaware that there are objections to the encroachment of central management. 'The expanded role' of the Civil Service Department was not to be 'allowed to develop into a takeover by central management of responsibilities that properly belong to other departments.' Still, it was to have 'a special part to play in assisting reorganization at the higher levels of departments; and in the last analysis it should be in a position both to call all departments to account for failure to use the recommended techniques, and to put in its own men to investigate any departmental organization and to recommend improvements'. Such a role is not negligible, and is the more unlikely to be neglected because with it goes a special influence over the careers of the more ambitious. The oddity, to put it no higher, of endowing with this power a department which has no expertise in the departmental policies which the respective organizations are meant to serve seems to have escaped notice. In practice, what Permanent Secretaries have to do, to look well at the centre, is to show an appropriate sensitivity to the need for the most 'modern' techniques, and whether or not a department is well organized is something which the Civil Service Department is not likely to know. Or if it does know, graver charges than ignorance would lie against it.

There was perhaps a false analogy at the back of the minds of the proponents of this system. They were perhaps thinking of the relationship of a company with its subsidiaries, but the *mutanda* are so many that no comparison holds. Apart from the fact that nothing like the standardization here practised would be dreamed of by any company not already far gone on the road to bureaucratization and decay, there is the fact that, however varied their activities and interests, companies are in the last analysis judged by the immensely simplified criterion of financial results. Those are the *results*, par excellence. That they may be achieved by chance or an easy market as well as by skill is beside the point. Number, in the form of money, has a final validity in business which it can never have in government, which rests on consent, aided more or less, according to the regime, by other means. The ambitious civil servant, therefore, has not so much to do well as to live plausibly. And this plausibility can be more stringently judged on the departmental scene than at the centre.

CAN ANYTHING BE DONE ABOUT IT?

One must not expect too much of an organization which has to take cognizance of all the muddled business which pushes itself before the attention of a modern government. It might be better if its existence was not admitted at all, as an entity, and there were just several hundred thousands of people, split up into groups more or less usefully and certainly very variously employed. The conception of the existence of the Civil Service as a corporate entity produces a dull intoxication, merely on account of numbers, and it even gives rise to the illusion that there are people who control it. At the same time, curiously enough, it produces a conviction that 'the old doctrine of ministerial responsibility' is 'a myth', though that doctrine has at least the merit of being part of an intelligible political system, and meaningful in a way that the conception of the responsibility of the bland officials who smile their way through successive changes of policy is not.

The recommendations put forward by the Fulton Committee were mostly pointed in the wrong direction – towards the melting of all classes into one, instead of the articulation of departmental and sub-departmental groups; and towards a conception of management detached from any intimate knowledge of the substance and purpose of particular pieces of work to be done. If there had to be a 'Civil Service Department' – and clearly it would not be practicable to pay so many people out of one purse without having some measure of co-ordination – it ought to have been established as a subordinate service department, leaving the major initiative and authority at various departmental points stretching out to the periphery. It is not self-evident that such a functionary as a Head of the Civil Service is wanted at all; he is the embodiment of a bogus unity. Of course there would be central questions to be settled, on which ministers would need some advice on a service-wide rather than on a departmental basis, but there is no reason why such questions should not be dealt with by a committee of Permanent Secretaries, with changing member-ship and, of course, changing chairmanship.

Within Departments, too, something ought to be done to diminish

259

the overweening, and sometimes nefarious, influence of Permanent Secretaries. This is a more difficult problem, but certainly not less urgent, for the harm which can be done by a bad Permanent Secretary is immense – something which can better be understood from below than from above. The key to this must be in the method of appointment, though the bad appointment can never be eliminated. It would be better, however, if such appointments were not made without some fairly wide canvass of the candidate's departmental colleagues, such as may take place before the appointment of the chairman of a company's board. It might be better, too, if the major policy issues were discussed by a departmental board, again of fairly wide membership, before formal advice was tendered to ministers. This would ensure that the advice had at least been tried in a circle of people who were not only generally knowledgeable about the background of the questions but about the people tendering the advice. The measure of internal openness which such a system would give would be at least some safeguard to a Minister and ensure that he was receiving something like the best Departmental advice and not merely the flattery of a courtier whose chief skill was in scenting what his master wanted to hear, and speaking accordingly. Combined with a system of canvassing views about possible promotions, it could in time exercise a considerable influence on the efficiency of the system.

The most urgent and immediate need in Whitehall, however, is undoubtedly for some way of getting rid of a very large number of senior officials quickly and soon. There is simply a superfluity, which will take years to work off, and which is being treasured at the moment in the certainty that, if nothing much in the system is changed, a further reflation of the Service will take place and it will be possible to use all the old bodies and promote a stream of new ones. A system for getting rid of people has become the more desirable because the fashion of early promotion to senior posts, which has prevailed for some years and which clearly has something to be said for it, must in a service from which people can hardly retire before sixty litter the place with former bright young men whose charm has left them. The need mainly arises, however, simply from the fact that there are too many cooks spoiling the broth, too many people meddling with the same things, too many layers through which advice goes without, necessarily, being improved. It is customary to represent the inflation of senior posts which regularly occurs in certain phases of government activity as merely marginal. But it is nothing of the kind. The distension is a form of organic disease which requires intermittent surgery.

Of course any radical change in the Civil Service must come from new ideas of government, not from Civil Service tinkering and techniques. The Civil Service is a subordinate institution and should always be treated as such. A much more rigorous analysis of function than has been customary for some years must take place, and Departments must be organized strictly to carry out those functions and not to 'think', an activity which, detached from performance, never got anyone anywhere, least of all a government. It is unfortunate that so many people in senior positions in the Service have never, before they reached their final eminence, had any experience of management to speak of. The typical career of the bright administrator is in essay-writing – which is usually called policy-making – and secretarial work of one kind and another. The direction of the eyes has always been upwards, to see what will please, not downwards, to see what is going on in the expensive organizations which are supposed to be under their control. This can result in an appalling incapacity in people who are rather intelligent than otherwise. Desirable though some technical improvement in management certainly is, in certain areas, it is the development of sensitivity down as well as up the line which is the greatest managerial need in Whitehall.

It does not do to expect too much of reform, or perhaps to think too much of general reforms at all. There are a number of particular problems rather than a general one. Nothing is easy, and all one can hope for is the removal of some of the prejudices which make things more difficult than they need be. Perhaps the era of freer discussion foreseen by Sir William Armstrong will help to alleviate the prejudices. That depends on how free the discussion is and there are, as Sir William has pointed out, strict limits to that, though in the realm of Civil Service organization they do not seem to be very serious ones. It is only the servants talking among themselves, about their own affairs, not about those of their masters, though to be sure radical action depends in the end on politicians. But the fact that Whitehall is parasitic though many of the executive organizations embedded in the Service, and serving the public directly, have their own *raison d'être* – should not make discussion impossible, though too many talking parasites would be a nuisance, one can see that. From that danger the desire to please, deeply institutionalized in the hierarchy of the Service, should protect us. A greater danger is the promotion of pseudo-discussion, with the pattern of right-mindedness determined from the top. From that, according to what we are usually taught, the robust traditions of our country should save us. I am not so sure, for vast modern organizations of their very nature induce pressures with a strong resemblance to those experienced, we understand, under the sway of the Czar of Muscovy.

It takes a long time for ideas to make their way in the world, and we must not complain too much if those which are being promulgated in Whitehall have a rather tatty look. It is the business of a democratic administration to pick up and diffuse ideas rather than to invent them, and too much novelty would hurt. But we should complain a little, because it is only in this way that cracks are opened through which hitherto unacceptable ideas filter in. Complaint comes better from influential quarters outside, and the source of much of what now passes for new in Whitehall is the academic thought of some years ago. But one of the dangers of leaving complaint entirely to outsiders is that they very rarely know enough to hit the mark exactly. Businessmen are aware of the pervasion of unfamiliar criteria, so that even where they see accountability they do not necessarily see what people are having to account for. Academics are apt to inflame themselves about obsessive questions of economics or sociology, or to pursue the dogmatism of a technique beyond what is reasonable. These points of view are valuable because of their lack of sympathy, but they supplement, and do not replace, criticism from within the Service itself. Admittedly the combination of one or two ideas with first-class practical experience must amount to something which is only just on the right side of insubordination.

W. A. Robson

The Relations of Nationalized Industries with the Public[1]

This inquiry into the relations of the publicly owned undertakings with the public is the second across-the-board type of inquiry which the Select Committee on Nationalized Industries has carried out.[2] The matter is one of the first importance.

The Committee's approach is to summarize briefly the relations between each industry and its consumers, then to consider the special machinery set up to represent consumers' interests, and finally to recommend such changes as the Committee thinks desirable. The Select Committee rightly emphasizes that the nationalized industries are subject to far more captious criticism from the public than any which is directed to the private sector. They do not, however, offer any explanation of this incontestable fact.

Relations with the public are not necessarily the same thing as relations with consumers, since 'the public' may be wider than or different from the body of consumers. Air lines, for example, must consider the reactions of people to whom aircraft noise constitutes a serious nuisance but who may never fly themselves. The National Coal Board's lack of concern with coal waste tips prior to the Aberfan disaster was a failure of relations with particular sections of the public. The Central Electricity Generating Board have difficult problems of public relations in connection with the siting of nuclear generating stations and the running of pylons across scenic landscape, but in neither case are the public concerned as consumers. The Select Committee does not seem to be aware of such non-consumer aspects of public relations.

The industries included in the report are coal, transport, electricity, gas, and the Post Office. It omits broadcasting, civil aviation, and steel together with a number of less ubiquitous activities such as forestry and the new towns.

Reprinted from *The Political Quarterly*, vol. 43, no. 2 (April–June 1972), pp. 229–232. By permission of the author and the publisher.

The report shows that the public corporations concerned are all anxious in principle to achieve or maintain good relations with their customers, but that the methods used and the degree of success achieved vary greatly. And so, too, do the status and functions of the statutory bodies which have been set up to represent the interests of consumers. The National Coal Board has very few direct contacts with consumers because nearly all of them buy their supplies from coal merchants, who may in turn obtain their supplies from wholesalers. The consultative machinery consists of the Domestic Coal Consumers' Council and a similar body for industrial consumers. There are no regional or local bodies to which complaints can be made. The Chairman of the DCCC told the Select Committee that although she would like to bring consumers' grievances to the notice of the Press she believed she is precluded from doing so and can only mention such matters in the Council's annual report – a slender document which receives little attention from Parliament or the Government. It is not surprising that the Council is almost unknown among the public and receives only fifty or sixty complaints a year.

The situation with the railways is worse so far as the official machinery is concerned, although there are regional committees as well as a Central Transport Consultative Committee, for since 1962 they have been forbidden to consider railway charges and reductions in services. Their main function is now confined to reporting on the hardship which a rail closure may cause and how it might be alleviated. The CTCC is not consulted on major questions of policy such as BR's five-year plan or the decision to electrify the Midland line from Euston. The Committee would like to be able to express their views on any question concerning the railway services, but the Railways Board regard the Committee 'without enthusiasm'. The responsible government department takes the view that the railways in their present competitive situation 'cannot be burdened with apparatus which seriously inhibits the discharge of their responsibilities'.[3] It is a strange view of the responsibilities of public enterprise which regards a statutory body representing the interests of those who use the railways as a 'burden'. For whom do the railways exist?

One of the anomalies is that there is no consultative body to represent the users of the National Bus Company, which runs nearly a third of all the bus and coach services. Yet when the NBC is required by the Minister to provide a service to replace a discontinued railway service, the obligation to do so lasts for only two years. At the end of that time, the passengers may be stranded without any public transport and with no official machinery through which to voice their complaints.

There is a much closer contact – too close according to some witnesses – between the area gas and electricity boards and their respective consumers' councils. The reasons for this close relationship are, first, a majority of the members of the Consultative Councils are nominated by local authority associations, and thus have a certain representative capacity for their constituents. Secondly, the Consultative Councils have much wider functions and are entitled to consider any matter affecting the supply of gas or electricity, including tariffs, facilities, and the provision of new or improved services. Thirdly, the Chairman of a Consultative Council is a part-time paid member of the area electricity or gas board and therefore has a direct voice in its decisions. Fourthly, although there is no central body, the chairmen of all the Consultative Councils meet the Electricity Council or the Gas Council once or twice a year to discuss national policy.

The Select Committee feels strongly that the consumers' councils should have a position of 'demonstrated independence'; that their essential purpose is that of representing the interest of consumers, and that this requires that they should be 'at arm's length from their industry and seen to be so'. In consequence, they recommend that overlapping membership shall cease. This would mean that representatives of the National Coal Board and the Gas Council would no longer be members of the Coal Consumers' Councils, and the chairmen of Consultative Councils would cease to be members of area gas or electricity boards. (This last recommendation was quite definite in the report but is omitted from the summary of recommendations. It is contrary to the views expressed by both councils and boards in the two industries.)

PRAISE FOR THE POST OFFICE USERS' COUNCIL

The Post Office comes out top of the class in the Select Committee's estimation as a watchdog for safeguarding consumers' interests – and seldom has such a defence been more sorely needed than at the present time, when the public is asked to pay the Post Office more and more for less and less. There is no common membership link between the PO Users' National Council and the Post Office Board. Below the Council are three Country Councils for England, Scotland and Wales. In addition there are about 200 voluntary local PO Advisory Committees of diverse origin and without statutory powers. They have a long history and have usually been initiated by chambers of commerce or local authorities.

The impressive feature of the National Council's work is that it has engaged actively in research, though it had to do this indirectly through the employment of management consultants and leading firms of accountants. If there were a large number of complaints about a particular sphere of Post Office work, the National Council would feel free to undertake its own independent research to discover the causes and also to seek the aid of research bodies to assist them if necessary. None of the other consultative organs have ever embarked on any research, either directly or indirectly, to discover causes of dissatisfaction or to test the correctness of the public corporation's statements, allegations, or excuses. This is, and always has been, a fundamental weakness of the consumer machinery.

LONG-TERM PLANS AND POLICIES

On the more general question of relations with the public, the Select Committee conclude that day-to-day communications between the industries and their customers are being developed with some care and that the result compares favourably with the situation in private enterprise. They rightly point out, however, that day-to-day relations are only one aspect. Long-term planning and capital investment have as important an impact on the consumer as the standard day-to-day management. The nationalized industries are urged, therefore, in order to cultivate good relations with the public, to publish a general review of their plans and future policies, possibly in a form similar to the Government's Green Papers.

The Consumer Councils are commended for the useful but limited work they have performed, and the Post Office Users' National Council is selected as the model which should be followed both in regard to its constitution and the way it has set about its work.

This investigation by the Select Committee on Nationalized Industries does not contain any new or startling ideas, but it confirms much of what certain academic researchers have remarked for some years. The Public Enterprise Group proposed some extremely interesting evidence about the importance of testing the quality of service and consumer attitudes towards quality, but the Select Committee declined to consider this large question. Their recommendations aim at emphasizing the need for the independence of the consultative bodies, widening the scope of some of them (or, in the case of gas, urging that a central body should be set up to consider the Gas Council's bulk tariffs), and increasing their effectiveness by giving them the right to employ expert assistance. No basic change in the structure is recommended, such as a unified system of consumer bodies to deal with all the nationalized industries, or the appointment of an Ombudsman or an administrative tribunal to inquire into individual complaints.

The volume of proceedings contains a paper prepared for the Committee by Professor Harry Hanson, which was written shortly before his much-lamented death. He had been appointed to advise the Committee and died while about to attend one of their meetings. In the paper he pointed out the tendency of the consultative organs to become cosy and complacent bodies on too good terms with their respective industries rather than a countervailing force to the power of the industries. The Committee accepted this view to the extent of declaring that the basic function of the committees is to safeguard consumers' interests.

NOTES

1. Second Report from the Select Committee on Nationalized Industries, Session 1970–71, 514. Relations with the Public. (HMSO, 616 and xlviii pp. £4.70 net.)
2. The first was on Ministerial Control. This was discussed at length in *The Political Quarterly*, Vol. 40, No. 1, at p. 103 (January–March 1969). See also Vol. 40 at p. 494.
3. Paras. 77, 79.

Part Five
Local Government and Regionalism

N. T. Boaden

Innovation and Change in English Local Government

It is being increasingly recognized that its present inadequacies, combined with the obvious centralizing pressures at work, could destroy our system of local government altogether. The result, drawing on both theoretical and practical arguments in favour of local government, has been a series of proposals to reform the system. These range from the Report of the Royal Commission[1] recommending a total reconstruction, to Departmental Circulars[2] offering more limited guidance to local authorities. Suggestions vary widely in scope and extent but also in the degree of compulsion which they embody. In some cases legislation has been introduced to compel the adoption of changes, while in others local authorities have been left free to act as they choose. Between these two extreme positions lie cases where proposals for change are accompanied by pressures or inducements in order to secure compliance. The variation in treatment reflects the complexity of any reform, but also the underlying dilemma inherent in a system of local government. National factors may suggest a need for reform, but the variety among local authorities makes it difficult to implement. At the same time an underlying theme of much reform concerns the desirability of local autonomy, and any attempt at compulsion is obviously at odds with this principle.

The varied treatment of reform by the central government arises from many causes. Different governments have been in office and various central departments have been concerned with different aspects of reform. The reforms themselves vary enormously in scope and cost to the central government, both factors which can affect their implementation, and thus the central pressure which might be applied. In addition, local response is important. The reforms affect various interests within local authorities. Professional interests, public relations and political positions are involved and can affect the degree of change which is both desirable and practicable. Educational reorganization perhaps best illustrates these complexities and their change over

Reprinted from *Political Studies*, vol. XIX, no. 4 (December 1971), pp. 416–429. By permission of the author and the publisher.

time. It was suggested for secondary schools in 1965 and agreement to change was slowly established during the next five years, as local authorities submitted plans for reorganization. At the same time the political control of local authorities was moving to the Conservatives, slowing down voluntary reform with the result that legislation to compel changes was introduced in 1970. The general election and the return of a Conservative central government put an end to this and Circular 10/70[3] reasserted the right of Local Education Authorities to decide for themselves about this aspect of local education. This cycle compares vividly with the acceptance of the Seebohm Report and the introduction of legislation to compel reorganization of the local services.[4]

These examples prompt important questions about the relationships between central and local government. What factors contribute to the variations shown? Is compulsion applied in any systematic way? How does the central government decide what it can and cannot compel? In addition, they raise interesting questions about local reaction to reform proposals when compulsion is not applied. The variations in those circumstances may reflect the wisdom of not trying to compel change, but this could arise from any of several causes. Indeed even where compulsion has been applied, local reactions have varied. Belated adoption of reform in the social services, and delay in appointing the new Directors of Social Service Departments, must affect the present and future work in those fields. The factors which account for that varied response may also condition reaction where local autonomy is greater. It is this varied reaction and the factors which account for it, that this paper will explore.

Our knowledge of the operation of local government has been greatly extended in recent years, but innovation and change within local authorities have not received wide attention. This partly reflects the widespread feeling that local authorities enjoy very little autonomy, but more the common view that they are seldom innovatory bodies. Neither of these views has prevented reform being left to local discretion. Where innovation and change have been studied it has normally been in individual authorities, reducing generalizability and giving rise to situational explanations.[5] To get away from such limitations a wider focus is necessary and the response of many local authorities to similar stimuli needs to be examined, using comparable measures. Location of those measures and of the characteristics which might explain innovation and change is by no means straightforward. There are, however, important suggestions in the literature on community politics and in varied work on organizational change and innovation which might be adopted.

The choice adopted here rests on a conception of local government as being a special case of the interaction between an organization and its environment. It is special both in terms of the form of organization and of the complexity of the environment. In addition the institutions and processes which link organization and environment are not as simple as in the case of many other organizations.[6] There is no 'market mechanism' as in most commercial cases, but there are elections and other alternative political devices which may be relevant.

Support for this view of local government can be found in many places. Friend and Jessup in their important study of local planning take as their basic framework 'the idea of a continuing dialogue between a governmental system and a community system'.[7] In their terms it is clear how innovation might result from the dialogue between the two systems, though it is also clear that the dialogue between the two systems may be unclear or misunderstood. The same general idea underlines most of the limited theoretical work on local government. It is made more or less explicit by Sharpe in his essay on the theory of local government when he concludes that 'the participatory value ... still remains as a valid one for local government' and justified local government 'as a reconciler of community opinion and as an agent for responding to rising demand'.[8] The interaction between and the responsiveness of, the local authority to its public, has an obvious bearing on the question of innovation and change and underlies our analysis.

ENVIRONMENTAL FACTORS

In considering the impact of the environment on the local authority, two facets are involved. Most obvious innovation and change in the authority may be prompted by changes in the environment. Environmental volatility is clearly important in a system designed to respond to external factors. Major changes of population impinge directly on services which have to be provided by law and which are supported by the prevailing norms about government provision. In addition, they may also affect the organizational structures necessary to making such provision, necessitating new appointments and new departments. In the same way changes in the character of a population may have a direct effect on the content of programmes and services. This is most obvious where the change involves coloured immigrants but could equally apply to changes caused by urban renewal. This is not to argue that such changes have produced innovation or change but that prima facie they might be likely to do so. In fact, of course, their impact is lessened by the characteristically slow rate of population change. Except when boundary changes occur, causing dramatic overnight variation, migration and mobility only take effect over quite long periods. Even so, they need to be incorporated in any examination of innovation and change.

If changes in the environment are important, so is its prevailing character. This may be conducive to change in the local authority or it may even exert a pressure for change. Equally it may operate in the reverse direction, accepting the status quo and reacting negatively to proposed changes. It is unlikely, however, that the nature of a community will dispose it to take a uniform line on innovation and change. Rather, some groups will support change in one aspect of council activity while others favour quite different developments. This distinction has been drawn by Banfield and Wilson in characterizing a 'public regarding' and 'private regarding' ethos in American cities.[9] The former is favourable to reforms of the government structure and to the development of policies improving the general welfare while the latter pursues a more sectional interest. The factors in a community giving rise to each kind of ethos are clearly outlined in terms of social class, religion and ethnicity. But no community is exclusively one or the other, the dominant ethos depending on the mixture of elements. If this is true of the United States it is even more so in Britain where urban local authorities are generally more heterogeneous and where religious and ethnic factors are less apparent. The idea is relevant here, particularly in view of the redistributive nature of much local government action, but social class would be the major determinant.

While such 'cultural' factors in the environment may facilitate innovation and change, they are often measured in research work by aspects of population structure. Values are attributed to groups in the population without always being reliably established. This difficulty of measuring 'culture' may account for the greater willingness of students to examine the direct impact of population structure on local political institutions and on local government policies. American research has established connections between community characteristics and the adoption of reformed politics.[10] In addition it has revealed connections between community structure and selected policy outputs, in some cases involving innovatory policies.[11] Research in England indicates similar connections and justifies the view that environment has an independent effect on the adoption of policy.[12] This does not often involve examination of innovation and change, but these could arise from such factors. In spite of reservations expressed about the findings of such research it appears to justify continued analysis.

Although much of the research argues as though environment had a direct impact on local government, it seems clear that the process is worked out through various intervening institutions. Several researchers have pointed to the causal sequence whereby social structure gives rise to reformed political institutions which in turn produce different policies.[13] At the same time others have explored the question of direct public involvement, or mobilization, and its effects on policy. Clark has shown a connection between group activity and urban renewal success,[14] and Aiken and Alford have pursued the same theme in that and other areas.[15] Other factors besides voluntary groups may be relevant although existing evidence suggests that this is doubtful. The electoral system is vitiated to a large degree by public indifference and by the rules of the electoral game (annual retirement and the aldermanic system). The local press, of whom much is hoped in assisting public participation, seem, on the available evidence, unlikely to have much effect.[16] Case studies of English local authorities suggest that groups and these other elements have varied impact but are not highly significant, though this is not yet confirmed as a general characteristic.

ORGANIZATIONAL FACTORS

If the character of the environment and the degree of public mobilization are important, so is the nature of the local authority. The interaction between the elected political element and the appointed professional one, underlies the whole question of local action. The politician responds to the manifest and perceived political and electoral consequences of his actions. His judgements about issues are derived from broad party positions, reinforced by the rules of party discipline. This is in contrast to the professional officer who is personally sheltered from direct electoral pressures and who is expected to behave in a politically neutral way. Such professionals do make value judgements based on different criteria established by colleagues and professional associations. In broad terms one would expect these to rest on more objective criteria and to be affected by different evidence from that which influences the politicians.

The interaction between these two sets of people varies widely between authorities. The quality of people involved obviously varies and the norms about the legitimate role of each group are not uniformly applied. Professions vary considerably both in terms of the certainty of their value positions and their ability and confidence in defending them. Local parties do not always reflect national party attitudes. Not only do they tend to be somewhat more extreme, but very long periods in office can also produce factionalism and division.[17] Besides these variations in each of the groups involved, the way in which their inter-relationships are organized is also relevant. Committee structures vary, as we shall see, and departmental organization is also diverse. Each of these affects the relative importance of councillors and officials. Recognition of this underlies many proposals for reform which hope to amend these structural factors and ultimately transform attitudes and processes.

Other features of the local authority position are also important. In the first place it is obvious that there is much less clarity of aim and purpose than in many others kinds of organization. Local authorities provide a wide and disparate array of services, which are judged by equally diverse criteria. Some trading services are similar in kind to commercial production, but social services and education do not lend themselves to the same production ideology. The absence of any market process and the use of tax or rate revenue to pay for services impose special strains and limitations on the organization. Such factors probably militate against innovatory activity, although uncertainty and diversity can facilitate change.

Moving to a more specific level Victor Thompson's description of the innovatory organization is interesting: 'departmentalism must be arranged so as to keep parochialism to a minimum. Some overlapping and duplication, some vagueness about jurisdiction, make a good deal of communication necessary. People have to define and redefine their responsibilities continually, case after case. They have to probe and seek for help. New problems can not with certainty be rejected as ultra vires.'[18] Local authorities vary, but in general they are not like this. Departmentalism is traditionally quite marked, jurisdiction is precise, hierarchy is developed and communication is limited both inside and outside the authority. Some suggestions for reform are aimed at changing this situation, but often without any certainty about the possible repercussions.

While these general features suggest that local authorities will not be innovatory, voluntary change is recommended and in some cases implemented. In organizational terms possible reasons are not hard to find. Organizational size would be one characteristic favourable to change.[19] The large authority will have the resources and the surplus capacity to implement change. Staff are likely to be better trained and better equipped to adopt new methods and new services. In addition the impact of any adopted change, short of major upheaval, is likely to be less severe in the context of a large authority.

Another feature, possibly related to size, is the degree of professionalism in an authority which should facilitate innovation and change. In the general comments just offered, it was clear that this varied between services, but was also affected by political pressures and the limitations of bureaucratic procedures. Local government has developed with the accretion of professional tasks, but these are carried out in an organizational setting which gives rise to limitations. Unlike central government there is not such a clear distinction between the specialist and the generalist. This means, however, that the specialist is subject to dual pressures and each role limits the other. Resolution of any ambivalence will depend on the profession concerned, the nature of political and other constraints and the personalities involved.

In terms of the politics of the situation reference has already been made to the possible effects of lengthy one-party control. These were intra-party effects, however, and the direction and extent of control obviously have implications for the whole authority. It will be argued below that the parties are likely to differ in their enthusiasm for innovation and change in terms of the substantive policy involved. They also vary in their attitudes towards professional autonomy and the proper role of officers. The extent of their control will obviously affect the degree to which they pursue such attitudes, but it would seem that marginal control reduces their effect. Some characteristic features of party control do vary directly with the degree of control.

TWO REFORMS

In order to assess the importance of these varied factors in England, two recent reforms will be examined. They have been chosen partly because they are available for analysis, but mainly because they offer wide scope to examine the effect of varied factors. Given the comments already made it was important to look at reforms which might vary according to some of the main features involved. In order to do this the internal management of the local authority and the reorganization of secondary education will be considered. Attention will be restricted to County Boroughs, but the analysis would be equally relevant in other areas.

INTERNAL ORGANIZATION

Reorganization within county boroughs had begun to take effect on a very small scale in the early 1960s, but was given great impetus by the Maud Report. This not only made explicit recommendations for change, but elaborated why they were necessary, giving pointed guidance as to likely reactions in localities. Reorganization of the committee system was proposed as a means of leaving officers free to conduct routine administration, and persuading members to consider major questions of policy.[20] It would also produce economies beneficial to ratepayers by saving time and effort wasted under the present system. Less clear, but implicit in the proposals, was a threat to the operation of party politics within the local authority. Increasing autonomy for officers would reduce the area open to councillor impact and could frustrate the implementation of party goals. Each of these aims suggests the likely response of the public and of those involved within local government.

Within the local authority one would expect fairly clear responses, though varying with the history and traditions of particular places. Local officials might welcome a movement towards reorganization of committees. It would free them from the contraints of excessive meetings and of detailed councillor interference in their daily work. Certainly such a reaction would be consistent with their professional standing and was shared by a number of chief officers interviewed in a study in four Merseyside county boroughs. They might also welcome an increased concern with policy among councillors. The same survey did not find all officers keen to take up the broader tasks left by councillors concentrating on details. While the norms about the legitimate role of each group are not universal, they are shared by many officials. Reaction to any new developments would, of course, be conditioned by the degree of autonomy which officers had already achieved in an authority.

For elected members the position is reversed but other factors create complications. There is a widespread tendency, among all parties, to remain attached to the traditional modes of operation. For the individual member they satisfy many of his motives in standing for the council as well as enabling him to meet many of the individual demands made on him as a representative.[21] The pressures of individual constituents on councillors and the rewards of satisfying them dictate concern with particularities and frustrate many attempts at reform. In addition to this individual reaction the parties occupy different positions on the question of officer and member roles. Reanalysis of material from Volume Five of the Maud Report shows Labour-controlled councils much more likely to limit officer autonomy and involve councillors in details.[22] This might reflect the different background of Labour councillors, the more programmatic nature of the party, the kind of wards represented or a general suspicion of professionals. Whatever its cause, it suggests that Labour controlled councils may be less willing to reorganize.

In part, of course, these attitudes vary with the age, length of service and position of the individuals. Maud's hope that younger men might be recruited in the future reflects the expectation that they would have different attitudes. If this is the case, the period since 1967 should have favoured reform. Change of political control to the Conservatives will have been reinforced by the introduction of new, younger councillors, less constrained by traditional concerns. They will have replaced long-serving members who would not welcome change. More importantly, the total change in committee chairmanships with the change in control would greatly facilitate reorganization. Some of this effect might be mitigated by the marginal control enjoyed by some Conservative councils. Marginality might increase electoral sensitivity, but this would diminish with time and would be less relevant given the nature of the issue.

This reform was chosen in part because it was unlikely to have much public impact. Reorganization might ultimately have repercussions on policy, as in the United States, but this would be indirect enough to limit public interest. Some kinds of environment might be favourable to reform, however, given arguments about economic and efficient administration and the removal of party politics. Each of these would seem to favour high ratepayers. Certainly many other reforms, such as planned programme budgeting, claim similar results, and also seem to rest on increased officer autonomy. Ratepayer effect might not be expressed, but would probably be anticipated.[23]

Table 1 shows the incidence of committee reorganization in relation to selected aspects of local environment and authority structure. These measures have been chosen as indicating the features which have just been discussed. Those relating to environmental character and popular mobilization are reasonably obvious. Those relating to the authority are somewhat less so. The number of departments has been used as one possible indicator of professional autonomy. This would indicate an increased potential for innovation, though the fragmentation involved, and the communication problems, might militate against this. The use of capital budgeting has therefore been included as further indication of autonomy for officers.[24] It suggests a long-term approach which favours professional decisions and inhibits both party involvement and the micro-concerns of many councillors. In these terms it would be most consistent with the aims of committee reform.

In fact this and most of the other expectations are supported by the evidence. Authorities with a higher domestic rate element are more likely to have reorganized as are those with a higher social class composition, though the effect is only small. It is much stronger for

Table 1. Reorganization of general committee structure related to selected aspects of county boroughs

Characteristic		Reorganized %	No.	Difference between groups %
Environmental character:				
Population size	Large	60	30	22
	Small	38	29	
Population change 1951–58	Large	65	26	21
	Small	44	25	
Per cent. social class IV and V	Large	47	30	5
	Small	52	29	
Domestic rateable values	High	53	28	8
	Low	45	31	
Popular mobilization:				
Local election turn-out 1967	High	57	30	16
	Low	41	27	
Character of authority:				
Elected:				
Party control	Labour	33	17	25
	Cons.	58	38	
Official:				
Number of departments	High	55	20	10
	Low	45	33	
Capital budgeting	Yes	58	36	38
	No	20	15	

larger authorities and those where electoral turn-out is higher. Population change too is related to reorganization, suggesting that environmental disturbance may create pressures on existing methods of operation. Each of these is important though the effects are not very dramatic. Given that this change was an internal one the relationship with environmental character is given added significance.

Appropriately the internal measures show much stronger relationships in the hypothesized directions. Party control is strongly related to reorganization, Conservative councils being much more ready to alter their committee arrangements. At the same time the relationship with capital budgeting confirms that reform may be part of a general orientation favourable towards official autonomy. The absence of such a clear relationship with the number of departments may reflect the smaller variation in this measure, or the fact that departmentalism is not favourable to innovation and change. In any event the figures leave a problem about the impact of officers and councillors and questions about the way in which their interrelationship operates.

Similar reservations must apply to the relationship with environmental factors as they are themselves interrelated. Examination of the independent effects of those factors which show considerable initial relationship with reorganization clarifies several issues. In terms of environmental character, size shows a sustained effect when each other factor is controlled, though its effect is most reduced by internal authority factors. Population change also maintains a relationship, though it again has less impact when internal factors are controlled. Environmental factors would seem to be relevant, but not overwhelmingly so.

Popular mobilization measured by electoral turn-out shows the least independent effect. It maintains substantial positive effect in relation to size but in every other case is seriously modified by the other variables. Although the measure does not capture important aspects of popular involvement, these results confirm an impression of low impact. Environmental effects would seem to depend on perceptions within the council, rather than on external pressures.

The two internal measures are less easy to distinguish because of small numbers in some cases. Using capital budgeting as indicative of officer effect, their influence is significant independently of each other factor. The effect of party is somewhat confused, particularly in relation to capital budgeting. In general terms, however, analysis confirms the favourable independent effect of Conservative control.

This brief examination confirms that change results from a complex interrelation between the environment and the organization. It indicates the pattern of features likely to secure favourable response to this kind of central suggestion. At the same time, of course, it confirms that a lot of authorities have not changed and suggests why they have not. For the future it would seem that the suggested basic reorganization of local government will facilitate this sort of internal reorganization. Larger authorities, modified in character quite suddenly with Conservative councils, should secure this kind of change. Whether they would be as favourable to other voluntary changes is a question to which we now turn.

EDUCATIONAL REORGANIZATION

The other issue chosen is of a very different kind. It involves one of the outstanding controversies in local government over the past ten years. Not only are major questions of social and educational principle involved, but the issues of public involvement and of central control are vitally at stake. Studies of individual movements to reorganize secondary education confirm the complexity of the decision and the variety of methods chosen to arrive at acceptable results. In many authorities the issue has remained at a symbolic level with little prospect of implementation in the short or medium terms. At that stage public involvement is less likely and practical questions of cost and form do not intrude very much. Subsequent adoption and development of schemes is a different matter. Schools, teachers and parents are affected and heavy capital spending can be involved. This raises other concerns and moves the debate on to an entirely different footing.[25] Testimony to the varied pressures in the two cases is to be found in the extensive submission of plans when compared with actual schemes in operation.

The submission of plans has been examined elsewhere[26] and here attention will be directed to the actual development of comprehensive schools. In terms of the environmental factors many of the arguments will be similar to those related to the question of submission, although the changing nature of the issue may modify their impact. The class structure of the population is still likely to indicate the pattern of support for reorganization. Comprehensive education is mainly designed to benefit the working class and any attack on grammar schools is clearly against middle class interests as normally conceived. At the same time, implementation of plans makes other aspects of the environment important. Large authorities may have greater difficulty in implementing reorganization. More schools are involved, creating obvious problems such as development on several sites, with all that that implies. In addition the normal zoning of population in large cities means that area schools will reinforce social patterns. In smaller authorities the necessary size of catchment areas obviates this to a considerable extent.

The question of public involvement and the expression of attitudes about reorganization is more obviously relevant here than in the previous case. This is an important action with major repercussions for most of the population, though this is not always reflected in public activity. Groups do become involved, though usually on a small scale and with little effect, except perhaps in the case of teacher unions. Cost factors are important in deciding to reorganize schools and one might expect ratepayers to be moved to take action. This is not reflected normally in education, however, despite the fact that it is such a dominant element in local government spending. Perhaps ratepayer antagonism is enhanced by the general opposition on social class lines. One is drawn to the conclusion that in spite of directives to consult parents and teachers, decisions are probably affected more by perceived than by manifest popular attitudes.

Within the authority important factors are involved. This is a party political issue and this aspect may be expected to dominate all other concerns. Conservative reticence about the social and educational principles involved is reinforced by the probable impact on their supporters and on the rate. Labour has not always been of one mind on the question, but since circular 10/65 comprehensives have become much more party orthodoxy. The inability of Labour councils to move towards reorganization often results from genuine difficulties in changing to an acceptable new system. The decision in principle is easy, but administration of a new system involves other considerations.

The attitudes of officials are obviously very relevant. Their attitudes are not so clear, however, though recognition of the political character of the decision would suggest cautious official involvement. Despite this, education departments are both large and professional, characteristics which favour independence from the politician. Professionalism might also enhance the willingness to adopt changes though size could produce an opposite effect in terms of the increased rigidity of organization. These somewhat opposed tendencies are reinforced by the absence of professional consensus about the principles underlying comprehensive reorganization. The general extent of officer autonomy remains an important factor. More important, given that this is a departmental issue, is the extent of departmental autonomy and development in education. Obviously the major feature of change in local government is the great variation between departments.

The relationship between these varied factors and the development of comprehensive schools is outlined in Table 2. Additional measures to those used in our first case relate directly to the provision of education. The complexity and scale of the school environment is one aspect. The level of educational spending is another, being taken as indicative of the quality and standing of the department and the service. Like the previous case, the picture is quite complex. Though relationships are smaller, there is still a need to sort out their interaction.

Party is directly relevant, Labour councils being more likely to have reorganized. In fact this measure of party control disguises the full impact of party. Among the councils defined as Conservative most introduced comprehensives while under Labour control. The incidence of this development during Conservative control is rare, only two cases clearly being of this type. At the same time official autonomy is also related to organization, but in a somewhat contradictory way. While the general measure of official autonomy shows a low or negative relationship, the measure of education department strength has a very positive effect. This would argue the importance of variation in departmental capability and would confirm that strong departments do best where the broader departmental climate is less favourable. Such claims must be checked more fully, however, as the variables used here are obviously interrelated.

Before doing that the other relationships demand some comment. Social composition does appear to favour reform. So does a large school age population, though this is itself closely related to spending on the service. Large authorities are more likely to have reorganized but not those with large numbers of schools. Population change does not facilitate reorganization, possibly because it sets up other pressures

Table 2. Reorganization of secondary education related to selected aspects of county boroughs

Characteristic		Reorganized %	No.	Difference between groups %
Environmental character:				
Population size	Large	45	38	9
	Small	36	42	
Population change 1951–58	Large	36	39	7
	Small	43	37	
Per cent. social class IV and V	Large	46	41	11
	Small	35	37	
Per cent. children school age	Large	46	41	13
	Small	33	40	
Number of schools	Large	36	44	7
	Small	43	37	
Popular mobilization:				
Local election turn-out 1967	High	43	44	10
	Low	33	30	
Character of authority elected:				
Party control	Labour	48	25	17
	Cons.	31	49	
Official:				
Number of departments	High	38	29	2
	Low	36	44	
Capital budgeting	Yes	45	52	3
	No	48	21	
Educational spending	High	55	40	34
	Low	21	39	

on educational resources which have to be met. These might include staffing problems, overcrowded accommodation and a pressure for new school buildings. Only the last of these would fit in easily to a general reorganization. Finally, turn-out shows a positive relationship despite its obvious correlation with higher class composition.

Further analysis sorts out some of these complexities though it does confirm that reorganization is the result of many factors. Environmental factors retain their connection though at quite different levels. Size is the most effective of them. Class composition and the proportion of children are interrelated and their effects are seriously muted when party is controlled. Electoral turn-out is less variable but again does not show much relationship independent of party or of size.

While it is reassuring to be able to note these environmental effects, internal variables remain more important. Educational spending shows a substantial and consistent relationship suggesting that officers are important whatever the conditions. Two cases deserve attention, however. Where Labour are in control this measure of spending does not have an effect, confirming perhaps the primacy of party. If there is a strong party pressure for reorganization it will be carried into effect regardless of official attitudes. Where party control is less dogmatic, official autonomy appears to be important. The other interesting case occurs where spending and capital budgeting are considered together. Where the former is high, suggesting a strong educational department, general official autonomy is very relevant. Strong education departments, as one would expect, do better in a less autonomous general climate. This may indicate the variety of departmental quality and its relevance for reform. Party is the most consistent factor, although modified by other influences.

As in the first case small numbers prevent any very exhaustive analysis of these complex relationships. The examination so far suggests that environmental factors are involved, but mainly it seems because of their formal impact on education or their indirect effect on officials and councillors. A complex relationship links the latter though in this case the party less favourable to official autonomy is in favour of the change. It is also generally favourable to educational spending, which means it may enhance education departments even where the general procedures maintain council involvement. This may have produced reforms in boroughs where Labour have lost office but created powerful allies in departments.

CONCLUSIONS

Two cases such as these provide no more than indicative findings.

They do, however, offer some comment on the adoption of new activity by local authorities as well as indicating possible future lines of research.

In the first place they indicate the limited effect of environmental factors. Aspects of a local authority area are related to the adoption of change, but the relationship is weak. This is in part a product of the nature of the changes examined. Overall effort in a particular service, or the development of some new aspect of service, might be much more closely related to the environment. In these two cases it seems that the impact of the new development is sufficiently tenuous to reduce the relationships. If this interpretation is correct it raises questions about the decision to leave discretion in local hands. One justification for such discretion would be the virtue of response to local conditions. This does not seem particularly relevant in these cases.

Another, less direct, justification would be that local representatives should enjoy autonomy, even if not always directly responsive to the public. These cases do show clear evidence of the impact of elected members. In both they exercise considerable independent impact. This evidence of the direct relevance of party is important. So is the fact that party alignments vary with different issues. Under Conservative control, organizational change is likely but the school system will tend to remain selective. Extension of local autonomy in any reorganized system of local government should take this into account. Political control will affect the patterns of activity and the rate of change. It would be interesting to know whether it affects other changes, and if so, in what ways.

Evidence about the impact of officials is less clear, but the data point to considerable effect. They also suggest that there may be variation between departments which should perhaps condition the granting of local discretion. Education is unlike most other departments and further research on other changes is clearly needed. Perhaps social work reform will offer a good example.

The interrelation between members and officers also needs further investigation. Both are important but the operation of the process of interaction requires investigation. When Conservative authorities have gone ahead with secondary school reorganization major questions arise. Is it the impact of an unusual group of Conservative members, or is it the officials who are playing a dominant role? Evidence from one County Borough in Merseyside suggests it may be a combination. Clearly either would be effective, but actual cases may depend on an alliance of members and officers. The question of cause becomes still more complicated if one examines the long-term relationships between members and officers and its effect on their relative impact. It is here that future attention must focus.

Independent environmental impact is small. Electoral turn-out is largely irrelevant. Evidence on the activity of local groups suggests that they are no more significant. The attitudes and perceptions of members and officers assume major significance. The manner of their interaction remains vital. Organizational change is likely to alter this interaction as well as changing attitudes. How this will work out is by no means clear on the basis of existing evidence. Only time will tell whether the reformers are right and the public interest served by the proposed changes.

NOTES

1. Royal Commission on Local Government in England 1966–69 (Report, HMSO, 1969).
2. E.g. Circular 10/65 issued by the Ministry of Education in June 1965, and dealing with the reorganization of secondary education.
3. Issued by the Department of Education and Science, October 1970.
4. The Committee on Local Authority and Allied Personal Social Services, Cmnd. 3703 (HMSO, 1968).
5. For one treatment of these topics see Robert R. Alford, 'The Comparative Study of Urban Politics', in Leo F. Schnore and Henry Fagin (eds), *Urban Research and Policy Planning* (Beverly Hills 1967).
6. Much of the literature is concerned with commercial organizations with a narrow productive task or with case-work agencies. By contrast the local authority is remarkably complex.
7. J. K. Friend and Neil Jessup, *Local Government and Strategic Choice* (London 1969), p. 101.
8. L. J. Sharpe, 'Theories and Values of Local Government', *Political Studies*, Vol. XVIII, No. 2, 1970, p. 174.
9. Edward C. Banfield and James Q. Wilson, *City Politics* (Cambridge, Mass. 1963).
10. See e.g. Robert R. Alford and Harry Scoble, 'Political and Socio-Economic Characteristics of American Cities', *Municipal Yearbook*, 1965.
11. E.g. Amos Hawley, 'Community Power and Urban Renewal Success', *American Journal of Sociology*, 1963.
12. Royal Commission on Local Government, Research Reports, Numbers 3, 4, 5 (HMSO, 1968).
13. Robert L. Lineberry and Edmund A. Fowler, 'Reformism and Public Policy in American Cities', in *City Politics and Public Policy*, ed. J. Q. Wilson (New York 1968).
14. Terry N. Clark, 'Community Structure, Decision Making, Budget Expenditures, and Urban Research in 51 American Communities', *American Sociological Review*, Vol. 33, 1968.
15. Michael Aiken and Robert R. Alford, *Community Structure and Mobilisation: The Case of War on Poverty*. Unpublished Disc. Paper, University of Wisconsin, 1968.

16. Banfield and Wilson, *City Politics*. Local research in Merseyside confirms similar tendencies in Britain.
17. R. Butterworth, 'Islington Borough Council: Some Aspects of Single-Party Rule', *Politics*, 1966.
18. Victor Thompson, 'Bureaucracy and Innovation', *Administrative Science Quarterly*, Vol. IV, 1965–66.
19. E.g. Lawrence B. Mohr, 'Determinants of Innovation in Organisations', *APSR*, Vol. 63, 1969.
20. Committee on the Management of Local Government, Vol. I (HMSO, 1967).
21. See e.g. J. Blondel and R. Hall, 'Conflict, Decision Making and the Perceptions of Local Councillors', Political Studies, Vol. XV, No. 3, 1967.
22. Noel Boaden, *Urban Policy Making* (Cambridge 1971).
23. Roy Gregory, 'Local Elections and the "Rule of Anticipated Reactions"', *Political Studies*, Vol. XVII, No. 1, 1969.
24. Robert R. Alford, *Bureaucracy and Mobilisation* (1970), pp. 120, 123.
25. Paul E. Peterson, *The Politics of Comprehensive Education in British Cities: A Re-examination of British Interest Group Theory*. Paper Delivered to APSA, 1969.
26. Noel T. Boaden and Robert R. Alford, 'Sources of Diversity, in English County Borough Decisions', *Public Administration*, 1969.

G. W. Jones

The Local Government Act 1972 and the Redcliffe-Maud Commission

The Local Government Act 1972 is hailed in some quarters as a radical and progressive reorganization of the antiquated structure of local government in England and Wales. Even Lord Redcliffe-Maud, who chaired the Royal Commission on Local Government in England (1969 Cmnd. 4040), has claimed that the Act 'will rank as the first major systematic and comprehensive measure which Parliament has placed on the Statute Book in the field of local democracy in this country'.[1] This article will examine the major features of the Act as it relates to England, and will show that it bears little resemblance to the proposals of the Royal Commission, that it is a far from radical measure, and that it seriously damages urban government.

The Royal Commission had been set up in 1966 after it had become clear that local government reform on the scale thought necessary by the then Labour government would never be achieved through the tortuous procedures laid down in the Local Government Act 1958.[2] The Commission was given broad terms of reference – nothing was excluded, claimed its chairman – and it had within its ranks eminent people with a first-hand experience of local government, whose voices carried considerable authority, including Lady Sharp, a former Permanent Secretary at the Ministry of Housing and Local Government; Dr A. H. Marshall, the former City Treasurer of Coventry; J. H. Longland, chief education officer of Derbyshire; T. D. Smith, the former leader of Newcastle upon Tyne city council; Mr Peter Mursell, chairman of the Local Government Computer Committee, and Sir Francis Hill, chairman of the Association of Municipal Corporations: Lord Redcliffe-Maud himself had been a councillor at Oxford in the 1930s and was a former Permanent Secretary at the Ministry of Education.

The Commission was the most remarkable of the twentieth century. It held in three years the most meetings, 181; it received evidence from the most witnesses, 2,156; it was the most expensive, £378,851;

Reprinted with some alterations from *The Political Quarterly*, vol. 44, no. 2 (April–June 1973), pp. 154–166. By permission of the author and the publisher.

it undertook and commissioned the most research; and it produced the longest report, three volumes of over 1,000 pages. If ever a topic had received a thorough and authoritative examination then it was certainly local government in England.

THE COMMISSION'S DIAGNOSIS

The Commission's diagnosis of the ills of the existing system of local government fell into four broad headings. First, there were too many too small authorities, lacking the areas, populations and resources to provide the specialized staff, equipment and institutions needed by increasingly technical and complex services, and catchment areas were too small to provide the necessary standards of service to the growing number of minority groups needing public help. Secondly, the existing areas of local government did not fit the facts of social life. Town and country, now socially and economically interdependent, were fragmented administratively; indeed the fatal defect of local government was the division between county and county borough. Suburbs were not governed by the towns from which they had emerged; conurbations, each now a single economic unit, were splintered into a variety of authorities, and urban districts were divorced from the rural districts whose core they composed. This administrative fragmentation damaged the provision of services to areas whose problems needed to be tackled comprehensively. Thirdly, this fragmentation meant that the citizens did not feel that local government units reflected anything meaningful in their daily lives. What they regarded as communities did not correspond to the areas of local authorities. And so they grew apathetic; indeed the very division of local authorities, outside the county boroughs, into tiers created a confusing system, hard for the citizen to comprehend and take an interest in. Very often the citizen did not know who provided what service. This ignorance was not thought to be a sound basis for democracy. Fourthly, the division of local government into competing authorities, unable to combine in a common front, and their inadequate areas, meant that the central government was increasing its control, and was likely to remove more functions from unreformed local government, leaving it with few important activities and increasingly unattractive for able people, either officials or members, to serve.

THE PROPOSED UNITARY AUTHORITIES

The Commission's solution, to ensure that local government would be both democratic and efficient, was the unitary authority. Over most of England would be fifty-eight unitary authorities, all-purpose authorities like the county boroughs, with a population range from 250,000 to just over a million and an average population of around 400,000. Above would be eight non-executive provincial councils for planning and strategy, and below a number of local councils, to represent local opinion, to be consulted by the unitary authority about the effects of its services on their areas, and to provide some amenities they were prepared to pay for. But in the three conurbations of the West Midlands, Merseyside and Greater Manchester the Commission made its fatal mistake by proposing a two-tier system, similar to London's, with three metropolitan county authorities and twenty metropolitan districts beneath. To the upper level were allocated the major environmental services, land use planning, transportation planning and traffic control, while to the lower level the personal and social services, education and housing. The force of the argument for the unitary authority was thus broken. If a two-tier system could be justified in one context, why, it was argued, would it not be relevant elsewhere. The Commission itself had provided ammunition for its opponents with its advocacy of the two-tier metropolitan system, even without Derek Senior's memorandum of dissent urging a two-tier system over the whole country and the Wheatley Royal Commission on Local Government in Scotland[3] proposing another type of two-tier system.

The case, however, for the unitary authority was powerful, but it found no influential group to defend it against the criticism of its enemies. The Commission disbanded after the publication of its report and so was unable to champion its proposals against the onslaught, and its chairman failed to stand up for his own recommendations.[4] The Association of Municipal Corporations, which had the most to gain from the reforms suggested by the Commission, was divided into factions representing the county boroughs and non-county boroughs; it preferred present unity to future expansion and so failed to support the Commission's proposals.

There are four basic justifications for the unitary authority. First, it is simple and easy to understand: one authority for all services. It ended the fragmentation of tiers, squabbles between different types of authority and the separation of town from country. It covered areas that were more meaningful to the daily lives of the citizens. Being more comprehensible it was likely to interest and involve the public. In short, it would enhance democracy. Secondly, services which were increasingly interrelated would be considered together by a single authority. It was argued that services now impinged on one another and could not be treated separately: housing was closely linked to the environmental cluster of functions, land use, transport and traffic, as well as to the personal and social services, welfare and education. The unitary authority allowed an integrated approach to the provision of the totality of services to the community. In short, it would ensure more rational and efficient services. Thirdly, it would enable the directly elected representatives of the community to assess the needs and problems of their community, to draw up a set of priorities for their community, and to allocate resources for that mix of services most appropriate for their community. The elected councillors of the community would be in control of the destiny of their community. This power of the local councillor to shape the development of his authority *in toto* would make the choices of the voters at local elections really meaningful. In short, it would be both efficient and democratic. Fourthly, the unitary system would enable local government to check the centre; stronger local authorities represented at the centre by a single local authority association would ensure that the tendencies to centralization would be reversed. Larger authorities would allow central civil servants to relax their controls and even to hand back services which had been lost.

The Labour Government in 1970 accepted the Commission's proposals, except that it added two metropolitan areas, South Hampshire and the West Riding of Yorkshire, and it moved education from the metropolitan districts to the metropolitan counties.[5] Labour's adherence to the unitary model was understandable; it looked like an extension of the county borough system where Labour was politically strong; it could be presented as an urban take-over of the counties and as ensuring that solutions to urban problems, the most pressing in Labour's eyes, would not be impeded by rural and suburban areas.

CONSERVATIVE OPPOSITION

It was also natural that the Conservatives should oppose it and champion a two-tier system of some sort, which could be portrayed as a continuation of the county and district pattern, in which they were politically predominant. In any case since they were in opposition it was conventional for them to oppose what Labour advocated. Further, they were able to exploit a weakness in the presentation of the Commission's case: the local council concept.

Opponents of Redcliffe-Maud argued that the unitary authorities would be too large and remote and that the local councils would be ineffective talking shops, offering little scope for people at the local level and potentially liable to be captured by unrepresented cliques with axes to grind. Local party activists, in both parties, felt that they would not find a worthwhile outlet for their public spirit in the local councils. The Labour government, whilst maintaining the unitary system, tried to meet their objections, to enable more people to take part in administration, by suggesting the creation of district committees of the unitary authority, composed also of local council members, to which the unitary authority would decentralize some of its administration.

THE TWO-TIER ALTERNATIVE

The Conservatives, however, came out for a clear two-tier system, and after winning the 1970 General Election issued their detailed proposals.[6] The main problem was: what set of functions to give to the bottom tier to make it attractive to members. The Government's first view was very little: mainly housing, which the existing districts already performed and which Conservative ideology did not enthuse over, and control of development, handling planning applications. For this service the bottom tier was not even to employ it own staff, but was to use the staff of the upper tier. The Conservative plan was for thirty-eight counties, a little larger than the unitaries, and about 300 districts with populations 'ranging upwards from 40,000, save in sparsely populated areas'. The metropolitan areas were raised to six (South Yorkshire and Tyne and Wearside were added and South Hampshire was dropped), with thirty-four metropolitan districts beneath, to which was moved back education.

When the Local Government Act was put on the Statute Book twenty-one months later this basic model remained intact. The main changes were an erosion of the powers of the counties and a consequent strengthening of the districts. The latter acquired their own planning staff, the right to make local plans, to operate building regulations, to maintain urban and unclassified roads, and under the so-called 'agency arrangements' to discharge many functions laid on the counties such as libraries, but not education, social services or police. The number of counties was increased by one, the Isle of Wight, to total thirty-nine; metropolitan districts grew by two to total thirty-six. The Local Government Boundary Commission advocated 296 districts.[7] Thus the existing structure of seventy-nine county boroughs, forty-five counties, 227 non-county boroughs, 449 urban districts and 410 rural districts, 1,210 authorities in all, is to be cut to around a third to 377. Metropolitan counties, although reduced in area, remained at six.

Despite Lord Redcliffe-Maud's praise for this system it is very far from the proposals of his Commission. Suppose that the Commission were reconstituted to assess the local government structure due to come into being in April 1974, how far would its diagnosis of the failings of the existing system still be appropriate First, the new authorities are too many and too small. Land use planning, which was in the hands of about 150 local authorities, will be spread to about 380, and in the absence of any provincial or regional level the crucial decisions on the regional framework or strategy of land use will be in the hands of central government civil servants. It is ironical that the land use planners who so strongly urged the need for local government reform should face a future system which is even worse from their point of view than the one they started with.

In the metropolitan areas the metropolitan districts seem too small to tackle the major problems of urban life. Only five are over 500,000; fourteen are under 250,000 and six are under 200,000.[8] They may not have the capacity to provide the housing, education and social services needed in the most under-privileged parts of the country. Urban problems are likely to increase in the future and yet in the six conurbations there is no authority responsible for providing these key services to the area as a whole. Power to act comprehensively is absent. A metropolitan wide approach is further checked by the provision that a rate equalization scheme, to reduce disparities in the rates levied in different districts of the county, can to be established only with the agreement of the council of every district, thus enabling the wealthiest and most reactionary parts to damage the interests of the poorer districts. The metropolitan counties are likely to be the weak elements of the new system, responsible only for strategic planning, transport, fire, police and consumer protection. They have had no pressure groups to champion them, unlike the districts, whose interests were promoted by the Association of Municipal Corporations, the Urban District Councils Association and the Rural District Councils Association, who were able to wring some important concessions from the Government. The metropolitan counties will get off to a bad start since they have no existing organization as a basis, as the Greater London Council had with the London County Council. Their role is likely to be an obstacle, or an irritant, to the metropolitan districts. Of the 296 districts outside the metropolitan areas two-thirds are under 100,000 and 111 between 25,000 and 75,000, too small to provide effectively housing, planning, and highways functions.

Secondly, the new areas do not fit the facts of social geography. The boundaries of the metropolitan counties have been drawn tight against the built-up areas, thus perpetuating the urban-rural division. The interdependence between the conurbation and its surrounding rural environment has been ignored, and each conurbation, hemmed into its urban straitjacket, is impeded in tackling its many social problems, especially housing. The metropolitan districts themselves, although too small for providing effectively their range of services, are too large to embody the communities to which people feel attached. The metropolitan districts are highly artificial.

In the districts elsewhere the facts of social life have also been neglected. Twenty-seven former county boroughs, not only denuded of their services like education, libraries and the social services, have been denied expansion to take in their own suburbs: their boundaries have been drawn tight around their existing areas. There has been no wholesale rearranging of boundaries to create urban or city regions at the district level, indeed four new districts, Bath, Cambridge, Hereford and Scunthorpe are totally surrounded by one single district whose centre they form. At the county level traditional boundaries, with many anachronisms, have been followed – deliberately so as to reduce administrative disruption during the transition to the new system. However, the consequence is that local government will still not reflect the living patterns of the population. The new local authorities will not consist of urban centres united with their service hinterlands and commuting zones.

Thirdly, the system of tiers still fragments local government and makes it hard for the citizen to comprehend; indeed the provisions for concurrent powers, for sharing functions, for enabling the staff of one authority to serve another, and for agency arrangements whereby one authority can agree with another to operate its functions, blur responsibility and contradict the Commission's and the Government's intention of allocating functions on a clear-cut and intelligible basis. In the new system it will be even harder for the citizen to know which authority is responsible for which function. The simple county borough, which Redcliffe-Maud found the most effective authority and the one which the public was most accurately informed about and most satisfied with, has been abolished in favour of a tangled complexity.[9]

CONFUSED ALLOCATION OF FUNCTIONS

Further, the failure to allocate functions on a clear-cut basis is a recipe for tension and conflict between authorities which have different interests and viewpoints. In land use planning the county is responsible for drawing up the structure plan, while the districts are to draw up the local plans (action, area and subject), and operate development control, within the context of the structure plan. But a further opportunity for contention is introduced by the provision for the county, in consultation with the districts, to draw up a development plan scheme to designate whether the county or a district will in fact prepare a local plan. Other services are split: the counties will plan the provision of public transport, the districts will provide the facilities; some roads will be in the hands of the counties, others are district responsibilities: the districts collect refuse, the counties will dispose of it; the counties will be the authorities for weights and measures and food and drug legislation, and the districts for food safety and hygiene.

In the Act, housing in the non-metropolitan areas is a responsibility of the districts, which means that it is severed from both the social and the environmental services in the hands of the counties. In the metropolitan areas housing as a responsibility of the metropolitan districts is separated from the environmental group of services, which is a metropolitan county responsibility. The division of housing from the social services is a major flaw in the Act, since the root of many social problems lies in poor housing. The Seebohm report on local authority social services concluded that a family service could not be fully effective unless the social service department and the education, health and housing departments were the responsibility of the same local authority. The division of housing from the environmental group of services is a further defect of the Act. The Royal Commission argued that housing was a major instrument of planning policy, linked intimately with decisions about development, re-development, conservation, and transport and traffic systems.[10] Thus the departure from the unitary system will damage both the social and environmental services.

The large number of concurrent powers, and provisions whereby the district can take some action if the county agrees, offer further scope for dissension: museums and art galleries; the acquisition and disposal of land for planning and development; the clearance of derelict land; conservation areas and the preservation of historic buildings; country parks; the provision of caravan sites; health education; entertainment; baths, parks and open spaces; physical training and recreation; emergencies; aerodromes and off-street car parks. Above all the confusion will be further confounded by the agency system, a confession of the failure of a tiered system to achieve a clear-cut allocation of functions. The 'agency' concept is that one authority can arrange for another to carry out a particular service, for instance a county might arrange for a district to provide libraries. If authorities cannot agree on a new 'agency' scheme then the Secretary of State is to arbitrate, which suggests a considerable amount of contention ahead.

AD HOC BODIES FOR HEALTH, WATER AND SEWAGE

Fragmentation is not only by tier, but also by function. Water, sewage disposal and some sewerage functions are to be removed from local government and put into new regional water authorities,[11] and existing local authority health services are to be allocated to the new regional health authorities and area health boards.[12] Social services and the health services will be quite separately administered. Interlocking problems will not be able to be tackled comprehensively. To overcome the disintegration to be caused by the new system, local government is advised to establish a network of joint-committees to co-ordinate the activities of the various authorities.[13] The prospect is that members and officials will spend much time quarrelling and bargaining on such committees to the detriment of the effective provision of the services, and to the confusion of the public.

It is ironical that, at the very time when corporate and community planning is fashionable,[14] a new system of local government should be established which will create many obstacles to its achievement. The Bains report on the internal structure of the new authorities calls for corporate management, 'the community approach', since local government is not 'limited to the narrow provision of a series of services to the local community.... It has within its purview the overall economic, cultural and physical well-being of that community.'[15] The new system is designed to frustrate corporate planning – or planning of any sort. One might suggest that it reflects Conservative ideology· where Labour is committed to planning and emphasizes co-ordination, the Conservatives stress decentralized decision-making, partisan mutual adjustment and a system of administrative competition similar to the classical market economy. A basic political approach or style is apparent in the shape and structure of the new local government system.

CENTRAL CONTROL UNTOUCHED

Fourthly, central control is not diminished. Despite the Government's early statement that it was intending to relax many of the thousand controls it exercises over local government,[16] there has been little change, and even the investigation of the controls has been discontinued since the Government now sees little point to it.[17] The Commission's hope that the National Health Service could be returned to a reformed local government system[18] has not materialized: indeed, local government now loses its remaining health services, home nursing, midwifery, maternity and child care, health visiting, ambulances, and the school medical and dental services to the appointed regional health authorities and area health boards. Water, sewage disposal and some sewerage functions are being lost also to a new regional system. The Housing Finance Act 1972 removes from local authorities the power to determine the rents of their council houses and threatens recalcitrant authorities with replacement by centrally appointed housing commissioners. Local authorities were prevented from giving free milk to children over seven. They are still not allowed without express statutory authority to spend on behalf of their community what they want, being limited now to the product of a 2p rate. Control of land use is still not in local government hands: land plans have to conform to regional strategies set by the centre and the regional offices of the departments. It is ominous that the regional arms of both the Department of Trade and Industry and of the Department of the Environment have recently been reinforced. So local government is not responsible for deciding about overspill, green belts or transportation networks. The centre has also not been able to allow local authorities to determine their own internal organization; still a statute lays down that local government has to set up certain committees, appoint certain officials, and accept central tutelage over some appointments. The continued fragmentation of local government into competing authorities will prevent the emergence of a powerful united local authority association to stand up against the central government. The conflicts within the local government system will result in calls on the centre to arbitrate; it will be pulled into local government affairs. And the continued dissension will enable civil servants to argue that local government is not fit to remain responsible for major services. The assertion, therefore, that a reformed system of larger authorities would be more trusted by the central government and allowed more discretion has not been borne out by the actions of the central government.

THE DECLINE OF CITY GOVERNMENT

Local government began in England as town government; most of the advances in services and functions began in urban areas; indeed, civilization is an urban phenomenon. The new local government system, however, marks the end of a long tradition of urban government. County boroughs lose their autonomy. Of the seventy-nine English county boroughs, thirty-seven are in metropolitan districts and forty-two become parts of districts, losing their education, library and social services. Important and influential urban centres like Portsmouth, Southampton, Leicester, Derby, Nottingham, Plymouth, Hull and Stoke are the main victims of the new system. It is significant that the new authorities are called counties and districts, symbolizing the take-over of the urban areas by the rural. The word 'take-over' is not used loosely, since the electoral system for the first election does not appear to end 'rural weighting'.[19] One man one vote value will not prevail at the start of the new local government system; the urban dweller will find that his vote counts for less than the rural dweller's.

POPULAR REPRESENTATION REDUCED

Indeed the implications for democracy of the new system are damaging, which is ironical given recent talk about the need for more popular participation. At the moment in England and Wales, if one excludes parish councillors, there are just over 40,000 councillors and aldermen. The reduction of the size of councils in the new structure and the abolition of aldermen will reduce the number of popular representatives to just over 22,000: a loss of 18,000, whose consequences to political parties and the vitality of democracy have not been seriously considered. In addition each councillor will serve on an authority covering a bigger area; his constituency will be larger and he will have more people to represent. There will be less contact between the citizen and his councillor. Local government will be more remote, while the councillor will find that his duties on the new authorities are more demanding. It is hard to see how the new system, therefore, will attract more interest from the citizen or the potential elected member than the old one, inadequate as that was.

A GREAT OPPORTUNITY MISSED

In the House of Lords Lord Redcliffe-Maud was quite gleeful at the coming 'holocaust of local authorities' who were going 'the primrose way to the everlasting bonfire'.[20] The near future offers for local government, he said, 'continuing turmoil while we change horses'.[21] There will be greater demands on staff and on members, and increased expenditure. The transition to the new system will be costly, and yet there is no certainty that services will be improved. Given the difficulties of achieving any reform it is tragic that the opportunity has been missed to bring about a radical change, instead of a conservative, indeed reactionary one. A radical scheme, like the Royal Commission's, might have enabled local government to have tackled major problems for the next generation. It is very strange that the man who was most well placed to lead the attack on such an inadequate Act should have been content to make it appear similar to his own Commission's recommendations. The Commission's diagnosis of the ills of the existing system of local government is just as valid for the new.

The Local Government Act is now on the Statute Book, the culmination of thirty years of effort to reform local government.[22] It is likely to last for a considerable time, since even the Labour Opposition has stated that it does not think it makes sense to repeal the Act totally and begin from scratch. But it remains 'free to amend either boundaries or the division of functions wherever these prove unworkable'.[23] The Act will not prove unworkable, since the skill of local government officials and the energy of members could make almost any system work, after a fashion; but it will prove inadequate for enabling a strong local governmental system to tackle and defeat the social problems of the future. An opportunity was missed – or thrown away.

NOTES

1. H.L.Deb., Vol. 335, Cols. 2040–41, October 19 1792.
2. The story of the establishment of the Royal Commission is told in G. W. Jones, 'Mr Crossman and the Reform of Local Government, 1964–1966', *Parliamentary Affairs*, Winter 1966–67.
3. Cmnd. 4150.
4. See Lord Redcliffe-Maud, 'Godspeed to Town Hall Revolution', *Sunday Times*, February 21 1971, and his speech in the House of Lords, H.L.Deb., Vol. 334, Cols. 54–63, July 31 1972.
5. *Reform of Local Government in England*, February 1970, Cmnd. 4276.
6. *Local Government in England*, February 1971, Cmnd. 4584.
7. *Local Government Boundary Commission for England*, Report No. 1, November 1972, Cmnd. 5148.
8. Department of the Environment, Circular 107/72, November 10 1972, *Local Government Reorganization in England: Areas of New Counties*.
9. *Royal Commission on Local Government in England*, Cmnd. 4040, 1969, paras. 252–253, and *Research Studies*, Vol. 9, *Community Attitudes Survey*, Section C, pp. 83–96.
10. See *Royal Commission on Local Government in England*, 1969, Cmnd. 4040, paras. 244–251. *Report of the Committee [Seebohm] on Local Authority and Allied Personal Social Services*, 1968, Cmnd. 3703, paras. 676–681. *Royal*

Commission. *[Wheatley] on Local Government in Scotland*, 1969. Cmnd. 4150, Chap. 12.

11. Department of the Environment, Circular 92/71, December 2 1971, *Reorganization of Water and Sewage Services: Government Proposals and Arrangements for Consultation.*

12. *National Health Service Reorganization: England*, August 1972, Cmnd. 5055.

13. The Bains Report, *The New Local Authorities, Management and Structure*, 1972, Chap. 8.

14. See J. D. Stewart, *Management in Local Government*, 1971.

15. The Bains Report, paras. 2.10 and 8.3. The 1972 Act does not conform with the contention of Mr K. Speel, Parliamentary Under-Secretary at the Department of the Environment, that 'Local Government reorganization would give the opportunity for a comprehensive approach to local problems, especially the improvement of the environment'. *Local Government Finance*, July 1972, p. 250.

16. Speech of Mr Peter Walker, Secretary of State at the Department of the Environment, to the Executive Council of the County Councils Association, March 24 1971. *County Councils Gazette*, April 1971, p. 96. Also see the White Paper of February 1971, Cmnd. 4584, para. 8.

17. See report of the Parliamentary and General Purposes Committee of the County Councils Association in the *Minutes of the Executive Council*, July 26 1971, p. 179, and *County Councils Gazette*, August 1972, pp. 219-220.

18. Royal Commission, paras. 359-367.

19. H. F. Wallis, 'The Role for County Interests', *District Councils Review*, May 1972, p. 139.

20. H.L.Deb., Vol. 334, Col. 59, July 31 1972.

21. H.L.Deb, Vol. 334, Col. 61, July 31 1972.

22. See W. A. Robson, *Local Government in Crisis*, 1966.

23. Speech by Mr C. A. R. Crosland to the Labour Party's Local Government Conference, 1972. *Partnership*, March 1972, p. 4.

1973 Ivan Yates

How to run Britain

The commissioners who have been examining our Constitution and structure of government for the last four years have come up with many different answers. Some want this sort of devolution, some want that; some want it for Scotland, some for Wales; some want the same for everyone, some urge variety, one thing for Scotland (and Wales) but quite another for England. Two of the thirteen who lived to sign last week's report have devised their own detailed blueprint; the other eleven group themselves somehow under one capacious umbrella.

But on two things all the commissioners are agreed. A great deal is wrong with the present set-up. The Executive, Government and bureaucracy, has got too powerful; Parliament's influence has declined, its procedures are congested, its members lack facilities and a role; local government, too, has lost out to the host of new nominated boards and authorities that run the hospitals and other public services. Everything has become more complex and more centralized. As Lord Crowther-Hunt and Professor Alan Peacock sum it up in their 'memorandum of dissent': there has been a decline this century in the extent to which we as a people govern ourselves.

All the members of the Kilbrandon Commission are agreed, too, that people, however vaguely, are aware of all this, are discontented and feel remote, powerless, even alienated. As a result, some now look outside official channels for some sort of 'direct action' or 'community politics' to achieve their aims.

In the face of this united testimony that all is not well with our system of government, it would be shortsighted, and in the long run probably self-defeating, for MPs to shelter behind the commissioner's inability to agree on a single sovereign remedy for our present discontents as an excuse to do nothing about them – whether their motive was the protection of Parliament's prestige or their own party's interests.

Reprinted from *The Observer* (4 November 1973), p. 12. By permission of the author and the publisher.

302

There is, however, one more respectable reason for caution, though not inaction. People are not always very good at diagnosing their own discontents. When they rail at the remoteness of government, at 'them and us', their real complaint may be the failure of successive Governments to cope with their own and the country's economic problems, to stop inflation at a stroke, and sometimes to do incompatible things at once. If these problems were solved, people might not worry so much about nationalism or devolution. Equally, nationalism and devolution may not help to solve them; for participation and effectiveness are two desirable, but different, things.

But though devolution will not necessarily help good government, it must assist democratic government. That is why all the commissioners (themselves, of course, nominated not elected for the task) looked to it in one form or another to give people a share in political power – at a time when, as the two 'dissenters' put it, 'a more educated citizenry has a greater capacity for playing a fuller part in the country's decision-making processes than ever before in our history'. The parties are falling over themselves in their anxiety to achieve a greater sense of participation in industrial affairs; it would be illogical, and suspicious, if they balked at closer participation in politics.

The commissioners divide in a curiously overlapping but symmetrical pattern. One issue that was crucial for them was whether the discontents that agitate Scotsmen and Welshmen are different in kind or only in degree from those that worry people in England. Eight of them (including the two Scotsmen, the two Welshmen and the Ulsterman) think they are, and, as a result, they would give Scotland a law-making Parliament, a Government, a Cabinet and a Prime Minister, and six of them would do the same for Wales.

They would fob England off, however, with a number of regional councils. These would have neither executive nor legislative powers: their function would be merely advisory and co-ordinating.

The other four (all, incidentally, Englishmen) see no essential difference between the nations and the regions, and they favour the principle of uniformity. They would give Assemblies and Governments, with executive but not legislative functions, to Scotland, Wales and a (different) number of English regions.

Two of them, a political scientist and an economist, have worked this out in a highly professional blueprint. The other two have gone along with the majority report, with its greater concern with the history and cultural traditions of the nations. This is a much less finished document: it doesn't, for instance, as Lord Crowther-Hunt and his colleague rightly complain, answer the vital question which of the particular discontents that people feel are justified and which are not.

On the other hand, the British Constitution, like Topsy, just growed: could it take in the dissenters' scheme in one mouthful? MPs, if they can be brought to consider the matter at all, may find the majority's rather amateurish approach more attractive; the excuse for it seems to be that the choice of which pattern of government to adopt is such an essentially political matter that it may be more sensible just to present alternative schemes, with their advantages, to be taken or left.

Even so, it is Crowther-Hunt's and Peacock's proposals that take full account of the effect on Parliament of the imposition of an intermediate range of regional authorities, and they have proposals for parliamentary reform in that situation; and it is they, too, who deal with the European dimension. They have seen the true importance of the proliferation of *ad hoc* nominated boards and authorities and nationalized industries, all organized on a regional basis, and of the infinitely various regional structures of central government departments, and the crying need to bring these under some form of political control if our democracy is to have full meaning.

Together with two of their colleagues on the other side of the fence, they believe uniformity of treatment is essential. Why should England be governed by a House of Commons containing even a reduced number of Scotsmen and Welshmen while Scotland and Wales, under the majority's proposals, to a large extent govern themselves? To which the only possible answer is: Scotland and Wales are different, and, if they are different, deserve different treatment: but there is no demand, and therefore no case, for either separate or federal Governments for England, Scotland and Wales, as all the commissioners concede.

But what of the realities of two-party politics? Could the Conservatives ever countenance a Wales as permanently Labour as Stormont was permanently Unionist? Could Labour stomach the reduction of MPs from Scotland and Wales at Westminster that would follow the establishment of Parliaments in those countries, if this would give, as it would, a marginally more Conservative complexion to the House of Commons? Only, perhaps, if the failure to do so also had unpleasant political consequences, because of the state of opinion in Scotland and Wales.

Even so, it was unkind of Lord Crowther-Hunt to twit the majority of his colleagues for neglecting these sordid considerations. All the more so, since his own memorandum of dissent contains some excellent proposals for curbing caucus rule and democratizing the political parties themselves, including 'primaries', or full meetings of party members, for the selection of candidates, and public subsidies for political parties, as in West Germany and Canada.

Dennis Johnson

Regionalism made Respectable

Perhaps the most curious thing about the report of the Royal Commission on the Constitution, published last week, was that it was not quite the flop that almost everyone said it was going to be. It is not that the Government is going to act on it soon – although the Prime Minister has promised early action on some aspects of it – but that it has succeeded in making the consideration of major constitutional reform respectable.

The commission, known as the Kilbrandon Commission after its second chairman, Lord Kilbrandon, was appointed four years ago by the Labour Government in response mainly to strong evidence that Scotland and Wales were beginning to channel their frustrations into nationalist movements. Some of the English regions, too, had been suffering from a sense of neglect and isolation from the centres of power.

Since then nationalism has appeared to wane. Mr Gwynfor Evans, the Welsh Nationalist leader, and Mrs Winifred Ewing, of the Scottish National Party, have both lost their seats in Parliament. Although Sir Alec Douglas-Home a few years ago came out in favour of a form of Scottish Assembly with some legislative functions, much of the drive which seemed to give urgency to constitutional reform in the sixties has been missing, at least when tested at the ballot box.

Hence it was predicted that the Kilbrandon report would make about as much impact on the public consciousness as the annual report of the White Fish Authority and be put conveniently away in ministerial filing cabinets, like the products of so many other Government-sponsored inquiries. In fact it was given a great deal of space in the 'serious' press and wrought at least one very significant change in the status of the whole question of devolution.

It is all very well for 'fringe' political parties to protest against over-centralization of government. They may well be – and certainly have been – supported to some extent by influential spokesmen in

Reprinted from *The Guardian* (10 November 1973), p. 17. By permission of the author and the publisher.

the main parties and by lobbyists concerned with economic 'imbalance' in various parts of the country. There has, indeed, been a very widespread demand for the introduction of more democratic government which would give the millions of people who live outside the London-dominated South-east a stronger sense of identity and a feeling that they were able to influence the decisions that affected them. The reforms in local government, to come into effect in April, are at least in a part a response to this pressure.

But until now the idea that there might be a case for separate Parliaments in Scotland and Wales and legislative assemblies in the English regions has lacked the authority which comes from being taken seriously by the 'establishment'. In many ways the Kilbrandon report is unsatisfactory and inconclusive, yet it is the outcome of a Royal Commission which has made a detailed study of the case for some fundamental devolution. Last week the argument about whether Scotland and Wales and the regions should be allowed to run their own domestic affairs stopped being the property of cranks, wild men, revolutionaries, and cultural fanatics and earned itself a place in the calendar of national debate.

It remains to be seen how much impact, in practical terms, the report will make, even in the long term. The Government has said there should be the 'widest possible public discussion' before any action is taken, and most observers believe that this means the report will be allowed to gather some dust. In England, though not so much in Scotland and Wales, 'regionalism' tends to be a yawn unless there is some very pressing reason to adopt it as a slogan, and, in any case, the task of making the new two-tier system of local government work is going to occupy attention for several years.

The Commission completely rejected the case for separate, sovereign Parliaments for Scotland and Wales. It also decided against a federal system of government. But it considered that devolution of central Government functions in some way 'which would preserve the essential political and economic unity of the United Kingdom' could do a great deal to reduce discontent with the present system.

It recommended Scottish and Welsh legislative assemblies, elected by proportional representation, and, for England, regional advisory councils with most members elected by the local authorities. A minority report, however, suggested a uniform system of elected assemblies with executive powers throughout the country.

What seems obvious is that no Government is going to legislate for too much fragmentation of control at a time when Britain needs all its corporate strength to deal with problems in the European Community. Nor has the majority of the commission recommended that it should. But the serious difficulty which 'intermediate' forms of government could run into is that they might worsen, rather than improve, the sense of frustration which has brought them into being. Assemblies set up for Scotland and Wales would need some very specific areas of activity over which they had clear control, and in the long run this could mean the kind of financial control and fund-raising responsibilities which central government would be reluctant to yield. The kind of regional advisory councils put forward for the English regions could not be much more than lobbyists and, to use the phrase on all the critics' lips last week, 'mere talking shops'.

The commission itself recognized a further problem. Nearly all complaints about the present system, it found, sprang either from the centralization of government in London or from developments in the style of administration – appointed rather than elected, boards represent a case in point – which run counter to democratic principles. But the commission points out that 'there is no inherent reason why regional government should be more democratic or more sensitive to public opinion than central government'.

This goes to the root of the matter. County councils, many of which have control over enormous budgets, have been remote and shadowy authorities to most ordinary people. Some of the big new metropolitan authorities which start work next year will have to work hard at keeping links with the public if they are to be any better. Regional governments would be a poor innovation – and possibly even a dangerous one – if all they appeared to do was to act as a kind of buffer between Westminster and the people.

Part Six
The Commonwealth

1966.

John Holmes

A Canadian's Commonwealth:
Realism out of Rhetoric*

... The one inescapable reality of the Commonwealth is that, improbable though it may seem, it exists. It is a fact of contemporary international life and of the international alignment of its members and we cannot ignore it, whether we consider it important or unimportant, a reactionary survival or a framework for progress. Its future is uncertain; but whether it lives or dies it requires attention because the manner of its passing could be as important as the manner of its living. Its disruption in anger would increase world tensions dangerously. On the other hand, it may pass by a serene sublimation into broader forms of international collaboration, leaving an afterglow of good will that would differ little in reality from the essence which distinguished it in its final institutional phase.

In estimating what future the Commonwealth may have, it is essential to recognize what the Commonwealth is not. It is not an economic organization, a diplomatic *bloc* or a defence alliance – and yet it is not without significance in all three fields. First of all, it ought no longer to be looked upon primarily as an economic organization – if indeed that ever was its purpose and justification. I must not, however, be too parochially Canadian. The commercial and financial advantages of membership have, for many years, been of less importance to Canada than to other members, and for this reason Canadians may have been guilty of underestimating the economic factor and stressing the political. The sensitivity of Canadian governments to Britain's flirtation with the European Common Market indicated that Commonwealth commercial advantage, although not of first importance, meant more to us than we had recognized. This crisis revealed also the dependence of other parts of the Commonwealth on the British market and on British finance, even though the United States and other countries

* This article is a revision of a lecture originally given at the Duke University Commonwealth-Studies Center, Durham, North Carolina.

Reprinted from *The Round Table* (October 1966), pp. 335–347. By permission of the author and the publisher.

were increasing in relative importance for them. Old patterns of commercial and financial association, a British sense of responsibility in once imperial areas, a common weakness for curried mutton and driving on the left, personal loyalties are assets which do not require institutional protection, although they must be continually promoted.

If one tries to analyze the reasons why Asian and African members have decided to remain within the Commonwealth, one is impressed – and perhaps worried – by the extent to which this is justified in their own words by the expectation of favourable economic terms. The late Prime Minister of Nigeria, for instance, speaking to his Legislature on the Independence motion of January 1960, said, 'The reason why I personally want to see Nigeria taken into the Commonwealth is this.... At present we are an under-developed country. In order to expand our economy we must seek investment from the richer and more developed countries, investments of both money and technical skill.' This was not his only reason, of course, but if the expectations of newer members, which extend not only to Britain but also to Canada and Australia and include capital as well as technical assistance, are disappointed, they may be more easily tempted to resign the first time they are irritated. Obviously their expectations cannot be fully satisfied from Commonwealth resources. Whether membership can continue to seem economically worth while is a major question.

INTERNATIONAL ECONOMIC ORGANIZATION

As an economic entity the Commonwealth is bound to be of declining significance. What still exists in the way of preferences and the sterling area cannot be abandoned on principle or surrendered without compensation. Preferences might be regarded as vestigal, as arrangements to be incorporated into broader international systems of commerce and currency if these can be achieved. If they cannot, then protective systems of all kinds will become important again – although regional systems may infringe on the old Commonwealth network. What the Commonwealth Economic Conference in Montreal in 1958 proved was that although consultation on economic problems among countries of such diverse interests was well worth while, that was not because the Commonwealth as an entity provided the means or resources to solve these problems.

We should accept as progress that many of the economic and political functions of the Commonwealth have merged into broader international organizations, just as the Colombo Plan, a Commonwealth initiative, was extended to include foreign peoples moving in the same direction. The Commonwealth can still be useful for some complementary purposes. It is of growing importance, for instance, as a framework for technical, especially educational, assistance programmes, because these are personal in application and the element of familiarity in a historical association is important. It is noteworthy that Canada has devoted almost its entire assistance programme to Commonwealth countries. A significant event this year is the conference to which Canada invited representatives of all Commonwealth countries in the Western Hemisphere for a broad discussion of common interests. The exchange throughout the Commonwealth of students, volunteers, engineers, teachers and civil servants strengthens the fabric of an association in which peoples on the whole get along better than governments. None of this work, however, can be exclusive, because other countries, and especially the United States, play an indispensable part in all those things that the Commonwealth is about.

I have said with circumspect brevity that the Commonwealth is not an economic unit. That the Commonwealth is neither a power *bloc* nor a diplomatic unit is also obvious enough. The idea that it should face the world as a unit with a single foreign policy persisted in some quarters until the end of the Second World War, but it was never a practical possibility. Certainly the new Commonwealth of many races would not have come into being if India, Ghana or Malaya, on achieving independence, had not felt themselves in a position to exercise their new freedom in foreign policy. Not even for the older members was a tight framework a possible alternative in an era when regional attractions were becoming stronger. Making a virtue of necessity in accordance with its genius, the Commonwealth proceeded to glorify its diversity and freedom. It found its justification not in unity of policy but in a common search for understanding, for the sharing of viewpoints, constant consultation: in the words of a Nigerian, 'the quality of listening to each other with forbearance'. It is beside the mark, therefore, when the Commonwealth is declared meaningless by a frustrated British Tory or a puzzled American computer simply on the grounds that its members don't stand shoulder to shoulder in UN voting.

I admit, however, that the complaint is not entirely irrelevant. Sympathetic consultation remains the essential justification of the Commonwealth. One cannot ignore the hollow sound this assertion sometimes makes. Our practice falls short of our pretensions. The denunciation of India's actions in Goa on the one hand or on the other hand of Britain's action in Rhodesia may be justifiable, but they have been shrill, unctuous, and unresponsive to the victim's explanations. Listening to each other with forbearance, indeed!

The withdrawal of South Africa removed one source of internal irritation, although at the cost of bitterness which has alienated many old Commonwealth supporters. The enmity within our circle of India and Pakistan, the mutual suspicions of Ghana and Nigeria, even the irritability which became an unhappy feature of Anglo-Canadian relations when they both had Conservative governments sap its strength. The Commonwealth never has been and never conceivably will be a happy band of concord, a heavenly choir in harmony; but there must always exist enough good will, enough candour and recognition of common interests to justify the institution. We must keep the quota of hypocrisy to an acceptable level so that it serves as a source of constructive inspiration rather than destructive cynicism.

STRENGTH THROUGH CRISIS

In considering its present disunity, the Commonwealth dare not hanker after a unity which is unattainable. Those who argue that the commitment to consultation and understanding was an inadequate alternative to the policy of a united front ignore the fact that the latter was never a possible alternative. We must nevertheless face up to the argument that the anxiety to stress freedom and the absence of commitment could land us in a hollow shell. Consultation has to be frequent enough and also serious enough to be worth while. The Commonwealth has suffered as much from a failure to face up to difficult issues as it has from public quarrelling over them. At the United Nations the regular meetings of Commonwealth representatives to exchange views on agenda items became a farce because only minor items were discussed. It was not worth while for senior members of delegations to attend; so they growled at each other in public sessions. In a way the Suez crisis, paradoxically, strengthened the Commonwealth. It split the membership (though not on racial lines); but for the first time in a long while Messrs Eden, Nehru, St Laurent, Menzies and others were talking to each other about desperately serious questions without blinking, expressing their disagreement frankly though respectfully and then trying to find some way out. Over South Africa and Rhodesia again they have been forced to face up to vital issues, but it has seemed to take an unavoidable crisis to induce the Prime Ministers to put anything controversial on their agenda.

It has also taken an expanded membership. Too many people, inspired by nostalgia rather than knowledge, tell us that with all these upstarts round a great big table at Marlborough House there can never be the intimacy and confidence experienced by the old guard European and Asian gentlemen in the Cabinet room at Number 10. May I give evidence as one who witnessed a number of those ancient rituals in Downing Street before the discovery of Africa? I was, of course, a bag-carrier in the back row but sounder of hearing than some in the front row. The intimacy was indeed such that there was a common will to omit from the agenda anything the discussion of which might interfere with the friendly relationship of which the communiqué was obliged to speak. Recent sessions of the Prime Ministers have been a great deal more vital. The Africans have shown signs of taking the Commonwealth seriously – and that has come as a shock in Whitehall. Another thing the Africans have done, I might add, is produce a healthy third force to triangulate the bipolarity of the white and brown Commonwealth which emerged after 1947.

The Commonwealth is confronted with grave internal issues in South Asia, Central Africa, the Caribbean and the English Midlands. The British, on the horns of appalling dilemmas over Rhodesia, Basutoland, Sarawak or British Guiana, and race problems at home, are resentful of advice from the Commonwealth or the UN. Much of this advice is so gratuitous and irresponsible that resentment is inevitable. Immigration questions, which effect not only Britain but also Australia, Canada, Ceylon, East Africa, have actually been exacerbated by the Commonwealth relationship, which makes restrictions seem particularly unacceptable. Nevertheless, there are paradoxes in this final stage of colonialism which must be resolved, and if this multi-racial fraternal society has any reason for existence it is to help resolve them. The responsibility for initiative and special concern in all these matters does not rest alone on those most deeply involved or passionately concerned; as a Canadian I feel bound to say that it rests also on those elder members who have long boasted of the magnanimity of spirit and purity of conscience with which a history unsullied by imperialism has endowed us.

USING THE COMMONWEALTH

One of the most encouraging features of the past year has been the greater disposition of members other than Britain to use the Commonwealth as an instrument through which to come to grips with deep-seated problems. The Lagos Conference of last January, which temporarily, at least, reduced the division between white and black countries over the Rhodesian issue, was called at the initiative of Nigeria, encouraged by Canada. The British were dubious, but fortunately the Labour Government, which understands much better

315

than the Conservatives this new Commonwealth it did so much to create, knew how to make use of such an opportunity. Sir Robert Menzies made his last and possibly his greatest contribution to the Commonwealth by sulking at home and then retiring. Coming to grips thus with the world's most insoluble problems is, of course, dangerous, and the Commonwealth hovers closer to the brink than it ever has been before. The increasing importance of the consultative function means that the Commonwealth is less likely to have a future at all, but, if it has one, it should be more rather than less worth while.

The third thing which the Commonwealth is not is a defence alliance. The old concept of an imperial defence system has been abandoned and the more powerful members are involved in regional military associations. The older members, including India and Pakistan, have recognized their dependence on United States power – or at least on the US-Soviet equilibrium. All this has been said often but recent events have indicated that we may have written off the residual military significance of the Commonwealth prematurely. Common service patterns are still of value. While Britain still bears most of the burden, Australia and New Zealand are helping in Malaysia. Canada, which has had a military training role in Ghana for some years, was asked last year by the Tanzanians to take over military training in that critical country and has responded. Of late, furthermore, Britain seems to have had second thoughts about her defence responsibility with the United States in that area. The future may see, therefore, some reversal of recent trends but in a pattern which is much more closely related to the United States and, if possible, the United Nations.

Another reality we must face is that a major problem area for the Commonwealth is Britain. The will to preserve the institution has to be encouraged not only at the periphery but also at the heart. The aim of Commonwealth enthusiasts used to be directed largely towards persuading recalcitrant Indians or Canadians of the value of this heritage. The fault of the British, if any, was that of behaving like too obviously clucking hens. Now the British have soured perceptibly. The trials of Suez, the burdens of Cyprus and Kenya, immigration policies at home, ingratitude and abuse in the United Nations have stimulated doubts about the value of empire. The hope of the Commonwealth as a power *bloc* to bolster their position in world diplomacy has been other than what was expected, and the attention of those Britons who crave great power ranking has been turned to association with Europe or the maintenance of nuclear status. The financial responsibilities of sustaining former colonies loom larger than the diminishing commercial advantages. It is not surprising, therefore, that in the anguishing debate over entry into the EEC the advocates of a European association, seeing in concern for the Commonwealth an obstacle to the fulfilment of their wishes, mounted a savage attack on it. What they attacked was rarely the new Commonwealth as it has flowered but a wild caricature of an empire that had existed only in the minds of the sillier breed of imperialists. The campaign has been anti-African, anti-Asian and anti-Canadian. The complaints were by no means entirely undeserved, but the result has been the mutual extension of bitterness rather than forbearance.

In recent years the Commonwealth and Europe have been set up quite unnecessarily as antithetical choices for Britain, although the European Community is a regional association with economic functions quite different from anything which the Commonwealth could provide. Responsibility for this misconception rests on both sides in the debate. It must be recognized, of course, that the European association is intended to have political significance. As an independent Atlantic state, Britain is more likely to give priority to Commonwealth interests than it would as a tightly knit associate of a European Community. Other members of the Commonwealth, however, must recognize that Britain cannot be prevented from this association if she is convinced that her prosperity lies in that direction To protest is only to make certain that Britain's affiliation with Europe, if it comes, would be accompanied by an angry renunciation of Commonwealth ties and responsibilities. We can only hope that the British, with their worldwide vision, will not, in whatever relations with Western Europe they contrive, become victims of a narrow and isolationist continentalism which it is the function of the Commonwealth to counter. The role of Britain in the Commonwealth is gradually being reduced to something more like equal status, but in many very practical ways it is still the *sine qua non*. The argument is logical that the Commonwealth could survive Britain's secession or the mere abdication of its role of *primus inter pares*, but the strength of historic concepts is such that I do not think it would last long.

DRAWING THE LINE

Another reality we cannot blink is what is happening to the free constitutional principles which we have claimed to be the heritage that binds the Commonwealth together. Here it is hardest to be objective, and one must tread warily. In the older established countries there has been a considerable effort to be fair about governmental trends in Pakistan, Ghana, Tanzania and now Nigeria. It is true that all too many people have delighted, like outraged spinsters, at the proofs Kwame Nkrumah has presented for their satisfaction that it was a mistake ever to let Africans out of the hands of their governesses. Nevertheless, a substantial body of opinion remains conscious of the sins we have all committed in our time in the name of effective government – in British Guiana, British Ulster or British Columbia. It recognizes the mixed history of colonial rule and the fruits of our racial intolerance, and acknowledges that we must not expect conformity to all the traditions of Westminster in countries where unity is frail, illiteracy high and the economy baffling. We cling long to the belief that, in spite of the restrictions on legitimate opposition and even interference with the courts, the recollection of free Commonwealth principles is still in some measure preserved. In our decision over South Africa we recognized that the principle of racial equality is as important as our British constitutional traditions in qualifying for membership. The Commonwealth philosophy, it must be recognized, now embraces the teachings of Gandhi, Nehru and Julius Nyerere. South Africa might have been read out of the family on either the older or newer principles, but it was because she denied racial equality rather than because she denied justice that she was allowed or forced to withdraw. It is on this same ground that common action has been taken against the Smith Government in Rhodesia. In the roundabout of history, however, people sometimes come to despise the freedom they fought for. Free principles of government may have an even harder time from anti-colonialists than they undoubtedly had from colonialists. It is hard to say how far we can go in tolerating in membership governments which deny either of the fundamental principles which are said to distinguish the Commonwealth system.

Yet we know that we cannot force the withdrawal of any of the non-white members except in extraordinary circumstances or as a result of conflict among themselves. It doesn't help us out of the dilemma merely to acknowledge that the non-Europeans are now enjoying a priority in Commonwealth affairs which we white folks used to exercise – although it is undoubtedly good for our souls to look at the situation from that perspective. The fact that Rhodesia was allowed representation at Prime Ministers' meetings many years ago while larger African and Asian countries had to await full self-government before they were graciously admitted is not easily – and ought not to be – forgotten. When these trends towards illiberal government are accompanied by shrill attacks on imperialism and neo-colonialism and critical situations ripen in the southern and eastern part of Africa, the chances of the Commonwealth blowing up are considerable. We shall not be saved by sweeping the realities under easy formulas. We may be saved, however, by patience born of a sense of history.

Recent Commonwealth Prime Ministers' meetings have been reassuring and encouraging. The leaders of the new nations showed a statesmanlike concern to avoid confrontation and seek constructive agreement. They even went beyond merely avoiding disruption to propose a common institution, a Secretariat, to promote the exchange of information. It is healthy that the older members such as Canada could overcome their Pavlovian reaction to proposals for common institutions and agree to this proposal, which came from newer members. No one drooled out loud – except the ineffable Sir Robert, who had always favoured common institutions when the good guys had a majority.

It should not be assumed, however, that this represents a reversal of the old decision against the Commonwealth as a centralized unity. What is sought now is a practical measure to make consultation more effective. One motive was to wrest control of Commonwealth machinery from Britain and persuade the British to join the Commonwealth as partners. This new attitude towards Britain is revealed in Julius Nyerere's comment on his quarrel with Mr Wilson over Rhodesia. He said: 'We shall not leave the Commonwealth – that is a multinational organization, not a British one, and is therefore, for the moment at any rate, unaffected by our decision.' With a zealous and imaginative Canadian as Secretary-General, the new institution has already proved its value in the Rhodesian crisis. The Secretariat, as I see it, is intended as a 'static conference machinery' rather than a 'dynamic instrument of governments' – if I might borrow Dag Hammarskjold's definitions for another purpose. Nevertheless, if the Secretary-General is dynamic and discreet enough to recognize the inescapable limitations imposed on the instrument by the loose nature of the association, he can make conciliation a by-product of communication.

ITS OWN HISTORY

The Commonwealth is a unique historical phenomenon. I apologize for that thundering cliché. If possible I prefer to eschew that nauseating pastime of Old Commonwealthers: rhapsodizing on the fragile mystery of our being, incomprehensible, of course, to foreign clods, 'lesser breeds without the law'. We were, in fact, caught so long admiring our navels that history almost passed us by. What I really wanted to say bluntly is that it is not an organization anyone would think up; it is a product of history – better explained perhaps by historians than by political scientists. It must work out its own history according to its own osmosis, never seeking to model itself on other institutions, particularly regional associations or defence alliances. Above all, it must abhor the federalist impulse. Nor is it a model UN. It is, however, a nucleus from which civilized principles of inter-governmental relations can expand. Because it shares its principles with many other countries and communities there may seem little excuse for it to carry on as a club with restricted and, what is worse, hereditary membership. But if it brings together some of the most important nations of the world and does good, it has the same mandate to exist as any benevolent association with selected membership. The world community is large and it requires within it societies of all kinds, as does any community. Ecumenicism can be carried too far.

Such a society, however, because of its own internationalist prin-ciples, is likely to grow less and less exclusive. This could lead to an honourable disintegration, or the Commonwealth could be strengthened because the idea caught on and offered members and others expanding opportunities. I have suggested that membership must be compatible with regional associations. I think also that NATO would be a lot healthier if it would reform itself along Commonwealth principles rather than grow more and more neurotic chasing after a constitutional structure to secure a unity which is unattainable. I would like to illustrate my point further by outlining another role I would like my own country to play.

In Canada the Commonwealth was too long regarded as a preserve of the Anglo-Saxons, a tie to Britain and the Crown, a bulwark against Yankees, wogs and frogs and other chaps who didn't know their place. This caricature obscured the nobler side of the British tradition and soured on the whole idea those who didn't qualify or didn't want to qualify for such a heavenly kingdom. Since the War, the new image of an inter-racial Commonwealth, an asset for Canada rather than a restraint, has spread slowly and inspired the most idealistic members of the Community. But the old idea dies hard. Non-Wasp Canadians remain unenthusiastic. In recent years the bicultural nature of our state has been reaffirmed by the new assertion of Quebec. If we are to satisfy both major elements in the country, we must project our bicultural character in our foreign policy. French Canadians would like our orientation to an English-speaking world matched by a closer affinity with French-speaking civilization. They have insisted that our aid programme for Commonwealth areas in Asia, Africa and the Caribbean be accompanied by similar programmes in the developing areas where French is spoken. The Government has wisely moved in this direction, although the sums for French-speaking countries are inevitably smaller because the Commonwealth areas are so very much more populous.

It seems to me that this twin policy makes good sense for the beneficiaries and makes good sense for Canada. It reconciles both elements of the community to external associations which singly they might not approve. The francophone Commonwealth has not even the loose links which the English-speaking (Anglo-saxophone?) Commonwealth still maintains, but it has its own identity. As the latter grows more informal, the two communities become more alike. For a country like Canada the vocation of serving and perhaps reconciling these great associations is to be encouraged. It is a grandiose conception, but Canada needs a touch of grandiosity to lift it from the failure of will and imagination from which it is at the moment suffering.

A LAPSED MEMBER

A distinguished Canadian professor once said that in the Commonwealth all roads lead to Washington. When Duke University gathered together on Lake Como in 1963 a group of Commonwealth and US citizens to talk about the Commonwealth, it was not easy to distinguish by the nature of their involvement the citizens from the non-citizens. Economically, culturally – even strategically – we are entwined. Inevitably we talked most of the time about problems of social and economic development, and here, of course, the preponderance of the US contribution and interest was obvious. As the institutional structure becomes not only looser but less important, the old distinctions fade. Is the 200-year-old schism in the Empire about to be breached? If so, whom will history record as the schismatics?

It is hard to present a logical argument for maintaining the Commonwealth organization without the United States. However, I think the organization should be perpetuated, and the United States, quite obviously, isn't the least bit interested in taking up its lapsed membership. The United States cannot easily tie itself to any restricted group, even an Atlantic or Western Hemisphere community, because it is a super-power, a world power. In its world mission, however, it can collaborate with limited associations which have complementary missions. The United States is deeply involved in Commonwealth affairs – in Australia or Rhodesia, Nigeria or Guiana – and there is no strong disposition in the Commonwealth to keep it out. Those voices crying 'Yankee, go home' are not doing so on the ground that theirs is a Commonwealth preserve. The continuing existence of the Commonwealth is, I believe, an important – though perhaps not vital

– interest of the United States. It was, for example, in the interest of the United States that the Commonwealth Prime Ministers assembled in Lagos and succeeded in keeping, for the time being at least, the major nations of Africa from falling apart over Rhodesia. It is in the interest of the United States that Canadians, rather than Czechs or Chinese, are training Tanzanians and that Commonwealth countries, because they are Commonwealth countries, feel a sense of responsibility in Asia and Africa. It is also in the interests of United States foreign policy, as now interpreted, that there should be a nucleus of Commonwealth power in the waters and islands south of Asia. Why otherwise are the British more understanding than most of the other allies of their terrible dilemma in Vietnam?

Although no one could reasonably complain of the benevolence of the United States to the members and the citizens of the Commonwealth, that benevolence has less often – outside North Carolina – extended to the institution itself. The traditional antipathy to the Empire from which the United States seceded was understandable. Before this present generation Americans had some reason, furthermore, to look upon us as a club whose exclusiveness was directed against them – an impression undoubtedly confirmed by the Commonwealth preference system which they have always viewed with deep, and in our eyes hypocritical, suspicion. For various reasons there has been less appreciation in the United States than seemed warranted of a noble institution based on principles of association which owe much to American inspiration. Americans helped instigate the Indians to self-government; but when they took this and stayed in the Commonwealth, this seemed an un-American activity to which liberals in the United States have never been reconciled. There has been less than full comprehension of the travail the United Nations has been spared by the invention of a framework through which was accomplished in unique tranquillity the largest quota of peaceful change in the history of mankind. It is true that the British are given their due appreciation for wisdom, and they deserve it, but this credit is less often extended to the institution that did the trick and which was much more than a British device. I am not saying that Americans have been hostile to the Commonwealth, they have just refused to take it seriously – and such is the influence of Americans that its members have therefore taken it less seriously. Dean Acheson referred liverishly to it recently as a body 'which has no political structure, or unity, or strength'. I think he was the man who first determined seventeen years ago that the Peking Government had no political structure, or unity, or strength. At any rate, like so many others, he was attacking the Commonwealth for not possessing features which it does not pretend to possess.

BRITAIN'S ROLE

I think that the inability in Washington to see the Commonwealth as an asset in the world-wide American mission is illustrated by its miscalculation about Britain's role in the world. So dedicated has been the Administration and the intellectual establishment to the chimera of a united West Europe and the dumbbell association of equal trans-Atlantic partners that their pressure has been directed towards encouraging Britain to shut itself up within Europe. President de Gaulle understood Britain's position as a maritime power better than did Washington, and it was on this by no means irrational ground that he rejected its entry into the EEC. Washington threw its strong weight behind those Europeans, on both sides of the Channel, who have accused the British of being isolationist and nostalgic because they wanted to maintain their contacts with their Commonwealth associates rather than seek refuge in a continent.

But who now are the isolationists and who are the friends of the United States? Those who called the Commonwealth 'a gigantic farce', the advocates of Little Englandism or Little Europism who not only want to withdraw British forces from East of Suez but also to give up any mission in the world at large? They would leave not only the Malayans and the Australians but also the Americans to go it alone. It has seemed to me myopic of Washington not to realize the importance for the United States of Britain's retaining its imperial or, in nicer language, Commonwealth vision. Its ally cannot be, of course, a revived British Empire, powerful in arms; there should be no illusion. If you are not to be left alone, however, you need allies who, like you, feel in their bones and their consciences the problem of equilibrium beyond their own continents and their own narrow interests.

The United States is becoming an imperial power in that it has acquired responsibility for maintaining an *imperium* – *imperium* in the sense of world order. The Soviet Union and China, although very differently, think in global terms. So does France, but for its own reasons. But who else is there to understand your burdens except those who long ago got accustomed to seeing themselves as pink blobs all over the map and avoiding the sunset?

The United States [as Alistair Buchan writes] has begun to feel the burden of loneliness in shouldering all the traditional security and political problems of the old colonial powers. Having done

323

much to foster a Europe that is provincial rather than universal in its interests, she is not happy with the consequences and is anxious to re-engage the interest and concern of Europe in the problems of world security.

I am not suggesting that the United States must choose between supporting a United Europe or the Commonwealth, for that would be to perpetuate an initial error. I suggest only that Washington might be less single-minded in the goals it pursues by recognizing that the Commonwealth and the EEC might be equally worthy of their blessing. You can never bet on a sure thing, but they might bear in mind that the Commonwealth exists, though its future is uncertain, whereas the union of Europe does not exist and its future is likewise uncertain.

TAKEN FOR GRANTED

The main threat to the Commonwealth is apathy. It no longer inspires strong hostility in Moscow or Dublin or Chicago. It is accepted, taken for granted but not taken very seriously. For many people, unaware of its transformation, it is unfashionable. Regional solutions – the European Community, Pan-Africanism, the Western Hemisphere, the Atlantic Community – are more in style, although the fact that the world gets smaller and regions less meaningful should make an intercontinental organization more rather than less significant. For the Africans there is a stronger emotional attachment to Africanism than to the Commonwealth, however inchoate as yet the common institutions of Africa. For many Britons Europe is more attractive, and for Canadians the continental or even the Western Hemispheric pull is strong. The Asian members are Asian first, and the Australians and New Zealanders are trying to adjust themselves to realities of their neighbourhood and a closer dependence on the United States. If we are going to regard these regional affiliations as irreconcilable with the interests of the Commonwealth, then I think the Commonwealth is a lost cause. This would resemble the mistake too many Canadians of an older generation made by assuming that Canada's destiny had to be either British or American. The Commonwealth cannot seek to force people into an unnatural framework, to set Malaysia apart from Asia, Trinidad from South America or Canada from the United States. It can recognize merely that nations need not and should not be total in their orientations, that they may with advantage vary their cultural and political – and their commercial – affiliations. It profits no one that the peoples of the world should be isolated in regions. To draw them together is, of course, a function of the UN, and it may be argued that the UN makes the Commonwealth unnecessary. The answer, I think, is that the ties which hold the races and continents in contact are frail and tenuous; all bonds which reinforce them are worthy of maintenance. The Commonwealth, we know from experience, can be a force for good working within the United Nations. It is counter-regional; its role is not to rival regional *blocs* but to serve as a link between them.

The Commonwealth cannot coast, however. Its very existence creates demands which must be continually fulfilled – for consultation, understanding, moral support and economic assistance. It might, of course, cease upon the midnight with no pain – and no regret and no harm done – having fulfilled its historic role as a framework during the perilous transition from an imperially controlled world to a world of independent states – a good chapter in the history books. There is danger, however, that it will expire in agony, strangled in its own rhetoric. If it does, then much of its historic mission as a bridge of harmony among the races will have been destroyed. Like all political institutions, it will eventually be supplanted and in our thinking we need not be dismayed or diverted by thinking that we must construct a framework for a thousand years. All we need know is that it has a useful function to perform for the time being, because ferment remains intense where the Empire's writ once ran and the world is still disorderly. The Commonwealth may not last long, but it is not doomed. Its fate is not pre-ordered. It is a matter of will on all sides.

Margaret Doxey

The Commonwealth in the 1970s

At the end of the 1950s, Professor Hedley Bull described the Commonwealth as an association exhibiting a continuous process of disintegration and suggested that too close an inspection of its operations might serve only to explode the myth and thus accelerate the process.[1] A notable attempt to explode the myth was made by the anonymous author of a series of articles published in *The Times* in April 1964. The author, identified only as 'a Conservative', dubbed the Commonwealth a 'gigantic farce', asserting that new and old members had 'no present real ties with Britain other than history might have left between any two foreign nations'.[2] Although he conceded that 'the unravelling of the tissue of law and practice which constitutes the Commonwealth fiction need not, indeed could not, be a sudden act', he advocated a restructuring of British policy in order to take account of reality.[3]

In 1972, with a membership of thirty-one countries,[4] plus one 'special member' (Nauru) and six associate (Caribbean) members, and with a total population approaching 1,000 million, this 'gigantic farce' has shown, at the very least, an ability to stage a very long run. At this point in time, it seems appropriate to discard any lingering scruples and hesitancies which may have induced reluctance to examine the Commonwealth too closely lest it prove too fragile to sustain analytical probing. Sentimental and nostalgic attitudes are no longer required and may in fact be counter-productive. To deplore what the Commonwealth is, is not, or might have been, is less useful than to investigate what activities are being sponsored within its framework and to assess its potential in a functional context.

I—THE COMMONWEALTH AND SYSTEM CHANGE

It was inevitable that a rapidly changing world environment coupled

Reprinted from *The Year Book of World Affairs 1973*, pp. 90–109. By permission of the author and the publisher.

with significant changes in status and alignment for old and new Commonwealth members would be reflected in the nature and structure of the association. In particular, the United Kingdom's membership of the European Economic Community (EEC), which took effect on 1 January 1973, transforms the status and alignment of the country which has stood in a sponsoring position to all other Commonwealth members at some period in their history. The United Kingdom was the imperial Power, the originator and leader of the group, and relations between each of the Commonwealth countries and Great Britain were historically closer than relations between the Commonwealth countries themselves. There was, and may still be, a 'special relationship'. It is pertinent, therefore, to ask whether the fact that the United Kingdom has become a full member of an enlarged EEC effectively pulls out the last vital piece of Commonwealth structural underpinning, so that the whole ramshackle edifice will now collapse into fragments. Even if some sections still remain shakily attached to others, will the whole system be in ruins?

Such an outcome would be in line with British pronouncements in the immediate post-war period. Although it has been official British policy since the date of the first application to join the EEC in 1961 that the Commonwealth and Europe were not mutually exclusive options for Britain, this was not the position taken in the earlier period. From the earliest days of the discussions on the Schumann Plan, through the debates on the proposed European Defence Community, to the negotiations between the Six which led to the Treaty of Rome in 1957, successive British governments consistently relied on arguments relating to Britain's position as a world Power and leader of the Commonwealth as reasons (or excuses) for avoiding European entanglements. It is possible to argue, however, that in the 1950s the Commonwealth did not preclude a closer relationship with Europe and that the two sets of alignments could have been reconciled.[5] Moreover, had the United Kingdom entered the EEC as a founder member, the special arrangements which proved so difficult to make for the Commonwealth preferential tariff system during the 1960s could have been more easily concluded. It is also interesting to note in this connection that the United Kingdom's reaction to the Treaty of Rome in 1957 was not to strengthen Commonwealth ties, but to form the European Free Trade Association (EFTA) to provide a bargaining force for negotiations with the Six.

In a much broader context, however, one can question whether the system of relationships which was then, or is now, described by the term 'Commonwealth' could be destroyed by British membership of the EEC. Now that British entry has at last been achieved, there is no multilateral cry that the Commonwealth is dead. Clearly, Britain's new involvement with Europe alters the nature of certain Commonwealth links, notably in respect of trade preferences – *of* which more will be said later – but it can be argued that the effects on the United Kingdom itself, and on British society, are likely to be more far-reaching than the effects on other Commonwealth countries. At the time of Britain's first application to join the EEC dire forebodings were expressed by the rest of the Commonwealth. For instance, at a meeting of the Commonwealth Economic Consultative Committee in Accra in September 1961, representatives of all governments except Britain expressed 'grave apprehension and concern' at the possible results of the British initiative[6] and even the typically bland communiqué issued after the acrimonious Commonwealth Prime Ministers' meeting held in London exactly a year later, while acknowledging the 'strenuous efforts' which the British Government was making to safeguard Commonwealth interests, noted that the representatives of Commonwealth governments had expressed 'anxieties' about the possible effects of Britain's membership of the EEC.[7]

As the 1960s progressed, however, and Britain persevered with her European policy, Commonwealth attitudes softened and some members, like Nigeria, made independent arrangements with the EEC. In recent years, the 'end of Commonwealth' has been forecast as a likely consequence not of the United Kingdom's membership of the EEC but of failure to deal satisfactorily with the problem of Southern Africa, and particularly Rhodesia. It seems that Southern Africa has been, and is likely to remain, a greater test of Commonwealth durability and adaptability than the relations between Great Britain and Western Europe. And to the Southern African problem should perhaps be added the question of migration as a factor likely to contribute to serious stress within the Commonwealth. This is not surprising: both these problems raise issues which are more fundamental to international relations and international co-operation in the last part of the twentieth century than the formation or enlargement of regional economic groupings. Failure to respond to them might indeed deal a death blow to the continuing vitality of the Commonwealth system. In general, however, the Commonwealth has not failed to respond and in so doing it has virtually transformed itself into a 'new' association. This newness is not only a product of decolonization, which has meant that twenty-seven members of the Commonwealth have achieved independence since 1947; it is also a reflection of the fact that, within the association, norms and communication systems, patterns of behaviour and the attitudes which inform them are themselves 'new', often bearing little relationship to the 'old' imperial links of defence and economic policy which were held together in London.

The object of this paper is to examine some important facets of this system change and to reassess the needs which the Commonwealth may be serving in the contemporary world. Limitations of space preclude anything more than a rather cursory survey, but it is hoped that this general analysis may point the way to further and more detailed studies.

(a) *The need for a multidimensional approach*

Analysis of the work of any international organization requires a multidimensional and open framework. Not only are unidimensional approaches unsatisfactory and misleading; there is the added problem that the organization cannot be studied as a closed system, operating in a vacuum. By its very nature, an international organization is a composite body, a collectivity, made up of States and of peoples, and it must be related to the external international environment in which it operates and from which it receives inputs which may require modifications in its functioning. It must also be viewed as a system whose own components are changing. Inputs received from its internal environment may be as important as, or even more important than, those received from outside. While it can be stated that failure to respond at all to significant changes will result in system breakdown, precise quantitative measures of changes in either of these two environments, or of capacity to respond to them, would be impossible to construct. Nor has integration theory developed to a point where it would permit confident statements about conditions or processes which will lead either to integration or disintegration. There are encouraging signs, however, that the study of international organization is breaking out of the normative 'integration' mould to which the 'uniting of Europe'[8] contributed both impetus and example, and that students of international organization are in the process of enlarging their fields of vision and devising more flexible schemes of analysis.[9] In particular, there could be advantages in placing less emphasis on integrative goals such as closer union, the formation of political communities and the replacement of several actors by one. Instead, effort might be devoted to constructing frameworks which permit the analysis of existing organizations as on-going systems of co-operation.[10] Within such a framework it should be possible to identify processes of expansion and contraction which are occurring simultaneously in different parts of the system, and at different levels of interaction.

(b) A 'Snakes and Ladders' analogy

From this perspective, the familiar children's game of snakes and ladders offers an over-simplified but useful illustration of what has been happening to the Commonwealth. On a board which has proved capable of rapid expansion to accommodate an increasing number of players, there have been some notable slides down ex-imperial 'snakes' and some important moves up a variety of functional 'ladders'. What has been happening on the snakes does represent a disintegrative process: a retreat from exclusiveness and centralized policy-making. What is happening on the ladders, however, is an altogether different process. These ladders can be seen as representing a spreading network of communication systems bringing functional co-operation at a number of different levels. This does not necessarily represent an *integrative* process, but it is conducive to further co-operation along similar lines, so that the ladders, unlike the snakes, are increasing in number. The current emphasis on functional co-operation is reflected in official communiqués which stress that the Commonwealth is an informal association which does not require its members to take collective action.[11]

If one looks for a 'watershed' which marks the change from the 'old' to the 'new' Commonwealth,[12] one should perhaps take the 1949 Declaration of London which permitted India to continue as a full member of the Commonwealth as a republic, acknowledging the monarch only as the Head of the Commonwealth.[13] General Smuts, who played a prominent part in Empire and Commonwealth from the early years of the century until the end of the Second World War, correctly noted that the Declaration of London was not a natural evolution, but a switch from what he termed the old 'organic line of development'.[14] But while he had accurately identified a discontinuity, he incorrectly analysed its significance. The Declaration itself, which referred to the 'traditional capacity of the Commonwealth to strengthen its unity of purpose while *adapting its organization and procedures to changing circumstances*',[15] was more accurate. An international body can only survive if organization and procedures are responsive to environmental changes, and this switch in Commonwealth policy, which filled Smuts with such misgiving, made possible the survival of the association. Ironically, in the 'new' Commonwealth there was to be no place for South Africa, for it was not the creation of 'two circles of Commonwealth, monarchies and republics'[16] which would place a brake on the wheel, but the acknowledgement of a new system norm which by installing racial equality at the hub was to keep it turning.

(c) Commonwealth norms

The whole question of norms is crucial to the kind of association which the Commonwealth has become: an interaction system generating horizontal co-operation of a functional nature rather than a goal-oriented system moving towards economic or political consolidation. In the most general sense, of course, it can be said that the Commonwealth does have a goal: it seeks to further the interests of its members by various means. But it is not seeking to organize peace and security by institutionalizing behaviour and providing for sanctions (which may serve only to discredit the institution when they fail to bring about the desired result). Experience suggests that security-oriented organizations are effective only when there is, within the organization, one strong, hegemonial Power which interprets security needs and defends the group from without, and if need be, from within.[17] There is today no question of the interests of the Commonwealth as a whole being interpreted, or met, by the United Kingdom; it is best seen as a co-operative enterprise designed to improve the wellbeing of all members, and particularly the majority who are plagued with the problems of poverty, economic and political modernization, and lack of trained personnel in all fields of endeavour.

In place of the formal structure of Councils and Assemblies, operating in terms of a charter or constitution, which are characteristic of the majority of international organizations, the Commonwealth operates on an informal basis. It has, however, developed a set of acceptable and accepted norms which facilitate interaction at all levels. These norms are both substantive and procedural. In the substantive category, multiracialism, non-intervention (of which the respect for independence and national sovereignty is the corollary) and equality are of primary importance. Procedurally, the norms governing discussions between heads of governments, or other governmental representatives, permit the frank expression of opinions and exchange of views in private; issues are not voted upon and decisions, where necessary, are based on consensus. Membership has been open to all Commonwealth dependent territories as they have achieved full independence, but there is no compulsion to join and members are free to withdraw at any time.[18] The convention remains that a change in constitution from monarchy to republic provides members with an opportunity to approve continued membership. All members acknowledge the Queen as symbolic head of the Commonwealth.

These norms, which are generally observed, give the Commonwealth credibility as an association whose aspirations and operations coincide fairly closely. In addition, the substantive norms fairly reflect the spirit of the times in that they minimize constraints upon national sovereignty while upholding respect for human worth, regardless of colour.[19] In retrospect, the Declaration of London, which was designed specifically to keep India in the Commonwealth, can be seen as a conceptual leap across a gap whose width was certainly not appreciated at the time. It represented a crucial piece of organizational engineering which enabled the expansion and conversion of the Commonwealth into an association of a kind which might not have been expected to evolve from a white man's empire.

II—DISMANTLING PROTECTIVE DEFENCE AND TRADE ARRANGEMENTS

Before looking at the functional activities which characterize the contemporary Commonwealth, it is worth considering briefly the extent to which the former protective arrangements for defence and trade have been dismantled.

(a) Defence

From a time when imperial defence was primarily the concern of the United Kingdom – and of the Royal Navy – the Commonwealth has passed through several stages. Before the First World War, the self-governing Dominions automatically sided with the mother country in time of war, but in the inter-war period this relationship came into question with the development of national foreign policies in the Dominions and doubts about Britain's continuing capacity to defend the whole area. It was noted at the 1937 Imperial Conference that it was the 'sole responsibility of the several Parliaments of the British Commonwealth to decide the nature and scope of their own defence policy'.[20] In the Second World War, Eire remained neutral and the vote in the South African Parliament on participation was close. By 1945 the world power configuration had changed completely, with the United States becoming the outstanding military Power in the West. The defence needs of Commonwealth members, including those of the United Kingdom herself, became a United States responsibility and American leadership of the non-Communist world led to a series of multilateral and bilateral defence pacts, of which NATO and SEATO were particularly relevant to Commonwealth members. Perhaps the most striking example of the end of imperial defence was the signing of the ANZUS pact in 1951 between Australia, New Zealand and the United States. Professor Geoffrey Barraclough notes that 'Great Britain was not even invited to participate' and quotes the phrase used by the Canadian historian, Frank Underhill: 'all roads in the Commonwealth lead to Washington.'[21] For more than a decade successive British governments have progressively whittled down over-seas defence responsibilities: an East of Suez role has been abandoned and military strength concentrated in Europe. This process certainly reflects shrinking capability and it may also be true that since the 1956 Suez escapade lack of capability has been equalled, if not sur-passed, by disinclination to retain burdensome overseas commitments. Abdication of hegemony is also reflected in non-intervention policies within the Commonwealth. One can contrast the Anglo-Boer War (1899—1902) with the rhetorical suspension of the Smith régime in Rhodesia after its unilateral declaration of independence (UDI) in 1965 to show how policy – and power – had changed in the intervening years.

It is neither possible nor necessary to apportion responsibility for this abandonment of a centrally organized protective defence system between the United Kingdom itself and other members of the 'old' Commonwealth. There is no doubt that in Canada, South Africa and Australia there was an increasing drive for autonomy in foreign policy, coupled with a growing realization that Britain could no longer provide the protection which might be needed. On the other hand, and particularly since the Second World War, British policy has inevitably reflected her inability to act as a world Power. In this context, the Suez affair in 1956 was an aberration, but it served to point out very sharply the limitations of British power. The enlarge-ment of the Commonwealth to include India, Pakistan and Ceylon meant that shared views on defence were no longer operative. India's policy of non-alignment under Nehru precluded the continuation of any specifically Commonwealth defence orientation, and as decolon-ization proceeded apace, the Commonwealth came to embrace a majority of members from Africa, Asia, the Caribbean and elsewhere who were anxious to diversify their external relationships. Although they were prepared to remain within the Commonwealth, they were generally averse to exclusive political or strategic ties with one country, particularly when that country had formerly exercised sovereignty over them. The United Kingdom's external Commonwealth defence commitments are today virtually limited to responsibility for her remaining dependent territories.

(b) Trade and Commonwealth preference

A distinguished Canadian economist noted in a recent article that the Commonwealth Preference System set up in Ottawa in 1932 had 'appeared progressively less and less relevant to the trading and politico-strategic interests of its members...'.[22] Measures originally designed to cope with the aftermath of Depression in the 1930s were not geared to the needs of the post-war world and arrangements made after 1945 for reducing tariffs and other barriers to trade were more broadly based. In the 1970s, there are problems of high growth rates and inflation in the industrialized countries and desperate needs for development and modernization in the rest of the world. The General Agreement on Tariffs and Trade (GATT), which in the 1950s and 1960s sponsored a number of multilateral tariff-cutting sessions, culminating n the Kennedy Round of 1964–66, has now been supplemented by the United Nations Conference on Trade and Development (UNCTAD), which was established in 1964 to serve the special interests of the developing countries. UNCTAD has proposed a generalized system of preferences which would enable these countries to obtain easier access to the markets of developed areas. Another important feature of the world trading picture has been the EEC's establishment of an internal common market and the conclusion of agreements with outsiders which offer them some of the advantages of duty-free access to this huge and prosperous market. Notable in this connection have been the two Yaoundé Conventions, which brought eighteen ex-French and Belgian colonies in Africa into association with the EEC, giving them access to the Common Market at zero tariffs, consultation through joint institutions and the right to draw on the European Development Fund for grants and loans.[23]

With these substantial changes in the external economic environment, the system of Commonwealth preferences inevitably became less significant. Although the trade of Commonwealth countries with each other has increased, it has become a less important ingredient of world trade[24] and nothing like a Commonwealth trading bloc can be said to exist. In addition – and this is a point which is particularly relevant to British membership of the EEC – a smaller proportion of exports from the Commonwealth now comes to Britain and a smaller proportion of Commonwealth imports is supplied by Britain. For instance in 1966 Australia sent 16 per cent. of her total exports to the United Kingdom, while India sent 17 per cent. and New Zealand 56 per cent. In 1970, however, the percentages had fallen to 12, 10 and 35 per cent. respectively.[25] Commonwealth imports from the United Kingdom have shown a similar pattern. Britain supplied 25 per cent. of Australia's total imports in 1966, 9 per cent. of India's and 37 per cent. of New Zealand's. In 1970 the corresponding percentages were 21, 6 and 28.[26]

Obviously the United Kingdom's membership of an enlarged EEC must have a direct effect on what is left of Commonwealth preference and having made the general observation that the system as a whole is of dwindling importance, it is still necessary to note that, in certain cases, hardship will certainly be felt by individual Commonwealth countries in spite of arrangements made to ease them through the transition period. In the White Paper issued by the British Government in 1971, it was stated that '... the interests of Commonwealth countries have been a major concern of Her Majesty's Government throughout the negotiations'.[27] Arrangements made for the Commonwealth were set out in detail in this White Paper and may be summarized briefly as follows:

1. Independent developing countries in Africa, the Pacific and Indian Oceans and the Caribbean may participate in the Association (Yaoundé) Agreement on the same terms as present members; alternatively they may make individual agreements with the EEC with particular emphasis on the removal of tariff barriers,[28] or trade agreements of the conventional kind. In any event, the status quo will continue until 31 January 1975.

2. Independent developing countries in Asia (India, Sri Lanka, Singapore, Malaysia and (presumably) Bangla Desh) will not have this option, but their problems will receive attention, and the applicability of the Generalized Preference Scheme will be considered.[29]

3. Australia and Canada will have to meet the Common External Tariff (CET) of the EEC by 1 July 1977, but it will be applied in four stages during the transition period and the White Paper promises 'speedy and effective action to deal with any abrupt dislocation of trade in agricultural products'.[30] In any case, there is a nil duty on raw wool, copper and metalliferous ores and other products important to Australia and Canada.

4. Special arrangements have been negotiated for New Zealand dairy products and lamb. The magnitude of this problem is indicated by figures which show that butter constitutes 11 per cent. and cheese 8 per cent. of New Zealand's total export earnings, and that 85 per cent. of exports go to the United Kingdom. The White Paper promises minimum guaranteed sales at prices equal to the 1969–72 average until 1977. In the third year following British accession, continuing arrangements for butter will be discussed. Lamb will be subject to a 20 per cent. tariff. The New Zealand Government expressed satisfaction with these arrangements.

5. Sugar presented another major area of difficulty and it has been agreed that all contracts made under the Commonwealth Sugar Agreement will be fulfilled until the end of 1974. Thereafter the EEC will make its own arrangements, but the White Paper notes that it will have 'as its firm purpose, the safeguarding of the interests of the developing countries concerned whose economies depend to a considerable extent on the export of primary products and particu-

larly of sugar'.[31] This is stated to be 'a specific and moral commitment' which is obviously of crucial importance to the sugar-producing countries of the Commonwealth Caribbean.

In spite of British assurances of her continuing concern for Commonwealth trade interests, and the fact that from inside the EEC she can exert direct influence over policy, it seems unlikely that in the future the United Kingdom will maintain a protective role for the economies of independent Commonwealth countries. Patterns of trade will obviously change over the next decade with the last vestiges of a Commonwealth trading bloc disappearing as the British tariff is merged with the CET and individual Commonwealth countries make their own adjustments and arrangements.[32]

III—THE GROWTH OF FUNCTIONAL CO-OPERATION

The enlargement of the Commonwealth to the point where it comprised an overwhelming majority of members from the Third World brought a new set of problems to the fore. These countries were all concerned with development – with raising national income and standards of living. Their needs have come to be strongly articulated in all international organizations to which they belong, and the Commonwealth is no exception. Under this stimulus, the Commonwealth has become increasingly technical-functional in character and over the past decades a variety of schemes for functional co-operation, both governmental and non-governmental, have been developed under its auspices. Some of these have their origins in existing activities; some are new; many are characterized by innovative procedures.

(a) Governmental co-operation

At the Governmental level, in addition to periodic meetings of Heads of Government (formerly called Prime Ministers' Meetings), there are regular meetings of Ministers (and officials) of Finance, Health and Education. Prior to 1965 there was no central Commonwealth agency, but in that year it was decided to establish a permanent Secretariat through which intra-Commonwealth activities could be co-ordinated.[33] For convenience, the Secretariat was located in London and in many respects it has taken over work formerly handled by the Commonwealth Relations Office (now merged with the Foreign Office). However, it has no aura of 'Britishness' about it. Mr Arnold Smith, a senior Canadian diplomat, was appointed as the first Secretary-General and his appointment was renewed for a second five-year term in 1970. He brought ability, stature and vigour to the position, in which he ranks as a senior High Commissioner and has the right of access to the Heads of all Commonwealth governments. He and his staff, which now numbers about 180, are representative of all parts of the Commonwealth; the Agreed Memorandum setting up the Secretariat requires them to 'be seen to be the servants of Commonwealth governments collectively'.[34] The Secretariat is financed by contributions from Commonwealth governments assessed on their capacity to pay in terms of national income and population. It operates on a modest budget which is still well under £1 million per annum.

In its relatively short life, the Secretariat has come to play a key role in facilitating intra-Commonwealth communication and co-operation at all levels. If it did not exist, it might well be considered essential to invent it. Its two main functions are:

(i) to service Commonwealth meetings which include: Heads of Government meetings; specialized conferences (for instance, the periodic Commonwealth Education and Medical Conferences); meetings of officials; meetings of the Sanctions Committee; and seminars (for instance, a seminar held in Singapore in 1970 on the organization of a diplomatic service).[35] These meetings are not confined to London but take place in a variety of Commonwealth settings.

(ii) to initiate new projects at the request of Commonwealth governments.

There are two particularly interesting aspects to the work of the Secretariat. One is the fact that a group of Commonwealth officials (who are not necessarily civil servants by profession) is working together to promote the interests of all member countries and, in the process, forming a close-knit circle of like-minded people who perforce develop habits and experience of practical co-operation. This experience is of benefit to the whole Commonwealth while they are with the Secretariat; ultimately it is fed back into national systems when the official's tour of duty comes to an end. An elite group of Commonwealth bureaucrats is thus in process of formation which, in some respects at least, can perhaps be compared to the servants of the EEC in Brussels; their existence constitutes an important factor in promoting the continuance of the Commonwealth association.

The value of this group of Commonwealth-oriented servants is enhanced because of the second point to be made about the Secretariat, which is its success in achieving its purposes. Commonwealth governments are tending to give the Secretariat more and more work, demonstrating their approval of what has been done and their confidence that the Secretariat can be authorized to meet new needs and perform new services. For instance, the original two-divisional structure (Administrative and Economic/International) has been greatly expanded at the request of Commonwealth governments. By 1972 the Secretariat had seven divisions: Administrative; International; Finance and Research; Trade and Commodities; Education; Legal; Information. Certain bodies, such as the Commonwealth Education Liaison Unit (set up in 1959) and the Commonwealth Economic Committee (dating from 1925) were absorbed into the Secretariat, which also maintains close liaison with such organizations as the Commonwealth Agricultural Bureaux, the Commonwealth Air Transport Council and the Commonwealth Telecommunications Organization.

Although the Queen remains the symbolic Head of the Commonwealth, it is the Secretariat today which, through a felicitous combination of diplomatic and bureaucratic procedures, has come to personify the contemporary Commonwealth. A political role for the Secretary-General is not precluded, and certain peacekeeping tasks have been undertaken,[36] but the main thrust of the Secretariat's work is at the functional level.

While it is not possible to give a detailed account here of the multifarious avenues of co-operation which are given official Commonwealth sponsorship, particularly in fields of education, health, communications, science and technology,[37] it is worth noting one recent venture in the provision of technical assistance which reflects the pragmatic, small-scale, efficient style of many Commonwealth ventures. This is the Commonwealth Fund for Technical Co-operation (CFTC), which was established within the Secretariat as an independent unit after the Heads of Government meeting in Singapore in 1971. The Fund, which was given initial finance of £400,000, had its origin in an earlier program for technical co-operation which was financed by the United Kingdom, Canada and New Zealand. The United Kingdom and Canada have pledged themselves to provide 70 per cent. of total contributions to the CFTC, but developing countries of the Commonwealth are also contributing on a voluntary basis, thus establishing a truly multilateral agency and blurring the rigid lines between donors and recipients which are an undesirable feature of many international aid projects and agencies. The CFTC deals in personnel who provide technical expertise particularly in studying and assessing development projects and needs, and in export market development. There is also provision for training courses in technical and vocational skills organized in *developing* countries for students from other developing countries. The Fund has a Board of Management, but day-to-day operations are handled by a (Canadian) Managing Director and an executive committee of ten members. It has been able to keep red tape to a minimum because of the relatively small number of Commonwealth countries compared with, say, the United Nations, and because of the small staff who can operate on a personal basis. Three full-time consultants are at present retained by the Fund to report on projects; other consultants can be employed on an *ad hoc* basis.

(b) *Non-governmental co-operation*

In the sphere of non-governmental co-operation, there is a network of transnational associations whose activities would repay more detailed investigation and analysis than they have yet received. Such bodies as the Commonwealth Parliamentary Association (founded in 1911) and the Association of Commonwealth Universities (founded in 1913) are known and respected in certain circles, but the activities of other bodies and groups are even less well publicized. In recent years the work of professional associations has received stimulus and support from the Commonwealth Foundation, another Commonwealth innovation. The purpose of the Foundation, which is a private body registered as a charity in the United Kingdom, is 'to administer a Fund for increasing interchanges between Commonwealth organizations in professional fields...'.[38] Like the Commonwealth Secretariat, with which it maintains close liaison, the Foundation was established following the 1965 Prime Ministers' meeting. Its terms of reference were few and under its Director, John Chadwick, and with a Board of Trustees made up of representatives of the twenty-eight subscribing governments and the Commonwealth Secretary-General, it has devised its own ground rules and developed its own policies.[39] In 1971, as a result of a decision taken at the Singapore Heads of Government Conference, its annual income was increased from £250,000 to £350,000 and the British Government pledged itself to meet 50 per cent. of this amount in the period 1972–77.

The record of assistance given by the Foundation to professional men and women in the Commonwealth over the period 1966–71 makes fascinating reading.[40] To mention only a few projects, the Foundation has: sponsored the establishment or financing of thirteen Commonwealth-wide professional associations; set up six national multidisciplinary professional centres in Uganda, Kenya, Trinidad and Tobago, Jamaica, Malta and Singapore; supported conferences, seminars and individual travel with grants; promoted the increased circulation of professional journals; and financed the publication of two new primary journals in the fields of tropical medicine and veterinary science. In encouraging the establishment and growth of professional associations, the Foundation has been concerned to support new areas of professional activity, such as youth leadership, management and accountancy, and food science. Its definition of a profession has been elastic enough to cover these and other areas of skill. In disbursing individual travel grants, the Foundation has sought to mitigate 'professional isolation' by financing short study courses of up to three months' duration in other parts of the Commonwealth. In all its activities it has sought to facilitate the adaptation of the professionalism of the 'old' Commonwealth to meet the needs of new members, without lowering of professional standards.

It is interesting to note that in the first five years, 22 per cent. of disposable grant income went to medicine and ancillary operations. Special efforts were made to cope with the problem of deafness among children in tropical African Commonwealth countries, and teaching, health and surgical projects were supported. The Foundation also supported refresher courses for public health nurses in East, Central and Southern Africa, and teaching and specialist interchanges between New Zealand and the South Pacific territories. In addition, funds were provided to enable nurses from all parts of the Commonwealth to meet in Montreal to discuss the establishment of a Nursing Federation and other matters of common concern.

A substantial grant (£59,000) has gone to provide travelling bursaries in race relations, so that teachers, social workers, police and others concerned with Commonwealth immigrants in their day-to-day work in Britain could travel to the countries of origin of these immigrants to study social conditions and to make contacts with their professional counterparts. The Foundation hopes that the British Government will be persuaded to finance this scheme when the present grant ends.

In all, the work of the Commonwealth Foundation, though modest in scale and scope, appears to be of considerable value in bringing together people from all parts of the Commonwealth who have something to learn from each other. Like the Secretariat, it is facilitating purposeful communication and its work is already showing practical results.

IV—FUTURE PROSPECTS

The growing demand for services, clearly revealed in the Reports of the Secretary-General, reflects the many and disparate needs of Commonwealth countries and a belief that the Commonwealth association can help to meet them. Five items taken at random from Mr Smith's Third Report illustrate the diversity of current Secretariat activity of a functional nature: (i) a study of methods of compiling the local costs of technical assistance, based on Guyanan experience; (ii) a study of tourism in general, and air fares in particular, with a recommendation that Commonwealth airline representatives should meet prior to IATA conferences; (iii) research papers on the Yaoundé Conventions and analysis of the advantages and disadvantages for developing Commonwealth countries of becoming associated with the EEC in this framework; (iv) a study of youth activities, focusing particularly on 'out of school' young people, with regional seminars organized in Nairobi in 1969 and Port of Spain in 1970 to which participants came as individuals and not government delegates; (v) the establishment of a legal division in the Secretariat to perform legal liaison duties among Commonwealth members.[41]

The scope for continuing and close co-operation in these and other areas is greater because of the common ability to communicate in English, both orally and in writing; comparable styles of political and bureaucratic behaviour; comparable education of relevant people and the manageable size of the organization. It is not expected that the Commonwealth will ever be open to all comers. The Secretary-General noted in his Third Report that membership is 'reaching its maximum'[42] and one suspects that a threshold of efficiency may exist beyond which useful co-operation becomes progressively more difficult to achieve. The Commonwealth is already large enough to permit some regional groupings, but not so large that the meetings become unwieldy and difficult to organize and the personal elements of communication and rapport are irretrievably lost. In this respect, the association has an advantage over the United Nations, especially in the area of functional co-operation where aid programs tend to get bogged down in multilateral bureaucratic mire.

The other advantages of the Commonwealth for the kinds of task which it is performing have already been noted in the course of this paper. The absence of anything resembling an authority structure, the fact that the Commonwealth does not threaten national identity with submergence – these are important contributors to its viability. But, in spite of all that has been said about functional co-operation in areas where 'high politics' do not intrude the work of the Secretariat in building up a utilitarian structure which largely fulfils expectations, there remain deep political divisions between members of the Commonwealth on a number of issues. In this area, expectations may not be fulfilled, and controversy and tension cannot be avoided.[43]

India and Pakistan have been at war twice: in 1965 and again in 1971. Both remained as members of the Commonwealth until the end of the second round of hostilities, when Bangla Desh emerged as an independent nation (and was subsequently admitted to the Commonwealth) and Pakistan decided to leave. Should Pakistan at some future date wish to re-enter the Commonwealth, however, it seems unlikely that her entry would be blocked.

The United Kingdom itself has placed heavy stress on the Commonwealth on several occasions, particularly in the Suez episode in 1956 when talk of leaving the Commonwealth was rife in both India and Ceylon.[44] The British Government's failure to consult Commonwealth partners before the Anglo-French ultimatum to Israel and Egypt was issued at the end of October 1956 was an assertion of the independent (if, in that instance, misguided) character of British foreign policy which has since been reasserted in the decision to negotiate entry to the EEC and the determination to sell arms to South Africa.

In a sense, the United Kingdom is now the only member of the Commonwealth which experiences collective pressure within the association. Demands for effective policies with regard to Southern Africa are understandable in the context of a multiracial Commonwealth in which sensitivity over racial discrimination and oppression is acute.[45] Nevertheless, it must be acknowledged that the norms of respect for national sovereignty and non-intervention are also basic to the continuance of the association. Recent Commonwealth heads of government meetings in Lagos and London in 1966 and even the Singapore meeting in 1971 have given grounds for concern that the old standards of tolerance and reticence were being abandoned in favour of confrontation techniques. It is to be hoped that this trend can be halted and even reversed, for if it continues, it could destroy the Commonwealth which depends on mutual confidence and respect. Edward Miles has noted correctly that public gatherings are often disintegrative in effect because rigidity increases and the possibilities for compromise diminish.[46] The Commonwealth has no need of a further move towards disintegration.

The special responsibility which the United Kingdom retains for dependent territories within the Commonwealth, particularly Rhodesia (and, perhaps, Hong Kong), makes it inevitable that there will be continuing Commonwealth pressure to influence British policies. For instance, at the beginning of 1972, the Canadian Prime Minister sent a special assistant to Nigeria, Tanzania and Uganda to persuade their governments not to carry out threats to walk out of the Commonwealth if the agreement between Britain and Rhodesia were to be implemented.[47] In the event, the settlement was not implemented, but the threats had been made. Clashes between the norms of non-intervention on the one hand and multiracialism on the other are not, of course, confined to the Commonwealth, but it is important that such clashes should be muted in order not to stultify the operations of the whole system. Pressure should be expressed in diplomatic and traditional Commonwealth forms, not only because such approaches are more conducive to achieving results, but because continued public denunciations of British policy can only be counter-productive. J. D. B. Miller notes the disastrous effect on British public opinion of the 1966 Commonwealth Conferences on Rhodesia,[48] and the vocal and influential segment of opinion in Britain which is anti-Commonwealth and hostile to Commonwealth immigrants draws strength from public condemnations of British policy by newer members of the group. Resentment over such 'pillorying', to which other Commonwealth members are not subjected, even where their own national policies would not always stand up to close scrutiny on criteria of human rights, could reach proportions where it effectively blocked a proper appreciation of what the Commonwealth actually offers as a continuing system of functional co-operation from which the United Kingdom, like all other members, can only benefit.

NOTES

1. H. Bull, 'What is the Commonwealth?', *International Political Communities: an anthology* (1966), pp. 459–468. Bull noted that there were ten members of the Commonwealth at that time and that 'their persistence in membership requires an explanation' (p. 461).
2. 'A Conservative', 'A Party in Search of a Pattern', part II: 'Patriotism based on Reality not on Dreams', *The Times*, 2 April 1964. Authorship of those articles has been attributed to Mr Enoch Powell.
3. *The Times*, 2 April 1964.
4. The members of the Commonwealth at the time of writing are: the United Kingdom, Australia, Canada, New Zealand, India, Ceylon, Ghana, Malaysia, Nigeria, Cyprus, Sierra Leone, Tanzania, Jamaica, Trinidad and Tobago, Uganda, Kenya, Malawi, Malta, Zambia, the Gambia, Singapore, Guyana, Botswana, Lesotho, Barbados, Mauritius, Swaziland, Tonga, Western Samoa, Fiji and Bangla Desh.
5. E.g. the Canadian Government did not disapprove of the Schumann Plan. See Canada, III H.C.Deb. (1950), p. 3192 (Statement by the Secretary of State for External Affairs, 5 June 1950).
6. See N. Mansergh (ed.), *Documents and Speeches on Commonwealth Affairs 1952–1962* (1963), p. 650.
7. Mansergh, *Documents*, p. 659.
8. The phrase was used by E. Haas as the title for his important work on regional economic integration, using the European Coal and Steel Community as a case-study (*The Uniting of Europe* (1958)).
9. See particularly J. S. Nye, *Peace in Parts* (1971) and the summer 1971 issue of *International Organization*, edited by J. S. Nye and R. Keohane, 'Transnational Relations and World Politics', 15 *International Organization*, No. 3, 1971. See, too, a stimulating article by Edward Miles, 'Organizations and Integration in International Systems', 12 *International Studies Quarterly*, June 1968, pp. 196–225.
10. D. Puchala's 'Concordance System' seems to be a most promising line of approach. 'Of Blind Men, Elephants and International Integration', 10 *Journal of Common Market Studies*, March 1972, pp. 267–284.

11. See e.g. *Commonwealth Prime Ministers' Meeting 1965*: Agreed Memorandum on the Commonwealth Secretariat, Cmnd. 2173, July 1965, p. 2.

12. An earlier 'watershed' is identified by N. Mansergh as the moment in 1917 when Smuts spoke of the need for a new name for what came to be called the British Commonwealth of Nations; at this point Mansergh suggests the balance shifted from the predominance of Empire to the predominance of Commonwealth. See N. Mansergh, *The Commonwealth Experience* (1969), p. 26.

13. The text of the Declaration which was issued as the Final Communiqué following the Prime Ministers' Meeting in London on 27 April 1949, is in N. Mansergh (ed.), *Documents and Speeches on British Commonwealth Affairs 1931–1952* (1953), pp. 846–847.

14. Statement published in the *Cape Argus* (Cape Town), 28 April 1949.

15. The Declaration as cited in note 13 above. Emphasis added.

16. Statement by Smuts as cited in note 14 above.

17. E.g. the Soviet Union assumes a protective role for Warsaw Pact countries *vis-à-vis* the West and is also prepared to act decisively to deal with what are seen as disruptive forces within the area covered by the Pact (e.g. Hungary 1956; Czechoslovakia 1968).

18. Eire and Pakistan have voluntarily left the Commonwealth; Burma and Southern Yemen elected not to join on attaining independence; South Africa was virtually forced to leave in 1961 on becoming a republic.

19. Problems of reconciling norms of non-intervention and multiracialism are discussed in the concluding section of this paper.

20. *Imperial Conference 1937: Summary of Proceedings*, Cmd. 5482, p. 20.

21. G. Barraclough, *An Introduction to Contemporary History* (1964), p. 73. Underhill's comment would have more accurately been phrased as 'all defence roads in the Commonwealth lead to Washington'.

22. H. G. Johnson in P. Streeten and H. Corbet (eds), *Commonwealth Policy in a Global Context* (1971), p. 85.

23. A third Yaoundé Convention is due to be negotiated in 1974 to come into effect when Yaoundé II expires on 31 January 1975.

24. See *Commonwealth Trade 1970*, the Commonwealth Secretariat (1971), p. vi.

25. *Commonwealth Trade*, Table 7, p. 122.

26. *Commonwealth Trade*, Table 7, p. 122.

27. *The United Kingdom and the European Communities*, Cmnd. 4715, p. 25.

28. The model for this type of agreement would probably be the Arusha Agreement signed between the EEC and Kenya, Tanzania and Uganda, which took effect in January 1971.

29. The EEC Council of Ministers agreed to activate this scheme, giving generalized preferences to developing countries within UNCTAD, on 22 June 1971. See *European Community*, Nr. 147, 1971, pp. 12–13.

30. Cmnd. 4715, p. 26.

31. Cmnd. 4715, p. 28.

32. The Sterling Area is also disappearing. The White Paper noted that the British Government was prepared to envisage 'an orderly and gradual run down of official sterling balances' after accession to the EEC (Cmnd. 4715, para. 127). The Sterling Area and the Commonwealth did not precisely coincide (Canada was not a member, and some non-Commonwealth countries were) but the overlap was considerable. However, in recent years, the significance of this currency area has been progressively diminishing and

controls over the export of capital to the Overseas Sterling Area announced in June 1972 by the Chancellor of the Exchequer (simultaneously with the decision to float the pound) can be considered as part of the move towards 'a progressive alignment of the external characteristics of sterling with those of other Community currencies' forecast by Mr Heath in June 1971. (Cmnd. 4715, para 127).

33. *Commonwealth Prime Ministers' Meeting 1965*: Agreed Memorandum on the Commonwealth Secretariat, Cmnd. 2713, July 1965.

34. Cmnd. 2713, pp. 2–3.

35. *Diplomatic Service*: *Formation and Operation* (Report on the Commonwealth Seminar, Singapore 1970) (1971).

36. Mr Smith has recorded his opposition to a Commonwealth peace mission to seek a cease-fire in the 1965 Indo-Pakistani war, which he felt was properly a UN task. See A. Smith, 'The Need for Commonwealth', *Round Table*, No. 223, July 1966, p. 225. On the other hand, he sent an observer team to report on the Gibraltar referendum in 1967 at the specific request of the British Government.

37. The three Reports of the Secretary-General covering the periods 1965–August 1966; September 1966–October 1968 and November 1968–November 1970 (published by the Commonwealth Secretariat, London) give an excellent picture of the agency's activities. Mr Smith does not minimize problems which must be faced if the association is to survive. See, too, D. Ingram, *The Commonwealth at Work* (1969) and R. H. Leach, 'The Secretariat', 26 *International Journal*, No. 2, 1971, pp. 375–400.

38. *Commonwealth Prime Ministers' Meeting 1965*: Agreed Memorandum on the Commonwealth Foundation, Cmnd. 2714, July 1965, p. 3.

39. See *The Commonwealth Foundation*: *The First Five Years, 1966–1971* (1971). The following account of the work of the Foundation is drawn from the material contained in this Report.

40. It is interesting to note that the Trustees need not be civil servants or diplomats; nor is the Foundation precluded from approaching private sources for additional financial support. The Trustees note, in the Report cited in note 39 above, that they hope that the 'second quinquennium will see the beginnings of worth-while co-operation between the public and private sectors in the broad Commonwealth professional interest' (p. 21).

41. *Third Report of the Commonwealth Secretary General* (1971), *passim*.

42. *Third Report*, p. v.

43. Professor Beloff ascribes disillusion with the Commonwealth to the 'failure of some countries to live up to ... expectations': M. Beloff, 'The Commonwealth – from Disillusion to Dissolution?', *Commonwealth*, April 1971, p. 38. In an interesting analysis of the sources of disillusion, he concludes that the 'element of expectation derives ... from an imperial situation' (p. 39). It is suggested that here many of these imperial consequences have in fact been dismantled.

44. See N. Mansergh (ed.), *Documents and Speeches on Commonwealth Affairs 1952–1962* (1963), for extracts from debates in the Lok Sabha and the Ceylon House of Representatives (pp. 523–534).

45. S. A. de Smith identifies these as 'colonial issues' which 'seem to be excluded from the scope of the (Non-interference) convention'. 'Fundamental Rules – Forty Years On', 26 *International Journal*, No. 2, 1971, p. 358.

46. E. Miles, in the article cited in note 9 above, p. 222.

47. Reported in the (Toronto) *Star*, 2 February 1972.
48. J. B. Miller, 'Reluctance about the Commonwealth', *Round Table*, No. 235, July 1969, p. 308.

An earlier publication edited by Professor Stankiewicz

CRISIS IN BRITISH GOVERNMENT

INTRODUCTION
W. J. Stankiewicz *The Need for Reform*

PART ONE CONSTITUTIONAL PRINCIPLES
J. A. Corry *The Prospects for the Rule of Law*
J. D. B. Mitchell *The Anatomy and Pathology of the Constitution*
Kingsley Martin *Monarchy's Future*
Geoffrey Marshall *Parliament and the Constitution*

PART TWO PARLIAMENT
Peter Bromhead *How Should Parliament be Reformed?*
Andrew Hill and Anthony Whichelow *The Root of the Evil*
Andrew Hill and Anthony Whichelow *Committees to Advise and Recommend*
Robert E. Dowse *The M.P. and His Surgery*
Henry Burrows *House of Lords – Change or Decay?*
Bernard Crick *Tackling the Lords*
Bernard Crick *The Prospects for Parliamentary Reform*

PART THREE GOVERNMENT AND THE ADMINISTRATION
SECTION I THE REFORM OF GOVERNMENT
William A. Robson *The Reform of Government*

SECTION II THE PRIME MINISTER AND THE CABINET
D. J. Heasman *The Prime Minister and the Cabinet*
G. W. Jones *The Prime Minister's Power*

SECTION III THE ADMINISTRATION, PLANNING, AND THE
CIVIL SERVICE
D. N. Chester *The Plowden Report: Nature and Significance*
Michael Shanks *What Future for 'Neddy'?*
Andrew Shonfield *The Planners and Whitehall*
S. C. Leslie *The New Planning System*
Geoffrey Owen *The Department of Economic Affairs:
An Experiment in Planning*
G. H. Daniel *Public Accountability of the Nationalized Industries*
R. G. S. Brown *Organization Theory and Civil Service Reform*
P E P *Government by Appointment*

'The editor is to be congratulated on a timely and well-chosen selection.'

Professor Elisabeth Wallace, *The Canadian Forum*

'Professor Stankiewicz has done his work of selection admirably.'

Rudolf Klein, *New Society*

'A valiant attempt to come to grips with this looming issue of current political thought.'

George Lochhead, *Daily Express* (London)

'Professor Stankiewicz makes two important suggestions: the creation of ginger groups to promote a favourable climate of public opinion towards reform; and the setting up of a Royal Commission on Reform.'

Oxford Mail

1967
02.977880.8. Paper £2.00

Index

China, 322, 323
Churchill, Sir Winston, 141, 182, 212
Civil Service, 4, 6, 18, 123, 193 211, 212, 213, 214, 219, 220-229; Fulton Committee on, 257-259; organization of in 'giant' departments, 245-246; problem of permanent secretaries, 259-260; structure and management after Fulton, 253-256; see also Reform
Civil Service College, 227, 257
Civil Service Commission, 227, 229
Civil Service National Whitley Council, 222, 225
Cobban, Alfred, 2, 4
Coleman, James, 3
Colombo Plan, 312
Committee on Ministers' Powers, 18-23, 34, 125; Report of, 19; W. A. Robson on, 21
Committee on Tribunals and Inquiries, 34, 37
Common Market, see European Economic Community
Commonwealth, 90; Britain's 'special relationship' to, 327; Change from 'old' to new', 329-330; and constitutional principles, 317; defence of, 332-333; and EEC, 327-328; future of, 340-343; growth of functions of, 336-339; heritage of, 317-319; historical nature of, 320-321, 325; membership of, 326-327; nature of, 311-316; norms in, 331-332; preference system in, 333; principles of, 318; role of Britain in, 316-317, 336; Secretariat, 319; threats to, 324; trade in, 333-336; and United Nations, 325; and USA, 321-324; usefulness of, 313, 315, 316, 325
Commonwealth External Tariff (CET), 335, 336
Commonwealth Fund for Technical Co-operation (CFTC), 338
Commonwealth Parliamentary Association (1911), 339
Commonwealth Foundation, 339-340
Commonwealth Relations Office, 336
Commonwealth Secretariat, 339
Compton Committee, 64
Confederation of British Industry (CBI), 159, 161, 165, 169, 204
Conseil d'Etat, 27, 33-34, 39, 40, 129, 130, 133, 197
Consent, 168, 169, 176, 177, 193
Constitution, the British, 1, 2, 3, 5, 11, 14, 75, 304; amendability of, 89-90; principles of, 6; relation to Commons of, 78-79; relation to Courts, 81-82; scope of written Constitution, 79-80; and social change, 1; and US, 12; value of a written Constitution, 92-93
Constitution of the Weimar Republic, The, 75
Constitutional conventions, and written constitution, 81
Constitutional Courts, jurisdiction of, 91-92
Constitutional Law, 4
Constitutional principles, 2, 3, 4, 6, 13, 19, 78, 317
Constitutional reform, 2
Control: judicial (in administration), 31-32, 34-35
Corbett, D. C., 3
Corporatism, 3
Council on Tribunals, 125, 132
Court of Star Chamber, 26
Courts, 87, 88; relation to written Constitution, 81-82
Courts Conciliar, 27-28, 32, 34
Cowen, D. V., 86
Crick, Bernard, 117
Criminal Law Revision Committee, The, 61
Crisis in British Government, 1, 6
Crossman, Richard, H. S., 11, 97, 118, 119, 121, 133, 178, 179, 180, 181, 182, 184, 187, 190, 192, 193, 197, 203, 205
Crown: and the law, 41-43; powers of, 15-16
Crown Proceedings Act 1947, 25, 41, 88
Crowther-Hunt, Lord, 302, 303, 304
Crowther Commission, see Royal Commission on the Constitution
Cyprus, 316

Davies, Edmund, Lord Justice, 61
Davies, S. O., 104, 230, 244
De Gaulle, Charles, 323
Delegated legislation, 18, 34
Deming, L. J., 39
Denmark, 112
Department of Economic Affairs (DEA), 164, 218
Department of the Environment (DOE), 234, 235, 241, 244, 246, 249, 250
Department of Health and Social Security (DHSS), 241
Department of Trade and Industry (DTI), 234, 235, 241, 244, 248, 249, 250